The Biology
and Utilization of Grasses

PHYSIOLOGICAL ECOLOGY

A Series of Monographs, Texts, and Treatises

EDITED BY

T. T. KOZLOWSKI

University of Wisconsin
Madison, Wisconsin

THE BIOLOGY
AND UTILIZATION OF GRASSES

Edited by V. B. Youngner
DEPARTMENT OF PLANT SCIENCES
UNIVERSITY OF CALIFORNIA
RIVERSIDE, CALIFORNIA

C. M. McKell
DEPARTMENT OF RANGE SCIENCE
UTAH STATE UNIVERSITY
LOGAN, UTAH

 1972

ACADEMIC PRESS   New York and London

ACADEMIC PRESS, INC.
111 Fifth Avenue, New York, New York 10003

United Kingdom Edition published by
ACADEMIC PRESS, INC. (LONDON) LTD.
24/28 Oval Road, London NW1 7DD

LIBRARY OF CONGRESS CATALOG CARD NUMBER: 77-154393

PRINTED IN THE UNITED STATES OF AMERICA

Contents

Chapter 1. The Evolution of the Grass Family
G. Ledyard Stebbins

Chapter 2. Polyploidy as a Factor in the Evolution and Distribution of Grasses
B. Lennart Johnson

Contents

Contents

Chapter 22.   Defoliation in Relation to Vegetative Growth
D. N. Hyder

Chapter 23.   Carbohydrate Reserves of Grasses
Dale Smith

Chapter 24.   Grass Reproduction
Arthur R. Berg

Chapter 25.   Inflorescence Induction and Initiation
Roy M. Sachs

Contents

Chapter 26. Differentiation in the Grass Inflorescence
June Latting

Chapter 27. Seed Production and Cultural Treatments
I. J. Johnson

Chapter 28. Future Needs in Grass Research

FUTURE NEEDS IN RANGE RESEARCH
Wesley Keller

RESEARCH NEEDS IN THE FORAGE GRASSES
A. A. Hanson

FUTURE NEEDS IN TURFGRASS RESEARCH
J. R. Watson

List of Contributors

Numbers in parentheses refer to the pages on which the authors' contributions begin.

ARTHUR R. BERG (334), Pacific Southwest Forest and Range Experiment Station, Forest Service, United States Department of Agriculture, Berkeley, California

O. T. DENMEAD (155), Division of Plant Industry, CSIRO, Canberra, Australia

R. M. ENDO (171), Department of Plant Pathology, University of California, Riverside, California

RAYMOND A. EVANS (230), Plant Science Research Division, Agricultural Research Service, United States Department of Agriculture, University of Nevada, Reno, Nevada

J. R. GOODIN (135), Department of Biology, Texas Tech University, Lubbock, Texas

ROY L. GOSS (278), Western Washington Research and Extension Center, Washington State University, Puyallup, Washington

A. A. HANSON (36, 405), Plant Science Research Division, Agricultural Research Service, United States Department of Agriculture, Beltsville, Maryland

CARLTON H. HERBEL (101), Jornada Experimental Range, Plant Science Research Division, Agricultural Research Service, United States Department of Agriculture, Las Cruces, New Mexico

DANIEL HILLEL (259), Faculty of Agriculture, The Hebrew University of Jerusalem, Rehovot, Israel

D. N. HYDER (304), Plant Science Research Division, Agricultural Research Service, Fort Collins, Colorado

S. K. JAIN (212), *Department of Agronomy and Range Science, University of California, Davis, California

B. LENNART JOHNSON (18), Department of Plant Sciences, University of California, Riverside, California

I. J. JOHNSON (400), Cal-West Seed Company, Woodland, California

WESLEY KELLER (404), Plant Science Research Division, Agricultural Research Service, United States Department of Agriculture, Logan, Utah

J. KIGEL (115), Department of Agricultural Botany, The Hebrew University of Jerusalem, Rehovot, Israel

WILLIAM R. KNEEBONE (90), Department of Agronomy, University of Arizona, Tucson, Arizona

D. KOLLER (115), Department of Agricultural Botany, The Hebrew University of Jerusalem, Rehovot, Israel

HORTON M. LAUDE (146), Department of Agronomy and Range Science, University of California, Davis, California

JUNE LATTING (365), Department of Plant Sciences, University of California Riverside, California

J. A. LONG (53), Biochemical Research, O.M. Scott and Sons Co., Marysville, Ohio

R. MERTON LOVE (66), Department of Agronomy and Range Science, University of California, Davis, California

O. R. LUNT (271), Laboratory of Nuclear Medicine and Radiation Biology, University of California, Los Angeles, California

C. M. McKELL (74), Department of Range Science, Utah State University, Logan, Utah

ROY M. SACHS (348), Department of Environmental Horticulture, University of California, Davis, California

DALE SMITH (318), Department of Agronomy, College of Agriculture, The University of Wisconsin, Madison, Wisconsin

*Present address: Genetics Section, Division of Plant Industry, P. O. Box 109, Canberra, Australia.

G. LEDYARD STEBBINS (1), Department of Genetics, University of California, Davis, California, and Center for Advanced Studies, Stanford University, Stanford, California

LEWIS H. STOLZY (247, 407), Department of Soil Science and Agricultural Engineering, University of California, Riverside, California

JAMES R. WATSON (203, 407), Toro Manufacturing Co., Minneapolis, Minnesota

JAMES A. YOUNG (230), Plant Science Research Division, Agricultural Research Service, United States Department of Agriculture, University of Nevada, Reno, Nevada

V. B. YOUNGNER (292), Department of Plant Sciences, University of California, Riverside, California

Foreword

The botanist Edgar Anderson has called attention to the paradox that our commonest plants are the least known, and that this perilous situation is very generally unsuspected by laymen and scientists alike. This is particularly true of the grasses, whose influence on man and civilization has been incalculable, and whose biology is almost neglected in both undergraduate and graduate studies in the biological and agricultural sciences.

Occasionally classes are taught in agrostology, and many of us do pick up enough systematics to identify those species of grasses common to the areas in which we live and do research. In general, however, our knowledge and understanding of grass biology remains rudimentary. Those of us who teach the principles of plant physiology, growth, and development favor the lofty dicotyledons and tend to gloss over the lowly grasses almost as if the monocotyledonous plants once pigeonholed are scarcely worthy of intensive study. Most students assume that the time spent talking about a subject is proportional to its significance. Thus, our students inherit our blind spots.

How important are the grasses to man? Almost 3000 years ago the Hebrew prophet Isaiah wrote: "All flesh is grass." For centuries that concept fascinated philosophers, poets, and theologians who in our more agrarian-oriented past understood that the idea was not only metaphorical but literal. In this technological era, we are likely to perceive only the metaphor, forgetting that the meat man eats is dependent upon grasslands and that wheat, rice, corn, and other cereal grains—primary staples of mankind since long before recorded history—are all grasses.

Nothing has changed. All flesh is still grass, and the grasses with their 7500 species not only far surpass all other vegetation of the world in abundance, but they remain the most important economic family of plants to man. More human beings depend upon rice for their food supply than any other plant. More agricultural acreage is devoted to wheat than any other crop. Grass provides the primary forage for man's domesticated animals. And, if anything, man has expanded his utilization of the grasses in this century by aiding nature. He has learned how to conserve soil by perennial grass covers, how to encourage wildlife maintenance by improving grassland habitats, and has developed new aesthetic uses of grass as turf.

Although taxonomic studies of grass have a long history, if one glances over the literature on grass biology and utilization one is immediately struck by how much of the work is of recent origin. The bulk of such research has been concentrated into the past few decades.

A number of factors are undoubtedly responsible for stimulating this sudden interest in the grasses. Development of systemic herbicides made it necessary for us to know much more about the physiology of mono-cotyledons. The enormous increase in use of grasses for aesthetic and recre-ational purposes accelerated turf studies. Rising costs of the livestock in-dustry made it essential to explore more efficient methods of range management. Our growing interest in ecology and restoration of denuded ecosystems has focused attention on the role of grasses in pioneering reveget-ation. All of these factors have generated new knowledge on the funda-mentals of grass genetics, morphology, physiology, ecology, and utilization.

Despite accelerated research on the grasses, much remains to be dis-covered about this extremely adaptable family whose species occupy all of the environmental extremes from the tropics to the tundra. We need to know more about seedling vigor, modification of growth responses with plant-growth regulators, the developmental physiology of tillering, and the utilization of carbohydrate reserves, and much else as well.

On an international scale there is rapidly expanding interest in the grasses. This isn't surprising when we reflect that arid lands occupy the bulk of the world's surface, and a high proportion of these are only suitable for grazing. Grasses may eventually offer us an opportunity for utilization of many of these wastelands. Grasses may also eventually prove to be a source of high quality protein in a famished world. At the moment, we can't look too far ahead because a better understanding of grass biology is basic to all future uses, and we know that the potential of grass to man remains relatively untapped.

H. M. DUGGER

Dean, College of Biological and Agricultural Sciences
University of California
Riverside, California

Preface

Grasses form one of the largest, most important, and most destinctive of families in the plant kingdom. Although the store of knowledge on grass biology is sizeable, it is for the most part poorly known to plant scientists other than grass specialists. One possible reason for this may be that there have been few attempts to bring together and summarize in a single volume the information scattered through numerous general biological and agricultural publications. The purpose of this book is to review the present knowledge in grass biology and to provide a broader understanding of the important role of grasses in man's existance. Many fundamental aspects of grass evolution genetics, morphology, physiology, and ecology are covered, emphasizing the relationship of these basic concepts to the use of grasses for forage, turf, and rangelands.

The first five chapters present basic information on grass evolution and genetics, followed by discussions of practical grass-breeding problems. Chapters 6 through 11 are concerned with vegetative growth and development of both the seedling and mature plant, while Chapters 12 through 16 consider grasses primarily from an ecological viewpoint. The next four chapters present both basic and applied information on soils and mineral nutrition as related to grass growth. Subsequent chapters are devoted to effects of defoliation (moving or grazing), carbohydrate reserves, physiology of flowering, and grass and production.

This book is the result of a symposium on grass biology held at Riverside, California in 1969. The symposium brought together outstanding specialists to provide an in-depth review of grass biology, emphasizing recent advances in the field. Although there have been a few changes in authorship and many revisions in the text, most of the contributions to this book are by the same authorities who discussed these topics at the symposium.

We hope that the comprehensive and up-to-date coverage of grass biology presented will make this book useful as a textbook or as a supplementary reference for courses in grass biology, forages, turfgrass management, range management, or general agronomy. In addition, many individuals concerned with the growing of grasses may find that the information presented will give them a better understanding of the crops they grow.

Thanks are extended to all the contributors for sharing their knowledge and experience. Special appreciation is extended to Mrs. Kimi Messenzehl for her assistance in many editorial tasks and to Mr. Sheldon Lisker for his help in organizing the original symposium that resulted in this book.

V. B. Youngner

C. M. McKell

Chapter 1

The Evolution of the Grass Family

G. LEDYARD STEBBINS

Origin and Relationships of the Grasses

As with all of the larger plant families, the origin of the grasses is buried in the antiquity of past geological ages and inaccessible to us. Although fossil leaves believed to be grasses have been found in a number of strata which date back almost to the earliest appearance of flowering plants in the Cretaceous period, the identity of these fossils is doubtful. They provide us with no clue at all as to what the earliest grasses were like and when they first appeared. The first undoubted fossils of grasses, both pollen and seeds, occur in deposits of mid-Tertiary age. The seeds are very similar to those of fairly advanced modern genera, such as *Stipa*, *Piptochaetium*, and *Phalaris* (MacGinitie, 1953; Beetle, 1958). One can hardly doubt that the first grasses evolved long before that time.

The ancestry of the grasses is equally obscure. Modern treatments of angiosperm phylogeny, such as those of Hutchinson (1934), Takhtajan (1959), Cronquist (1968), and Thorne (1968), all agree in placing the family at one of the highest points of the evolutionary "tree" of flowering plants. The apparent simplicity of both their vegetative and reproductive structures results from phylogenetic reduction and is a sign of extreme specialization. One would think that in the case of such a specialized family, less

1

specialized ancestral forms would still be living and clearly recognizable. Such, however, is not the case. The similarity between grasses and the other large family of grasslike plants, the sedges (Cyperaceae), is only superficial and is no indication of a true relationship. Sedges differ radically from grasses in the structure of their spikelets and flowers, as well as in their chromosomes, which have the peculiar condition of multiple centromeres (Tanaka, 1949; Östergren, 1949). In all of these features Cyperaceae are more like Juncaceae, or rushes, than grasses. These two families are very probably derived from a common ancestor. Some anatomical features of both rushes and grasses suggest affinities with the group of monocotyledons known as Farinosae, which is essentially equivalent to the Class Commelinidae of Cronquist (1968). The primitive representatives of this group which have flowers that have no sign of reduction in their parts are such families as the spiderworts (Commelinaceae) and yellow-eyed grasses (Xyridaceae), which are quite different from lilies. There is good reason to believe, therefore, that grasses and sedges have converged in their superficial appearance through similar reductions in floral parts associated with wind pollination. The original ancestors from which the reductional trends began were quite different for the two evolutionary lines (Takhtajan, 1959).

The only other families that may have stemmed from the same line of phylogenetic reduction as the grasses are three groups, rather little known to botanists of the Northern Hemisphere, which are distributed principally in the tropics and the Southern Hemisphere; the Restionaceae, Centrolepidaceae, and Flagellariaceae. All three of these families have high degrees of specialization along lines of their own, and the Flagellariaceae, consisting of only three small genera, are relictual. They do not provide us with any sound clues as to what the ancestors of the grasses were like.

What Were the Oldest Grasses Like?

Botanists are equally at a loss to construct a replica of the earliest ancestral members of the grass family itself. All of the modern tribes of grasses are specialized in one way or another. With respect to reproductive characteristics, bamboos are the least specialized of living grasses. This has led some botanists, such as Bews (1929) and Prat (1936), to regard this tribe as primitive and similar to the common ancestor of all modern grasses. On the other hand, bamboos are highly specialized with respect to most of their vegetative characteristics (Arber, 1934). Their woodiness is secondary, being derived not from the activity of a typical cambium, but through the multiplication of separate vascular bundles and the proliferation of sclerenchyma tissue. Their branching pattern involves a complex alternation of elongate and much shortened internodes, so that the branches appear superficially as if they were emerging from the main stem in bundles. Their leaves have sheaths and petioles that are far more elaborate and specialized than are those of most grasses; although in many species the young primary stems bear simpler, nonpetiolate leaves. In their physiology of flowering, bamboos are also highly specialized. Many of them have built-in "time clocks," which cause a particular clone to grow vegetatively for many years and then to flower simultaneously in all subdivisions of the clone no matter where they may have been carried and replanted by horticulturists. Finally, all members of the bamboo tribe that have been studied cytologically are high polyploids, having somatic chromosome numbers of $2n = 48$ or higher. All of these features have led Arber and the present writer (G. L. Stebbins, 1956) to regard bamboos as not primitive but archaic. They certainly are ancient, but from the evolutionary point of view they are a mixture of primitive and advanced characteristics. They have evolved along their own lines of specialization, which are quite different from those other grasses followed. The same conclusion is reached with respect to another grass that has primitive features in its florets, the small genus *Streptochaeta* of tropical America.

   A frankly speculative reconstruction of the most primitive and now extinct members of the grass family is as follows. They were probably low-growing perennials, somewhat tufted but perhaps with short rhizomes and with relatively short leaves. Among North American grasses, a *Distichlis* without rhizomes or a perennial *Blepharidachne* would approximate my idea about their growth habit.

   The primitive grass inflorescence probably consisted of a small number of spikelets arranged in a short raceme. Although most agrostologists regard the panicle as the most primitive kind of inflorescence in grasses, the ontogenetic evidence does not support this point of view. The grass panicle develops in a very peculiar and complex fashion (Bonnett, 1937). The individual spikelets develop in an acropetal fashion, with the lowest florets maturing first and the upper ones maturing later. The panicle, on the other hand, matures basipetally, the uppermost spikelet being the first to develop. In the spike of the wheat–barley tribe (Hordeae), on the other hand, the middle spikelets develop first, followed by the lower and upper spikelets. These complex patterns of development do not exist in other monocotyledons and seem to have originated *de novo* in the Gramineae. The same is true of the fasciculate arrangement of the lower panicle branches and the great elongation of these branches in most grasses, involving as it does the combined activity of a strongly developed intercalary meristem and excessive elongation of the cells in the branches. For these reasons I regard as most primitive the kind of racemiform inflorescence now found in the genus *Brachypodium*.

4

. *Ledyard Stebbins*

The florets of the primitive grasses were probably already somewhat modified from their primitive trimerous condition, but much less so than in most modern grasses. The lemma was many nerved and short awned or awnless. The palea may well have consisted of two separate organs, as in the modern genus *Streptochaeta*. For reasons that are too lengthy to be incorporated in this review, I follow the relatively few morphologists (Schuster, 1910) who have suggested a homology between the palea and two sepals of the primitive flower. The third sepal of the original flower probably disappeared during the evolution of grasses from their ancestral forms. The lodicules, which probably represent reduced petals, were three in number, flat, and many nerved, as in bamboos and some other grasses such as *Danthonia*. There were six stamens and an ovary with three stigmas, containing a single orthotropous ovule.

Anatomically the primitive grasses probably produced all of the kinds of specialized cells on their epidermis that we now find in bamboos and in most other subfamilies except for the Festucoideae. Epidermal cells of these kinds occur in the genus *Joinvillea*, belonging to the neighboring family Flagellariaceae (Smithson, 1957). Their leaf chlorophyll bearing parenchyma were evenly distributed, and the specialized bundle-sheath chloroplasts found in species of Panicoideae and Eragrostoideae had not evolved. Their embryos were relatively small compared to the endosperm but were equipped with epiblast and cotyledonary node. Cytologically they probably had a gametic number of $n = 6$ or $n = 7$ and relatively small chromosomes.

Ecologically these grasses were probably adapted to semiarid situations, perhaps steppes or savannas. Through the action of bulliform cells, their leaves were probably able to become inrolled during periods of drought. They probably had already developed enough of a basal intercalary meristem to enable the leaves to recover from grazing. Their silica content evolved during the differentiation of the family from its ancestors, increasing their resistance to grazers, particularly the relatively inefficient grazing mammals or reptiles existing at that time, as well as to many kinds of insects. The modification of petals into lodicules enabled their florets to open during periods of favorable moisture and close during periods of excessive moisture or drought. Finally, wind pollination is generally an adaptation to dry regions where pollinating insects are relatively scarce and winds are strong.

Adaptive Radiation within the Grass Family

Starting with primitive grasses of the kind just described, the evolution of the family consisted of adaptive radiation along several lines. With respect to vegetative characteristics the most general trend was an increase in size.

This was accomplished by the increased activity of intercalary meristems. Those in the leaves became responsible for their great elongation, as we see it in most modern grasses, including particularly the ones that are most valuable for forage. Intercalary meristems in the stems gave rise to elongate rhizomes to elevated culms; and in bamboos, *Arundo, Saccharum,* and other genera, they gave rise to tall stems having many nodes. These intercalary meristems in the stem could not have been functional and adaptive until the specialized leaf sheath had become fully evolved. Unless protected by overlapping sheaths, the meristematic tissue of grass stems is too weak to support the stem.

The most general trends in the spikelets and florets consisted of various kinds of reductions. The reduction of lodicules from three to two, of stamens from six to three, and of stigmas from three to two took place in nearly every radiating line. The primitive condition with respect to some or all of these organs is retained only in species of Bambusoideae, and a few species belonging to the Arundoideae, Oryzoideae, and Festucoideae. The retardation of reductional trends in the florets of bamboos is probably related to their long life and infrequency of reproduction by seed. Under such conditions, selective pressure would be much less on reproductive than on vegetative characteristics.

Reduction of the number of florets per spikelet is an even more familiar general trend, since it has been used as the basis for recognizing tribes and genera in the traditional taxonomic systems. As is well known this reduction has proceeded in an enturely different way in the Festucoid and Panicoid subfamilies.

Among the more interesting specialized trends of adaptive radiation in grasses have been adaptations for seed dispersal and establishment of seedlings. Seed dispersal by wind is often aided by bristlelike structures that surround the dispersal unit, usually the lemma, palea, and caryopsis. In each of the various groups in which this mechanism has evolved, very different original structures have been modified into bristles. In *Aegilops umbellulata* and polyploids of which it is one parent, as well as in genera of the tribe Pappophoreae, the dispersal mechanism of bristles consists of numerous awns of the lemma itself. In *Sitanion* much divided sterile glumes have the same function. In *Hordeum jubatum* this function is carried out by the long-awned and very slender glumes and lemmas of the sterile lateral florets that flank the fertile floret on each node of the rachis. Turning to the subfamily Panicoideae, we find that in *Setaria* and *Pennisetum* the same function is performed by secondary branches of the inflorescence, which no longer bear spikelets. In *Andropogon, Saccharum,* and related genera, as well as in *Arundo, Phragmites,* and other genera of the subfamily Arundoideae, and in *Calamagrostis* of the *Agrostideae,* wind transport is facilitated by the development of large unicellular trichomes surrounding the base of the lemma.

Wind transport of entire spikelets is achieved in *Hilaria* by modification of the glumes and lemmas of lateral staminate spikelets into papery, wing-like structures.

Mechanisms for seed dispersal by animals are even more diverse. The most familiar ones are long, rough awns or beards that penetrate the hair and feathers of mammals or birds, or even the skin, especially near the mouth parts of grazing mammals. In other instances, particularly among species of which the caryopses and surrounding lemmas are small and light, trichomes on the surface or at the base of the lemma help it to adhere to animal fur. The webby pubescence of *Poa*, which is often used in taxonomic keys to the species of the difficult genus, is a good example. In *Bromus mollis*, *B. purgans*, and other species of *Bromus* as well as of other genera, surface hairs on the lemma itself, and occasionally on the empty glumes, aid in dispersal. An extreme instance of this kind is the bur of *Tragus*, in which strong, hooked hairs developed on the sterile glumes convert the entire spikelet into an easily dispersed unit. In *Cenchrus* an equally functional bur has evolved through coalescence of sterile branchlets of the inflorescence around a fertile spikelet.

Some mechanisms for dispersal by animals render the caryopsis and its surrounding envelopes attractive for ingestion by birds, and at the same time at least partially resistant to their digestive juices. In *Oryzopsis*, *Phalaris*, and *Milium* the lemma has been modified to carry out this function, but in *Coix* the hard shiny covering of the dispersal unit is the modified sheath of a bract.

Evolution at the Species Level

Grasses have a reputation for being taxonomically difficult. This reputation is fully deserved. The difficulty of delimiting species of Gramineae is through no fault of the excellent taxonomists who have studied them. It exists because grasses break almost all of the rules that many other groups of animals and plants observe, and which make life easier for the monographer. Species can most easily be delimited when they consist of a series of reasonably similar populations, separated from each other by sharp, easily recognized gaps of morphological and genetic discontinuity. This condition is rare among genera of grasses. I know it only in the genus *Melica*, and in Californian species of *Bromus*, sect. *Bromopsis*. In both of these groups, species are easily delimited because they are all diploid, and hybrids between them are all highly sterile (Joranson, 1944; Jacob, 1954). Furthermore ecotypic variation within these species is not great.

Other groups of grasses possess one or more of the following conditions which tend to blur species boundaries: (1) A large amount of racial or ecotypic variation within an interfertile complex of populations; (2) partial phenotypic discontinuities between sympatric races or inbred lines because of the extreme development of self-fertilization; (3) varying degrees of partial hybrid sterility in crosses between related populations; (4) strongly developed barriers of hybrid sterility between phenotypically similar populations, both sympatric and allopatric; (5) altered segregation ratios and fertility relationships resulting from polyploidy; (6) stabilization of sterile hybrid derivatives through facultative or obligate apomixis.

Reproductive isolation, since it is one of the principal mechanisms for the origin of species, deserves particular attention. The "biological species concept," which maintains that species should be delimited on the basis of genetic continuity within a species and the presence of reproductive isolation for the separation of species, continues to generate much heated controversy. One must admit that in grasses and many other groups of plants, this concept does not provide a purely objective, nonarbitrary basis for delimiting species as Simpson (1951) and Mayr (1963) have claimed for animals. This is because even without the complicating factors provided by different levels of polyploidy combined with hybridization, the amount of reproductive isolation between populations having the same chromosome number may vary over a whole spectrum of intermediate degrees, even among a group of closely related races. Nevertheless the fact that reproductive isolation by itself does not provide infallible criteria for delimiting species any more than do other kinds of characters does not justify the complete rejection of this phenomenon as basic to the process of speciation. The importance of reproductive isolation between sympatric populations is that it permits each population thus isolated to develop its own adaptive system and to evolve in its own particular direction. Without reproductive isolation, which begins at the species level, evolutionary diversity could not exist.

Nevertheless in considering the evolution of grasses at the species level, we must consider four complicating features that are often found with respect to their patterns of reproductive isolation. The first of these is the presence of strongly developed barriers of hybrid incompatibility between closely similar, often sympatric populations, which all taxonomists regard as belonging to the same species. This condition was observed by the present author in the widespread species of western North America, *Elymus glaucus*, and was intensively studied by Snyder (1950, 1951). In this species nearly all crosses between populations inhabiting different geographical regions either fail completely or produce highly sterile hybrids. Moreover, some localities contain as many as five or six different "races," which can be recognized on the basis of slight differences in external morphology and habitat preference, and which are separated from each other by barriers of hybrid incompatibility or F_1 sterility. These are truly sibling species in the sense of Mayr (1963). How many such sibling species exist in *Elymus glaucus* as recognized by taxonomists is unknown and could only be determined by a very large number of hybridizations; there are certainly hundreds of them. Field observations, as yet unsupported by experimental data, suggest that the same situation exists in the related species *Sitanion hystrix* and *S. jubatum*.

The second complication is the existence of strong barriers of reproductive isolation between populations inhabiting regions widely separated from each other geographically, whereas populations inhabiting intermediate regions can form partly fertile hybrids with both extremes. This condition has been found by the writer in *Bromus* subgenus *Ceratochloa* (G. L. Stebbins and Tobgy, 1944; G. L. Stebbins, unpublished data). When strains of *B. carinatus* from coastal California are crossed with *B. marginatus* from the mountains of Arizona, the F_1 hybrid, in spite of nearly regular chromosome pairing at meiosis, is almost completely sterile. On the other hand, strains of *B. marginatus* from the Sierra Nevada will form partly fertile hybrids with both Arizona *marginatus* and coastal *carinatus*. On the basis of these results, as well as their pattern of morphological and ecological variation, *B. carinatus, B. marginatus*, and *B. breviaristatus* are all regarded as well-marked subspecies of a single species. If, however, the intermediate strains should become extinct, the extreme populations could behave as separate species even without any further evolutionary divergence.

Polyploidy as a Factor in Grass Evolution

The third condition that has blurred and obscured the boundaries between species of grasses is the combination of hybridization with the doubling of entire chromosome sets, or polyploidy. I have repeatedly stressed my conviction that successful polyploidy in higher plants is nearly always associated with hybridization, but that this hybridization need not be of the extreme kind that gives rise to species agreeing with the classical concept of allopolyploids (G. L. Stebbins, 1949, 1950, 1956, 1959, 1971). For the evolutionist, the most useful definition of hybridization is crossing between populations having widely different adaptive norms or reaction systems. Such parental populations often form fertile F_1 hybrids at the diploid level, as in orchard grass, *Dactylis* (G. L. Stebbins and Zohary, 1959). Polyploids derived from such hybrids, in spite of their hybrid origin, possess all of the cytogenetic characteristics of autopolyploidy (McCollum, 1958). If, therefore, we retain the classical categories of autopolyploids and allopolyploids, we must recognize the presence of many autopolyploids that are actually of hybrid origin. This category is hard to fit into the usual division of polyploids into auto- and allopolyploids, as is also the category of segmental allopolyploids (G. L. Stebbins, 1950), which result from doubling the chromosome number of hybrids between species having partially homologous genomes. In my opinion the best way of avoiding confusion in discussing the evolutionary origin of polyploids is to discard completely the typological categories of auto- and allopolyploids. We can then analyze polyploids with respect to two kinds of characteristics that are separate and not necessarily correlated with each other: (1) The degree of morphological and ecological differentiation between ancestral diploid populations, and (2) the degree of cytogenetic homology between ancestral diploid genomes, leading to varying percentages of multivalent formation and tetrasomic inheritance in the polyploids themselves.

The degree to which distinctions between ancestral diploid populations have become blurred is greatest in examples of polyploids derived from hybridization between ecotypes of the same species or between closely related species having partly homologous genomes. An excellent example of this blurring is the polyploid complex of *Dactylis* or orchard grass. It contains several different diploid ecotypes, which are widely separated from each other geographically, and are for the most part easily distinguishable on the basis of morphological characteristics. Were it not for the existence of tetraploids derived from them, these diploids would certainly qualify as different species (G. L. Stebbins and Zohary, 1959). Hybrids between them may be fully fertile and vigorous in the F_1 and F_2 generations (G. L. Stebbins, 1962), or they may be separated by slight barriers of hybrid sterility (Borrill, 1961). Nevertheless, polyploids derived either from individual diploid populations or from hybrids between them are fertile, vigorous, and freely able to exchange genes with each other. Moreover, triploids occur not uncommonly in regions where diploids and tetraploids occur sympatrically. Although highly sterile, these triploids can nevertheless produce some vigorous and fertile offspring through backcrossing with tetraploids, and thus form a one-way bridge for gene flow from diploid to tetraploid populations. Hence the result of repeated natural doublings from different diploid strains, followed by backcrossing, hybridization at the tetraploid level, and segregation has produced a complex web of tetraploid variants, which completely bridge the morphological gaps between diploids, and render the subdivision of the complex into morphologically recognizable entities extremely difficult. The existence of this situation in *Dactylis* and many other genera of grasses was not imagined by any of the botanists who originally described species of the family. One must not be surprised at the failure of attempts to produce clear-cut classifications of such complexes on the basis of conventional methods. One may still debate the question of how they should be classified; but in my opinion no classification of them will be meaningful unless it takes into account their evolutionary history of both hybridization and chromosome doubling.

Distinction between ancestral diploid populations can also become blurred through secondary hybridization between polyploid species having quite different origins. This happens most often in contacts between two polyploids that have one of their two component genomes in common (G. L. Stebbins, 1971). Using the conventional letter system for designating genomes, we can conceive of two polyploids, $AABB$ and $AACC$, which originated independently from hybridizations and doublings involving the diploid species AA, BB, and CC. The buffering effect produced by the common genome AA will make gene exchange between the tetraploid species $AABB$ and $AACC$ much easier than between the ancestral diploid BB and CC. Based upon extensive field observations and artificial hybridizations, Zohary (1965) has recognized a series of such hybridizing tetraploids which center about the diploid species *Aegilops umbellulata*. The success of these tetraploids and their hybrid derivatives is due largely to the adaptive character of the seed dispersal mechanism possessed by *Ae. umbellulata*. Its genome is designated as a *pivotal genome* for the series of tetraploids.

After learning about this situation from Dr. Zohary, I realized that we had found two examples of pivotal genomes in our cytogenetic studies of grasses, but had failed to realize their significance. One of them is the widespread group of perennial bunch grasses that are usually placed in *Agropyron*, *Elymus*, and related genera: *Agropyron trachycaulum*, *A. parishii*, *Elymus glaucus*, *E. canadensis*, *E. villosus*, *E. virginicus*, and the genera *Sitanion* and *Hystrix* in North America; *A. caninum*, *E. dahuricus*, and *E. sibiricus* in Eurasia; and *A. breviaristatum*, *A. scabriglume*, *A. tilcarense*, *E. patagonicus*, and their relatives in South America (Hunziker, 1966), as well as many other species related to these. The results of a number of hybridizations have shown that the North American tetraploids of this complex (as well as *A. caninum*,) contain one genome derived from either the diploid *Agropyron spicatum* or some closely related species (G. L. Stebbins and Snyder, 1956). The results of morphological comparisons and hybridizations indicate that a genome essentially homologous to that of *A. spicatum* is widespread in Asia, being found in *A. caespitosum* of Iran and Asia Minor and probably also in *A. Gmelinii* of Siberia (G. L. Stebbins and Pun, 1953). The success of the tetraploids and hexaploids that contain the *A. spicatum* genome may well be due to the marked drought and cold resistance that genome carries.

Natural hybrids between them are well known, and evidence is abundant that the complexity of their variation pattern has been increased by introgression (G. L. Stebbins, 1957; Church, 1967, Hunziker, 1967). The alternative genomes that entered into the various tetraploids are still unidentified, and the diploid species that carried them may be extinct. There is some reason for believing that they were primitive ancestors of the modern perennial diploid species of *Hordeum*.

The second polyploid complex based upon the principle of a pivotal genome consists of the octoploid members of the complex of *Bromus carinatus*. These species or subspecies all contain three genomes made up of medium-sized chromosomes and one genome consisting of considerably larger chromosomes. Hybrids between them have somewhat irregular chromosome behavior at meiosis, with pairing considerably more disturbed between the large chromosomes that the medium-sized ones (G. L. Stebbins and Tobgy, 1944). Analyses by means of hybridizations indicate that the three genomes having medium-sized chromosomes are derived from hexaploid species of the subgenus *Ceratochloa* which are now natives only to South America; whereas the genome having large chromosomes in homologous to that carried by diploid species of the subgenus *Bromopsis* (G. L. Stebbins, Jr., 1947). When the various octoploids, such as *B. carinatus*, *B. marginatus*, *B. breviaristatus*, and *B. laciniatus*, are compared morphologically with different diploid North American species of subgenus *Bromopsis*, some of them are seen to resemble more closely *B. vulgaris*, others *B. Orcuttianus*, and still others *B. anomalus*. Moreover, these morphological resemblances are correlated with the geographical and ecological distribution of the octoploids. This example is best explained by assuming that a single hexaploid, or a few very closely related hexaploid species hybridized in different localities with several different diploids, producing a number of octoploid derivatives which at first were quite distinct from each other. Later, however, different octoploids came together and were able to hybridize and exchange genes because of the buffering effect of the three genomes derived in common from the ancestral hexaploid. In this example, therefore, the three *Ceratochloa* genomes are pivotal.

An extension of this principle, which includes additional hybridizations and one-way introgression between tetraploids and distantly related diploids, has been found by De Wet and Harlan (1966) in perennial species belonging to several genera of the tribe Andropogoneae. They have designated the enormously variable complex of populations that results from these processes a *compilospecies*. In the Andropogoneae the complexity is greatly increased by the presence of asexual or apomictic seed production, which serves to preserve and spread genotypes which by sexual reproduction would be completely sterile.

Polyploidy and Apomixis in Grasses

Along with the Rosaceae and Compositae, the Gramineae are noteworthy for the high frequency with which seed production by asexual means, or apomixis, appears in various genera. In addition to the long-known examples of *Poa* and *Calamagrostis* (G. L. Stebbins, 1950), apomixis has been found in *Panicum* (Warmke, 1954), *Paspalum* (Snyder, 1957, 1961), *Pennisetum* (Narayan, 1955a,b, Snyder *et al.*, 1955; Gildenhuys and Brix, 1959), *Setaria* (Emery, 1957), *Bouteloua* (Harlan, 1949; Kapadia and Gould, 1964), *Bothriochloa* and related genera of Andropogoneae (De Wet, 1968), and several other genera (Brown and Emery 1957, 1958; Emery and Brown, 1958, Rychlewski, 1961). Each of these genera is notorious for its taxonomic difficulty. This is due largely to the fact that genotypes of hybrid origin which are sexually sterile can be preserved indefinitely and spread over large areas by apomictic reproduction. A further complication exists in grasses because of the very frequent presence of facultative apomixis. Many clones which usually reproduce apomictically can occasionally produce sexual offspring. Because the original clones are highly heterozygous on account of their hybrid origin, their sexual offspring may deviate widely from the parental clone, and may perpetuate this deviation by renewed apomictic reproduction (Clausen, 1954). In genera that have had such an evolutionary history, the delimiting of clearly recognizable species is impossible.

The fact that apomixis exists in grasses that have a high value for forage, such as bluegrass (*Poa pratensis*) and guineagrass (*Panicum maximum*), represents both a problem and a challenge to plant breeders. The challenge is provided by the fact that an economically valuable clone, once it has been obtained, can be perpetuated indefinitely by means of apomictic seed production. The problem exists because of the difficulty or impossibility of using many genotypes of these groups as parents of hybrids. One way of breaking through this barrier is to locate facultatively apomictic genotypes, and to increase by artificial means the proportion of seed they produce via sexual reproduction. Experiments to show that this can be done have been carried out in *Poa* (Grazi *et al.*, 1961; Nygren and Almgård, 1962) and the Andropogoneae (Knox and Heslop-Harrison, 1963; Knox, 1967). These experiments show that the desired goal can be reached by means of both environmental manipulation and radiation of seeds to produce mutations. Many more such experiments are, however, needed before the problem can be regarded as solved.

Synthetic Evolution in Grasses

Most experimental studies of evolution continue to be analytical rather than synthetic. The investigator attempts to discover the evolutionary processes that are active in a particular population or group of populations or to trace the past evolutionary history of a group. The final demonstration that we understand the processes of evolution will, however, come from successful experiments in which new, adaptively successful races or species have been synthesized from known ancestors by carefully controlled methods. Moreover, the value of evolutionary knowledge to mankind depends on the ability to use these methods for the production of some economically valuable crop plant or domestic animal.

With respect to speciation in the absence of polyploidy, I have shown (G. L. Stebbins, 1957) that new microspecies or sibling species of the *Elymus glaucus* complex can be synthesized by hybridization between *E. glaucus* and the closely related but morphologically very different species *Sitanion jubatum*, followed by backcrossing and selection for fertility. That this result does not inevitably result from such a procedure is evident from the difficulty which Grant (1966) has had in performing similar experiments in the genus *Gilia*. The greater success which was experienced in *Elymus* is probably based upon the fact that in the F_1 hybrid of *Elymus* × *Sitanion* chromosome pairing is intimate and crossover frequency is high, so that many new gene combinations can be generated. Because of the virtual absence of pairing in the F_1 hybrids of *Gilia*, recombination for the most part involved entire chromosomes, so that rare but potentially valuable new combinations of genes almost never arose.

Speciation by means of polyploidy is more or less instantaneous. Consequently this kind of evolution is much more easily duplicated by the experimenter, who has relatively little time at his disposal, than are the longer, more complex pathways for the origin of species by means of mutation, genetic recombination, and selection. I have had some success with this kind of synthesis, both with an without accompanying hybridization.

The successful autopolyploid was produced by colchicine treatment from a strain of the South African species *Ehrharta erecta* spontaneous on the Berkeley campus of the University of California. In nearly every location in which seeds of this artificial autotetraploid were sown along with those of the parental diploid, the diploid proved to be much more successful in competition under seminatural conditions than the tetraploid. In one locality, however, near the Botanical Garden of the University of California, the tetraploid has been very successful. Twenty-five years after the initial planting, it has spread several hundred feet from the original site. It occupies a habitat recognizably different from that occupied by the diploid that was planted at the same time and has spread equally far. The tetraploid grows in deep shade under oak trees, on relatively steep slopes with good drainage, whereas the diploid tends to grow in partial shade, and on less well-drained soils. New experiments, started a few years ago and using the same strains, are producing similar results.

This artificial autotetraploid *Ehrharta erecta* has most if not all of the characteristics of a valid species. It can be distinguished morphologically from the diploid on the basis of growth habit and particularly its larger spikelets. Although the established populations have been studied during 25 years, no natural hybrids between diploids and tetraploids have been found. They would be easily recognizable because, being triploids, they would be highly sterile. Gene exchange between diploids and tetraploids in this example is therefore minimal or lacking altogether. Finally, the newly synthesized tetraploid occupies its own distinctive ecological niche, where it successfully resists competition from other species, even such weedy grasses as *Hordeum leporinum*. Its origin can therefore be regarded as the synthesis of a successful new population that has many characteristics of a new species.

A similar synthesis has been carried out with respect to a hybrid polyploid. Artificial hybrids between *Elymus glaucus* and *Sitanion jubatum* were produced in 1950, and polyploids were obtained from them with the aid of colchicine (G. L. Stebbins and Vaarama, 1954). In 1952 seed of these polyploids were planted on various natural sites. On one of these sites, in the North Coast Range of California west of Capay Valley, Yolo County, the *Elymus-Sitanion* polyploid maintained itself for 15 years but is now gone. A few plants of *S. jubatum* were on the site at the original time of planting and have persisted but not increased in number. The site is too dry for *E. glaucus*. Hence it appears that on this particular site, the hybrid polyploid *E. glaucus–S. jubatum* was more successful than either of its parental species.

These experiments, although they are all on a very small scale, nevertheless tell us that we know enough about the processes of evolution so that we can duplicate under seminatural conditions some steps of evolutionary change.

References

Arber, A. (1934). "The Gramineae—A Study of Cereal, Bamboo, and Grass." Cambridge Univ. Press, London and New York.

Beetle, A. A. (1958). *Piptochaetum* and *Phalaris* in the fossil record. *Bull. Torrey Bot. Club* **85**, 179–181.

Bews, J. W. (1929). "The World's Grasses; Their Differentiation, Distribution, Economics, and Geology." Longmans, Green, New York.

Bonnett, O. T. (1937). The development of the oat panicle. *J. Agr. Res.* **54**, 927–931.

Borrill, M. (1961). The pattern of morphological variation in diploid and tetraploid *Dactylis*. *J. Linn. Soc. London, Bot.* **56**, 441–452.

Brown, W. V., and Emery, W. H. P. (1957). Some South African apomictic grasses. *J. S. Afr. Bot.* **23**, 123–125.

Brown, W. V., and Emery, W. H. P. (1958). Apomixis in the Gramineae: Panicoideae. *Amer. J. Bot.* **45**, 253–263.

Church, G. L. (1967). Taxonomic and genetic relationships of eastern North American species of *Elymus* with setaceous glumes. *Rhodora* **69**, 121–162.

Clausen, J. (1954). Partial apomixis as an equilibrium system in evolution. *Caryologia* **7**, 469–478.

Cronquist, A. (1968). "The Evolution and Classification of Flowering Plants." Houghton, Boston, Massachusetts.

De Wet, J. M. J. (1968). Diploid-tetraploid-haploid cycles and the origin of variability in *Dichanthium* agamospecies. *Evolution* **22**, 394–397.

De Wet, J. M. J., and Harlan, J. R. (1966). Morphology of the compilospecies *Bothriochloa intermedia*. *Amer. J. Bot.* **53**, 94–98.

Emery, W. H. P. (1957). A study of reproduction in *Setaria macrostachya* and its relatives. *Bull. Torrey Bot. Club* **84**, 106–121.

Emery, W. H. P., and Brown, W. V. (1958). Apomixis in the Gramineae, tribe Andropogoneae: *Heteropogon contortus*. *Madrono, San Francisco* **14**, 238–246.

Gildenhuys, P. J., and Brix, K. (1959). Apomixis in *Pennisetum dubium*. *S. Afr. J. Agr. Sci.* **2**, 231–245.

Grant, V. (1966). The origin of a new species of *Gilia* in a hybridization experiment. *Genetics* **54**, 1189–1199.

Grazi, F., Umaerus, M. and Åkerberg, E. (1961). Observations on the mode of reproduction And the embryology of *Poa pratensis*. *Hereditas* **47**, 489–541.

Harlan, J. R. (1949). Apromixis in side-oats grama. *Amer. J. Bot.* **36**, 495–499.

Hunziker, J. H. (1966). Una especie nueva de *Agropyron* de la flora Argentina. *Kurtziana* **3**, 121–125.

Hunziker, J. H. (1967). Chromosome and protein differentiation in the *Agropyron scabriglume* complex. *Taxon* **16**, 259–266.

Hutchinson, J. (1934). "The Families of Flowering Plants," Vol. II. Macmillan, New York.

Jakob, K. M. (1954). The cytogenetics of some hybrids and an allopolyploid in the genus *Bromus* (Section Bromopsis). *Proc. Int. Congr. Genet., 9th, 1953* p. 1180–1182.

Joranson, P. N. (1944). The cytogenetics of hybrids, autotetraploids, and allotetraploids in the grass genus *Melica* L. Ph. D. Thesis, University of California.

Kapadia, Z. J., and Gould, F. W. (1964). Biosystematic studies in the *Bouteloua curtipendula* complex. IV. Dynamics of variation in *B. curtipendula* var. *caespitosa*. *Bull. Torrey Bot. Club* **91**, 465–478.

Knox, R. B. (1967). Apomixis: Seasonal and population differences in a grass. *Science* **157**, 6–15.

Knox, R. B., and Heslop-Harrison, J. (1963). Experimental control of aposporous apomixis in a grass of the Andropogoneae. *Bot. Notis.* **116**, 127–141.

McCollum, G. (1958). Comparative studies of chromosome pairing in natural and induced tetraploid *Dactylis*. *Chromosoma* **9**, 571–605.

MacGinitie, H. D. (1953). Fossil plants of the Florissant Beds, Colorado. *Carnegie Inst. Wash. Pub.* **599** 1–198.

Mayr, E. (1963). "Animal Species and Evolution." Harvard Univ. Press. Cambridge, Massachusetts.

Narayan, K. N. (1955a). Cytogenetic studies of apomixis in *Pennisetum* I. *Pennisetum latifolium* Spreng. *J. Mysore Univ.* **14**, 401–410.

Narayan, K. N. (1955b). Cytogenetic studies of apomixis in *Pennisetum* I. *Pennisetum clandestinum* Hochst. *Proc. Indian Acad. Sci.* **41**, 196–208.

Nygren, A., and Almgård, G. (1962). On the experimental control of vivipary in *Poa. Kogl. Lantbruts-Hoegsk. Ann.* **28**, 27–36.

Östergren, G. (1949). *Luzula* and the mechanism of chromosome movements. *Hereditas* **35**, 445–468.

Prat, H. (1936). La syntématique des Graminées. *Ann. Sci. Natur.: Bot. Biol. Veg.* **10**, 167–258.

Rychlewski, J. (1962). Cyto-embryological studies in the apomictic species *Nardus stricta L. Acta Biol. Cracov. Ser. Bot.* **4**, 1–24.

Schuster, J. (1910). Über die Morphologie der Grasblüte. *Flora (Jena)* **100**, 213–266.

Simpson, G. G. (1951). The species Concept. *Evolution* **5**, 285–298.

Smithson, E. (1957). The comparative anatomy of the Flagellariaceae. *Kew Bull.* **3**, 491–501.

Snyder, L. A. (1950). Morphological variability and hybrid development in *Elymus glaucus. Amer. J. Bot.* **37**, 628–635.

Snyder, L. A. (1951). Cytology of inter-strain hybrids and the probable origin of variability in *Elymus glaucus. Amer. J. Bot.* **38**, 195–202.

Snyder, L. A. (1957). Apomixis in *Paspalum secans. Amer. J. Bot.* **44**, 318-324.

Snyder, L. A. (1961). Asyndesis and meiotic non-reduction in microsporogenesis of apomictic *Paspalum secans. Cytologia* **26**, 50–61.

Snyder, L. A. Hernandez, A. R., and Warmke, H. E. (1955). The mechanism of apomixis in *Pennisetum ciliare. Bot. Gaz.* **116**, 209–221.

Stebbins, G. L. (1945). Unpublished data.

Stebbins, G. L., Jr. (1947). The origin of the complex of *Bromus carinatus* and its phytogeographic implications. *Contrib. Gray Herb. Harvard* **165**, 42–55.

Stebbins, G. L. (1949). The evolutionary significance of natural and artificial polyploids in the family Gramineae. *Proc. Int. Congr. Genet., 8th, 1948* pp. 461–485.

Stebbins, G. L. (1950). "Variation and Evolution in Plants." Columbia Univ. Press, New York.

Stebbins, G. L. (1956). Cytogenetics and evolution of the grass family *Amer. J. Bot.* **43**, 890–905.

Stebbins, G. L. (1957). The hybrid origin of microspecies in the *Elymus glaucus* complex. *Proc. Int. Genet. Symp., 1956* pp. 336–340.

Stebbins, G. L. (1959). The role of hybridization in evolution. *Proc. Amer. Phil. Soc.* **103**, 231–251.

Stebbins, G. L. (1962). Unpublished data.

Stebbins, G. L. (1971). "Chromosomal Evolution in Higher Plants." Addison-Wesley, Reading, Massachusetts.

Stebbins, G. L., and Pun, F. T. (1953). Artificial and natural hybrids in the *Gramineae*, tribe *Hordeae*. V. Diploid hybrids of *Agropyron. Amer. J. Bot.* **40**, 444–449.

Stebbins, G. L., and Snyder, L. A. (1956). Artificial and natural hybrids in the *Gramineae*, tribe *Hordeae*. IX Hybrids between western and eastern North American speices *Amer. J. Bot.* **43**, 305–312.

Stebbins, G. L., and Tobgy, H. A. (1944). The cytogenetics of hybrids in *Bromus*. I. Hybrids within the section *Ceratochloa. Amer. J. Bot.* **31**, 1–11.

Stebbins, G. L., and Vaarama, A. (1954). Artificial and natural hybrids in the *Gramineae*, tribe *Hordeae*. VII. Hybrids and allopolyploids between *Elymus glaucus* and *Sitanion* spp. *Genetics* **39**, 378–395.

Stebbins, G. L., and Zohary, D. (1959). Cytogenetic and evolutionary studies in the genus *Dactylis*. I. Morphology, distribution, and interrelationships of the diploid subspecies. *Univ. Calif., Berkeley, Publ. Bot.* **31**, 1–40.

Takhtajan, A. (1959). "Die Evolution der Angiospermen." Fischer, Jena.

Tanaka, N. (1949). Chromosome studies in the genus *Carex*, with special references to aneuploidy and polyploidy. *Cytologia* **15**, 15–29.

Thorne, R. F. (1968). Synopsis of a putatively phylogenetic classification of the flowering plants. *Aliso* **6**, 57–66.

Warmke, H. E. (1954). Apomixis in *Panicum maximum. Amer. J. Bot.* **41**, 5–11.

Zohary, D. (1965). Colonizer species in the wheat group. *In* "The Genetics of Colonizing Species" (H. G. Baker and G. L. Stebbins, eds.) pp. 403–423. Academic Press, New York.

Chapter 2

Polyploidy as a Factor in the Evolution and Distribution of Grasses

B. LENNART JOHNSON

The development of range grasses for higher forage yields under natural competition with other species requires the preservation of greater adaptability than that needed by crops grown in pure culture under the artificial environment of cultivation. The versatility of polyploids, indicated by their striking role in the evolution of the *Gramineae*, suggests that induced amphiploidy in particular has a place among techniques for the breeding of such grasses. This paper will present some speculations regarding factors determining the evolutionary success of polyploids and will consider the impact of amphiploidy in the evolution and distribution principally of the *Stipeae*. Examples will be drawn also from the *Triticinae*. In the latter, amphiploidy at the level to be discussed is apparently of relatively recent origin but sufficiently stabilized to demonstrate its enhancement of colonizing ability. In the former, amphiploidy, although abviously of great age, is still a persistent force in the exploration and occupation of new habitats.

Factors Determining the Evolutionary Advantage of Polyploidy

No convincing evidence exists to indicate that the mere replication of chromosomes accounts for the evolutionary advantage of polyploids. Nevertheless the preponderance specifically of amphiploids in the *Gramineae* attests to a potential for their superiority. The basis for this superiority appears to entail the interaction of various phenomena among which heterosis (hybrid vigor) is conspicuously implicated.

The sterile hybrid (AB) between related diploid species (AA and BB) commonly exhibits heterosis, which, interpreted in terms of the classical theory of East (1936), is due to the occurrence of functionally allelic genes ($r_1{}^A$ and $r_2{}^B$) with somewhat divergent roles (suggested by the subscripts 1 and 2) at corresponding (homoeologous) loci in the respective genomes (A and B). The fertile amphiploid $AABB$, derived by doubling of the chromosome complement of the primary hybrid, ostensibly has the competitive advantage of the adapted genomes of both parents. Furthermore it retains the functional heterozygosity at homoeologous loci and the attendant vigor of the primary hybrid, and thus presumably would have a competitive advantage at least in the environment supporting the parental ecotypes. Thereafter its ability to surpass the geographic ranges of its parents probably involves other factors including: (1) the obligate perpetuation of heterozygosity; (2) greater enzyme versatility provided by the initial gene combination; (3) an enhanced opportunity for new enzyme mutations at duplicated gene loci; and (4) an assertedly enhanced facility to acquire genes from other sources by introgressive hybridization.

Perpetuation of Heterozygosity

A frequently cited evolutionary advantage of amphiploids over diploids involves the perpetuation of heterozygosity between homoeologous loci with its associated hybrid vigor over successive generations. In random mating populations of diploids or amphiploids a maximum of 50% heterozygosity would be expected to be retained at a given locus, but the initial heterozygosity between functional alleles on homoeologous chromosomes of amphiploids would not be reduced by segregation except in the rare event of pairing between homoeologues. In inbreeding populations any heterozygosity at strictly homologous loci would be expected to decline at the same rate in diploids and amphiploids, but without any effect on the heterozygosity between homoelogous loci of the latter.

Autoploids, which will not be considered further in this discussion, typically do not have the advantage of homoeologous loci to perpetuate functional heterozygosity, all of the functional alleles being at the same locus. However, the expected frequency of various heterozygotes maintained at a given locus under random mating is much higher for an autoploid than for a diploid, as stressed by Barber (1970). For example, three auto-tetraploid heterozygotes ($r_1r_1r_1r_2$, $r_1r_1r_2r_2$, $r_1r_2r_2r_2$) are possible compared with one diploid heterozygote (r_1r_2). Under inbreeding the rate of reduction in heterozygosity is slower for autoploids than for diploids, but this difference can be of little significance on an evolutionary time scale.

THE INITIAL GENE COMBINATION

Barber (1970) suggested that by virtue of its more versatile enzymes the polyploid might actually outdistance the adaptational range of its parents, and that in this way polyploids may have dominated the short-term evolution of plants. Greater versatility of the enzymes of the polyploid is attributable to oligomerization of the peptide chains coded by the functional alleles. The classical work with hemoglobin (cf. Ingram, 1963) and more recent studies including those of Bonner et al. (1965) clearly indicate that interactions between different polypeptide chains are significant in the expression of enzyme activities; and the widespread occurrence of multiple forms of enzymes suggests that they have evolutionary advantages (Wieland, 1968). Good evidence for dimerization of esterases in hexaploid wheat was presented by Barber et al. (1968).

The greater enzyme diversity of polyploids was illustrated by Barber (1970) by reference to the octoploid rye–wheat hybrid Triticale (*AABBDDEE*). This alloploid, carrying functional alleles at four corresponding loci, assertedly can produce not only the four pure dimeric enzymes r^Ar^A, r^Br^B, etc., characteristic of the respective diploid progenitors, but also six hybrid dimeric enzymes r^Ar^B, r^Ar^D, etc., each with a presumably increased rate of activity. In contrast, a diploid heterozygous (r_1r_2) at a given locus can produce only one hybrid dimeric enzyme in addition to the two pure ones.

It should be pointed out, however, that tetraploids clearly have much less advantage over diploids attributable to enzyme diversity than do octoploids, yet they are more numerous and appear to be as competitive as octoploids on the basis of available geographic distributional data. Thus with reference to the homoeologous loci r^Ar^B, each of which is initially homozygous, the tetraploid *AABB*, like the diploid, can produce only one heterozygous dimeric enzyme and two pure ones. Therefore the primary factor in the short-term evolutionary advantage of polyploids would appear to be the perpetuation of the hybrid enzyme rather than the initial amount of enzyme diversity.

DUPLICATED GENE LOCI

While perpetuation of the initial heterozygosity at homoeologous loci provides a short-term advantage, attendant restrictions on the genetic flexibility of amphiploids tend to handicap them in the long run. They are reproductively isolated from the parental species and other possible sources of preadapted genes. Their initial complete homozygosity at strictly homologous loci does not provide for ready reassortment of genes to derive more highly adaptive combinations. Furthermore the specific genotypes comprising the initial genomes A and B inferentially represent local diploid ecotypes which are not likely to endow the amphiploid with a gene combination competitively superior on its own merits to all ecotypes encountered throughout the ranges of both parents.

Despite these innate handicaps, however, amphiploids commonly surpass the geographic ranges of their progenitors and frequently displace them in the evolutionary succession. This suggests the operation of a long-term phenomenon that is not dependent solely on the initial level of heterozygosity. Evidence from the evolution of enzymes in other organisms (Watts and Watts, 1968) links this phenomenon with the reduplicated gene loci.

Upon doubling of the chromosomal complement of the sterile hybrid AB, all of its gene loci are abruptly reduplicated. This doubling, while initiating fertility, apparently does not per se confer any other immediate competitive advantage on the polyploid as compared with the sterile primary hybrid; that is, two doses of r_1^A or of r_2^B are not known to be superior to one of each. However, the polyploid emerges with a plethora of surplus, precoded loci now available for mutation and diversification of enzyme systems without imperiling the meiotic balance of the genome or the vital functions of the original enzymes.

The unlikelihood "that a new enzyme activity can evolve unless the genome contains extra DNA with suitable coding properties such as is provided by the duplication of a gene for a functionally related enzyme" was pointed out by Watts and Watts (1968). The potentially greatly accelerated rate of evolution provided by the convertible loci presumably enhances the adaptability of the amphiploid on all geographic fronts over an indefinite period of time. Coupled with this advantage, a relatively high level of obligate inbreeding tends to purge the amphiploid population of disadvantageous enzyme mutants. Among 24 species whose world-wide or local success as colonizers was attributed by Allard (1965) to their self-fertilizing system of mating, 16 are, in fact, polyploids; six include polyploid or aneuploid forms; only two are strictly diploids.

Enhanced Facility for Gene Exchange

A hypothesis attributing the colonizing ability of polyploids in the *Aegilops–Triticum* group to hybridization was proposed by Zohary and Feldman (1962). This hypothesis further explicated by Zohary (1965) presumes that the ability of polyploids to acquire adaptive genes from related polyploids and diploids is enhanced by a mechanism involving a "pivotal" genome and one or more modifiable genomes. The four tetraploid species, *Ae. ovata* L. (C^uM^o). *Ae. triaristata* Willd. (C^uM^t), *Ae. biuncialis* Vis.(C^uM^b) and *Ae. columnaris* Zhuk. (C^uM^c) assertedly were derived by amphiploidy (Kihara, 1954) from the diploid *Ae. umbellulata* Zhuk. (C^u) and *Ae. comosa* Sibth. et Sm. (*M*). The tetraploids were assigned the indicated genome formulas by Kihara to suggest that the *comosa* genome varies among them whereas the *umbellulata* genome does not. The subsequent hypothesis by Zohary and Feldman asserts that the pivotal (C^u) genome provides a buffering effect that permits the second (*M*) genome to become modified by hybridization.

Evidence presented from mixed stands of *Aegilops* species suggests that introgressive hybridization has indeed contributed to the morphological variability of some of these polyploids. Whether introgressive hybridization provides an appreciable impetus to their greater colonizing aggressiveness and greater geographic dispersal as compared with diploids, however, can be questioned. Hybridization in mixed stands is a localized phenomenon likely to provide only localized adaptational advantage, since the prevailing inbreeding system of new polyploids, at least, does not provide for dispersing the acquired genes. The validity of the pivotal genome hypothesis rests heavily on the original cytological evidence of Kihara (1945, 1954) interpreted to show that observed differences in chromosome pairing affinities in interspecific hybrids were confined to one of the two genomes (the *M* genome). As pointed out by Waines (1969) the published evidence to support this interpretation is inconclusive largely because a distinction could not be made between auto- and allosyndesis. If, in fact, polyploids in general have an advantage over diploids in acquiring genes by hybridization, this could, alternatively, be due to the duplicated loci on all of the chromosomes (in this case both the C^u and *M* genome) that could be traded off without impairing survival ability.

According to more conventional interpretation, the four *Aegilops* amphiploids referred to were derived from at least four different hybrid combinations, possibly at different times as suggested by marked differences in the extent of their geographic ranges. On the basis of this assumption the various *M* genomes of the tetraploids are attributable to divergence in homology within the population of *Ae. comosa* (*M*) prior to the origin of the tetraploids. Waines (1969) found the protein electrophoretic pattern among accessions of *Ae. comosa* to be the most variable among all of the diploid species of *Aegilops*, whereas the pattern of *Ae. umbellulata* (C^u) and of the four tetraploids showed relatively little variation.

If enzyme mutations at the convertible loci largely account for the colonizing success of amphiploids, the expected effect on the population would be relative morphological homogeneity as compared with the effects expected from hybridization. Many polyploids, in fact, are strikingly uniform compared with related diploids. The widely distributed tetraploid *Ae. cylindrica* Host. (*CD*), apparently of relatively recent origin, is morphologically very uniform compared with its diploid progenitors, *Ae. caudata* L. (*C*) and especially *Ae. squarrosa* L. (*D*). It is also very uniform compared with those diploids with respect to the seed protein pattern produced by electrophoresis (Johnson, 1967). From each variable parental species a specific type can be selected whose protein extracts when mixed will produce a pattern that essentially duplicates the ubiquitous type of the tetraploid. This suggests that the tetraploid could have originated essentially from these two parental types and that subsequent hybridization was not a significant factor in its evolution.

Evolution of the Alloploid Series in the *Stipeae*

The chromosome numbers among species of *Stipa* and *Oryzopsis* comprise a series from $n = 11$ to $n = 41$. These numbers can be accounted for as a result of recurrent amphiploidy (Fig. 1) beginning with a theoretical basic number of six followed by a postulated change to five in one of the diverging lines. All of the chromosome numbers in the diagram other than the basic numbers of six and five represent actual counts for existing species and hybrids. The number of species represented by each count and their continental distribution are shown in the columns at the right. Extrapolation from the confirmed high chromosome counts back to the theoretical basic number is based upon several studies clearly demonstrating reticulation between diverging evolutionary lines at the higher chromosome levels by the formation of sterile hybrids and fertile amphiploids. Thus an otherwise rather arbitrary evolutionary scheme assumes a degree of plausibility.

Intergeneric Hybridization and Spontaneous Amphiploidy

Sterile intergeneric hybrids are very common in the *Stipeae*. Morphological and cytological evidence obtained by Johnson and Rogler (1943)

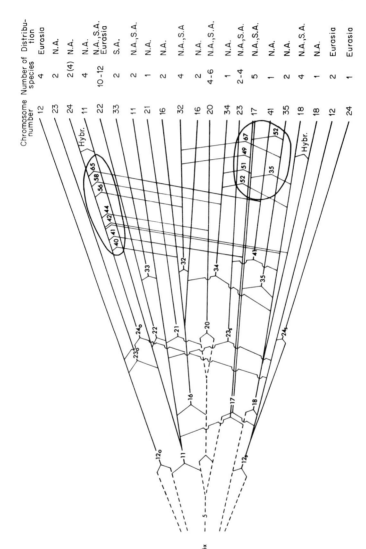

Fig. 1. The postulated manner of origin and convergence of phylogenetic lines with different chromosome numbers in *Oryzopsis* (o) and *Stipa* (s).

showed *Oryzopsis caduca* Beal to be a hybrid between *O. hymenoides* (Roem. and Schult.) Ricker ($n = 24$) and *Stipa viridula* Trin. ($n = 41$). The count of $n = 65$ for *O. caduca* is shown together with counts for other intergeneric hybrids in the encircled area of the diagram (Fig. 1, upper right). Subsequently morphological and geographic distributional data (Johnson, 1945a) from herbarium specimens revealed that *O. hymenoides* crosses spontaneously with various species of *Stipa* to produce sterile hybrids which in the past have all been classified in the herbaria under the specific name of *O. bloomeri* (Boland.) Ricker. Sporadically distributed west of the 100th meridian in the United States, these hybrids appear where the more generally prevalent *O. hymenoides* shares a common habitat with a species of *Stipa*. To date such hybrids involving 11 different species of *Stipa* have been reported (Johnson, 1945a, 1960, 1962a, 1963; Webber, 1957), and for all but two of these (Table 1, Fig. 1) the chromosome number ($n = 40$–65) has now been confirmed from material transplanted from the wild.

In favorable years and under advantageous conditions of habitat disturbance hundres of individuals have been observed in some hybrid swarms.

TABLE 1

NATURAL STERILE HYBRIDS IN *STIPA* AND *ORYZOPSIS*, AND THEIR CHROMOSOME NUMBERS

Hybrid	Chromosome number (n)	Previous report of chromosome number
Oryzopsis hymenoides × *Stripa viridula*[a]	65	Johnson and Rogler, 1943
Oryzopsis hymenoides × *Stipa elmeri*[b]	42	Johnson, 1962a
Oryzopsis hymenoides × *Stipa occidentalis*[b]	42	Johnson, unpublished
Oryzopsis hymenoides × *Stipa columbiana*[b]	42	Johnson, unpublished
Oryzopsis hymenoides × *Stipa thurberiana*	41	Johnson, unpublished
Oryzopsis hymenoides × *Stipa scribneri*[b]	44	Johnson, unpublished
Oryzopsis hymenoides × *Stipa robusta*	—	
Oryzopsis hymenoides × *Stipa neomexicana*	—	
Oryzopsis hymenoides × *Stipa speciosa*[b]	56	Johnson, 1960
Oryzopsis hymenoides × *Stipa nevadensis*[b]	58	Johnson, 1962a
Oryzopsis hymenoides × *Stipa pinetorum*	40	Johnson, 1963
Stipa lepida × *Stipa pulchra*	49	Love, 1954
Stipa cernua × *Stipa pulchra*	67	Love, 1957
Stipa lepida × *Stipa cernua*	52	Love, 1957
Stipa elmeri × *Stipa thurberiana*	35	Johnson, unpublished
Stipa elmeri × *Stipa nevadensis*	52	Johnson, unpublished
Stipa nevadensis × *Stipa thurberiana*	51	Johnson, unpublished

[a]A spontaneous amphiploid was recovered from this hybrid (Nielsen and Rogler, 1952).
[b]Synthetic amphiploids recovered from these hybrids are reported here for the first time.

Their recurrence from repeated hybridization and their persistence owing
to the perennial habit provide a constant opportunity for polyploidization.
However, no amphiploids have been recovered under strictly natural conditions. A single caryopsis was found but unfortunately destroyed in the
process of massive harvests from *O. hymenoides* × *S. nevadensis* B. L. Johnson. Repeated harvests from nursery grown plants of *O. hymenoides* ×
S. viridula finally yielded a single seedling (Nielsen and Rogler, 1952) which
proved to be a fertile, true-breeding amphiploid. It was subsequently increased and tested as a potential forage grass.

SYNTHETIC AMPHIPLOIDS

Since then synthetic amphiploids have been produced readily by colchicine treatment of rooted crown divisions from natural hybrids involving
O. hymenoides with seven different species of *Stipa* (Table 1). These potential
new species, featuring *Stipa* parents as diverse as the high montane *S.
pinetorum* Jones ($n = 16$), the arid desert *S. speciosa* Trin. and Rupr. ($n = 32$),
and the mesic *S. viridula* ($n = 41$), leave little doubt that the recombination of
genetically divergent evolutionary lines in the *Stipeae* has been a factor in
the colonization of diverse habitat. The rate of recovery of meiotic regularity
(Fig. 2A) and seed fertility varies greatly among the amphiploids, but in two

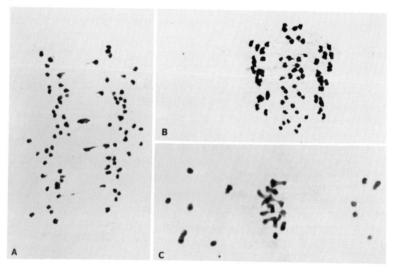

FIG. 2. Meiotic chromosome figures. A. Anaphase I in the fertile first generation amphiploid from *Oryzopsis hymenoides* × *Stipa elmeri* ($2n = 84$). B. Anaphase I in the sterile hybrid,
Stipa elmeri × *S. nevadensis* ($n = 52$) showing dividing univalents. C. Unoriented univalents
and dividing bivalents in the sterile hybrid, *S. elmeri* × *S. thurberiana* ($n = 35$).

instances a practical level of fertility was reached in three generations of selfing. For the plant breeder the amphiploids provide a broad genetic base for the selection of adapted forage types for a wide range of environments.

INTERSPECIFIC HYBRIDIZATION

The role of amphiploidy in the evolution of the *Stipeae* is further illustrated by hybrids between widely dissimilar lines within the genus *Stipa*. At least six sterile natural hybrids between different species of *Stipa* have been collected or previously reported in the literature (Table 1). Their chromosome numbers (Fig. 1, encircled area lower right) varies from $n = 35$ to $n = 67$. The three possible hybrids among *S. lepida* Hitchc. ($n = 17$), *S. pulchra* Hitchc. ($n = 32$), and *S. cernua* Stebbins and Love ($n = 35$) were reported by Love (1954), and the three possible hybrids among *S. elmeri* Piper and Brodie ex Scribn. ($n = 18$), *S. thurberiana* Piper. ($n = 17$), and *S. nevadensis* ($n = 34$) are reported here for the first time. Probably many more interspecific hybrids could be found were they as easily detected as the *O. hymenoides* × *Stipa* hybrids.

GENOME HOMOLOGIES

Although the occurrence of spontaneous hybrids and the artificial production of fertile amphiploids demonstrate only a potential for alloploidy in the *Stipeae*, the evolutionary role of that phenomenon can be traced more directly through genome homologies among established species. Thus meiotic pairing in the hybrids described by Love (1954) indicated that the *cernua* ($n = 35$) and the *pulchra* ($n = 32$) chromosomal complements each includes most of the *lepida* ($n = 17$) complement, and that the *lepida* complement itself is derived from more than one genome. Similarly meiotic divisions in the *S. nevadensis* × *S. elmeri* hybrid (Fig. 2B), consistently featuring 16 to 18 bivalents and an approximately equal number of univalents, indicate that the *nevadensis* ($n = 34$) complement includes essentially the *elmeri* ($n = 18$) genome. Homologies between the *nevadensis* and *thurberiana* ($n = 17$) complements estimated from their hybrid are more equivocal, and the high frequency (12 to 15) of univalents at meiosis in the *S. elmeri* × *S. thurberiana* hybrid (Fig. 2C) suggests relatively distant affinities between the $n = 17$ and $n = 18$ evolutionary lines.

NATURAL AMPHIPLOIDY

The amphiploid origin of two species of *Stipa* (Fig. 3A, B) has been documented by detailed evidence regarding both parents. *Stipa latiglumis*

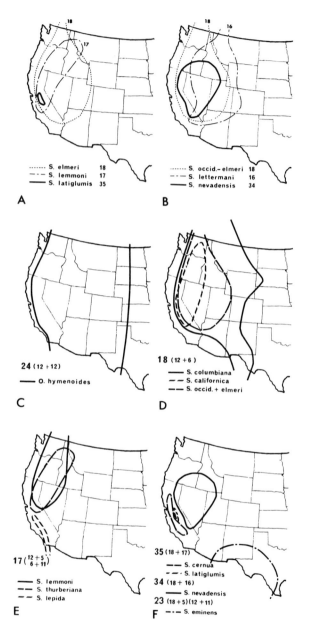

FIG. 3. Geographic distribution of species of *Stipa* and *Oryzopsis*. A, B. The amphiploid species *S. latiglumis* and *S. nevadensis*, and their presumed parental species. C–F. Species distributions suggesting the former persistence of types with *n* = 6 or 12 chromosomes in western North America.

Swallen ($n = 35$), according to Pohl (1954), was clearly derived from a cross between *S. lemmoni* Vasey (Scribn.) ($n = 17$) and *S. elmeri* ($n = 18$). Similarly *S. nevadensis* ($n = 34$), according to Johnson (1962b), was derived from a cross between *S. lettermani* Vasey ($n = 16$) and *S. occidentalis* Thurb. or *S. elmeri* ($n = 18$), the last two being regarded as a single species. The limited geographic range of *S. latiglumis* and the extensive range of *S. nevadensis* possibly suggest a more recent origin of the former. In both instances the amphiploid is sympatric with its postulated progenitors.

A suggestion of more ancient amphiploidy is provided by the North American endemics *O. racemosa* (J. E. Smith) Ricker ($n = 23$) and *O. asperifolia* Michx. ($n = 23$) which are strikingly intermediate between American 11-chromosome diploids such as *O. pungens* (Torr.) Hitchc. or *O. canadensis* (Poir.) Torr. and the 12-chromosome diploids of the Balkan Peninsula and the Near East (Johnson, 1945b). Bowden (1960) reported chromosome counts of $2n = 48$ for *O. racemosa* and *O. asperifolia* and a count of $2n = 24$ for *O. pungens* which, if correct, still do not negate the possible amphiploid origin for the first two. The affinities of *O. hymenoides* ($n = 24$) are puzzling. Its geographic range (Fig. 3C) and hybridization pattern suggest affinity with *Stipa* but morphologically it resembles the Balkan *O. virescens* (Scop.) Beck. ($n = 12$). Possibly it originated by amphiploidy between the 12-chromosome line of *Stipa* and the 12-chromosome line of *Oryzopsis* (Fig. 1).

Further speculation (Fig. 1) regarding the origin of chromosome numbers in the *Stipeae* by alloploidy is done largely without the benefit of evidence from gross morphology or chromosomal homology, recognizing that in some instances the counts might more logically be explained by the addition or loss of chromosomes. Three species with $n = 13$ or $n = 14$ chromosomes are not included in Fig. 1. Some discrepancies are unavoidable owing to variations in the reported chromosome number for a few species.

Conceivably the 12-chromosome species of *Oryzopsis* and *Stipa* arose by amphiploidy involving different hypothetical 6-chromosome lines. With one questionable exception they are all confined to Eurasia. The American 11-chromosome species mostly referred to *Oryzopsis* possibly arose by amphiploidy involving 5- and 6-chromosome lines. By further reticulation among the increasing number of amphiploid lines the chromosome number presumably climbed to a record height of $n = 41$ in *S. viridula*, to $n = 65$ in hybrids between *Oryzopsis* and *Stipa*, and to $n = 67$ in hybrids between different species of *Stipa*.

Gene and Chromosomal Exchange

The conspicuous role of alloploidy tends to obscure other evolutionary phenomena in the *Stipeae*. *Stipa californica* Merr. and Davy ($n = 18$), which exhibits some ability to borrow genes from either *S. occidentalis* ($n = 18$) or *S. columbiana* Macoun. ($n = 18$), may have originated as a hybrid between those two species (Johnson, 1962b) or as a morphologically intermediate evolutionary line. *Oryzopsis contracta* (B. L. Johnson) Shechter ($n = 24$), long regarded as a form of *O. hymenoides* ($n = 24$) was postulated by Shechter and Johnson (1968) to have evolved by hybridization between the latter species and *O. micrantha* (Trin. and Rupr.) Thurb. ($n = 11$), followed by backcrossing and gross restructuring of the *hymenoides* genome to include segments of *micrantha* chromosomes.

GEOGRAPHIC DISTRIBUTION

Any attempt to relate the geographic distribution pattern of *Stipa* and *Oryzopsis* to amphiploidy is handicapped by the fact that chromosome counts are available for only about 25% of the species, mostly those endemic to the United States. Furthermore, detailed studies on genome homologies are lacking. Some 300 species of *Stipa* have been reported from temperate and tropical areas of all of the continents. *Oryzopsis* probably includes less than 30 species confined largely to North America and Eurasia.

Available counts indicate the occurrence of species with $n = 12$ chromosomes among the Eurasian but not among the American *Stipeae*. A possible exception involves the count of $2n = 24$ by Bowden (1960) as compared with $2n = 22$ by Johnson (1945b) for *O. pungens*. Four Eurasian species of *Oryzopsis*, two of *Stipa*, and one of the related genus *Phaenosperma*, having $n = 12$ chromosomes, suggest three diverging lines at this ploidy level. A single Eurasian polyploid species of *Stipa* with $n = 24$ chromosomes has been reported.

However, the distribution of species with chromosome numbers hypothetically involving a basic number of $n = 12$ or 6 (Fig. 3C–E) suggests that 12-chromosome types may have persisted for a long time in western North America before becoming extinct if, in fact, they are extinct. Geological evidence (Elias, 1942) attests to a great proliferation of highly specialized *Stipeae* in the high plains of Nebraska during the Tertiary. *Oryzopsis hymenoides* with $n = 24$ (presumably $12 + 12$) and four species of *Stipa* with $n = 18$ ($12 + 6$) chromosomes are generally distributed west of the 100th meridian as are three species of *Stipa* with $n = 17$ ($12 + 5$ or $6 + 11$) chromosomes. Four higher polyploid species (Fig. 3F) having one putative parent with 18 ($12 + 6$) chromosomes are also largely confined to this area. One of these *S. eminens* with $n = 23$ chromosomes could alternatively be interpreted to represent a $12 + 11$ combination.

Chromosome counts of $n = 11$ occur among American species of the

Stipeae. Five mostly unspecialized North American species of somewhat uncertain classification as *Oryzopsis* or *Stipa* probably represent relicts of a primitive 11-chromosome complex. Among related genera one North American species of *Brachyelytrum* and three South American species of *Piptochaetium* have $n = 11$ chromosomes. No species with $n = 11$ chromosomes have been reported from Eurasia, but seven species with $n = 22$ are reported from America and Eurasia, and two species with $n = 33$ chromosomes are reported from South America, attesting to the success of polyploidy also in the 11-chromosome series.

Two of the $n = 11$ species, *O. canadensis* and *O. pungens* occur in the Great Lakes–New England area and three of them, *O. exigua* Thurb. Little, *O. micrantha*, and *O. kingii* (Boland.) Beal in the western states (Fig. 4A). The ranges of the presumed amphiploids *O. asperifolia*, *O. racemosa*, and *S. spartea* Trin. with $n = 23 (11 + 12)$ chromosomes include the Great Lakes–New England region and extend westward beyond the 100th meridian where the basic chromosome number of 6 or 12 seems to prevail (Fig. 4B). *Stipa comata* Trin. and Rupr. (Fig. 4C) with reported counts of $n = 22$ and $n = 23$ chromosomes also spans the disjunct areas of the 11-chromosome species distribution, and ranges throughout the western states. *Stipa neomexicana* (Thurb.) Scrib. ($n = 22$) has a more restricted distribution in the southwest. Considering the geographic distribution of the species, the count of $n = 23$ could be less probably interpreted as $5 + 18$. However, until the discrepancy between Bowden's (1960) count of $2n = 48$ and Johnson's (1945b) count of $2n = 46$ for *O. asperifolia* and *O. racemosa* is resolved, the distribution of these amphiploids probably suggests that the focal point of polyploidization in the *Stipeae* may have been in North America. Beetle (1959) speculates that if *O. hymenoides* ($n = 24$) is of intergeneric origin, its *Oryzopsis* parent must have entered the New World via Greenland whereas the *Stipa* parent migrated across an Alaskan land bridge.

The basic chromosome number, $x = 6$, is related to the second hypothetical basic number, $x = 5$, through the addition or subtraction of a chromosome. The latter number is inferred from the existence of 11-chromosome species (Fig. 4A) and polyploids presumably involving one or more 5-chromosome progenitors (Fig. 5). The concentration of such polyploids in southwestern United States suggests that 5-chromosome types may have persisted in that area for some time. Thus three species with $n = 20$ chromosomes found in California and in the southern Rocky Mountain states presumably are octoploids from a basic number of $x = 5$. Four species with $n = 16$ chromosomes distributed largely throughout the Rocky Mountain states may represent alloploids involving 5- and 11-chromosome progenitors. Another three species with $n = 16 (5 + 11)$, $n = 21 (5 + 16)$, and $n = 23$ $(5 + 18)$ chromosomes, occurring in the southwestern states and northern

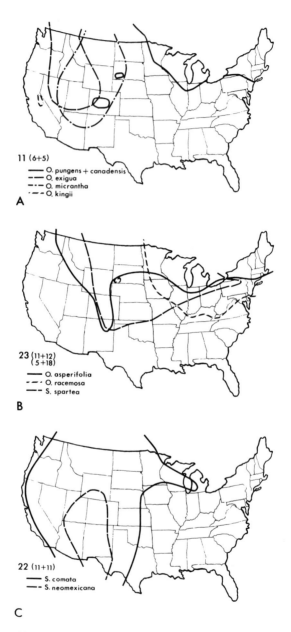

FIG. 4. Geographic distribution of 11-chromosome species of *Oryzopsis* and of higher polyploid species of *Oryzopsis* and *Stipa* presumably involving 11-chromosome parents.

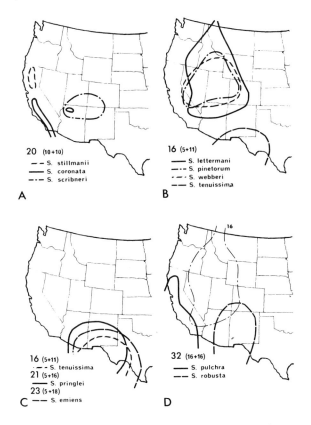

FIG. 5. Geographic distribution of species of *Stipa* suggesting the former occurrence of types with $n = 5$ chromosomes in southwestern United States and Northern Mexico.

Mexico, can be interpreted as amphiploids involving a 5-chromosome progenitor in each case. Three species with $n = 17$ chromosomes ranging from Baja California to British Columbia (Fig. 3E) could be construed as amphiploids involving either 12- and 5-chromosome or 11- and 6-chromosome lines. Morphological similarities between the $n = 18$ and $n = 17$ species favors the former interpretation. *Stipa robusta* (Vasey.) Scribn., (Fig. 5D) with $n = 32$ chromosomes, could represent a tetraploid involving 16-chromosome lines, but it would be more difficult to interpret similarly *S. pulchra* (cf. Love, 1954).

Stipa viridula, with the highest chromosome count ($n = 41$) reported for a species of the *Stipeae*, ranges from the Rocky Mountains to the Great Lakes over the area occupied by three or four polyploids having $n = 23$ chromosomes (Fig. 4B). It bears no marked resemblance to any of these. At the western end of its range it has broad contact with *S. columbiana* ($n = 18$, Fig. 3D) which it resembles closely. It is tempting to speculate that *S. viridula* is an amphiploid between an 18-chromosome type such as *S. columbiana* and a 23-chromosome type that has not yet been found. To identify the latter probably would involve systematic chromosome counts of biotypes in *S. viridula* and in the related sympatric *S. richardsoni* Link. for which a count apparently has not yet been reported.

References

Allard, R. W. (1965). Genetic systems associated with colonizing ability in predominantly self-pollinated species. *In* "The Genetics of Colonizing Species" (H. G. Baker and G. L. Stebbins, (eds.), pp. 49–76. Academic Press, New York.

Barber, H. N. (1970). Hybridization and the evolution of plants. *Taxon* **19**, 154–160.

Barber, H. N., Driscoll, C. J., Long, P. M., and Vickery, R. S. (1968). Protein genetics of wheat and homoeologous relationships of chromosomes. *Nature* (*London*) **218**, 450–452.

Beetle, A. A. (1959). Distribution as a key to the age and origin of grasses. *Recent Advan. Bot.* **1**, 111–116.

Bonner, D., DeMoss, J. A., and Mills, S. E. (1965). The evolution of an enzyme. *In* "Evolving Genes and Proteins" (V. Bryson and H. J. Vogel, eds.), pp. 305–318. Academic Press, New York.

Bowden, W. M. (1960). Chromosome numbers and taxonomic notes on northern grasses. III. Twenty-five genera. *Can. J. Bot.* **38**, 541–557.

East, E. M. (1936). Heterosis. *Genetics* **21**, 375–397.

Elias, M. K. (1942). Tertiary prairie grasses and other herbs from the high plains. *Geol. Soc. Amer., Spec. Pap.* **41**, 1–176.

Ingram, V. M. (1963). "The Hemoglobins in Genetics and Evolution." Columbia Univ. Press, New York.

Johnson, B. L. (1945a). Natural hybrids between *Oryzopsis hymenoides* and several species of *Stipa. Amer. J. Bot.* **32**, 599–608.

Johnson, B. L. (1945b). Cyto-taxonomic studies in *Oryzopsis. Bot. Gaz.* **107**, 1–32.

Johnson, B. L. (1960). Natural hybrids between *Oryzopsis* and *Stipa*. I. *Oryzopsis hymenoides* × *Stipa speciosa. Amer. J. Bot.* **47**, 736–742.

Johnson, B. L. (1962a). Natural hybrids between *Oryzopsis* and *Stipa*. II. *Oryzopsis hymenoides* × *Stipa nevadensis. Amer. J. Bot.* **49**, 540–546.

Johnson B. L. (1962b). Amphiploidy and introgression in *Stipa. Amer. J. Bot.* **49**, 253–262.

Johnson, B. L. (1963). Natural hybrids between *Oryzopsis* and *Stipa*. III. *Oryzopsis hymenoides* × *Stipa pinetorum. Amer. J. Bot.* **50**, 228–234.

Johnson, B. L. (1967). Confirmation of the genome donors of *Aegilops cylindrica. Nature.* (*London*) **216**, 859–862.

Johnson, B. L., and Rogler, G. A. (1943). A cyto-taxonomic study of an intergeneric hybrid between *Oryzopsis hymenoides* and *Stipa viridula. Amer. J. Bot.* **30**, 49–46.

Kihara, H. (1945). Genomanalyse bei *Triticum* und *Aegilops*. IX. Systematisches Aufbau der Gattung *Aegilops* auf genomanalytischer Grundlage. *Cytologia* **14**, 135–144.

Kihara, H. (1954). Considerations on the evolution and distribution of *Aegilops* species based on the analyzer method. *Cytologia* **19**, 336–357.

Love, R. M. (1954). Interspecific hybridization in *Stipa*. II. Hybrids of *S. Cernua, S. lepida* and *S. pulchra. Amer. J. Bot.* **41**, 107–110.

Nielsen, E. L., and Rogler, G. A. (1952). An amphiploid of X *Stiporyzopsis. Amer. J. Bot.* **39**, 343–348.

Pohl, R. A. (1954). The allopolyploid *Stipa latiglumis.* Madrono, San Francisco **12**, 145–150.

Shechter, Y., and Johnson, B. L. (1968). The probable origin of *Oryzopsis contracta. Amer. J. Bot.* **55**, 611–618.

Waines, J. G. (1969). Electrophoretic-systematic studies in *Aegilops.* Ph.D. Thesis, University of California Riverside.

Watts, R. L., and Watts, D. C. (1968). Gene duplication and the evolution of enzymes. *Nature (London)* **217**, 1–15.

Webber, W. A. (1957). A new intergeneric natural hybrid involving *Oryzopsis* and *Stipa* (Gramineae). *Rhodora* **59**, 273–277.

Wieland, T. (1968). Multiple forms of enzymes. *In* "Homologous Enzymes and Biochemical Evolution" (N. V. Thorai and J. Roche, eds.), pp. 3–18. Gordon & Breach, New York.

Zohary, D. (1965). Colonizer species in the wheat group. *In* "The genetics of Colonizer Species" (H. G. Baker and G. L. Stebbins, eds.), pp. 403–423. Academic Press, New York.

Zohary, D., and Feldman, M. (1962). Hybridization between amphiploids and the evolution of polyploids in the wheat (*Aegilops-Triticum*) group. *Evolution* **16**, 44–61.

Chapter 3

Breeding of Grasses

A. A. HANSON

No organized attempts were made to select improved grass varieties in the United States until 1889 when Willet M. Hays made a number of timothy selections at the University of Minnesota. In 1937 grass breeding work was in progress at 38 locations. Most of these breeding projects were of very recent origin, although at a few of the locations listed in the *1937 Yearbook of Agriculture* selection studies had been in progress for from 10 to 20 years. A review of the objectives given for these programs is instructive for it reflects favorably on the imagination of the investigators leading these projects. It is particularly noteworthy to call attention to the program at the W. K. Kellogg Demonstration Farm, Augusta, Michigan, where in 1930 A. B. Dorrance started to select bermudagrass, *Cynodon dactylon* (L.) Pers., for improved winter hardiness—an objective that has been of concern in recent investigations.

The origin of current varieties as depicted in Table 1 shows clearly the impact of ecotypic selection in grass improvement. Many of the varieties that trace to a single identifiable source could also be classed as ecotypic varieties because the original source may well represent a specific ecotype. In general, most ecotypic varieties display improved persistence in the area where they were selected, but gains in yield and quality are not impressive except when they are compared with unadapted varieties and ecotypes. It is evident that many varieties have been named and released solely on the basis of adapta-

TABLE 1

<small>PERENNIAL GRASS VARIETIES IN THE UNITED STATES, 1969</small>

Source	Species		
	Indigenous	Introduced	
		Forage	Turf
Ecotype	15[a]	37[a]	17[a]
Selection			
Single Source	5	34	18
Other	13	67	22

[a]Direct increase—selection limited to roguing off-type plants.

tion to a given environment, so that a recognized adapted seed source would be available for seeding purposes. Many named grass varieties have not enjoyed wide acceptance.

The modest success and failure of many grass breeding programs can be attributed to the lack of fundamental information on population genetics, breeding behavior of polyploids, and the heritability of specific traits. The consequences of these deficiencies can be underscored by such extreme examples as selection practiced within species that later studies have shown to be obligate apomitics. Breeding progress has also been impeded by the lack of appropriate screening procedures for pest resistance and physiological characteristics and because of complex problems involved in evaluating species that are consumed by livestock. In addition, the major differences that separate perennial grass breeding from breeding grain and vegetable crops are not always recognized in research planning and budgeting. Notable advances have been made in developing superior grass varieties, especially when plant breeders can take advantage of either vegetative reproduction or apomictic seed set to increase improved varieties. Although several outstanding examples of progress can be cited, serious deficiencies remain in the store of basic information that can be applied in organized efforts to develop superior grass varieties. Thus it is necessary to draw on experimental evidence from other crops to illustrate those principles that are of significance in grass breeding.

Genetic Diversity

The origin of our major grasses is an important factor in any consideration of grasses and their improvement through breeding. Most of the grasses used for hay, pasture, and turf, and many species adapted for range seeding in arid and semiarid regions were introduced to the United States from other continents. The pattern of introduction was established soon after the settlement of the Eastern seaboard. "English grass," a collective term for mixtures of bluegrasses (*Poa* spp.), ryegrasses (*Lolium* spp.), bentgrasses (*Agrostis* spp.), fescues (*Festuca* spp.), and white clover (*Trifolium repens* L.) were seeded by early settlers in New England. The "seed" was obtained in the form of chaff collected from immigrant ships. In Rhode Island hay seed chaff was used to plant hay meadows as early as 1647, and by 1650 there was some movement of hay seed among the New England colonies (Colby, 1941).

The poor quality of native forage species in the southern colonies in North America was more serious than further north. Here the cool-season grasses and legumes were not adapted, and livestock production did not flourish on indigenous grasses. Certain large plantation owners and government officials became interested in locating tropical and subtropical species that would meet the needs of the region. Bermudagrass, *Cynodon dactylon*, which was brought to Savannah, Georgia, in 1751 by Governor Harry Ellis, was considered to be one of the most important grasses in the southern United States by 1807 (Burton, 1951). This observation is substantiated in early agricultural reports from the U.S. Commissioner of Patents (Anonymous, 1850). Guineagrass, *Panicum maximum* Jacq., was introduced as early as 1813 into Mississippi, and johnsongrass, *Sorghum halepense* (L.) Pers., was sent to South Carolina from Turkey in 1830. The accidental introduction of dallisgrass, *Paspalum dilatatum* Poir., from South America is thought to have occurred before 1850.

Organized public support for the introduction of forage crops into the United States began with the establishment of the U.S. Department of Agriculture on May 15, 1862, and the Land-Grant College Act on July 2, 1862. Plant exploration efforts sponsored by the Department of Agriculture, as well as plant exchange activities conducted by individual scientists, furnished a wide array of useful forage species and germplasm for plant breeding work. Systematic exploration activities received a tremendous stimulus from Vavilov (1949–1950), the Russian agronomist who first proposed a worldwide collection of plants for use in crop improvement. His example encouraged other countries to improve their approach to plant collection work. In time plant explorers were sent out to accumulate comprehensive collections of individual species and to search for germplasm within species that might furnish superior resistance to particular plant pests or provide other specific characteristics.

Experience gained from chance introductions and organized research can be used to illustrate some of the basic problems and opportunities in the collection and evaluation of perennial grasses.

DEVELOPMENT OF NEW ECOTYPES

The transfer of exotic germplasm to a new environment provides an immediate opportunity for new ecotypes to evolve by natural selection, provided that some portion of the original introduction survives. Differences in photoperiod, temperature extremes, available moisture, soil fertility, drainage, disease organisms, and insects contribute to the origin of adapted ecotypes.

The advantages of locally grown clover seed were recognized as early as 1850 in the United States (Fergus and Hollowell, 1960) and many field experiments have served to confirm this point. Similarly, in smooth brome, *Bromus inermis* Leyss. (first introduced from Hungary by the California Agricultural Experiment Station in 1884, and from Russia by the U.S. Department of Agriculture in the period 1896 to 1899) two major types were recognized in 1943—namely, northern adapted and southern adapted material (Newell and Keim, 1943). The origin of these two types may trace in part to differences in original seed sources and in part to the environment under which the introductions were grown in North America. In the past 25 years several ecotypic varieties have been selected from old fields of southern smooth brome.

The superior adaptation of local ecotypes has prompted some plant breeders to discard unadapted introductions after preliminary testing. It is imperative to evaluate new introductions not only for adaptation but also for specific plant characteristics such as resistance to disease and drought in order to realize the full benefit from an investment in plant introduction. Under some circumstances it may be necessary to cross poorly adapted introductions with adapted varieties or ecotypes to insure an acceptable level of vigor for preliminary evaluation.

Comparatively little attention has been given to the possibility of entirely new species developing as a result of plant introduction work. Good opportunities may be provided for extensive hybridization, especially in the grasses, when exotic germplasm is grown in close association with its near relatives in experimental plots, in field plantings, or as escapes near research stations.

Johnsongrass, *Sorghum halepense*, provides an example of major changes that might occur. This tetraploid species is reported to have been brought from Turkey to South Carolina in 1830 and from there to Alabama in about 1840. J. R. Harlan and DeWit (personal communication) have drawn attention to the fact that tetraploid johnsongrass is not native to the Mediterranean region. Johnsongrass is represented in that region by a small, weak, diploid form. These workers suggest that tetraploid johnsongrass may have developed in Alabama from a natural cross between two diploid species, the diploid from Turkey and diploid guinea corn [*Sorghum bicolor* (L.) Moench.]

that came to the United States via the West Indies. If this hypothesis proves correct, then johnsongrass is a new species that originated in North America from two introduced diploids.

REGIONAL EVALUATION

The success of any given introduction often reflects the degree to which the new environment matches that prevaling in the area from whence the introduction was received. Thus armed with sufficient facts on environmental conditions, research workers should be capable of selecting the one site best suited for evaluating any particular introduction.

Crested wheatgrass, *Agropyron desertorum* Fisch. ex Link, is a major cool-season grass extensively used for seeding depleted range and abandoned cropland in the northern Great Plains and intermountain regions of the United States. The development of crested wheatgrass to this prominent position was described by Dillman (1946) and will illustrate the advantages and safeguards provided by the wide evaluation of new accessions.

Professor N. E. Hansen, who traveled to Russia for the U.S. Department of Agriculture in 1897–1898, obtained five samples of crested wheatgrass from Director V. S. Bogdan of the Valuiki Experiment Station, Samara Government. These samples were sent to Alabama, Indiana, Michigan, Colorado, and Washington in 1899. No reports were received on this distribution even though we now know that the grass is well adapted in both Colorado and Washington. There is some evidence that Professor Hansen's collections were planted at Highmore, South Dakota, but the plantings were lost when the grass nurseries were plowed in 1908. Professor Hansen's efforts to introduce crested wheatgrass ended in failure.

In 1906 the Division of Forage Crops in the U.S. Department of Agriculture obtained 4- to 5-lb samples of six accessions of crested wheatgrass from Director Bogdan. These seed lots were distributed over the period from 1907 to 1913. Although the grass looked promising at several locations, the only seed increase was at Newell, South Dakota. Seed produced at Newell was sent to Mandan, North Dakota, and Ardmore, South Dakota, to establish yield trials (Table 2). The crested wheatgrass experiments initiated at the Northern Great Plains Field Station, Mandan, North Dakota, attracted much attention during the dry years from 1916 to 1921, and this played a key role in the early distribution and establishment of crested wheatgrass in the United States. Furthermore the need for replacement vegetation on wheatland abandoned during the severe drought of the 1930's contributed greatly to the rapid acceptance of crested wheatgrass.

Despite the rather extensive distribution of seed, only one station increas-

TABLE 2

RECORD OF CRESTED WHEATGRASS DISTRIBUTION FROM NEWELL, SOUTH DAKOTA

Year received	Location	Results
1915 and 1918	Mandan, North Dakota	Yield tests showed potential
1913 and 1916	Ardmore, South Dakota	Yield tests showed potential
1915	Mocassin, Montana	Looked promising

RECORD OF CRESTED WHEATGRASS DISTRIBUTION FROM MANDAN, NORTH DAKOTA AND DIVISION OF FORAGE CROPS

Year received	Location	Results
1917 and 1921	Seed distributed to county agents in Montana	
1920	Dickinson, North Dakota	Promising
1922	Dickinson, North Dakota	2 to 3 acres planted

First extensive planting at Dickinson, North Dakota, in 1927.

ed seed, and only one station conducted any significant research. In the absence of extensive regional distribution and testing, crested wheatgrass may not have been available when it was so urgently needed in the 1930's.

LIMITED GERMPLASM

History would suggest that some well-established introduced grasses may trace to one or perhaps a small number of introduced seed lots which are not representative of the total variability available for exploitation. The possibility that this may have occurred is subject to speculation, except for a few well-documented introductions such as intermediate wheatgrass, *Agropyron intermedium* (Host) Beauv.

Practically all the intermediate wheatgrass grown in the United States traces to one seed lot received from the Soviet Union in 1932 (A. A. Hanson, 1965). The original introduction contained an appreciable amount of variability as evidenced by the distinct varieties developed for forage planting (Table 3). On the other hand it is reasonable to assume that additional progress could be made from a thorough examination of the variability available at or near this species' center of origin.

Further restrictions can be placed on genetic diversity by inadvertently limiting seed collections to locations where the species has been introduced

TABLE 3

SOURCE OF INTERMEDIATE WHEATGRASS [*AGROPYRON INTERMEDIUM* (HOST) BEAUV.]
VARIETIES IN THE UNITED STATES

Named Varieties[a]	Source	Data released
Chief (Canada)	USSR sources and Ree (98568)	1961
Greenar (Washington)	PI 98568 from	1945
Nebraska 50 (Nebraska)	Maikop region	1950
Oahe (South Dakota)	in USSR	1961
Ree (South Dakota)	received in 1932	1945
Amur (New Mexico)	PI 131532 Manchuria, China	1952

[a]Fine experimental varieties trace to PI 98568.

within comparatively recent times. This practice can be serious if investigators assume that they have secured a truly representative sample of available germplasm.

The efficacy of a plant introduction as the source of a new forage variety or as new germplasm for plant breeding and genetic research depends heavily on the accumulation of collections representative of the variability within the species.

It is generally possible to utilize known climatic and ecological data in locating regions from which potentially useful source material can be secured. Hartley (1954) has attempted to develop improved procedures for planning forage exploration work, and his agrostological index may have some merit in organizing collection work. In practice major activity will be centered in those regions of countries from which adapted or useful germplasm has been obtained in the past. Collections that have a very narrow objective (that is, to locate winter-hardy germplasm in a single species) can be planned with comparative ease. However, in the absence of good guidelines as to species, objectives, and ecological conditions, plant explorers should make every attempt to sample extensively throughout the region to which they have been assigned.

Germplasm Pools

The commitment that grass breeders make to evaluating initial selections provides a strong argument for upgrading the source material from which these selections are made. Germplasm pools help in achieving this goal by (a) increasing genetic diversity for selection, (b) improving the utilization of diverse plant collections, and (c) maintaining and improving the frequency of genes for a substantial number of potentially valuable characteristics.

H. V. Harlan and Martini (1929) pioneered in increasing the genetic diversity of bulk populations. Since that time many variations have been applied in the development of germplasm pools within both self- and cross-fertilized crops. In barley, Suneson (1956) proposed the assembly and study of seed stocks from diverse evolutionary origins, recombination by hybridization, bulking the F_1 progeny, and subsequent prolonged natural selection of the progeny in successive natural cropping environments. Dudley *et al.* (1963) practiced recurrent selection in two alfalfa germplasm pools. This procedure was selected because it offered the combined advantages of preserving genetic variability at low cost, breakup of linkage blocks, and flexibility for the subsequent subjection of the pools to more complex breeding methods.

Results obtained from composite crosses and other broad-based populations subjected to recurrent selection have been promising. Germplasm developed in these programs often exhibits outstanding characteristics and, depending on the species, could conceivably be released for direct use. The general pattern, however, is to make these pools available to plant breeders for the isolation and evaluation of superior types.

Breeding Methods

The impression is created on occasion that breeding method is the ultimate consideration in predicting degree of success from a particular improvement program. This is true insofar as appropriate methods must be chosen for self-fertilized, cross-fertilized, and apomictic species. On the other hand there are dangers in excessive dedication to a specified breeding procedure to the exclusion of alternative methods. In fact, in certain crops a rigid approach may be harmful because of inadequate knowledge of population structure and the origin and maintenance of genetic variability. It is now recognized that "mass selection," which may have been discarded in favor of more sophisticated methods, can be extremely useful. Factors affecting progress through mass selection include stage of breeding program, genetic character sought, and the effectiveness of the selection pressure applied.

"Recurrent selection" has gained in stature on the basis of demonstrated successes in increasing desirable gene frequency. In simple terms recurrent selection implies that each cycle of selection will be conducted within populations created by intermating selected plants from the previous cycle. Recurrent selection may be based entirely on phenotype in conjunction with mass selection but most often includes replicated progeny tests of selected plants.

"Backcrossing" is a valuable breeding method in solving certain types of problems. In general the objective is the transfer of a single desired character to an otherwise superior line or variety (the recurrent parent) without inducing other changes. Success from this approach depends very largely on (a) the availability of a good recurrent parent, (b) the identification of the transferred character in segregating populations, (c) populations of sufficient size being grown, and (d) undesirable characters not being closely linked with the desirable character to be transferred from the nonrecurrent parent. The method has been very useful in transferring simply inherited characters, especially major genes for resistance. It has been resorted to with variable success in transferring characters that are not simply inherited.

Cytogenetics and Breeding Behavior

Cytogenetic investigations have been invaluable in clarifying the taxonomy and phylogeny of the Gramineae, in determining the type and nature of polyploidy, in explaining the nature of self- and cross-sterility, and in confirming the mode of reproduction, especially the existence and type of apomixis. Genetic studies have been impeded by the presence of polyploidy, cross-pollination, and varying degrees of sterility with both self- and cross-pollination.

Structural disturbances in chromosome behavior are usually related to one another but their relationship to pollen quality and seed set has often been poor. Nielsen (1966) presented information suggesting that physiological or metabolic disturbances may account for much of the sterility encountered within grasses. This is especially evident in wide crosses where an imbalance could exist between the nucleus and the surrounding cytoplasm. In his judgment physiological disturbances result in either micro- or megasporocyte degeneration and are recognized in microsporocytes by extrachromosomal accumulations, complement fractionation (bi- and polynucleate prophase sporocytes; multipolar spindles and split plates at metaphase I; multiple spindles at anaphase I; and pollen grains of different size classes in the same anther), and upsets in timing (nonsynchronous chromosome separations; precocious bivalent separation; and the precocious formation of exinelike walls as early as late prophase).

Seed set in cross-fertilized grasses seldom reaches 100% under open pollination (Nilsson, 1934). When self-pollinated, the perennial grasses are largely sterile or have low frequencies of seed set. Research on fertility relationships has been complicated by the known effect of environmental conditions on both open-pollination and on enforced self-pollination. In addition little data are available on the genetics of incompatibility in the grasses. However, there is evidence from the work of Lundquist (1955, 1963) that incompatibility mechanisms exist. He reports that incompatibility in *Festuca pratensis* is based on two loci, each with multiple alleles. A pollen tube was incompatible in the style when both of the genes it carried were present in the style. A similar incompatibility system was reported by Hayman (1956) in *Phalaris coerulescens* Desf.

The rate of reduction in vigor that accompanies inbreeding is thought to reflect the rate of approach to homozygosity. According to the theory of inbreeding autotetraploids, diploids are expected to exhibit more inbreeding depression than autotetraploids and, similarly, inbreeding depression in autotetraploids should exceed that in autohexaploids. Dewey (1966) found that the vigor reduction in diploid, tetraploid, and hexaploid crested wheatgrass populations did not follow the accepted pattern. His results showed the greatest loss in vigor in the hexaploid population followed by tetraploid and diploid populations in that order. The severe inbreeding depression found in tetraploid and hexaploid populations was attributed to chromosome aberrations that accumulate in species buffered by autoploidy.

In smooth brome and timothy, Nielsen and Drolsom (1966) and Drolsom and Nielsen (1969) concluded that selection of plants that possess some self-fertility, even though relatively low, offers greater possibilities of success in breeding than the selection and use of wholly self-sterile plants. On the basis of their observations they suggest that a modest degree of self-fertility, which is usually associated with meiotic regularity, offers opportunities for gene exchange and the isolation of new, desirable combinations.

Apomixis

"Apomixis" is a general term covering all types of asexual reproduction that substitute for the sexual method. Although this definition includes vegetative reproduction of plants incapable of producing seeds, the term "apomixis" is often used as a synonym for reproduction by asexual seeds. Grass breeders are concerned primarily with those forms of apomixis that lead to the production of asexual seed. Both facultative and obligate forms of apomixis are relatively common in the Gramineae.

Apomixis was regarded by some investigators as an evolutionary "dead end" because of the obvious limitations imposed on recombination and segregation. It has become apparent, however, that apomixis in perennial grasses is an effective evolutionary force both in the creation and maintenance of new species under highly competitive conditions.

In facultative apomicts variability is stored and released by means of the delicate competitive balance between sexual and apomictic embryo sacs in the same ovule. In these species enrivonmental conditions can influence the relative proportions of sexual and apomictic seed (Knox, 1967). Environmental effects together with the frequent fertilization of unreduced eggs restricts the value of most genetic analyses. Although inheritance studies have been inconclusive, there appears to be little question regarding the existence of genetic control over the basic processes governing apomixis.

Obligate apomixis by definition would not seem to lend itself to inheritance studies. On the other hand hybrids have been produced between sexual and apomictic species found within certain genera or a "species complex." Many or most of the hybrids from these wide crosses result from the fertilization of unreduced female with reduced male gametes.

Genetic data have been obtained by crossing obligate apomicts with closely related sexual biotypes. These crosses have had the advantage that the parent plants are capable of only one method of reproduction (apomixis vs. sexuality), and there is no evidence that obligate apomixis is influenced by environmental effects. Thus Burton and Forbes (1960) obtained segregation for apomixis and sexuality by crossing the obligate apomict common bahiagrass ($2n = 40$) onto sexual, induced autotetraploids of Pensacola bahiagrass (*Paspalum notatum* Flugge). Their F_2 data suggest that apomixis is recessive to the sexual state and controlled by a very few recessive genes. There was no evidence that facultative apomixis developed in the F_2 generation from sexual plants. Similarly, the isolation of a "rare" sexual biotype enabled Taliaferro and Bashaw (1966) to study the inheritance of apomixis in the obligate apomict *Cenchrus ciliaris* L. (= *Pennisetum ciliare* (L.) Link). Their results suggest that the inheritance of apomixis is relatively simple in buffelgrass. It was postulated that mode of reproduction was controlled by two genes and epistasis.

Hybridization of obligate apomicts with sexual plants provides an opportunity to develop new vigorous recombinations that can be stabilized and increased via apomixis. Higgins buffelgrass is the first apomictic variety produced through the manipulation of obligate apomixis (Bashaw, 1968). This variety possesses characteristics not observed previously in naturally occurring populations of *C. ciliaris*.

Induced Polyploids

The intensive study of polyploidy in plant improvement began with the discovery that colchicine, an alkaloid found in the autumn crocus, could be used to double the chromosome number (Blakeslee and Avery, 1937).

Since some induced polyploids were larger and more vigorous than naturally occurring diploids in the same group, great expectations were expressed for this approach to plant improvement. Additional study has shown that induced polyploidy is not an answer to all breeding problems, but that it can be used, either directly or indirectly, in the development of useful varieties within certain crops. Generally, induced autopolyploids have been most successful in crops grown for their vegetative parts rather than for seed, especially if they have a low chromosome number and are cross-rather than self-fertilized (Levan, 1948; Love, 1952). Rather good autopolyploids have been obtained by doubling the chromosome number of sugar beet, turnip, mangel, rye, mustard, red clover, alsike clover, ryegrass, grape, and a number of flowers.

Induced autopolyploids are usually lower in fertility than their diploid prototypes. This is not especially serious in ornamentals in which reduced fertility and increased seed costs are of less importance than the size and beauty of the flowers.

Different genotypes within a species may react differently to chromosome doubling, and for this reason success is often associated with the number of induced polyploids available for study. In addition, "new polyploids" are rarely, if ever, successful without further selection for improved stability and fertility. Cross-pollination of newly created polyploids provides opportunities for the recombination of genes conditioning fertility and genotypic balance.

In groups characterized by differences in level of polyploidy among natural species, artificial polyploidy may serve as a step in transferring a valuable characteristic from one species to another across the barrier of hybrid sterility. An excellent example is provided by *Nicotiana* where resistance to the necrotic type of mosaic was transferred from *N. glutinosa* to *N. tabacum* by means of the amphiploid *N. digluta* (Valleau, 1952).

Sterile hybrids between distantly related species have been rendered fertile by doubling the chromosome number (amphiploidy). As a rule these artificial allopolyploids have been less successful than induced autopolyploids. They are often distinguished by extremes in genic sterility, unstable chromosome numbers, and the preferential segregation of chromosome sets or genomes. Polyploid breeding is a specialized approach with demonstrated merit in certain species, and the possibilities of utilizing this method in plant breeding are far from exhausted.

Interspecific and Intergeneric Hybridization

The contribution of hybridization to variation within grass species is well recognized and extensive introgression has been reported within certain species. The study of genome relationships in hybrids and some extensive biosystematic investigations have been most helpful in clarifying taxonomic relationships. On the other hand, pairing relationship must be interpreted with care, for there is a possibility that chromosome pairing may be under genotypic control (Müntzing and Prakken, 1940).

The ease with which many species and genera can be hybridized has presented an interesting challenge to geneticists and plant breeders. The production of viable hybrids does not necessarily mean that such hybrids will contribute to population diversity (Nielsen, 1966). In general, the products of many wide crosses will only contribute to populations when hybridization is followed by some form of chromosome doubling.

Ryegrass (*Lolium* spp.), fescue (*Festuca* spp.) hybrids have received more attention from plant breeders than any other wide cross. Workers have met with considerable success, but they have yet to solve the problem of producing stable fertile plants that combine the best features of both species. R. C. Buckner at Lexington, Kentucky, was the first to develop a substantial number of amphiploids ($2n = 56$) by doubling the chromosome number of sterile F_1 hybrids produced by crossing annual ryegrass ($2n = 14$) with tall fescue ($2n = 42$) (Buckner *et al.*, 1965). A fair degree of fertility was achieved in the amphiploid but stability remains a serious problem. It seems conceivable that further selection will yield hexaploid ($2n = 42$) hybrid derivatives that will retain portions of ryegrass chromosomes. Because the rate of exchange among ryegrass and fescue chromosomes is thought to be limited, large numbers of hybrids will be needed so ryegrass characteristics can be accumulated at the hexaploid level ($2n = 42$) through backcrossing and recurrent selection.

The use of wide crosses in breeding requires great patience as in many of these programs the investigator will not be greeted with instant success. He may have to accept comparatively small, difficult-to-recognize exchanges among chromosomes and devote much time to accumulating these transfers in an acceptable, fertile type. Ryegrass-fescue crosses are apparently typical of those interspecific and intergeneric F_1 hybrids in which there is little or no natural recombination of characters. The tendency of crosses of this nature to segregate toward the parental types in the absence of recombination or interchange mechanisms is well known.

Sterility problems can be readily circumvented in *Cynodon* and other species where the sterile products of wide crosses can be propagated vegetatively. Likewise, wide crosses that involve facultative apomicts provide an opportunity to select hybrids that produce seed asexually.

Another promising alternative is available in which chromosome races exist within the same species complex. This has been demonstrated by Dewey and Pendse (1968) who produced vigorous, fertile tetraploid hybrids by crossing *Agropyron desertorum* ($2n = 28$) with induced tetraploids of *A. cristatum*. The induced tetraploids were obtained by colchicine treatment of open-pollinated seed from diploid fairway wheatgrass.

Induced Mutations

Mutation breeding based on the treatment of grasses with chemical mutagens and ionizing radiation has been somewhat controversial. However, the potential value of induced mutations is supported by the obvious value of natural somatic mutations in developing successful varieties of many fruits and flowers. Research has shown that there are no essential differences between induced and spontaneous mutations (Muller, 1954; Müntzing, 1951).

Although most induced mutations are of no practical value, available data show that beneficial mutants can be isolated and used in crop improvement. Mutations can be sought in specific characteristics where the range of natural variation is limited. An excellent example of progress has been provided by Sears (1956) who used X-ray treatments in the successful transfer of leaf rust resistance from *Aegilops umbellulata* to wheat.

Mutagenic agents provide an opportunity to induce reproducible mutants in apomictic grasses. Changes in growth habit have been reported from ionizing radiation in the obligate apomict, *Paspalum dilatatum*, (Burton and Jackson, 1962; Bashaw and Hoff, 1962), and for disease resistance in the facultative apomict, *Poa pratensis* (A. A. Hanson and Juska, 1962). Although mutations within apomictic species may prove useful in the direct development of promising varieties, mutations within some characteristics may prove to be either very rare or unobtainable. Thus improved seed set which had been one of the objectives in *Paspalum dilatatum* was not observed following ionizing radiation treatments (Burton and Jackson, 1962; Bashaw and Hoff, 1962).

Elliott (1958) suggested irradiation of sterile interspecific and intergeneric F_1 hybrids to increase interchanges, which on fixing by selfing could be propagated without the sterility effects commonly associated with heterozygous interchanges. The appeal in this approach must be tempered by the known effects of irradiation in increasing chromosomal abnormalities and by the limitations imposed by population size and self-sterility.

Individual investigators must decide whether mutation research or some other method of increasing variability is applicable to the species with which they are working. In these deliberations attention must be given to the variability available in plant collections or that can be created in germplasm pools.

The Consequences of Selection

There is a growing realization that certain "good" breeding objectives may have unrecognized and perhaps undesirable side effects. In the search for insect tolerance in forages, questions are raised with respect to the response of animals feeding on insect-resistant varieties. Could increased palatability and an improvement in forage intake result in toxicity when the original forage shows little or no evidence of creating animal toxicity problems? These and similar questions have encouraged the growth of cooperative research among geneticists, plant physiologists, biochemists, and animal nutritionists. It has been demonstrated, for example, that estrogenic activity in alfalfa is closely allied with damage from foliar diseases (C. H. Hanson, 1966). Thus coumestrol level in alfalfa can be reduced by selecting for resistance to foliar diseases.

Isogenic lines are powerful tools in showing the consequences of selection for specific characteristics. They were used to demonstrate that awnlessness in wheat is not compatible with maximum grain production (Atkins and Norris, 1955). The widespread use of isogenic lines in evaluating the significance of specific traits is restricted by the time required to develop such lines and the danger that they may not be representative. Burton (1966) has proposed the use of near isogenic populations rather than near isogenic lines in studying the effect of specific characteristics on yield. The principle advantage of this approach lies in the speed with which answers can be obtained. Both near isogenic lines and populations are valuable tools in measuring the possible usefulness of individual characteristics.

Opportunities for developing and using either isogenic lines or populations are limited in complex polyploids. However, there is evidence from other crop plants that grass breeding not only requires the development of more effective breeding methods and screening techniques but also investigations on changes, both desirable and undesirable, that may accompany intensive selection.

References

Anonymous (1850). "Report of the Commissioner of Patents for the Year 1849," Part II. Agriculture. Washington, D.C.

Atkins, I. M., and Norris, M. J. (1955). The influence of awns on yield and certain morphological characters of wheat. *Agron. J.* **47**, 218–220.

Bashaw, E. C. (1968). Registration of Higgins buffelgrass. *Crop Sci.* **8**, 397–398.

Bashaw, E. C., and Hoff, B. J. (1962). Effects of irradiation on apomictic common dallisgrass. *Crop Sci.* **2**, 501–504.

Blakeslee, A. F., and Avery, A. G. (1937). Methods of inducing doubling of chromosomes in plants. *J. Hered.* **28**, 393–411.

Buckner, R. C., Hill, H. D., Hovin, A. W., and Burrus, P. B., II. (1965). Fertility of annual ryegrass x tall fescue amphiploids and their derivatives. *Crop Sci.* **5**, 395–397.

Burton, G. W. (1951). The adaptability and breeding of suitable grasses for the Southern United States. *Advan. in Agron.* **3**, 197–241.

Burton, G. W. (1966). Plant Breeding—Prospects for the Future. *Plant Breeding* Iowa State Univ. Press, Ames.

Burton, G. W., and Forbes, I. (1960). The genetics and manipulation of obligate apomixis in common bahiagrass (*Paspalum notatum* Flugge). *Proc. Int. Grassland Congr., 8th, 1960,* pp. 66–71.

Burton, G. W., and Jackson, J. E. (1962). Radiation breeding of apomictic prostrate dallisgrass, *Paspalum dilatatum* var. *pauciciliatum*. *Crop Sci.* **2**, 495–497.

Colby, W. G. (1941). Pasture culture in Massachusetts. *Mass., Agri. Exp. Sta., Bul.* **380**.

Dewey, D. R. (1966). Inbreeding depression in diploid, tetraploid, and hexaploid crested wheatgrass. *Crop Sci.* **6**, 144–147.

Dewey, D. R., and Pendse, P. C. (1968). Hybrids between *Agropyron desertorum* and induced-tetraploid *Agropyron cristatum*. *Crop Sci.* **8**, 607–611.

Dillman, A. C. (1946). The beginnings of crested wheatgrass in North America. *J. Amer. Soc. Agron.* **38**, 237–250.

Drolsom, P. N., and Nielsen, E. L. (1969). Use of self fertility in the improvement of *Bromus inermis* and *Phleum pratense*. *Crop Sci.* **9**, 710–713.

Dudley, J. W., Hill, R. R., and Hanson, C. H. (1963). Effects of seven cycles of recurrent phenotypic selection on means and genetic variances of several characters in two pools of alfalfa germ plasm. *Crop Sci.* **3**, 543–546.

Elliott, F. C. (1958). "Plant Breeding and Cytogenetics." McGraw-Hill, New York.

Fergus, E. N., and Hollowell, E. A. (1960). Red clover. *Advan. Agron.* **12**, 365–436.

Hanson, A. A. (1965). Grass varieties in the United States. *U.S. Dep. Agr., Agr. Hand.* **170**, 1–102.

Hanson, A. A., and Juska, F. V. (1962). Induced mutations in Kentucky bluegrass. *Crop Sci.* **2**, 369–371.

Hanson, C. H. (1966). Foliar diseases and forage quality. *Proc. Int. Grassland Congr., 9th, 1965,* pp. 1209–1213.

Harlan, H. V., and Martini, M. L. (1929). A composite hybrid mixture. *J. Amer. Soc. Agron.* **21**, 487–490.

Hartley, W. (1954). The agrostological index. A phytogeographical approach to the problems of pasture plant introduction. *Aust. J. Bot.* **2**, 1–21.

Hayman, D. L. (1956). The genetical control of incompatibility in *Phalaris coerulescens* Desf. *Aust. J. Biol. Sci.* **9**, 321–331.

Knox, P. B. (1967). Apomixis: Seasonal and population differences in grasses. *Science* **157**, 325–326.

Levan, A. (1948). Svalöf 1886–1946. [History and Present Problems] pp. 304–323. Carl Bloms Boktryckeri A.-B, Lund.

Love, R. M. (1952). The value of induced polyploidy in breeding. *Proc. Int. Grassland Congr., 6th, 1952* vol. 1, pp. 291–298.

Lundquist, A. (1955). Genetics of self-incompatibility in *Festuca pratensis* Huds. *Hereditas* **41**, 518–520.

Lundquist, A. (1963). The nature of the two-loci incompatibility system in grasses. II. Frequency of specific incompatibility alleles in a population of *Festuca pratensis* Huds. *Hereditas* **52**, 189–196.

Muller, H. J. (1954). The nature of the genetic effects produced by radiation. "Radiation Biology." pp. 353–473. McGraw-Hill, New York.

Müntzing, A. (1951). "Genetics in the 20th Century—Genetics and Plant Breeding," pp. 473–492. Macmillan, New York.

Müntzing, A., and Prakken, A. (1940). A mode of chromosome pairing in *Phleum* twins with 63 chromosomes and its cytogenetic consequences. *Hereditas* **26**, 463–501.

Newell. L. C. and Keim, F. D. (1943). Field performance of bromegrass strains from different regional seed sources. *J. Amer. Soc. Agron.* **35**, 420–434.

Nielsen, E. L. (1966). New interpretations of the cytogenetics and breeding behavior of polyploid grasses. *Proc. Int. Grassland Congr., 10th, 1966*, pp. 676–679.

Nielsen, E. L., and Drolsom, P. N. (1966). The use of self-fertility in breeding polyploid species. *Proc. Int. Grassland Congr., 9th, 1965* Vol. 1, pp. 151–154.

Nilsson, F. (1934). Studies in fertility and inbreeding in some herbage grasses. *Hereditas* **19**, 1–162.

Sears, E. R. (1956). The transfer of leaf-rust resistance from *Aegilops umbellulata* to wheat. *"Genetics in Plant Breeding."* pp. 1–21. Brookhaven Nat. Lab., Upton, New York.

Suneson, C. A. (1956). An evolutionary plant breeding method. *Agron. J.* **48**, 188–191.

Taliaferro, C. M., and Bashaw, E. C. (1966). Inheritance and control of obligate apomixis in breeding buffelgrass, *Pennisetum ciliare*. *Crop Sci.* **6**, 473–476.

Valleau, W. (1952). Breeding tobacco for disease resistance. *Econ. Bot.* **6**, 69–102.

Vavilov, N. I. (1949–1950). "The Origin, Variation, Immunity, and Breeding of Cultivated Plants." Chronica Botanica, Waltham, Massachusetts.

Chapter 4

Developing Superior Turf Varieties

J. A. LONG

Improved turfgrasses have been developed and placed in use largely within the past two decades. The lack of progress in the breeding of improved turf varieties until recently has been primarily due to insufficient support for programs of this nature. Emphasis has been placed on breeding programs for important agricultural crop species. Rapid urbanization in the United States as well as other countries appears to be largely responsible for increased interest.

Initial programs in variety improvement were the selection of desirable biotypes that were already present in nature (Brittingham, 1943; Funk, 1969). Such selections were then released directly as improved varieties after limited testing to define characteristics. A number of turf varieties used at the present time were developed primarily for pasture applications from earlier forage breeding programs. The varieties Kentucky 31 and Alta within the species *Festuca arundinacea* and Argentine and Paraguayan varieties within the species *Paspalum notatum* are examples.

Recent advances in turf variety improvement are indicated in Table 1. A general comparison is given for the number of varieties for several turf species for 1954 and 1968. A significant number of varieties introduced in the past five years has been from plant breeding programs in Europe (Anonymous, 1968). In sharp contrast to breeding programs in the United

TABLE I

A COMPARISON OF THE NUMBER OF TURFGRASS VARIETIES FORM DIFFERENT SPECIES IN 1954 AND 1968[a]

Common name	Species	Number varieties	
		1954	1968
Bentgrasses	*Agrostis* spp.	4	18
Bermudagrass	*Cynodon* spp.	4	15
Kentucky bluegrass	*Poa pratensis*	2	38
Red fescue	*Festuca rubra*	4	16

[a]Compiled from "List of Cultivars Eligible for Certification Under the OECD Scheme 1968" (Anonymous, 1968), and Juska and Hanson (1964).

States, breeding programs in Europe are largely funded and carried out by private firms instead of public agencies which has been the trend in the United States.

Turf Variety Improvement Goals

The general goal of the plant breeder working on turf species is to modify plant genotype through appropriate breeding procedures that will better fit the plant to its environment and to its intended use. As with other economically important plants it is necessary to assist plant adaptation to environment and use situations by employing cultural treatments which include supplemental fertilization, irrigation, mechanical renovation, and pesticides.

The use to which varieties are subjected in various turf situations has an important bearing on goals for improvement and the direction that breeding programs take. For example, the goals and selection of source species in a breeding program of improved varieties for highway slopes will differ from those for varieties for golf greens. One of the most critical phases of any breeding program is the development of procedures that apply accurate and realistic selection pressure to breeding stocks. Turf varietal candidates intended for use on golf greens must have the capacity to produce dense turf cover under frequent mowing at heights of 0.64 to 1.28 cm whereas those intended for highway slopes would be mowed at heights of 10 to 30 cm on an extended mowing frequency. Drought tolerance would be an important requirement of highway turf, but would have limited importance for golf greens turf. In this example evaluation procedures for screening experimental selections for golf greens should include a moving height and frequency comparable to that used on greens. In addition it would be important to use cultural practices including fertilization and irrigation that would also simulate greens conditions.

Burton (1951) in reviewing the status of breeding grasses for the southeastern states stated that the plant breeder must first take inventory of the features of the environment before proceeding with an improvement program. Features of the environment that he discussed included climate with special emphasis on temperature extremes, soil fertility, and soil drainage.

Youngner and Nudge (1968) evaluated Kentucky bluegrass varieties for response to varying temperatures and pointed out that such varieties were being used throughout the general area of Kentucky bluegrass adaptation with few attempts to assign any specific regions of adaptation. Results of this investigation showed that turf density and carbohydrate reserves of the varieties Merion, Newport, and 0217 differed in response to various soil temperatures. The Newport variety showed a low tolerance to warm temperatures and a distinct adaptation to cool temperature. Carbohydrate accumulation and tillering of Newport increased with decreasing heat units. Results of this research indicated an association between temperature response and the climate of origin of the varieties studied. Since the capacity of Kentucky bluegrass to maintain a turf appears to be influenced by maintenance of a proper carbohydrate reserve, breeding goals should consider this behavior when developing improved varieties for fringe areas of adaptation.

Lobenstein (1962) studied growth characteristics of several Kentucky bluegrass varieties and found that in one variety adapted to shade, rhizomes were frequently found 25.6 to 30.7 cm deep. He suggested that the variety may have been able to survive in the shade because of greater competitive ability for soil moisture or mineral nutrients. This observation suggests that rhizoming depth might be used as a selection factor in screening types for shade adaptation.

In developing dwarf-type grasses the plant breeder may encounter growth behavior requiring some adjustment in goals for improvement. Very slow growth rates of dwarf types may not be acceptable to the consumer. Lobenstein (1962) observed that a dwarf Kentucky bluegrass variety produced essentially no tillers throughout an entire season when clipped at 1.92 cm in height. A similar observation was made on stolon growth of a dwarf St. Augustinegrass selection in Scotts breeding program (personal observation). Over an eight-week period Floratine yielded 21 and 40 gms of stolons at 1 and 4 kg of nitrogen per hectare, respectively. During the same period the dwarf variety produced no stolons at either rate of nitrogen fertilization. These examples suggest that it may be necessary for the plant breeder to adjust breeding goals to produce intermediate dwarf types that would have a more acceptable rate of establishment.

Fusarium patch caused by the pathogen *Fusarium roseum* is a major lawn disease in the upper Midwest and mid-Atlantic areas of the United States. Turf breeding programs for grasses to be used in these regions must give some priority to selecting for resistance or tolerance to this pathogen since no commercially available fungicides effectively control the disease. Goals of breeding for resistance to some turf pathogens may be questionable where effective fungicides are available to combat the disease. Rust resistance for Kentucky bluegrasses and gray leafspot resistance for St. Augustinegrass are two minor diseases that may be given a lower priority in breeding programs for these species.

Problems related to air pollution which have developed recently in some large populations centers such as Los Angeles add another dimension to goals of developing improved turf varieties. A selection program carried out by Youngner (1966) on bermudagrass which evaluated effects of air pollution demonstrated significant differences among varieties on tolerance to air pollution. The improved bermudagrass variety Santa Ana was found to be more tolerant to air pollution than were the varieties Tifway and Tifgreen.

One major consideration that has been a factor in discouraging initiation of turfgrass breeding programs is the high cost of a moderate sized program. Costs of cultural practices in turfgrass breeding programs are high compared to those of small grains. Most turf evaluation systems require continual mowing and very frequent irrigations to provide conditions simulating turf in home lawns, golf courses, and athletic fields. The turfgrass breeder must exploit all possibilities in employing simulated evaluation systems in the laboratory and greenhouse to assess characteristics of breeding stocks. If such practices are not followed, development costs for improved turf varieties become excessive.

Species and Breeding Progress

Kentucky Bluegrass (*Poa pratensis*)

Varieties of this species represent the dominant turf used across the northern United States; the mountainous sections of the upper South and Southwest; and extending to below Los Angeles in the West. Ability of Kentucky bluegrass to produce a dense turf through the production of tillers and rhizomes and rapid regrowth under frequent clipping gives it excellent adaptation to turf use.

Extensive cytogenetic and cytological studies have produced much literature relating to the method of reproduction and breeding behavior of this species (Akerberg, 1963a,b, 1939; Armstrong, 1937; Engelbert, 1940; Müntzing, 1933; Nilsson, 1933; Tinney and Aamodt, 1940; Tinney, 1940). Since these reviews provide thorough treatment of the subject, this discussion will be restricted to recent developments and those earlier investigations that had significant bearing on this recent work.

Brittingham (1943) was one of the first workers to suggest breeding methods that would appear to be workable for this species. Methods he discussed were (1) selection of desirable apomictic biotypes, (2) inbreeding, (3) intraspecific hybridization, (4) strain building, and (5) interspecific hybridization. The view that intraspecific hybridization would be a method of varietal improvement was not shared by most plant breeders working with Kentucky blue grass at that time. Clausen (1962) suggested that the inability of the plant breeder to identify intraspecific hybrids was a limitation to this method of breeding. In addition the difficulty encountered in crossing procedures no doubt represented another factor discouraging the breeding method.

Julen (1954) provided another important contribution to the use of intraspecific hybridization as a significant breeding method for Kentucky bluegrass. Reports of variation resulting from X-ray irradiation of Kentucky bluegrass (Gustafsson, 1944, 1951) led to further evaluation of the effects of X-ray. He found that X-rays produced a high percentage of plants with both sexual and apomictic seed formation. The breakdown in apomixis seemed to be independent of morphological characteristics in some plants. He observed that in the second generation progeny of sexual plants segregated into apomictic, partially sexual, and sexual types. Controlled crosses between plants with induced sexuality and normal apomicts produced progeny of wide variation. This was the first significant use of intraspecific hybridization to produce considerable numbers of hybrids.

Funk (1969) in the United States later demonstrated that intraspecific hybridization was effective in combining desirable characteristics into hybrids. Funk suggested that Kentucky bluegrass hybrids should be superior to their parents as breeding material for a new cycle of hybridization because they will contain a recombination of desired characteristics from both parents and through transgressive segregation are likely to produce progeny superior to both parents for a given characteristic. Although evaluation of the first Kentucky bluegrass hybrids is presently being carried out, it does appear that significant advances can be expected in this species through intraspecific hybridization.

Based on results of Julen's investigations (1954), breeding methods now used for the improvement of other sexual and cross-fertile grasses appear to be feasible for improving Kentucky bluegrass. Inbreeding followed by hybridization of superior sexual lines plus apomictic restoring lines may offer considerable flexibility in breeding programs. Superior cross-fertile lines could also be selected on the basis of polycross testing followed by production of synthetic varieties.

Clausen's investigations (1952) of interspecific hybridization also suggest a potential for developing hybrids with unique adaptation characteristics. The interspecific hybridization method would provide a broader germplasm base than would be possible through intraspecific hybridization.

BERMUDAGRASS (*CYNODON* SPP.)

Bermudagrass is used throughout the southern region of the United States (Burton, 1947). Where low temperatures limit the use of St. Augustinegrass for home lawns in this region, bermudagrass is the next choice. It is the dominant species used on golf courses throughout the South—on putting greens, tees, and fairways. In certain sections of Southern California and the interior valley extending to north of Sacramento, bermuda as well as dichondra and Kentucky bluegrass are used for home lawns.

As with Kentucky bluegrass considerable research had been devoted to the breeding behavior and mode of reproduction of bermudagrasses (Burton, 1947; Hurcombe, 1946, 1947; Juska and Hanson, 1964) before significant advances were made in varietal improvements.

Varieties used for turf are classified within at least three species: *C. dactylon, C. magennisii,* and *C. transvaalensis.* Bermuda is one of the few turfgrasses in which improved varieties have been developed through interspecific hybridization, intraspecific hybridization, and selection (Burton, 1947). Early improved varieties were selected from superior clones without further breeding modification. More recently the improved varieties have been developed through hybridization. Effective improvement in growth habit, disease resistance, and vigor has been achieved through systematic breeding. Table 2 shows a comparison of characteristics of a number of improved varieties developed in the breeding program at Tifton, Georgia. The varieties listed in Table 2 with the exception of common are propagated and distributed vegetatively.

Horn (1967) points out that high maintenance costs and necessity of frequent mowing are major drawbacks to the use of bermudagrasses for home lawn applications. The improved bermudagrass varieties appear to require more careful attention in moving maintenance than the widely used common.

Disease resistance, nematode resistance, and modification of growth

TABLE 2

COMPARATIVE CHARACTERISTICS OF SEVERAL BERMUDAGRASS VARIETIES
USED FOR TURF PURPOSES[a,b]

Variety	Chromosome number	Disease resistance	Density	Fineness	Softness	Type green
Tifway	27	1	2.3	1	3	Very dark
Tiffine	27	1	2.5	1	2	Light
Tiflawn	36	1	2.9	3	4	Dark
Tifgreen	27	1	2.2	1	1	Dark
Common	36	5	6.5	4	4	Medium

[a]Burton (1959). Unpublished data from USDA, ARS, CRD, Coastal Plains Experiment Sta., Tifton, Georgia.
[b]Ratings nearest 1.0 were most resistant to disease, had the greatest sod density, the finest leaves, and made the softest turf.

habit are characteristics that should be given priority in breeding programs for this species. The great variation observed in plant collections would seem to provide sufficient genetic base for further varietal improvement. Since bermudagrass can be propagated vegetatively with relative ease, additional flexibility is provided in breeding programs.

St. Augustinegrass (*Stenotaphrum secundatum*)

St. Augustinegrass is the dominant turfgrass used in home lawns throughout the Gulf Coast area of the United States (Long and Bashaw, 1961). It has limited use in Arizona and Southern California.

As recently as 1951, Burton reported that no organized attempt had been made to improve the species by plant breeding. One recognised improved variety, Floratine, was released in 1961 by the Florida Agricultural Experiment Station (Wilson, 1961). Three other varieties are described and used primarily in Florida (Horn, 1967). All of these varieties are selections of naturally occurring clones.

A breeding program was initiated in 1957 by the Texas Agricultural Experiment Station for developing improved varieties. During the period from 1957 until 1961, breeding behavior and method of reproduction were determined for the species (Long and Bashaw, 1961). This research demonstrated that the mode of reproduction is sexual, that variability exists in the species, and that it is possible to use several breeding methods for turf improvement. Intraspecific hybridization is now being used for St. Augustine-

TABLE 3

RESPONSE OF VARIETIES AND EXPERIMENTAL HYBRIDS OF ST. AUGUSTINEGRASS

Grasses	Chromosome number[a]	Gray leafspot[b]	Chinch bug		Sod webworm injury[d]
			number	injury[c]	
Floratine	27	90	75	5	9
Bitterblue	27	—	30	4	9
Ea 67-3[e]	18	15	4	1	4
Ea 66-90[e]	18	10	134	2	8
Ea 65-30[e]	18	15	242	5	7

[a]Unreduced
[b]Percent leaves infected
[c]Number chinch bugs/6m²
[d]Injury: 10 = turf killed; 1 no visible effect
[e]Hybrid
[f]To gray leafspot, chinch bug, and sod webworm, Apopka, Florida, 1968

grass improvement. Characteristics of several experimental F₁ hybrids are compared with present varieties in Table 3. As with Kentucky bluegrass it appears that a potential exists for combining and recombining desired turf characteristics through hybridization cycles resulting in progeny superior to both parents.

FINE-LEAVED FESCUES (*FESTUCA RUBRA* AND *F. OVINA*)

Red fescue and the botanical variety *commutata* are used for turf primarily in blends with Kentucky bluegrass. Such blends are used generally throughout the same region as Kentucky bluegrass with the exception of the southern range of bluegrass adaptation where most varieties have not possessed sufficient heat tolerance.

The history of fescue breeding is similar to that for other turf species in which desirable appearing types were selected in mass or individually, increased, and then released. The variety Illahee was selected in a growers field on the basis of vigor and seed yield without consideration for turf quality. Marketing preceded testing.

Systematic breeding programs have been effective in producing improved varieties of both species. The most widely practiced breeding method employs the polycross technique of selecting clones that combine well, followed by the production of synthetics (Hanson and Carnahan, 1956). Synthetic varieties such as Pennlawn often show adaptation to a wider range of climatic conditions than do nonsynthetic varieties.

The use of multiple clones (in excess of six) in synthetic fescue varieties by European plant breeders has not been demonstrated to be of significant value in turf performance tests to date.

Research on orchardgrass by Weiss *et al.* (1951) indicated little advantage in varying clones from four to ten in synthetic combinations relative to performance of recombinations in Syn 1 and Syn 2 generations. Apparently any gains made from multiple clones (over six) could be offset by problems in clonal maintenance. More information is needed on late generations of synthetics to assess optimum generation numbers for maximum synthesis (Graumann, 1952).

Present breeding work is centered in Europe. A number of recently developed synthetic varieties as well as straight varieties from the European programs are under test in the United States at this time. With the diversity of varieties under test it is anticipated that additional improved varieties of both red and chewing fescue will be available within the next five years. Recent research (unpublished, Research Division, O. M. Scott & Sons Co.) evaluating improved varieties within the species *F. ovina* variety *duriuscula* have shown these to be better adapted to high temperatures than the red fescues. The synthetic variety C-26, within this species, has also shown greater tolerance to dollarspot and leafspot. Jenkens (1955) was successful in producing interspecific hybrids between *F. rubra* and *F. ovina* which suggests a potential for combining superior characteristics of these two species.

PERENNIAL RYEGRASS (*LOLIUM PERENNE*)

Renewed interest in ryegrasses for use in turf appears to be the result of introduction of several improved perennial varieties within the past decade. The improved varieties are better adapted to turf culture than older forage-type ryegrasses as demonstrated by Funk and Engel (1968). The synthetic variety Manhattan was found to have increased resistance to brownpatch disease, to produce less upright growth, and to possess finer leaf texture. Adaptation of the improved varieties is still limited to coastal areas of the northern States where mild winters are experienced. Some tendency to lose density during midsummer appears to be a characteristic of all perennial ryegrasses including the newer varieties when used in monoculture. The improved varieties perform well when used in blends with Kentucky bluegrass where ryegrass does not exceed 50% by seed weight.

Increased cold and heat tolerance plus improvement in resistance to leaf diseases still challenge the plant breeder working with the perennial ryegrasses. Polycross evaluation for parental selection and release as synthetic varieties is the dominant breeding method presently used for perennial ryegrasses.

BENTGRASS (*AGROSTIS* SPP.)

The bentgrasses used in turf culture are classified as either colonial or creeping types. The colonial bentgrass types are placed in the species *Agrostis tenuis* whereas the creeping types are placed in the species *Agrostis palustris*. One additional species that has limited use for golf greens is *Agrostis canina*, commonly called "velvet" bentgrass.

Colonial bentgrass is used primarily in turf where Kentucky bluegrass is not well adapted. Geographically this would include golf course areas in the northeastern and northwestern coastal regions of the United States. Wide use is made of colonial bentgrass in Europe for lawn plantings. It is usually blended with red or chewings fescue and bluegrass. Winter overseeding of turf for winter greening in the southern United States represents another use for this species. Natural selection of superior clones or mass selection of uniform populations has represented the route of improvement until very recently.

Synthetic varieties now are increasing in use. Considerable potential exists for improvement of the colonial bentgrasses based on evidence from various breeding investigations. Interspecific hybridization (Jones, 1956) may offer a means of altering growth habit of this species which would be a significant advance. Improved varieties of recent introduction include Holfior, Bardot, Tracenta, and Exeter (Anonymous, 1968).

Creeping bentgrasses and bermudagrass are the most important grasses for golf greens. Numerous vegetatively propagated improved varieties of creeping bentgrass were used intially for greens application. These are being replaced in many areas by the improved variety Penncross which is planted from seed. The vegetatively propagated varieties were selected as superior clones in old turf areas. Plant breeders developing improved creeping bentgrass varieties must devote close attention to evaluation systems providing accurate assessment of disease resistance.

CENTIPEDEGRASS (*EREMOCHLOA OPHIUROIDES*)

Centipede is used in lawn plantings in the southeastern United States. Varietal improvement has been very limited. One improved variety, Oaklawn, is reported to have increased cold tolerance which has been one of the characteristics limiting the use of the species. Tennessee hardy and several green- and red- stem selections represent other strains within this species that are used for lawn plantings (Horn, 1967). Limited information on the breeding behavior of the species has been a factor contributing to lack of improvement. Susceptibility of centipedegrass to nematodes and ground pearl are the major weaknesses of presently used strains.

BAHIAGRASS (*PASPALUM NOTATUM*)

Bahiagrass is used to a limited extent in home lawn areas in Florida. It is also popular for use on highway shoulders, school grounds, and industrial grounds where limited maintenance is employed. The use of superior selections from plant introductions is the method of improvement to date (Burton, 1951). Both apomictic and sexual types occur within the species. Of the improved varieties, developed primarily for pasture, Argentine is the most widely used for turf. Principle disadvantages are unsightly seedhead production, mowing difficulties and lack of turf forming growth habit. Improvement in these characteristics will be required before the species finds wide acceptance for fine turf.

ZOYSIAGRASS (*ZOYSIA* SPP.)

Three species of Zoysiagrass (*Z. tenuifolia*, *Z. japonica*, and *Z. matrella*) are used for lawn plantings in the United States (Daniel and Roberts, 1966). The varieties Meyer and Emerald represent the two most widely used for turf purposes. *Zoysia matrella* is used as a lawngrass in Alabama, Georgia, and California, but no recognized variety is reported for this species. The variety Meyer is a superior clonal selection, tested and distributed for lawn use. Emerald is a vegetatively propagated F_1 hybrid selected from crosses between *Z. japonica*, *Z. matrella*, and *Z. tenuifolia*. Progress in further improvement of the species listed has been limited due to a lack of breeding programs devoted to this grass.

TALL FESCUE (*FESTUCA ARUNDINACEA*)

Tall fescue produces an excellent turf through the upper South and is a popular choice for the home lawn. Cowan (1956) in reviewing tall fescue characteristics stated that "toughness of this grass, its drought resistance and dense deep sod, makes it an ideal turf for airports, playgrounds, athletic fields, and other areas where a durable, firm, wear-resistant turf is essential."

Cowan (1956) points out that the degree of variability that exists between individuals is most tall fescue plant populations would indicate great potential for selection to improve the species for turf applications.

Varieties used for turf are from forage breeding programs, as there has been little progress in breeding turf varieties. Sufficient data are available on breeding behavior and method of reproduction to provide a basis for effective breeding progress once the plant breeders give the problem attention.

References

Akerberg, E. (1936a). Bastard mellan *Poa pratensis* L. X *Poa alpina* L., Artificiellt framställd. *Bot. Notis.* pp. 563–566.

Akerberg, E. (1936b). Studien über die samenbildung bei *Poa pratensis* L. *Bot. Notis.* pp. 263–269.

Akerberg, E. (1939). Apomictic and sexual seed formation in *Poa pratensis. Heriditas* **25**, 359–370.

Anonymous. (1968). "List of Cultivars Eligible for Certification Under the O.E.C.D. Scheme." Directorate for Agriculture and Food, 2 rue André-Pascal, Paris-16.

Armstrong, J. M. (1937). A cytological study of the genus *Poa. Can. J. Res. Sect. C* **15**, 281–287.

Brittingham, W. H. (1943). Type of seed formation as indicated by the nature and extent of variation in Kentucky bluegrass and its practical implications. *J. Agr. Res.* **67**, 225–264.

Burton, G. W. (1947). Breeding bermudagrass for the southeastern United States. *J. Amer. Soc. Agron.* **39**, 551–569.

Burton, G. W. (1951). Breeding grasses for southeastern United States. *Advan. Agron.* **3**, 197–240.

Burton, G. W. (1959) Comparative characteristics of several bermudagrass varieties used for turf purposes. Unpublished Data.

Clausen, J. (1952). New bluegrasses by combining and rearranging genomes of contrasting *Poa* species. *Proc. Int. Grassland Congr., 6th, 1952* Vol. 1, pp. 216–221.

Clausen, J. (1962). Personal communication.

Cowan, J. R. (1956). Tall fescue. *Advan. Agron.* **3**, 283–318.

Daniel, W. H., and Roberts, E. C. (1966). Turfgrass management in the United States. *Advan. Agron.* **18**, 260–323.

Engelbert, V. (1940). Reproduction in some Poa species. *Can. J. Res. Sect. C* **18**, 518–521.

Funk, C. R, (1969). Advances in breeding cool season turfgrasses. *Conf. Proc. 40th Annu. GCSAA Conf.* p. 24–28.

Funk, C. R., and Engel, R. E. (1968). Manhattan perennial ryegrass for turf. *Turfgrass Times* **4**, No. 1.

Graumann, H. O. (1952). The polycross method of breeding in relation to synthetic varieties and recurrent selection of new clones. *Proc. Int. Grassland Congr., 6th, 1952* Vol. 1, pp. 314–319.

Gustafsson, A. (1944). The X-ray resistance of dormant seeds in some agriculture plants. *Hereditas* **30**, 165–178.

Gustafsson, A. (1951). Induction of changes in genes and chromosomes. II. Mutations, environment and evolution. *Cold Spring Harbor Symp. Quant. Biol.* **16**, 263–281.

Hanson, A. A., and Carnahan, H. L. (1956). Breeding perennial forage grasses. *U.S., Dep. Agr., Tech. Bull.* **1145**, 1–116.

Horn, G. C. (1967). Turfgrass variety comparisons. *Proc. Fla. Turf Mgt. Conf.* **15**, 91–99.

Hurcombe, R. (1946). Chromosome studies on *Cynodon. S. Afr. J. Sci.* **42**, 144–146.

Hurcombe, R. (1947). A cytological and morphological study of cultivated *Cynodon* species. *J. S. Afr. Bot.* **13**, 107–116.

Jenkens, T. J. (1955). Interspecific and intergeneric hybrids in herbage grasses. XV. The breeding affinities of *Festuca rubra. J. Genet.* **53**, 125–130.

Jones, K. (1956). Species differentiation in *Agrostis. J. Genet.* **54**, 370–390.

Julen, G. (1954). Observations on X-rayed *Poa pratensis. Acta Agr. Scand.* **4**, 585–593.

Juska, F. V., and Hanson, A. A. (1964). Evaluation of bermudagrass varieties for general purpose turf. *U.S., Dep. Agr., Agr. Handb.* **270**, pp. 1–54.

Lobenstein, C. W. (1962). Observing bluegrasses. *Midwest Turf Conf. Proc.* pp. 66–69.

Long, J. A., and Bashaw, E. C. (1961). Microsporogenesis and chromosome numbers in St. Augustinegrass. *Crop Sci.* **1**, 41–43.

Long, J. A. (1964). Growth rate of Floratine and a dwarf selections of St. Augustinegrass. Unpublished Data.

Long, J. A. (1968). Performance of varieties within the species *Festuca ovina.* Unpublished Data.

Mützing, A. (1933). Further studies on apomixis and sexuality in *Poa hereditas* **26**, 115–190.

Nilsson, F. (1933). Själv-och hors-befruktning: rodsvingel (*Festuca rubra* L.), ängsgröe (*Poa pratensis* L.), och ängskavle (*Alopecurus pratensis* L.). *Bot. Notis.* pp. 221–223.

Tinney, F. W. (1940). Cytology of parthenogenesis in *Poa pratensis. J. Agr. Res.* **60**, 351–360.

Tinney, F. W., and Aamodt, O. S. (1940). The progeny test as a measure of the types of seed development in *Poa pratensis* L. *J. Hered.* **31**, 457–464.

Weiss, M. G., L. Taylor, L. H., and Johnson, I. J. (1951). Breeding behavior of orchardgrass plants, correlations with clonal performance. *Agron. J.* **43**, 594–602.

Wilson, F. (1961). A comparison of lawn grasses for Florida. *Fla., Univ., Agr. Ext. Serv., Circ.* **210**, pp. 1–7.

Youngner, V. B. (1966). Santa Anna, A new turf bermudagrass for California. *Calif. Turfgrass Cult.* **16**, p. 23–24.

Youngner, V. B., and Nudge, F. J. (1968). Growth and carbohydrate storage of three *Poa pratensis* L. strains as influenced by temperature. *Crop Sci.* **8**, 455–457.

Chapter 5

Selection and Breeding of Grasses for Forage and Other Uses

R. MERTON LOVE

Agronomists have generally concentrated their attention on producing cultivars adapted to (1) forage production with a companion legume for intensively managed irrigated pastures, (2) hay production, (3) forage production on nonirrigated sites. From a survey of the papers presented at the Tenth International Grassland Congress in Finland, 1966, in Section III: Herbage Plant Breeding and Seed Production, it is evident that grass breeders still have rather general objectives. These can be listed as (1) higher dry matter yields and animal product per acre (Julen and Lager, 1966; Murphy and Lowe, 1966), (2) hay types (Fejer, 1966), (3) forage types (Rogers and Lazenby, 1966, Fejer, 1966), (4) higher seed yield of good forage types (Carlson, 1966; Griffiths et al., 1966), (5) stand establishment and seedling vigor (Barclay and Armstrong, 1966; Smith and Drolsom, 1966), (6) disease resistance (Drolsom et al., 1966). These are all laudable objectives but, except for the last one, are rather too general for specific breeding objectives.

Grass breeders often have to work with several species and even genera and so their efforts are somewhat less than concentrated. Even so there are many quite satisfactory improved cultivars of grasses in use today. However, most advances in productivity of grasslands involving the efforts of plant breeders and geneticists have been either from introduced material itself or selections therefrom, rather than resulting from sophisticated plant breeding procedures.

Grass breeders, perhaps more than most others, must also be as strong in taxonomy, cytology, and ecology as in genetics. Love (1947) pointed out that the systematists have been remarkably successful in delineating groups of populations into genera and populations into species. Nevertheless the grass breeder must realize that the material must often be reinvestigated to determine more accurately the genetic limitations and potentialities of the species in question. Love (1949) further emphasized the importance of cytology as a practical aid to the grass breeder. He pointed out the importance of a knowledge of chromosome numbers in the species under improvement and gave several examples where such knowledge could have saved time and money in the breeding program (in *Stipa: S. cernua* vs. *S. pulchra* (Stebbins and Love, 1941 a,b); in *Ehrharta calycina*; aneuploidy (Love, 1948; Tothill and Love 1964). Chromosome behavior of meiosis and the type of polyploidy in the species must also be known [examples: in *Bromus inermis* (Elliott and Love, 1948); in *Stipa* (Stebbins and Love, 1941 a, b]. A study of interspecific hybrids is also very helpful (Stebbins *et al.*, 1946).

The production of improved cultivars through the induction of polyploidy has appealed to many breeders. Success has been something less than spectacular. One reason is probably that the plant breeder has used rather high polyploid species to start with. Love (1952) wrote, "A great deal of research is needed to provide fundamental knowledge necessary to the development of a sound, scientific program of plant improvement through induced alloploidy." No one could have guessed on agronomic grounds which diploid species formed the basis of our cultivated wheats. This means that the plant breeder cannot expect to know how to select the parents to be hybridized. He must be prepared to expend time and effort obtaining basic information on related species at the diploid level. It is encouraging to learn that Mansat *et al.* (1966) were doing this in their work with clovers.

In spite of the fact that Carnahan and Hill reported the *Festuca–Lolium* cross in 1955, breeders are still hopeful that a stable cultivar will be attained. There were several promising reports on the cross at the 1966 International Grassland Congress in Finland.

An important concern of the breeder has been to locate a species that fits into a particular econiche. In this regard forage grass breeders are literally thousands of years behind the cereal breeders. Cereal breeders are generally well aware of the niche into which their product must fit and this, of course, has been gained from thousands of years of experience with the growing of cereals. On the other hand, not as much is known about the environment in which range, improved pasture, or even irrigated pasture forages are to be used. The environment is more complicated, especially with respect to management, because livestock harvest the forage crop. Perenniality of the grass crop complicates the matter further.

As the farming operations became more efficient, plant breeders could be satisfied with the lesser degrees of improvement because the farm operator, through intensive management, was able to take advantage of the genetic improvement provided by the plant breeder. A 10% increase in grain yield attained by the breeders is meaningful and is likely to be attained by the grower. With forage grasses, and especially range grasses, the picture is very different. First of all, little is known about the details of management placed on new varieties by the livestock operator who, incidentally, is not likely to be as concerned with intensive management as is the field crop or vegetable crop grower. Therefore if an improved range forage cultivar is to be distributed to the livestock operator, it must be a greater than 100% improvement over the grasses it is to replace.

The practical aspect of forage grass research is that it is useful to know not only the present distribution of the proposed introductions, but also the factors that determine distribution. Hartley and Williams (1956) determined the average percentage of species of each of the major grass tribes in the total grass flora of the world, and from these data they derived the average proportion of each tribe of the world. They mapped the existing distribution of each tribe in relation to these averages which facilitated comparisons of the distribution with that of environmental factors. Pertinent to this discussion are their findings concerning the natural distribution of the more important cultivated pasture grasses. One center of origin is Eurasia—the main center of origin of cultivated pasture grasses because 24 of the 40 species are indigenous there. The second center is East Africa, including parts of Kenya and Uganda. The third center is subtropical eastern South America extending northward from the province of Buenos Aires in Argentina. They indicated that *Bromus marginatus*, (Western United States), *Digitaria procumba* (Transvaal), and *Sorghum sudanense* (Sudan) are the only three cultivated species of importance that are not indigenous to the three centers mentioned.

Hartley and Williams regard the Mediterranean as a subregion of the Eurasian center of origin. In support of this conclusion they named three genera that have close relatives in both areas and advanced the idea that

Mediterranean Taxon	Eurasian Taxon
Dactylis glomerata	*Dactylis glomerata* ssp. *glomerata*
Lolium rigidum (Wimmera)	*L. perenne* and *L. multiflorum*
Phalaris tuberosa var. *stenoptera*	*P. arundinacea*

these Mediterranean species may, therefore, be expected to hold promise as good forage plants.

Their conclusions concerning the origins of grass species now in commercial production are of considerable interest. They point out that few, if any, of the important cultivated grasses are constituents of the flora of the major grasslands of the world. Ecologically the typical meadow grasses of Europe (*Poa, Festuca, Lolium, Dactylis*) are allied to and probably derived from woodland and forest margin types.

Grazing animals of the family Bovidae constituted an important segment of the herbivores. It appears that they evolved in northern Eurasia during the Pliocene and Pleistocene. During late Pliocene, they invaded Africa in large numbers, but few species were established in North America. Hartley and Williams think that if there was a significant evolutionary development of grass species and grazing animals during the same period, Pliocene and Pleistocene, this may have led to grasses especially adapted to grazing. If, as seems to be the case, domestication of animals occurred in the same region, the predecessors of the meadow grasses would have been subjected to these more intensive grazing pressures in the communities of neolithic man as he colonized Europe. This would help explain (1) the abundance of cultivated pasture species from Eurasia and the center of tropical Africa, (2) the scarcity of such grasses in the indigenous flora of North America, and (3) the significant affinity between pasture grasses of the Mediterranean and northern Eurasian region. It would not, of course, explain the South American center. This concept also applies to the tropical grasses such as elephantgrass and guineagrass. On the other hand, Hartley and Williams feel that the great grassland regions of the world, such as the tall grass and short grass prairies have not contributed to the pool of cultivated pasture species because these grasses have developed in regions of lower rainfall and lower soil fertility than is found in the woodlands and forest margins. I think that is why work on *Bouteloua, Andropogon, Elymus,* and *Sporobolus* has not resulted in a significant development of commercial grasses from these primitive grassland types.

Those concerned with Mediterranean-type climates should concern themselves first with species, subspecies, and ecotypes from the Mediterranean region which are closely allied taxonomically to the important Eurasian cultivated grasses. *Phalaris tuberosa* var. *stenoptera*, which is called "Hardinggrass" in California, was introduced by P. B. Kennedy from the Toowoomba Botanical Garden in Australia and named by Mr. Kennedy after the director of that garden. It is rather interesting to note that McWilliam (1963) in Australia described a selection of *Phalaris tuberosa* which holds its seed longer and as a result more seed can be harvested. McWilliam received this material as an introduction from Argentina. We happen to know that this material was taken to Argentina by one of our graduate students many years ago. It may well be that the situation in Argentina was such that more diversity exhibited itself and so McWilliam had an opportunity to make a selection for retention of seed.

Years ago seed of *Ehrharta calycina* was received from Australia. This species is native to South Africa. It was a very unsatisfactory grass from the standpoint of seed production since each seed shattered as it ripened. The seed producer was lucky to harvest 50 to 100 lb of seed per acre. A mutant arose in Australian material and a year or two later it was found in our own material in California. As a result we were able to put out a new strain which we called "Mission Veldt" (Love, 1963). Presumably it has one gene that has the dual effect of altering the formation of the abscission layer, so that the seed is retained in a contracted panicle.

A third nonshattering species with a contracted panicle has recently been certified. It is *Dactylis glomerata* cv. Palestine, a selection originating in the Carmel Mountains of Israel (Love, 1969). It would appear, therefore, that mutants or types with contracted panicles generally retain seed better than the open types. We are now looking into the biochemical, developmental, and anatomical aspects of this phenomenon.

Perhaps just as interesting is another Mediterranean grass, *Oryzopsis miliacea*, which was introduced by Professor Hilgard in 1879. It has such weak seedling vigor that its use was extremely limited. On the best of grassland seed beds it was very difficult to get a stand of *Oryzopsis miliacea* but in the ash of a brush burn it was very simple to get a stand. The main reason for success in burned areas was the lack of competition since where there was heavy brush, very little herbaceous vegetation existed. We had found the proper niche for this grass. No more selection needed to be done on this grass since it was ideally adapted to rough rocky sites from the northern coast of California to San Diego County. In fact, in many places it has now become part of the flora.

The time has now arrived when we can take advantage of the work of the plant physiologist and biochemist to pinpoint our objectives more discretely. For example, the work of Whalley and McKell (1967) on the disappearance of starches and sugars during the germinating period of grass seeds opens the way to studies of this kind. Whereas *Phalaris tuberosa* seed requires 10 to 14 days for the starches to be converted to sugars, the sugars to disappear, and the seed to germinate, their work with the rapidly growing weedy annual grass, *Schismus arabicus*, shows that these events transpire in the course of 24 to 48 hours. McKell and his colleagues have demonstrated three sets of systems concerned with metabolism of the germinating grass seed: (1) breakdown of starch in the endosperm with glucose as the end product in the root and shoot; (2) synthesis and transport of sugars, mainly sucrose, to the growing points, with glucose as the end product in the root and shoot; (3) anabolic and catabolic systems associated with the utilization of this glucose to support cell division and expansion.

Laude and colleagues (Sankary *et al.*, 1969) have indicated a genetic basis for summer dormancy in *Phalaris tuberosa*. Summer dormancy among collections from Israel varied from 30 to 127 days in families grown at Davis, California. As expected, plants from the more arid sites of origin tended to exhibit the longer dormancy. But there were exceptions. These, together with the diversity of behavior in the material, suggest that genotypes may be selected with a potential for later growth in the spring or earlier growth in the autumn.

Drought resistance or tolerance is another characteristic of great value to the agronomist, but it has too many facets to be used as a breeding objective per se. Here the physiologists could assist tremendously. Love (1956) pointed out that in all the reports by physiologists none related drought tolerance to the type of soil. He mentioned two grasses, *Phalaris tuberosa* and *Ehrharta calycina*, that have a high degree of drought tolerance but the former required heavy clay soils and the latter light sandy soils.

To summarize, agronomists have generally concentrated their attention on producing varieties adapted to growth in harmony with legumes in intensively irrigated pasture or to survival and potential for production of more feed than native or resident range species.

Our objectives in selection and breeding of grasses should include the above, which we may group together as grasses for intensive ultilization or management. We must also extend our horizons and develop grasses especially useful for preventing soil erosion where forage production is secondary or negligible or even undesirable. For example, *Schismus*, a weedy annual immigrant on California's drier ranges, could be an ideal plant on fire denuded brush areas of southern California. Its forage production potential is probably lowest of any grass and thus provides little fuel for accidental fires. On the other hand, it appears to be one of the fastest to germinate and produce a root system. We also need to develop grasses whose performance lies between that of turf grasses and range grasses for park areas much used by man. Grasses are needed for use in forested areas that have been burned and require a temporary ground cover but there is no desire for a high volume plant material that would compete unduly with seedling trees transplanted into the area. Other uses for grasses include forage for big game and other wild animals, grasses to improve wildlife habitat, and grasses to provide attractive ground cover for outdoor recreation areas.

There is a new horizon for grass breeders. The increasing importance of wildlands for outdoor recreation means that we shall have to substitute a management approach for the custodial approach used in the past. Improved grassland species adapted to wildland sites, together with our knowledge of vegetation manipulation practices, allow us now to embark on a program of wildfire hazard reduction in our brush and forest areas. These tools provide the scientific knowledge that can be used to help reduce the misery of our under-employed people. The private sector, as well as the local state, and Federal agencies could provide meaningful employment to such persons to enhance the environment of the great out of doors (Love, 1962, 1970a, b).

References

Barclay, P. C., and Armstrong, J. M. (1966). Certain aspects of chromosome number and seed size in induced tetraploid pasture plants. *Proc. Int. Grassland Congr., 10th, 1966* pp. 667–670.

Carlson, I. T. (1966). Clonal and topcross evaluation of selections of reed canarygrass, *Phlaris arundinacea* L. *Proc. Int. Grassland Congr., 10th, 1966* pp. 637–640.

Carnahan, H. L., and Hill, H. D. (1955). *Lolium perenne* L. *tetraploid Festuca elatior* L., triploid hybrids and Colchicine treatments for inducing autoallohexaploids. *Agron. J.* **47**, 258–262.

Drolson, P. N., Nielsen, E. L., and Smith, D. C. (1966). Studies of foliar and seedling disease organisms affecting *Bromus inermis* Leyss. *Proc. Int. Grassland Congr., 10th, 1966* pp. 745–748.

Elliott, F. C., and Love, R. M. (1948). The significance of meiotic chromosome behavior in breeding smooth bromegrass, *Bromus inermis* Leyss. *J. Amer. Soc. Agron.* **40**, 335–341.

Fejer, S. O. (1966). Selection methods for breeding hay- and pasture-varieties of forage plants. *Proc. Int. Grassland Congr., 10th, 1966* pp. 618–624.

Griffiths, D. J., Lewis, J., and Bean, E. W. (1966). The problem of breeding for improved seed yields in grasses. *Proc. Int. Grasslands Congr., 10th, 1966* pp. 749–753.

Hartley, W., and Williams, R. J. (1956). Centers of distribution of cultivated pasture grasses and their significance for plant production. *Proc. Int. Grassland Congr., 7th, 1956* pp. 190–199.

Julen, G., and Lager, A. (1966). Use of the *in vitro* digestibility test in plant breeding. *Proc. Int. Grassland Congr., 10th, 1966* pp. 652–657.

Love, R. M. (1947). Interspecific and intergeneric hydridization in forage crop improvement. *J. Amer. Soc. Agron.* **39**, 41–46.

Love, R. M. (1948). Preliminary cytological studies of *Ehrharta calycina* Smith. *Amer. J. Bot.* **35**, 358–360.

Love, R. M. (1949). Cytology as a practical aid to forage crop improvement. Lilloa **19**, 89–96.

Love, R. M. (1952). The value of induced polyploidy in breeding. *Proc. Int. Grasslands Congr., 6th, 1952* pp. 291–298.

Love, R. M. (1956). Better adaptation of plants to arid conditions. *In* "Future of Arid Lands," Publ. No. 43, pp. 343–367. *Amer. Ass. Advance. Sci.*, Washington, D.C.;

Love, R. M. (1962). Fire as a tool in forest management and protection. *Proc. Soc. Amer. Forest., N. Calif. Sect.* pp. 3–5.

Love, R. M. (1963). Registration of Mission Veldtgrass. *Crop Sci.* **3**, 367–368.

Love, R. M. (1969). Registration of Palestine Orchardgrass. *Crop Sci.* **9**, 523.

Love, R. M. (1970a). The rangelands of the western U. S. *Sci. Amer.* **222**; 89–96.

Love, R. M. (1970b). Better watershed management. *Proc. Int. Grassland Congr., 11th, 1970* pp. 16–19.

McWilliam, J. R. (1963). Selection of seed retention in *Phalaris tuberosa* L. *Aust. J. Agr. Res.* **14,** 755–764.

Mansat, P., Picard, J., and Berthou, F. (1966). Value of selection at the diploid level before tetraploidization. *Proc. Int. Grassland Congr., 10th, 1966* pp. 671–675.

Murphy, R. P., and Lowe, C. C. (1966). Methods of breeding perennial forage species of the temperate zones of the United States. *Proc. Int. Grassland Congr., 10th, 1966* pp. 607–613.

Rogers, H. H., and Lazenby, A. (1966). Selection criteria in breeding of grasses. *Proc. Int. Grassland Congr., 10th, 1966* pp. 630–632.

Sankary, M. M., Laude, H. M., Love, R. M., and Fox, R. E. (1969). Variation in summer dormancy among collections of *Phalaris tuberosa* at Davis, California. *J. Brit. Grassland Soc.* **24,** 134–137.

Smith, D. C., and Drolson, P. N. (1966). Parent and progeny evaluation in the improvement of smooth bromegrass, *Bromus inermis. Proc. Int. Grassland Congr., 10th, 1966* pp. 633–636.

Stebbins, G. L., and Love, R. M. (1941a). An undescribed species of *Stipa* from California. *Madrono San Francisco* **6,** 137–141.

Stebbins, G. L., and Love, R. M. (1941b). A cytological study of California forage grasses. *Amer. J. Bot.* **28,** 371–382.

Stebbins, G. L., Valencia, J. I., Valencia, R. M. (1946). Artificial and natural hybrids in the Gramineae, tribe *Hordeae. I. Elymus, Sitanion* and *Agropyron. Amer. J. Bot.* **33,** 338–351.

Tothill, J. C., and Love, R. M. (1964). Autecological studies on *Ehrharta calycina. Advan. Front. Plant Sci.* **8,** 69–107.

Whalley, R. D. B., and McKell, C. M. (1967). Interrelation of carbohydrate metabolism, seedling development and seeding growth rate of several species of *Phalaris. Agron. J.* **59,** 223–236.

Chapter 6

Seedling Vigor and Seedling Establishment

C. M. McKELL

Differences in success of establishment among grass species are well known and have been attributed to differential plant response to such environmental conditions as the permeability of the soil to seedling roots, soil moisture content, low or high temperature, and light intensity. Species that consistently show a rapid germination rate, fast rates of root and top growth, a robust growth habit, or resistance to stress are often referred to as having seedling vigor. Success in seedling establishment may be enhanced, therefore, by either providing favorable environmental conditions or by selecting species that have a high degree of vigor during the seedling stage.

Growth of a new grass plant starts with activation (Mayer and Poljakoff-Mayber, 1963) of the embryo and other seed parts and proceeds through the seedling stage to the period of rapid vegetative growth and finally maturity of the established plant (R. F. Williams, 1964) (Fig. 1). With the emergence of the radicle, seedling establishment begins and may not be considered a success until the plant has developed an adequate root system and leaf area to sustain in a high rate of growth (Fig. 2). Whalley et al. (1966a) consider the seedling stage in three phases: (1) the heterotrophic stage which occurs from inhibition to the initiation of photosynthesis; (2) the transition stage during which time the seedling obtains complex organic compounds

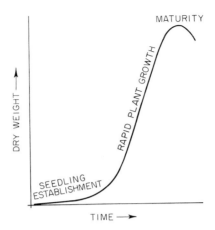

FIG. 1. Relative growth curve of barley. Adapted from data of R. F. Williams (1964).

from both photosynthesis and the remainder of the endosperm; and (3) the autotrophic stage which occurs after the seedling has exhausted the endosperm and is completely dependent on its own photosynthetic products. During the establishment stage, intense competition from within the species and from other species may be very great and result in the lost of many seedlings. Under unfavorable environmental conditions only those plants with a high degree of seedling vigor will be able to survive. With such exceptions as the cereals, members of the *Gramineae* do not have large seeds with the attendant advantage of extensive food reserves, and as a result have evolved various seedling characteristics which aid in establishment.

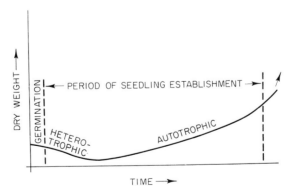

FIG. 2. Period of grass seedling establishment showing relative importance of the various stages of seedling growth.

Seedling Vigor

There is no single attribute that would adequately characterize seedling vigor in grasses. Most definitions used in the literature refer to limited features of seedling growth that may be useful in a specific situation. Kittock and Law (1968) consider ability of seedlings to emerge as "seedling vigor." A common use of the term appears in ratings of plant performance in breeding programs (Kneebone and Cremer, 1955; Tossell, 1960; Robinson and Thomas, 1963; Mahadevappa, 1967) and field performance of commercial grass such as *Bromus inermus* (Al-Ansary, 1960) and *Agropyron* varieties for seedling dry land pastures (Kittock and Patterson, 1962).

Resistance to seed or soil-borne microorganisms was considered by Isley (1957) to be an expression of seedling vigor. However, a differential response to temperature may be a large factor in the resistance to pathogens as Hoppe (1955) showed when he employed a cold temperature to test for seedling vigor in corn. Seeds were incubated for 10 days at 45 to 50° F and then germinated at 86° F. *Pythium* sp. were active at the low temperature as contrasted with relative inactivity of the corn, and the incubation period thus became a test for resistance to attack by the pathogens.

Most biologists use the term "seedling vigor" in its broadest sense to describe a vigorous growth habit that involves a more rapid size increase than that of competing plants of the same age. Prompt seedling growth, as soon as conditions become favorable, is an obvious advantage toward successful establishment. Seedlings with a fast root and top growth must be supported by efficient enzyme systems with which to mobilize stored food reserves in the endosperm tissue. Rapid transport of soluble sugars to growing points and areas of high metabolic demand is a further necessity for a vigorous seedling.

Seedling vigor is of critical importance in plant competition. The traditional view of Clements (1907) and later of Donald (1963) holds that competition is a physical process of plants drawing from a pool of such factors as air, light, nutrients, and water. When the pool is limited or subject to depletion, then the more vigorous seedling that draws rapidly from the pool or can explore a greater volume of the environment will be the successful competitor.

Tests for seedling vigor have been proposed by numerous authors as a means of evaluating or quantifying certain aspects of seedling growth. Delouche and Caldwell (1960) reviewed seed vigor tests from the seed analyst's point of view.

Emergence force of germinating seeds of wheat, oats, barley, and rye through various depths of brick dust was described as "triebkraft" by

Lindenbein and Bulot (1955) and Lein (1956). This method gave a close correlation with other tests for seedling vigor. W. A. Williams (1956) evaluated the emergence force of germinating small-seeded legumes by measuring the height they could elevate various lengths of glass rods in glass tubing.

Emergence from deep planting has been used by numerous workers as a test for seedling vigor. Lawrence (1963) reported that emergence from various sowing depths correlated well with other aspects of seedling vigor in *Elymus junceus*. Seed size and speed of germination also correlated well with ratings of seedling vigor.

Rate of seedling growth and development is a common criteria of seedling vigor (Plummer, 1943; Gullakson *et al.*, 1964; Whalley, 1965). Thomas (1966) used the term, "parameters of vigor," in his study of *Lolium perenne* in which length, width, area of leaves, rate of leaf appearance, and number of tillers correlated well in the initial growth stages with seed size and long-term production. Haydecker (1960) questions the possibility of measuring seedling vigor but proposes that accumulated measurements of root or shoot length are good tests for seedling vigor.

Tests for biochemical and physiological activity may also provide an estimate of seedling vigor. The degree of reduction of TTC (2,3,5 triphenyl-2H-tetrazolium chloride) by germinating seeds of wheat (Kittock and Law, 1968) was not significantly correlated with seedling vigor but showed a correlation to the nongenetic factors associated with seed quality. No clear answer is available from other reports which indicate a high correlation between respiration of germinating corn seeds and seedling vigor (Woodstock and Feeley, 1965) and a contrasting report (Throneberry and Smith, 1955) that oxygen consumption and TTC reduction were not well correlated with vigor ratings on corn. Major problems that could be causing such differences are the nonspecific nature of the term "seedling vigor" and the interaction of plant growth and seedling environment. Inasmuch as seedling vigor is the result of increased biological activity rather than a cause, considerable study of the physiology and nature of seedling vigor is needed before definitive tests can be perfected.

Resistance to disease and environmental stresses as related to the seedling has been tested in a variety of ways. Exposure of seedlings to microorganisms and then measurement of survival or vigor of growth were reported by Isley (1957) and Hoppe (1955). Helmers *et al.* (1962) subjected seeds of crimson clover to various temperatures and relative humidities prior to germination. They found that seedling response to the extreme conditions imposed on the seeds gave a good index of seedling vigor. Mark and McKee (1968) used stress tests of cold and hot flooding, accelerated aging, and immersion in an acid solution to evaluate vigor and potential field performance of reed canarygrass. They found that the hot flood test gave a good indication of field performance and in lieu of the hot flood test, results of the standard germination test should be reduced by one third to predict comparable results in the field. Resistance to mechanical injury, high temperatures, or storage at unfavorable conditions appears to be a function of the type of seeds in so far as germination and seedling vigor is concerned (Webster and Dexter, 1961). A high percentage of germination is not always a guarantee of seedling vigor if germination is spread over too long a time period.

Characteristics Important in Seedling Vigor

SEED SIZE AND WEIGHT

Seed size and weight are extremely important characteristics associated with seedling vigor. Davies (1967) summarized results with commonly used British grasses stating that, "Under normal field conditions, the size of the endosperm is an important factor in determining the potential ability of a epecies to establish itself." Considerable variation in seed size exists in seeds produced from the same plant according to Whalley *et al* (1966c). They also reported that commercially harvested seeds of *Phalaris tuberosa* var. *stenoptera* may contain a high proportion of immature seeds. Germination percentage and rate were lower in small and immature seeds than in large mature ones. Within species, seed weight is of greater significance to seedling vigor than it is between species or genera. Kittock and Patterson (1962) concluded that, "The closer the genetic background of compared lines, the higher the correlation between seed weight and seedling vigor."

In one of the earliest papers published in the *Journal of the American Society of Agronomy*, Zavitz (1908) reported consistently greater yields from plantings of large well-filled cereal seeds than from small well-filled seeds. A large portion of the increased yields may have occurred as a result of genetic selection from the great amount of diversity present at the time. However, many reports emphasize the importance of a greater volume of endosperm food reserve in relation to subsequent seedling size or rate of growth (Hove and Klinendorst, 1957; Demivlicakmak *et al.*, 1963; Kneebone and Cremer, 1955). Whalley *et al.* (1966a) showed that large seeds had longer seedling growth than small seeds of the same species (Fig. 3). One extremely small seeded species, *Schismus arabicus*, grew at a fast rate but in the absence of light was through growing even before radicle emergence of larger seeded species had started.

Seed size and weight are not as important as the plant responses de-

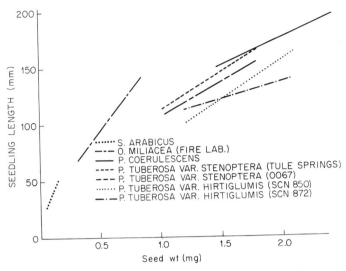

FIG. 3. Seed weight in relation to total seedling length. *Schismus Arabicus* and *Oryzopsis miliacea* show a greater degree of correlation between seed weight and seedling length than do the various *Phalaris* species and varieties.

pendent on them, such as emergence from soil depths, early seedling root growth, and embryo size. In areas subject to rapid drying of the soil surface, deeper planting of grass seeds is important for successful establishment and survival. Rogler (1954) and Vogel (1963) working with *Agropyron* spp. reported a close correlation between seed weight and total emergence from depths greater than 1 in. Increasing the seeding depth decreased the rate of emergence. Similar results were reported by Multamaki (1962) and Kalton *et al.* (1959).

Early seedling root growth is almost equally important as emergence and has been shown to be correlated with seed size (Plummer, 1943; Kittock and Patterson, 1962; Tadmor and Cohen, 1968). Early root growth is largely dependent on endosperm reserves because photosynthetic activity of leaves is delayed after emergence (Anslow, 1962) and is initially insufficient to support root growth and metabolism.

The effects of embryo size versus endosperm size on emergence of wheat seedlings were compared in an experiment by Bremner *et al.* (1963). In contrast with little or no effect from embryo size, the volume of endosperm had a considerable effect on seedling growth. Thus increased seedling vigor attributable to seed size and weight is a result of greater reserve materials within the seed.

Rapid Germination

Rapid germination is another plant characteristic that may contribute to a vigorous and successful seedling. The statement of Kittock and Patterson (1962) that the spread of germination over a broad period can have little survival value is particularly appropriate for grass establishment in arid regions or even in irrigated pastures and turf areas where the soil may be subject to intermittent drying. Rapid germination is often a characteristic of weedy grasses that invade grass communities when a short period of favorable conditions occurs (Major *et al.*, 1960). The same internal biochemical systems that are active in the germination process continue to operate in the seedling stage and even beyond, thus sustaining a vigorous growth habit.

Seed Age

Seed age can be a negative factor in seedling vigor unless stored under conditions that retard embryo and endosperm deterioration. Older seeds have been shown (Kittock and Law, 1968; Crocker, 1948) to germinate more slowly, they may produce malformed seedlings, and the resulting seelings are often slower in their growth.

Biochemical and Physiological Activity

A high level of biochemical and physiological activity of seedlings is basic to seedling vigor. Seedlings with high physiological activity generally are those with a high rating for vigor. Mayer and Poljakoff-Mayber (1963) discuss the many systems and processes that may be involved in supporting seedling growth. After imbibition, storage products are enzymatically changed to soluble forms; metabolism and further breakdown of storage products such as carbohydrates, lipids, proteins, and phosphorus-containing compounds increases as a function of increased enzyme activity; and respiration increases resulting in high demands for energy-rich substrate and oxygen. Cell division and elongation in growing points are highly dependent on efficient transport systems in order to sustain high growth rates.

Reports on metabolic rate as an index of physiological activity in vigorous seedlings are conflicting. Mahadevappa (1967) reported that leaf tissues of pearl millet failed to show any differences in the rate of respiration nor could he find a correlation between respiration capacity and growth rate. Earlier, Throneberry and Smith (1955) reported essentially the same result with germinating corn seeds. However, Kittock and Law (1968) and Woodstock

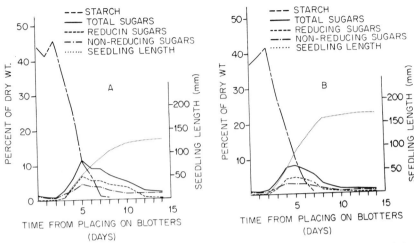

FIG. 4. Conversion of starch to sugars during germination and seedling growth of (A) *Phalaris tuberosa* var. *stenoptera*, (Tule Spring) which is rated low in seedling vigor, and (B) *P. coerulescens* which is rated high in seedling vigor.

and Feeley (1965) report close correlations between respiration rates and seedling vigor.

Rapid mobilization of endosperm reserves and transport appears to be another factor in seedling vigor. Whalley *et al.* (1966a) and Whalley and Mckell (1967) show that the degree of availability of sugars or the lack of sufficient transport to the growing seedling may partially account for differences in seedling vigor among several species of *Phalaris* (Fig. 4). Considerable study is needed before a clear picture can be drawn of the rate of biochemical and physiological activity in vigorous seedlings.

FORCE OF GROWTH

Force of seedling growth is a valuable plant attribute that may be critical in survival. Where rapidity of emergence depends on a high growth rate of the coleoptile and shoot, the force of emergence may be more dependent on endosperm reserves and a durable epidermis. Kalton *et al.* (1959) made observations on the relation between seed size and emergence from different depths. Emergence was delayed or reduced with an increase in seedling depth but the difference in seedling emergence between large and small seeds increased. Lawrence (1963) sowed seeds of *Elymus junceus* at depths of from 0.5 to 1.5 in. and reported a positive correlation between total emergence and seed size. Subsequently, seed yield and forage yield were also correlated.

RATE OF GROWTH

Rate of growth, being one of the most obvious characteristics, is often regarded as evidence of seedling vigor. Both rapid top growth and root growth can be a distinct advantage in seedling establishment. Early achievement of an adequate leaf area supplies the needs of the developing seedling for products of photosynthesis in addition to occupying surface area that would otherwise be used by competing species. Loomis and Williams (1963) suggest that the time required for attainment of an optimum leaf area and thus increased productivity can be shortened by planting more seeds per unit area or by planting seeds that produce a large initial leaf area per plant. Thomas (1966) showed that leaf size is correlated with seed size but that the relationship decreases with time. Shibles and MacDonald (1962) compared two varieties of birdsfoot trefoil which were known for low and high seedling vigor. Even though both varieties were equal in net photosynthetic rate per unit area of cotyledon, the variety known for its high seedling vigor had a higher rate of production of photosynthetic surface even though seeds of the same size were used.

ROOT SYSTEM DEVELOPMENT

Rapid development of a root system sufficient to garner water and nutrients for the young seedling is perhaps a higher priority than early top growth if endosperm reserves in large seeds are still available. Plummer (1943) attributed the success or failure of establishment of 12 range grasses to total root development prior to summer drought. The most successful species, *Agropyron cristatum*, produced a greater total root length in the seedling stage. Differential response of tops and roots to temperature must be considered. Brouwer (1966) reviewed the literature concerning factors affecting root growth rates and presented information showing that at low temperatures root growth is favored more than top growth. An increase in temperature results in a burst of top growth giving an increase in shoot root ratio. Other factors such as low nitrogen, moisture stress, and shade also cause low shoot/root ratios.

Cohen and Tadmor (1969) reported large differences among 10 species of grasses and legumes in seedling root growth. Seedling root elongation in the upper soil layer (2 to 12 cm) was greatest at 25°C. whereas in the deeper layer (12 to 22 cm) 20°C appeared to be the most favorable temperature. Seed size also correlated well with rate of root elongation. *Phalaris tuberosa* seeds were the smallest in their study and had the slowest elongation rate whereas the opposite was true for wheat and barley. Low temperatures accentuated these differences. For species like *Phalaris* which is adapted to Mediterranean climates larger seed varieties must be developed to provide increased vigor of root growth to overcome the adverse effects of low soil temperatures during the moist season.

RESISTANCE TO UNFAVORABLE ENVIRONMENT

Resistance to physical and biological environment may be a direct expression of seedling vigor caused by a tough epidermis, an anatomical or physiological makeup that makes a seedling nonsusceptible to plant pathogens, or a physical constitution that enables a seedling to withstand mechanical damage of various types. Conversely, resistance as an aspect of seedling vigor may merely be the result of a high rate of growth, the ability to grow at an unusual temperature regime, or the ability to withstand other environmental stresses because of a high level of biochemical or physiological activity. Whatever the case, a resistant seedling may easily be classed as a vigorous seedling if it results in a substantial advantage in establishment. Several studies give examples of the significance or resistance. High temperatures and high humidity prior to germination were shown by Helmers *et al.* (1962) to eliminate seeds that did not have the potential for high seedling vigor. Disease resistance (Isley, 1957) is another aspect of plant vigor but one which draws on more fundamental seedling characteristics such as anatomy and physiology. Resistance of reed canarygrass seedlings to flooding or acid conditions was correlated with field performance (Mark and Mckee, 1968) thus indicating the importance of this type of vigor in the seedling stage for overall plant performance.

Possibilities for Increasing Seedling Vigor

GENETIC IMPROVEMENT

Genetic improvement of seedling vigor can be obtained by selecting for the characteristic mentioned previously. Inasmuch as seed size seems to be so interrelated to a number of other vigor characteristics, considerable progress could be made in selecting for larger size seeds.

Another area that should receive intensive sutdy is the role of various biochemical and physiological processes in seedling vigor and the heritability of such processes. Genetic selection could then be intensively applied to produce seedlings of greater vigor.

GROWTH REGULATING CHEMICALS

Growth regulating chemicals used in the seedling stage have shown considerable promise as a means of increasing grass seedling vigor. The general result attributed to the use of gibberellins on grass seedlings is an increase in cell division and elongation. Seedlings treated with gibberellic acid under experimental conditions appear to grow faster than untreated ones. Recent work of Paleg 1960) has shown how naturally occurring gibberellins stimulate the enzymatic activity of the aleurone layer causing an increase in starch hydrolysis and the level of reducing sugars. Additional gibberellic acid applications further increase the rate of starch breakdown, create extra supplies of reducing sugars, and thus increase the growth rate of seedlings. Hurd and Purvis (1964) reported that gibberellins stimulated cell division in quiescent meristems thus removing the need for vernalization. Whalley (1965) reported a differential stimulation of seedling growth rates of two species of *Phalaris*. His data show that the increase consisted primarily of root growth rather than top growth. Reducing sugars and glucose concentrations were also increased by gibberellin treatment.

FERTILIZATION

A cultural practice such as fertilization is an easy way to increase seedling vigor and may be particularly effective in cases where differential species responses can be predicted. Not all grass species utilize nitrogen with the same degree of efficiency but through better knowledge of how plants respond to external nitrogen the practice of fertilization can be used to increase seedling vigor. Folkes *et al.* (1952) reported that nitrogen present in the endosperm of barley is mainly transferred to the growing seedling during the first two to six days. During this time a peak in respiration occurs and growth at the expense of reserves is mainly completed by the eight day. When external nitrogen is available, growth and differentiation are increased but there is also an increase in respiration from the fourth day onward. Ayeke and McKell (1969) showed that moderate amounts of external nitrogen during the first six days of germination accelerated the decrease in starch content of *Lolium multiflorum* and *Oryzopsis miliacea* seeds but without a corresponding increase in seedling growth. Very low amounts of nitrogen plus phosphorus gave an increase in top and root growth of *L. multiflorum* but higher rates significantly reduced root growth and increased the top growth. *Oryzopsis miliacea* seedlings did not increase in growth at very low nitrogen–phosphorus rates and grew even less as the nitrogen–phosphorus rates increased.

Germination may be delayed and emergence reduced when fertilizers are placed in close proximity to the seeds. Chapin and Smith (1960) reported that rates of 20 lb nitrogen per acre plus 83 lb potassium per acre had little effect on germination when the soil was at field capacity but when the concentration of the fertilizer was increased by a decrease in soil moisture content, emergence was decreased.

The problem therefore appears to be one of time and amount. In the early seedling stage small amounts of external nitrogen may stimulate growth and mobilization of reserves in certain species. Excess nitrogen in the very early seedling stage can be a negative influence by increasing respiration and favoring top growth at a time when there is a greater need for the development of an adequate root system, particularly if the danger of soil surface drying is imminent. By the use of slow-release fertilizers or placement of fertilizers at a sufficient distance to allow early development under low nitrogen levels, vigorous seedling growth during the autotropic stage can be obtained by having adequate fertilizer readily available.

Favorable growing conditions for the parent generation may have a significant influence on seed quality and thus raise the vigor of subsequent seedlings. Kidd and West (1919) first suggested the possibility but little has been done directly. Seed certification standards reflect the general philosophy that seed fields should be well cared for and that seeds should be high in germinability. Whalley *et al.* (1966b) found that application of nitrogen and phosphorus to parent plants of *O. miliacea* increased the number of seeds per plant and the mean seed weight. Both the seedling growth rates and the ultimate seedling lengths in the dark were increased by the fertilizer application to the parent plants. Water stress imposed on the parent plants decreased the seed yield per plant but increased the mean seed weight. Seedling growth, independent of seed weight, was not affected. Thus it would appear that proper attention to fertility requirements of the parent generation can result in seeds being produced that have a higher potential seedling vigor than seeds produced under conditions of inadequate fertilization.

Seedling Establishment

VIGOROUS SEEDLINGS

Establishment of grass seedlings starts with the emergence of the coleorhiza and the coleoptile and continues until a high rate of growth is achieved. Establishment is a success only when the plant has developed an adequate root system of sufficient depth and lateral spread to obtain water and nutrients at a rate equal to or greater than competing seedlings. In a like manner top growth must not only be in proportion to root growth but greater than competing seedlings.

Plant Density Reduction

Under both natural and cultivated conditions a large reduction in seedling numbers is likely to occur. High seeding rates are always recommended for improved pastures and turf areas as insurance against disease, environmental stresses, and poor management. In drill seedings of rangeland the seed rates are proportionately lower than under cultivated conditions. Species that are naturally self-reseeding generally produce a large volume of seed. Thus a high degree of intraspecific competition occurs in cultivated grasslands and in drill-seeded rangelands competition is generally interspecific in nature. Self-reseeding grasslands have both types of competition. As an example of the magnitude of seedling number reduction in annual range, Heady (1956) found the number of plants early in the growing season to vary from 20 to nearly 100/in.^{2} But the end of the growing season the number of plants per square inch may range from one to ten.

Climatic and Environmental Conditions

Grass establishment occurs over a wide range of climatic conditions to form the grasslands that occupy about one fifth of the land surface of the globe. In addition, grasses may be found intermixed with the three other great plant formations; forest, desert scrub, and tundra. Obviously, grass seedlings must be able to grow rapidly during short periods of favorable temperature or soil moisture in difficult environments and to endure or escape the stress conditions during the unfavorable seasons of the year. The time available for grass establishment varies with the environment. Under cultivated conditions moisture may be supplied during turf establishment and unfavorable temperatures are often the greatest hazard. In irrigated pastures the time requirement for establishment may be longer than for turf areas but careful grazing management is necessary to prevent serious seedling damage. On arid rangelands seeded with *Agropyron* species establishment is not generally assured until the beginning of the second season because root and top growth must have been sufficient to carry the plants through the dry and cold seasons of the year. Seedling establishment on annual rangeland with annual grasses and legumes may be considered a success if sufficient seeds are produced to provide seed for the next growing season.

Perennial grasses are not considered established until the beginning of the following growing season.

Conditions for Success

Conditions required for success in seedling establishment are three: vigorous (adapted) seedlings, reduced competition, and favorable environment. Not all three conditions may be required together depending on the severity of the environment and on the possibilities for environmental modification. Under present-day knowledge and conditions it is increasingly possible to insure greater success in seedling establishment. Improved grass varieties have been selected for desired forage, turf, or ground cover attributes but in addition for as many vigor characteristics as can be identified. Not all characteristics show favorably in the rows of the breeder's nursery and should be tested in separate studies (O. B. Williams, 1960).

Cultural practices used in grass establishment may be elaborate or relatively simple but techniques are now available for competition reduction and modification of the seedling environment. Plant competition can be reduced by tillage, selective herbicides and sprays, or by such mechanical means as scraping an area free of litter and weed seeds prior to seeding.

References

Al-Ansary, M. M. (1960). Variation in seed and seedling characters of bromegrass, *Bromus inermis* Leyss., in relation to environment. *Diss. Abstr.* **20**, 3913.

Anslow, R. C. (1962). A quantitative analysis of germination and early seedling growth in perennial ryegrass. *J. Brit. Grassland Soc.* **17**, 260–263.

Ayeke, C. A., and McKell, C. M. (1969). Early seedling growth of Italian ryegrass and smilo as affected by nutrition. *J. Range Manage.* **22**, 29–32.

Bremner, P. M., Eckersall, R. M., and Scott, R. K. (1963). The relative importance of embryo size and endosperm size in causing the effects associated with seed size in wheat. *J. Agr. Sci.* **61**, 139–145.

Brouwer, R. (1966). Root growth of grasses and cereals. *In* "The Growth of Cereals and Grasses" F. L. Milthorpe and J. D. Ivins, eds.). p. 359. Butterworth, London.

Chapin, J. S., and Smith, F. W. (1960). Germination of wheat at various levels of soil moisture as affected by applications of ammonium nitrate and muriate of potash. *Soil Sci.* **89**, 322–327.

Clements, F. E. (1907). "Plant Physiology and Ecology." Holt, New York.

Cohen, Y., and Tadmor, N. H. (1969). Effects of temperature on the elongation of seedling roots of some grasses and legumes. *Crop Sci.* **9**, 189–192.

Crocker, W. (1948). "Growth of Plants. Twenty years Research at Boyce Thompson Institute." Reinhold, New York.

Davies, W. (1967). Seeds Mixture Problem. Soil germination, seedling and plant establishment with particular reference to the effects of environment and agronomic factors. Field trials, *Welsh Plant Breed Sta. Bull.* Series H. **6**, 39–63.

Delouche, J. C., and Caldwell, W. P. (1960). Seed vigor and vigor tests. *Proc. Ass. Off. Seed Anal.* **50**, 124–129.

Demivlicakmak, A., Kaufmann, M. L., and Johnson, L. P. V. (1963). The influence of seed size and seeding rate on yield and yield components of barley. *Can. J. Plant Sci.* **43**, 330–337.

Donald, C. M. (1963). Competition among crop and pasture plants. *Advan. Agron.* **15**, 1–114.

Folkes, B. F., Willis, A. J., and Yemm, E. W. (1952). The respiration of barley plants. VII. The metabolism of nitrogen and respiration in seedlings. *New Phytol.* **51**, 317–341.

Gullakson, G., Foote, L. E., and Jackobs, J. A. (1964). Seedling vigor of *Festuca arundinacea, Panicum virgatum* and *Bothriochloa caucasia* and their response to added nutrients. *J. Range Manage.* **17**, 214–216.

Haydecker, W. (1960). Can we measure seedling vigor? *Proc. Inst. Seed Test. Ass.* **25**, 498–512.

Heady, H. F. (1956). Evaluation and measurement of the annual type. *J. Range Manage.* **9**, 25–27.

Helmers, J. D., Delouche, J. C., and Lienhard, M. (1962). Some indices of vigor and deterioration in seed of crimson clover. *Proc. Ass. Off. Seed Anal.* **52**, 154–161.

Hoppe, P. E. (1955). Cold testing seed corn by the rolled towel method. *Wis. Agr. Expt. Sta. Bull.* **507**.

Hove, H. J., and Klinendorst, A. (1957). The influence of seed size on the youth development of Lolium perenne L. *Mededel. Inst. Biol. Scheikundig Onderz Landbouwgew.* **179**, 39–46.

Hurd, R. G., and Purvis, O. N. (1964). The effect of gibberellic acid on the flowering of spring and winter rye. *Ann. Bot. (London)* **28**, 137–151.

Isley, D. (1957). Vigor tests. *Proc. Ass. Off. Seed Anal.* **47**, 176–182.

Kalton, R. R., Delong, R. A., and McLeod, D. S. (1959). Cultural factors in seedling vigor of smooth bromegrass and other forage species. *Iowa State J. Sci.* **34**, 47–80.

Kidd, F., and West, C. (1919). Physiological predetermination: the influence of the conditions of seed upon the course of subsequent growth upon yield. II. Review of literature. *Ann. Appl. Biol.* **5**, 112–142.

Kittock, D. L., and Law, A. G. (1968). Relationship of seedling vigor to respiration and tetrazolium chloride by germinating wheat seeds. *Agron. J.* **60**, 286–288.

Kittock, D. L., and Patterson, J. K. (1962). Seed size effects on performance of dryland grasses. *Agron. J.* **54**, 277–278.

Kneebone, W. R., and Cremer, C. L. (1955). The relationship of seed size to seedling vigor in some native grass species. *Agron. J.* **47**, 472–477.

Lawrence, T. (1963). A comparison of methods of evaluating Russian Wildrye grass for seedling vigor. *Can. J. Plant Sci.* **43**, 307–312.

Lein, A. (1956). Triebkraft, ein fester Begriff der Pratis ["Triebhraft," (seedling vigor) a well-established definition in practice]. *Saatgut Wirt.* **8**, 178–180.

Lindenbein, W., and Bulot, H. (1955). Treibkraft, Ziegelgruswert, und Tetrazolium wert. [Germinating energy, the brickdust value and the tetrazolium value.] *Saatgut Wirt.* **7**, 315–319.

Loomis, R. S., and Williams, W. A. (1963). Maximum crop productivity: An estimate. *Crop Sci.* **3**, 67–72.

Mahadevappa, M. (1967). Investigations on seedling vigor in pearl millet. (Pennisetum *typhoides* Staph. and Hubb.) *Proc. Indian Acad. Sci., Sect. B* **66**, 87–91.

Major, J., McKell, C. M., and Berry, L. J. (1960). Improvement of medusahead-infested rangeland. *Calif., Agr. Exp. Sta., Ext. Serv. Leaflet.* **123**.

Mark, J. L., and Mckee, G. W. (1968). Relationships between five laboratory stress tests, seed vigor field emergence, and seedling establishment in reed canarygrass. *Agron. J.* **60**, 71–76.

Mayer, A. M., and Poljakoff-Mayber, A. (1963). "The germination of seeds," *Int. Ser. Monogr. Pure Appl. Biol., Plant Physiol. Div.* Macmillan Co., New York.

Multamaki, K. (1962). [The effect of seed size and depth of seeding on the emergence of grassland plants]. *Mastaloustieteellinen Aihakauskirja* **34**, 18–25.

Paleg, L. G. (1960). Physiological effects of gibberellic acid. 1. On carbohydrate metabolism and amylase activity of barley endosperm. *Plant Physiol.* **35**, 293–299.

Plummer, A. P. (1943). The germination and early seedling development of twelve range grasses. *J. Amer. Soc. Agron.* **35**, 19–34.

Robinson, L. R., and Thomas, H. L. (1963). Combining ability for seedling vigor in *Bromus inermis* Leyss. *Crop Sci.* **3**, 358–359.

Rogler, G. A. (1954). Seed size and seedling vigor in crested wheat. *Agron. J.* **46**, 216–220.

Shibles, R. M., and MacDonald, H. A. (1962). Photosynthetic area and rate in relation to seedling vigor of birdsfoot trefoil (*Lotus corniculatus*). *Crop Sci.* **2**, 299–302.

Tadmor, N. H., and Cohen, Y. (1968). Pre-emergence seedling root development of Mediterranean grasses and legumes. *Crop Sci.* **8**, 416–419.

Thomas, R. L. (1966). The influence of seed weight on seedling vigor in *Lolium perenne. Ann. Bot.* **30**, 111–121.

Throneberry, G. O., and Smith, F. G. (1955). Relation of respiratory and enzymatic activity to corn seed viability. *Plant Physiol.* **30**, 337–343.

Tossell, W. E. (1960). Early seedling vigor and seed weight in relation to breeding in smooth bromegrass, *Bromus inermus* Leyes. *Can. J. Plant Sci.* **40**, 268–280.

Vogel, W. G. (1963). Planting depth and seed size influence emergence of bearded wheatgrass seedlings. *J. Range Manage.* **16**, 273–274.

Webster, L. V., and Dexter, S. T. (1961). Effects of physiological quality of seeds on total germination, rapidity of germination and seedling vigor. *Agron. J.* **53**, 297–299.

Whalley, R. D. B. (1965). Physiology of seedling vigor in grasses. Ph.D. Dissertation, University of California, Riverside.

Whalley, R. D. B., and McKell, C. M. (1967). Interrelation of carbohydrate metabolism, seedling development and seedling growth rate of several species of *Phalaris. Agron. J.* **59**, 223–226.

Whalley, R. D. B., McKell, C. M., and Green, L. R. (1966a). Seedling vigor and the nonphotosynthetic stage of seedling growth in grasses. *Crop Sci.* **6**, 147–150.

Whalley, R. D. B., McKell, C. M., and Green, L. R. (1966b). Effect of environmental conditions during the parent generation on seedling vigor of the subsequent seedlings of *Oryzopsis miliacea* (L.) Benth. and Hook. *Crop. Sci.* **6**, 510–512.

Whalley, R. D. B., McKell, C. M., and Green, L. R. (1966c). Seed physical characteristics and germination of hardinggrass (*Phalaris tuberosa* var. *Stenoptera* (Hack.) Hitch.). *J. Range Manage.* **19**, 129–132.

Williams, O. B. (1960). The selection and establishment of pasture species in a semi-arid environment—an ecological assessment of the problem. *J. Aust. Inst. Agr. Sci.* **26**, 258–265.

Williams, R. F. (1964). The quantitative description of growth. *In* "Grasses and Grasslands" (C. Banard, ed.), pp. 89–101. Macmillan, New York.

Williams, W. A. (1956). Evaluation of the emergence force exerted by seedlings of small seeded legumes using probit analysis. *Agron. J.* **48**, 273–274.

Woodstock, L. W., and Feeley, J. (1965). Early seedling growth and initial respiration rates as potential indicators of seed vigor in corn. *Proc. Ass. Off. Seed Anal.* **55**, 131–139.

Zavitz, C. A. (1908). The relation between the size of seeds and the yield of plants of farm crops. *Proc. Amer. Soc. Agron.* **1**, 98–105.

Chapter 7

Breeding for Seedling Vigor

WILLIAM R. KNEEBONE

Seedling vigor leads to better stand establishment. It is therefore an essential selective criterion in most grass breeding programs. Many things enter in the final product, and "seedling vigor" and attempted definitions tend to become either ambiguous or partial. Simply stated, seedling vigor may be defined as realized capacity for rapid growth in the seedling stage. Isely (1957) emphasized two features: seed attributes and environmental stresses, both of which are an inevitable part of any consideration of this subject. Increased seedling vigor increases the *probability* of stand establishment. *Absolute* values of either change widely with environments. However defined, "seedling vigor" is an inclusive term probably best approached by considering the major factors that affect it. Use of the term "seedling vigor" presupposes starting with live, nondormant seed. Thus it is essential to consider the continuous process of growth from imbibition of water by the seed through to true autotrophism. This essentially includes the first six weeks from seeding for most plantings having available moisture. This period corresponds to Tossell's (1960) period of "early seedling vigor."

Pathways to Seedling Vigor

LARGE SEED

Within any given species, seedlings from large seed emerge faster (Knee-bone and Cremer, 1955; Rogler, 1954; Tossell, 1960) from deeper plantings (Lawrence, 1963; Rogler, 1954; Tossell, 1960) and grow faster once emerged (Kneebone and Cremer, 1955; Tossell, 1960; Trupp and Carlson, 1967) than seedlings from smaller seed. The importance of seed size is emphasized by the data in Table 1 showing its close relation to stand establishment. Of all the selective criteria affecting seedling vigor, from which a breeder can choose, seed size is probably the most important and promises the most im-mediate progress. A physiological basis for vigor differences due to seed size has been demonstrated by work at Arizona (McDaniel, 1969) with barley which shows that larger seeds have more mitochondrial protein than smaller seeds and their higher rates of respiration and energy release thus contribute to more rapid growth.

Seed size effects appear to be largely related to the size of the seed itself whatever the reason for the size differential. In reciprocal crosses of sand

TABLE I

CORRELATIONS BETWEEN SEED SIZE AND MEASURES OF ESTABLISHMENT OBTAINED BY VARIOUS WORKERS

Authority	Species	Character	Correlation
Rogler, 1954	*Agropyron desertorum* (Fisch.) Shult.	Field emergence 7.6 cm planting depth	0.85[b]
Hunt and Miller, 1965	*Agropyron intermedium* (Host.) Beauv.	Greenhouse emergence 7.6 cm planting depth	0.80[b]
Kneebone, 1956	*Andropogon hallii* Hack	Field emergence	0.88[b]
Tossell, 1960	*Bromus inermis* Layss.	Field vigor rating	0.82[b]
Tossell, 1960	*Bromus inermis* Layss.	Field vigor rating	0.60 [a]
Robison and Thomas, 1963	*Bromus inermis* Leyss.	Total plant weight— greenhouse	0.68[b]
Robison and Thomas, 1963	*Bromus inermis* Leyss.	Total plant weight— field	0.44
Lawrence, 1963	*Elymus junceus* Fisch.	Field emergence 7.6 cm planting depth	0.84[b]
Slinkard, 1963	*Elymus junceus* Fisch.	Field emergence	0.36[a]

[a]Significant at 0.05 level.
[b]Significant at 0.01 level.

bluestem (*Andropogon hallii* Hack.), for example, seedlings from seed produced on the large seeded parent as female were more vigorous than those from the small seeded parent as female (Kneebone, 1959). Where reciprocal crosses of intermediate wheatgrass (*Agropyron intermedium* (Host.) Beauv.) differed in seed size, Hunt and Miller (1965) found that more seedlings emerged from the large seed. Where a cross and its reciprocal were similar in seed size, their seedling emergence values were also similar. Large seed from apomictic sideoats grama (*Bouteloua curtipendula* (Michx.) Torr.) varieties produced more vigorous seedlings than did small seed from the same varieties (Kneebone and Cremer, 1955). Although seed size studies within barley (*Hordeum vulgare* L.) varieties may involve more than one genotype, there is certainly very close genetic correspondence between large and small seed, yet seedlings from the two sizes show distinct differences in performance (Kaufmann, 1968; McDaniel, 1969). Varieties that regularly produce large seed, grown for seed production under optimum conditions, provide the first line of attack on poor stand establishment.

SEEDLING VIGOR

Differences in seedling vigor attributes unrelated to seed size have been shown by many workers (Kneebone and Cremer, 1955; Kneebone, 1956; Lawrence, 1957, 1963; Robison and Thomas, 1963; Trupp and Carlson, 1967; Voigt and Brown, 1969; Whalley *et al.*, 1966a). Hunt and Miller (1965) compared large and small seed separates from clones of intermediate wheatgrass which themselves varied in average seed size. Average emergence was 83.0 for "large" seed of all clones and 58.8 for "small" seed from all clones. In several instances, however, "small" seed from one clone gave greater emergence than "large" seed from another even though the "large" seed was larger.

COLEOPTILE LENGTH

One of the advantages of seedlings from large seed has been their ability to grow from greater planting depths. Other things being equal, a greater planting depth provides greater protection from drought stress during heterotrophic and transitional stages. Greater initial depths for the seminal roots allow utilization of water from a greater range of soil depths. For a seedling to emerge from greater depths, it must be capable of greater coleoptile growth. Coleoptile growth has been shown associated with seed size in barley (Kaufmann, 1968), *Agropyron* spp. (Rogler, 1954; Hunt and Miller, 1965), *Phalaris* and *Oryzopsis* spp. (Whalley, *et al.*, 1966a,b). It is also subject to heritable controls independent of seed size effects (Hunt and Miller, 1965; Lawrence, 1957; Allen *et al.*, 1961, 1962, 1965; Kaufmann, 1968) and can therefore be increased by direct selection and recombination.

RESISTANCE TO STRESSES

Since seedling growth, particularly in the transitional stage, is extremely vulnerable to stresses, resistance to those stresses becomes an important consideration in any breeding program that is aimed at greater seedling vigor and improved establishment. Here, too, seedlings from large seed tend to withstand stresses better than seedlings from smaller seed (Kneebone, 1957). In some respects the effect of seed size can be equated with that of heterosis, increasing vigor and providing a homeostatic effect over an array of stress situations. Seed size effects and seedling heterosis are separable phenomena; however, working with mitochondrial heterosis in barley at Arizona, Dr. McDaniel has found sufficient differences related to seed size so that he must make his comparisons with equivalent size seed in order to distinguish seedling heterosis from size related vigor. There are heterotic increases in seedling growth unrelated to seed size but closely related to mitochondrial activity and efficiency (barley, McDaniel, 1969; corn, McDaniel and Sarkissian, 1967).

Rapidity of growth can provide a measure of resistance to some stresses by means of lowered exposure time. The critical period for susceptibility of orchardgrass seedlings (*Dactylis glomerata* L.) to heat and cold appears to be shortly after endosperm exhaustion (Dotzenko *et al.*, 1967) in late transition and early autotrophic stages. In earlier or later stages susceptibility is less. The more rapidly a seedling can pass through this stage, the less likely is it to suffer from extremes of heat or cold. Hanson and Carnahan (1956) reviewed earlier work showing genetic potentials in several grasses for heat resistance in this vulnerable stage.

Heat stress is often associated with drought stress and some form of moisture stress is often found with grass seedlings because of their shallow planting depths. Seedlings under rangeland conditions are by definition involved with moisture limitations. Seedling drought tolerance then becomes an important attribute toward seedling vigor and establishment. Studies at Arizona by Wright (1966) have demonstrated that seedling drought tolerance is a heritable trait in blue panicgrass (*Panicum antidotale* Retz.), lehmann lovegrass and boer lovegrass (*Eragrostis* spp.). Seedling drought tolerant selections of the lovegrasses are being tested for establishment under range conditions in southern Arizona and have shown better stands than standard checks (Wright and Jordan, 1970). Literature relating to evaluation of genetic material under drought stress has been reviewed by Wright and Streetman (1960).

Seedling diseases cause or contribute to the death of a high percentage of most potential plants in grass seedlings, particularly in more humid areas. Bean and Robison (1963) found distinct differences in emergence among varieties of smooth bromegrass (*Bromus inermis* Leyss.) inoculated with various isolates of *Rhizoctonia solani* Kuhn. The varieties with best emergence had been selected for seedling vigor and for disease resistance. Rapid emergence allows a minimum of exposure during the susceptible heterotrophic and transitional growth stages and may intensify the advantage of natural resistance. Resistance, on the other hand, allows growth to proceed unhampered by pathogens. The young seedling is thus doubly provided with greater vigor to withstand other stresses.

COMPETITIVE ABILITY

Competition effects may be very keen since most grass seedings involve an excess of seed, are seldom free from stress conditions, and often involve more than one species either in a compounded mixture or with a so-called "nurse" crop. Varieties used must be good competitors to become effectively established. Obviously the vigor factors already considered contribute greatly to competitive effectiveness. Rhodes (1968a) has shown with *Lolium multiflorum* Lam. and *Phalaris coerulescens* Desf. that differences between seedlings favoring large seed over small seed were increased several fold when the two sizes were grown together in comparison to the two sizes grown separately. Accessions of *Phalaris coerulescens* with high numbers of nodal roots and tillers at early seedling stages were better competitors than those with less (Rhodes, 1968b). Harper (1963) emphasized that plants live in populations and their existence involves interferences with each other. He suggested that breeders should be concerned with "ecological combining ability" as well as the capacity to produce good hybrids.

Japanese workers with rice (*Oryza sativa* L.) and with barley have considered competitive ability as a trait by itself and selected for it. Akihama (1968) was able to show differences in behavior in mixed versus pure stands of rice and to shift population performance in mixed stands in either direction by selection. Sakai (1961) proposed that competitive ability be used like any other vigor character with tests for general and specific competitive ability by appropriate mixed planting designs.

Differences in ability to obtain necessary nutrients from the soil, particularly during the transitional and early autotrophic stages of growth, might be critical to survival, particularly under competition. Such differences do exist, can be demonstrated, and can be selected for as shown by the work of Mouat (1962) with cation exchange capacity differences in roots from different ryegrass sources. Related to this as well as to stress resistance are genetic differences in salt tolerance where salt concentrations may be limiting to establishment. Kneebone (1967) has shown wide differences among bermudagrass selections in the ability of their open pollination seed to germinate in high salt concentrations.

Jowett (1958) demonstrated that copper tolerant seedlings could grow at very low levels of available calcium at which noncopper-tolerant seedlings were unable to grow. Snaydon and Bradshaw (1961) demonstrated genetic differentials in response to calcium in *Festuca ovina* L. and emphasized the importance of such "edaphic ecotypes."

Breeding Procedures

SEED SIZE

Seed size is not only important because of its close relationship to seedling vigor but also because of positive correlations in many species with desirable mature plant traits such as seed yield (smooth bromegrass, Christie and Kalton, 1960a; sand bluestem, Kneebone, 1956, intermediate wheatgrass, Slinkard, 1963; Russian wildrye, *Elymus junceus* Fisch., Lawrence, 1963; blue panicgrass, Wright, 1969) and parental vigor (Lawrence, 1963; Hunt and Miller, 1965; Schaaf *et al.*, 1962; Whalley *et al.*, 1966a) it may be used as an additional selective tool for these traits. In crested wheatgrass (*Agropyron desertorum* (Fisch.) Schult.) there is little or negative association between seed size and seed yield, apparently because low seed sets contribute to high seed size (Schaaf and Rogler, 1963). This emphasizes the importance of knowing the situation in the individual species being studied. Generalizations about "grasses" must be modified to fit a particular "grass."

Seed size is highly heritable (Table 2). Wherever progenies have been tested, combinations of high seed weight parents have given progeny with higher seed weights than combinations of low seed weight parents. Progeny values have tended to reflect the averages of their parents. With high heritability and primarily additive genetic variance, most rapid progress is likely to be made by direct selection of large-seeded parents. The high heritability values and the decided disadvantages of small seed suggest that initial screening of collections might involve an actual screening with elimi-

TABLE 2

HERITABILITY ESTIMATES FOR SEED SIZE IN GRASSES OBTAINED BY VARIOUS WORKERS.

Authority	Species	Variance Ratio Among:	Heritability
Christie and Kalton, 1960a	*Bromus inermis* Leyss.	S₁ segregates	84%
Christie and Kalton, 1960a	*Bromus inermis* Leyss.	"High" polycross progenies	92%
Kneebone et al., 1963	*Bouteloua curtipendula* (Michx.) Torr.	Clones, 5 locations	80%
Schaaf et al., 1962	*Agropyron cristatum* (L.) Gaert.	Clones, 1 location	97%
Wright, 1969	*Panicum antidotale* Retz.	Clones, 1 location	73%

Authority	Species	Parent vs. Progeny Correlations	Heritability
Christie and Kalton, 1960a	*Bromus inermis* Leyss.	S₁ progenies	.83[a]
Kneebone, 1956	*Andropogon hallii* Hack	OP progenies	.34
Schaaf and Rogler, 1963	*Agropyron desertorum* (Fisch.) Schult.	Polycross progenies	.84[a]

[a]Significant at 0.01 level.

nation of the lower 20% to 25% of the seeds in the laboratory before planting.

The usual procedure in comparing plants for seed size has been to sample polycross, topcross, or open-pollination seed by counting and weighing, using some standard convenient number for the sample such as 100-200-500 seed depending on the species and its seed size. An alternative procedure might be to screen known weights of seed, recording the percentage exceeding a given screen size or sizes.

A simple selection procedure for large seed size would be to grow large composited populations of cross-pollinated species, harvest in bulk, mechanically screen the seed, and use the largest seed fractions as source material for further selection. Additional selection from the large seed fractions might be made by specific gravity using air columns or gravity tables. Seed density may contribute to seed size effects as described by Sung and Delouche (1962) for rice and by Kneebone and Cremer (1955) for buffalograss (*Buchloe dactyloides* (Nutt.) Engelm.

SEEDLING VIGOR

One of the simplest schemes for sceening for seedling vigor per se is to select for rapidity of germination either under standard laboratory conditions (Isely, 1957; Maguire, 1962; Tucker and Wright, 1965) or under some induced stress (Delouche and Caldwell, 1960). A high respiration rate during the heterotrophic stage of growth has been reported to be closely related to seedling vigor. Direct respirometer tests or chemical indicators (tetrazolium) have been suggested as measures of seedling vigor (Kittock and Law, 1968; Woodstock and Feeley, 1965). Differences in seed respiration rates can be detected shortly after imbibition and are probably the first measurable attribute for seedling vigor. Germination percentage itself, unless some stress is applied, is not a measure of vigor but rapidity of germination is. Woodstock and Feeley (1965) found that heated corn kernels, for example, showed lowered respiration rates and subsequent losses in seedling vigor with no reduction in germination.

Coleoptile length achieved during a given period of time within a laboratory test is a direct measure of seedling vigor as well as an important character in its own right. Emergence from deep plantings provides another direct measure of seedling vigor, although coleoptile lengths are confounded with this measure and it is likely that disease-susceptible seedlings would also tend to be eliminated (Rogler, 1954; Lawrence, 1963; Hunt and Miller, 1965). Deeper planting, where feasible, is desirable and increased coleoptile length adds to its feasibility. Since disease resistance is also highly desirable, deep plantings have multiple selective value.

Robison and Thomas (1963) used total seedling weight produced per field plot or greenhouse pot from plantings of equivalent numbers of polycross seed to evaluate combining abilities of 47 clones of smooth bromegrass for seedling vigor.

Field sowings at high rates or with competitive species allow natural selection for competitive ability. Voigt and Brown (1969) found that seedlings grown from seed produced on a drilled increase of seed from their original parent selections approached the vigor of seedlings whose parents had been specifically selected for seedling vigor.

Large numbers of seedlings are easily handled in the greenhouse and growth chamber. Selection under some stresses such as low nutrient levels or toxic substances can be done most efficiently under those controlled conditions. The field is, however, the final arena and considerable progress has been made in field performance as a result of control chamber, greenhouse, and nursery-type tests. Many seedling vigor attributes are positively correlated with desirable attributes in mature plants and perhaps breeding programs should be reoriented to begin with the seedling and work toward

98   *William R. Kneebone*

the mature plant. Since seedlings and seedling characters lend themselves most readily to screening procedures for very large numbers, this approach is doubly logical.

References

Akihama, T. (1968). Inheritance of the competitive ability and effects of its selection on agronomic characters. *Jap. J. Breed.* **18**, 12–14.
Allen, R. E., Vogel, O. A., Burleigh, J. R., and Peterson, C. J., Jr. (1961). Inheritance of coleoptile length and its association with culm length in four winter wheat crosses. *Crop Sci.* **1**, 328–332.
Allen, R. E., Vogel, O. A., and Peterson, C. J., Jr. (1962). Seedling emergence' rate of fall sown wheat and its association with plant height and coleoptile length. *Agron. J.* **54**, 347–350.
Allen, R. E., Vogel, O. A., Russell, T. S., and Peterson, C. J., Jr. (1965). Relation of seed and seedling characteristics to stand establishment of semi-dwarf wheat selections. *Crop Sci.* **5**, 5–8.
Bean, G. A., and Robison, L. R. (1963). Pathogenicity of *Rhizoctonia solani* on *Bromus inermis*. *Crop Sci.* **3**, 345–347.
Christie, B. R., and Kalton, R. R. (1960a). Inheritance of seed weight and associated traits in bromegrass, *Bromus inermis* Leyss. *Can. J. Plant Sci.* **40**, 353–365.
Christie, B. R., and Kalton, R. R. (1960b). Recurrent selection for seed weight in bromegrass, *Bromus inermis* Leyss. *Agron. J.* **52**, 575–578.
Delouche, J. C., and Caldwell, W. P. (1960). Seed vigor and vigor tests. *Proc. Ass. Off. Seed Anal.* **50**, 124–129.
Dotzenko, A. D., Cooper, C. S., Dobrenz, A. K., Laude, H. M., Massengale, M. A., and Feltner, K. C. (1967). Temperature stress on growth and seed characteristics of grasses and legumes. *Color., Agr. Exp. Sta., Tech. Bull.* **97** (West. Reg. Res. Publ.).
Hanson, A. A., and Carnahan, H. L. (1956). Breeding perennial forage grasses. *U.S., Dep. Agr., Tech. Bull.* **1145**.
Harper, J. L. (1961). The nature and consequence of interference amongst plants. *Genet. Today, Proc. Int. Congr., 11th. 1963* Vol. 1, pp. 465–482.
Hunt, O. J., and Miller, D. G. (1965). Coleoptile length, seed size, and emergence in intermediate wheatgrass, *Agropyron intermedium* (Host.) Beauv. *Agron. J.* **57**, 192–195.
Isely, D. (1957). Vigor tests. *Proc. Ass. Off. Seed Anal.* **47**, 176–182.
Jowett, D. (1958). Populations of *Agrostis spp.* tolerant of heavy metals. *Nature (London)* **182**, 816–817.
Kaufmann, M. L. (1968). Coleoptile length and emergence in varieties of barley, oats, and wheat. *Can. J. Plant Sci.* **48**, 357–361.
Kittock, D. L., and Law, A. G. (1968). Relationship of seedling vigor to respiration and tetrazolium chloride reduction by germinating wheat seeds. *Agron. J.* **60**, 286–288.
Kneebone, W. R. (1956). Breeding for seedling vigor in sand bluestem, (*Andropogon hallii* Hack.) and other native grasses. *Agron. J.* **48**, 37–40.
Kneebone, W. R. (1957). Selection for seedling vigor in native grasses under artificial moisture stress. *Agron. Abstr.* p. 55.
Kneebone, W. R. (1959). Seed size in relation to germination and establishment of native range grasses. *Agron. Abstr.* p. 77.
Kneebone, W. R. (1967). Differential germination of open pollination seed lots from different selections of bermudagrass. *Proc. West. Grass Breed. Work Plan. Conf., 19th.* pp. 7–10.

Kneebone, W. R., and Cremer, C. L. (1955). The relationship of seed size to seedling vigor in some native grass species. *Agron. J.* **47**, 472–477.

Kneebone, W. R. Hackerott, H. L., Barnett, F. L., McCully W. C., and Streetman, L. J., (1963). Adaptation and breeding potentials for sideoats grama varieties as demonstrated by uniform tests of clones and their progenies at widely separated locations. *Agro. Abstr.* p. 83.

Lawrence. T. (1957). Emergence of intermediate wheatgrass lines from five depths of seeding. *Can. J. Plant Sci.* **37**, 215–219.

Lawrence, T. (1963). A comparison of methods of evaluating Russian wild ryegrass for seedling vigor. *Can. J. Plant Sci.* **43**, 307–312.

McDaniel, R. G. (1969). Relationships of seed weight, seedling vigor and mitochondrial metabolism in barley. *Crop. Sci.* **9**, 823–827.

McDaniel, R. G., and Sarkissian, I. V. (1967). Mitochondrial heterosis in maize. *Genetics* **59**, 465–475.

Maguire, J. D. (1962). Speed of germination–aid in selection and evaluation for seedling emergence and vigor. *Crop Sci.* **2**, 176–177.

Mouat, M. C. H. (1962). Genetic variation in root cation exchange capacity of ryegrass. *Plant Soil*, **16**, 263–265.

Rhodes, I. (1968a). The growth and development of some grass species under competitive stress. 1. Competition between seedlings, and between seedlings and established plants. *J. Brit. Grassland Soc.* **23**, 129–136.

Rhodes, I. (1968b). The growth and development of some grass species under competitive stress. 3. The natural competitive stress and characters associated with competitive ability during seedling growth. *J. Brit. Grassland Soc.* **23**, 330–335.

Robison, L. R., and Thomas, H. L. (1963). Combining ability for seedling vigor in *Bromus inermis* Leyss. *Crop Sci.* **3**, 358–359.

Rogler, G. A. (1954). Seed size and seedling vigor in crested wheatgrass. *Agron. J.* **46**, 216–220.

Sakai, K. I. (1961). Competitive ability in plants: Its inheritance and some related problems. *Symp. Soc. Exp. Biol.* **15**, 245–263.

Schaaf, H. M., and Rogler, G. A. (1963). Breeding crested wheatgrass for seed size and yield. *Crop Sci.* **3**, 347–350.

Schaaf, H. M., Rogler, G. A., and Lorenz, R. J. (1962). Importance of variations in forage yield, seed yield, and seed weight to the improvement of crested wheatgrass. *Crop Sci.* **2**, 67–71.

Slinkard, A. E. (1963). Relationship between seed size and seedling vigor in Russian wildrye, *Elymus junceus* Fisch. *Proc. West. Grass Breed. Work Plan. Conf., 17th* pp. 29–30.

Snaydon. R. W. and Bradshaw, A. D. (1961). Differential response to calcium within the species *Festuca ovina* L. *New Phytol.* **60**, 219–234.

Sung, T. Y., and Delouche, J. C. (1962). Relation of specific gravity to vigor and viability in rice seed. *Proc. Ass. Off. Seed Anal.* **52**, 162–165.

Tossell, W. E. (1960). Early seedling vigor and seed weight in relation to breeding in smooth bromegrass, *Bromus inermis* Leyss. *Can. J. Plant Sci.* **40**, 268–280.

Trupp, C. R., and Carlson, I. T. (1967). Progress report of improvement of stand establishment of smooth bromegrass by recurrent selection for increased seed weight. *Proc. West. Grass Breed. Work Plan. Conf., 19th* pp. 17–21.

Tucker, H., and Wright, L. N. (1965). Estimating rapidity of germination. *Crop Sci.* **5**, 398–399.

Voigt, P. W., and Brown, H. W. (1969). Phenotypic recurrent selection for seedling vigor in side-oats grama *Bouteloua curtipendula* (Michx.) Torr. *Crop Sci.* **9**, 664–666.

Whalley, R. D. B., McKell, C. M., and Green, L. R. (1966a). Seedling vigor and the early non-photosynthetic stage of seedling growth in grasses. *Crop Sci.* **6**, 147–150.

William R. Kneebone

Whalley, R. D. B., McKell, C. M., and Green, L. R. (1966b). Effect of environmental conditions during the parent generation on seedling vigor of the subsequent seedling of *Oryzopsis mileacea* (L.) Benth. and Hook. *Crop Sci.* **6**, 510–512.

Woodstock, L. W., and Feeley, J. (1965). Early seedling growth and initial respiration rates as potential indicators on seed vigor in corn. *Proc. Ass. Off. Seed Anal.* **55**, 131–139.

Wright, L. N. (1966). Drouth tolerance evaluation among range grass genera, species, and accessions of three species using program-controlled environment. *Proc. Int. Grassland Congr., 9th 1965* **1**, pp. 165–169.

Wright, L. N. (1969). Sampling and clonal variability in seed weight and seed yield of blue panicgrass, *Panicum antidotale* Retz. *J. Ariz. Acad. Sci.* **5**, 245–247.

Wright, L. N., and Jordan, G. L. (1970). Artificial selection for seedling drouth tolerance in boer lovegrass (*Eragrostis curvula* Nees). *Crop Sci.* **10**, 99–102.

Wright, L. N. and Streetman, L. J. (1960). Grass improvement for the southwest relative to drouth evaluation. *Ariz., Agr. Exp. Sta., Tech. Bull.* **143**.

Chapter 8

Environmental Modification for Seedling Establishment

CARLTON H. HERBEL

Under rangeland conditions most grasses should not be seeded deeper than 2 cm. Harsh environmental conditions in the surface soil often prevent successful seedling establishment. Army and Hudspeth (1960) and Hudspeth and Taylor (1961) reported that under field conditions in the southern Great Plains sufficient moisture for seedling emergence of grasses planted at the customary shallow depths could not be maintained on bare surface soil except under extremely favorable weather conditions. The average annual precipitation in that area ranges from 36 to 58 cm. Environmental modification, particularly of the moisture and temperature, is imperative to insure greater success in grass establishment. Artificial and natural mulches and land-forming procedures offer increased possibilities for obtaining seedling establishment under difficult environmental conditions.

Natural Mulches

In forage establishment a covering of plant residue improves soil moisture and protects the soil surface against wind and water erosion (Duley, 1952).

Mannering and Meyer (1963) used a rainfall simulator to show that infiltration increases and runoff decreases as the amount of plant residue on the soil surface increases. Mulches reduce the impact force of raindrops on soil, so that soil is not puddled or sealed at the surface.

One of the most economical methods of obtaining mulch is to use stubble, trash, or other materials left on the soil surface during land preparation. Moldenhauer (1959) reported that emergence of grass occurred at a lower level of watering when the soil surface was covered with chopped sorghum stover at the rate of 4500 kg/ha, as compared with no cover. The mulch was much less beneficial when maximum daily temperatures were less than 21°C during the germination period than when they were about 35°C.

Stubble mulching has been used for seedling grasses in the Great Plains for several years (K. L. Anderson, 1959). The method consists of planting a residue-producing crop such as sorghum a year before the grass is to be seeded. The sorghum crop is seeded in mid to late summer to prevent seed formation before frost but yet make 15 to 20 cm of growth. Grasses are seeded the following spring with a drill designed for shallow seeding. Residue from the sorghum crop protects the grass seedlings from soil erosion around the root zone.

A mulch of over 3360 kg straw per hectare encouraged damping-off diseases to the point where mulched seedings were less satisfactory than the unmulched (Willard, 1952). However, in a dry season better initial stands were obtained under a heavy mulch than under no mulch. Increased insect populations in plant residues may also present problems in grass establishment.

In an Arizona trial emergence of grass seedlings was 4 to 20 times greater under light coverings of straw and cotton gauze than on bare ground (Glendening, 1942). Soil moisture in the surface 2.5 cm and at 15- and 30-cm depths was consistently greater under the straw and gauze than on the untreated area. Straw mulch, jute mesh, and twisted-paper mesh were effective in stabilizing the soil surface and aiding in grass establishment on earthen dams, roadsides, terrace channels, ridges, and waterways (U.S. Department of Agriculture, 1962).

In turf seedings a 3-mm cover of moist, pulverized sphagnum peat is a good mulch (Willard, 1952).

It is difficult to reduce evaporation from the soil surface. Hanks and Woodruff (1958) compared straw, black-painted gravel, aluminum-painted gravel, and plastic film mulches with bare soil. The total difference in evaporation in a year between the check and other treatments was not more than 2.5 cm of water.

Artificial Mulch

Because they are expensive, the use of artificial mulches for grass establishment is limited. However, they can be used effectively on lawns, roadsides, waterways, or other high-value areas.

Polyethylene mulches have been used to control surface evaporation in establishing turfgrasses and crops (U.S. Department of Agriculture, 1962). In dryland areas plastic mulches increased the efficiency of water use by crops. Incorporating hexadecanol into the surface soil can be used to reduce evaporation.

In Texas poor grass establishment was obtained in summer seedings under clear and black polyethylene because of the 50°C soil temperatures (Army and Hudspeth, 1959). White polyethylene has a high reflectivity index and substantially reduces maximum soil temperatures when it is used as a mulch covering. Such soil coverings as plastic, aluminum and black paint sprays, roofing paper, and aluminum foil improved moisture conditions in the seed zone (Army and Hudspeth, 1960).

Large sheets of clear polyethylene have been used successfully in lawn establishment (Army and Hudspeth, 1960), probably because lawn grasses are seeded in the spring when high soil temperatures are not a problem. Seedings made in the cool part of the year also often benefit from the higher soil temperatures obtained under black coverings.

In an exploratory test in Colorado emergence and growth of blue grama [*Bouteloua gracilis* (H.B.K.) Lag. ex Steud.] were hastened by an asphalt mulch (Bement et al., 1961). There was more soil moisture at the 2.5-cm depth under the asphalt mulch than in the check. Further a cationic emulsion of asphalt mulch held soil moisture for a longer period than an anionic emulsion of asphalt mulch.

In Israel a synthetic rubber spray formed a durable crust that temporarily stabilized sand dunes (Harpaz et al., 1965). However, it had no detrimental effect on the emergence or growth rate of the seeded grasses.

Land-Forming Procedures

The primary objective of various land-forming and seeding methods is to place the seed in a favorable environment for germination and establishment of the seedling. Water conservation in site preparation is essential in dry areas. Staggered pits or interrupted contour furrows are effective in increasing soil moisture (D. L. Anderson and Swanson, 1948). They may be constructed with eccentric or cutaway disks. Pitting followed by cultipacker seeding was the most consistent method of successfully seeding ranges in Arizona (D. Anderson *et al.*, 1957). Ripping and contour furrowing were also good methods of seed-bed preparation on fine-textured bottomland soils.

In the northern Great Plains pitting accompanied by seeding has been an unsuccessful practice for seedling establishment (Barnes *et al.*, 1958). Thus additional moisture does not always insure seeding success.

An intensive study of the effects of ripping in New Mexico revealed that runoff and erosion were decreased by the treatment, but attempts to seed forage species during three years were mostly unsuccessful (Dortignac and Hickey, 1963).

Branson *et al.* (1966) evaluated the effects of the following mechanical soil treatments on water storage: interrupted furrows made with a Model B Contour Furrower, broad-base furrows made with a motor grader, trenches made with a motor grader, pits made with spike-tooth or rotary pitters, pits made with an eccentric disk pitter, ripping with an augur ripper, and ripping with an augur ripper equipped with a furrow opener. The most effective treatments were contour furrowing at intervals of 0.9 to 1.5 m and depths of 20 to 25 cm, and broad-base furrows that had low dikes 0.5 m high. The most consistent beneficial responses occurred on medium- to fine-textured soils.

In some Arizona trials Judd (1966) compared the following seedbed and planting methods: disk-broadcast seed-cultipack-mulch with native brush; disk-broadcast seed-cultipack; disk-broadcast seed-harrow; broadcast seed-disk; broadcast seed-harrow; and broadcast seed. The protective brush mulch was highly important for stand establishment and maintenance.

Deep-furrow drilling generally results in better grass stands on dry sites (Plummer *et al.*, 1955). McGinnies (1959) found that furrows only 10 cm deep significantly increased available soil moisture and improved seedling establishment over an unfurrowed check. In unstable soils the furrows were often filled by soil from local erosion in a relatively short time.

Hyder and Bement (1969) designed a microridge roller for seeding on light-textured soils. Small interrupted furrows are formed to concentrate water on the seeded rows.

Seedling Establishment Research at the Jornada Experimental Range

The climate at the Jornada Experimental Range is typical of the arid phase of the semidesert grassland. The average annual precipitation is 22.9 cm and the average during the summer growing season (July to September) is

12.7 cm. The average annual evaporation from a Weather Bureau pan is 229 cm or 10 times the precipitation. Spring is generally dry and windy. The average maximum temperature for July is 35°C and the average minimum is 18°C. Soil temperature and moisture data were collected for many of the trials.

Hay Mulch

A hay mulch was applied in a 30-cm strip over seeded rows at the rate of 2240 kg/ha and held in place with a light covering of an asphaltic emulsion. Maximum soil temperatures at the 1.3-cm depth averaged 51°C on the checks and 41°C under hay cover. Available soil moisture at the 1.3-cm depth was greater under the hay mulch.

Polyethylene

White polyethylene (0.1 mm thick) was compared with checks on seeded furrows at two sites and a flat seeded area at one site. The soil was dry when the furrows were seeded. The plastic was perforated over the seeded row so that in effect the rain water was concentrated on the seeded area. After 3.8 cm of precipitation, a flat area was seeded to determine if the plastic would hold the moisture long enough for seedling establishment.

On a fine sandy loam site an excellent stand of seedlings emerged in the plastic-covered furrows whereas there was only a very sparse stand on the check furrows. Parts of the plastic were removed one week, two weeks, and six weeks after emergence. The few seedlings that emerged in the check furrows all died within two weeks. Many of the seedlings died in the plastic-covered furrows when the plastic was removed one or two weeks after emergence. This occurred even though there was adequate moisture. There were 12.9 cm of precipitation at this site during the 57 days after seeding. The soil moisture potential at the 1.3-cm depth was between 0 and 1 bar for 7 days in the furrowed check rows and 45 days in the plastic-covered furrows. By the end of the summer a fair grass stand was established where the plastic was removed one week following emergence, a good stand was established where the plastic was removed one week later, and an excellent stand was established where the plastic was left in place for six weeks following emergence.

On a loamy fine-sand site, seedlings emerged later because of less favorable moisture conditions than at the fine sandy loam site. There were 9.3 cm of rainfall at this site during the 57 days after seeding. The soil moisture potential at the 1.3-cm depth was between 0 and 1 bar for 6 days in the fur-

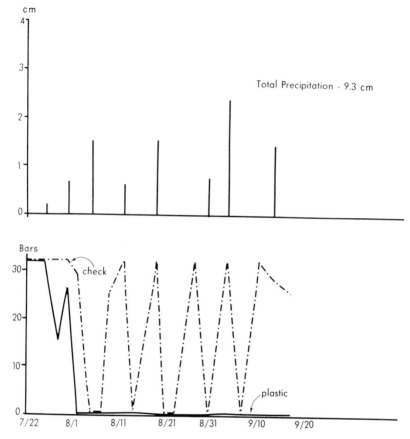

FIG. 1. Daily precipitation (cm) and soil moisture potential (bars) at the 1.3-cm depth in furrows with and without white polyethylene covering on a loamy fine sand site.

rowed check rows and 46 days in the plastic-covered furrows (Fig. 1). By the end of this period there was a fair grass stand in the plastic-covered furrows and a very poor stand in the check furrows.

On the fine sandy loam site, some seedlings emerged under the plastic on the flat area by 9 days after seeding. Many of those seedlings died during a dry period in August but later seedlings survived. No emergence occurred on the flat check area. There were 9.1 cm of rainfall on this site during the 46 days following seeding. The soil moisture potential at the 1.3-cm depth was between 0 and 1 bar for 2 days on the uncovered flat area and 36 days on the plastic-covered flat area (Fig. 2).

During the summer study period, the mid-day soil temperatures at the

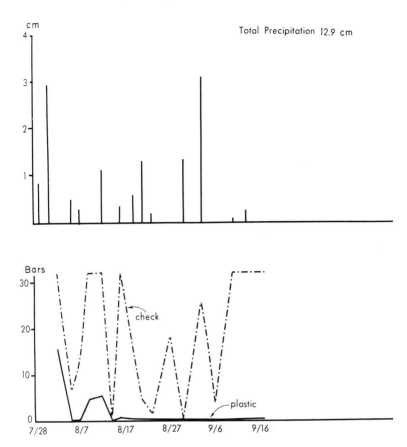

Fig. 2. Daily precipitation (cm) and soil moisture potential (bars) at the 1.3-cm depth on a flat area with and without white polyethylene covering on a fine sandy loam site.

1.3-cm depth under plastic ranged from 29 to 47°C whereas in the checks it ranged from 29 to 62°C. Soil temperatures at the 1.3-cm depth generally were 10 to 18 degrees cooler under the plastic than the checks on hot, sunny days. Only small temperature differences were observed on cool, cloudy days.

Stand establishment under white polyethylene on the sandy loam site could be attributed to more favorable soil moisture and temperature conditions. Even the two-to-three-week-old seedlings benefited from lower temperatures and possibly from protection from high solar radiation. The seedlings did not become etiolated under the plastic. Water concentration in furrows was successful when the seedlings were protected.

PITS AND FURROWS

A fine sandy loam site was treated with a pitter disk seeder. The maximum summer soil temperatures at the 1.3-cm depth were 10°C lower (41°C vs 51°C) in the pits than on adjacent flat areas. There were 10.5 cm of rainfall during the 66 days following treatment. The soil moisture potential at the 1.3-cm depth was between 0 and 15 bars for 36 days but none was recorded on the flat area (Fig. 3). A fair stand of grasses emerged on the pitted area in September.

North-south and east-west furrows, 30-cm deep, were established on a loamy fine-sand site in early summer. Grasses were seeded on the middle of each slope and in the bottom of each furrow. Excellent emergence was obtained on all the slopes within a few days after seeding. However, as seedlings emerged in the bottoms they were covered by drifting sand. The average maximum air temperature 10.2 cm above ground surface during the summer was 34°C. The average maximum temperatures at the 1.3-cm depth

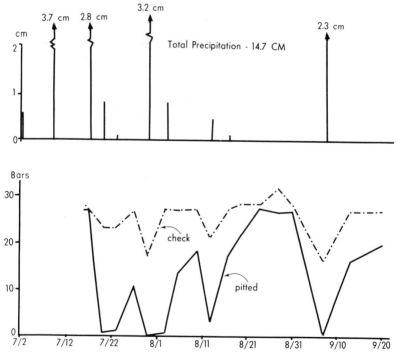

FIG. 3. Daily precipitation (cm) and soil moisture potential (bars) at the 1.3-cm depth in the bottom of pits and a flat area.

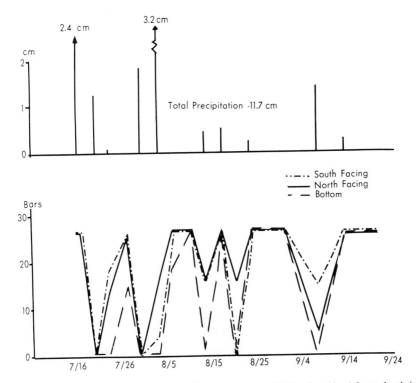

FIG. 4. Daily precipitation (cm) and soil moisture potential (bars) at the 1.3-cm depth in the bottom of a furrow and the middle of the north- and south-facing slopes of a furrow.

were 43°C, 44°C, 48°C, and 43°C for the north-, east-, south-, and west-facing slopes, respectively. During a 66-day summer period, 11.7 cm of rainfall was recorded. Moisture potential at the 1.3-cm depth was between 0 and 1 bar for 4 days on the slopes of the furrows and 13 days in the bottoms of the furrows (Fig. 4).

Concentrating moisture by employing various land-forming procedures does not always insure seedling establishment. The surface soil still dries rapidly and, particularly on medium to heavy textured soils, forms a heavy crust. If the surface could be further protected to reduce evaporation and hence delay crusting, seedling emergence would be greatly enhanced.

ROOTPLOWING AND SEEDING

Fine sandy loam and gravelly sandy loam sites infested with brush were rootplowed. This was followed by a till-and-pack seeder which pressed most

of the brush into the soil. Some grasses emerged in September, primarily in
the tractor tracks, on the fine sandy loam site. On the gravelly sandy loam
site, a large number of seedlings emerged in July but died during August;
other seedlings emerged in September. The maximum air temperature 10 cm
above the surface of the ground ranged from 29°C to 34°C during the latter
half of July and the early part of September. During August it ranged from
38°C to 40°C. The minimum relative humidity ranged from 27% to 57%
during July and September and 16% to 17% during August. Maximum soil
temperatures at the 1.3-cm depth averaged 51°C with no ground cover and
38°C under sparse brush cover. A high temperature of 59°C was recorded
at the 1.3-cm depth with no surface cover and 41°C under brush cover.

During an 82-day period, 12 cm of rainfall was recorded from July 2 to

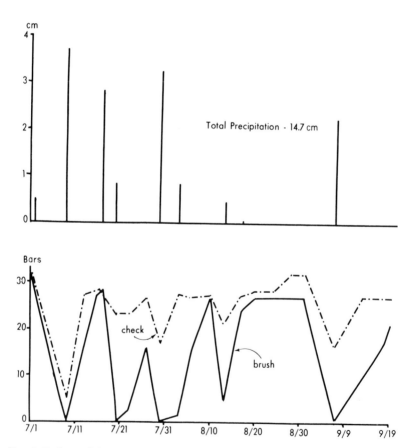

Fɪɢ. 5. Daily precipitation (cm) and soil moisture potential (bars) at the 1.3-cm depth without surface cover and under brush cover.

August 3 on the fine sandy loam site, followed by 2.3 cm on September 7. Moisture potential at the 1.3-cm depth was between 0 and 15 bars for 5 days on the area with no cover and 42 days on the area with brush cover (Fig. 5). On the gravelly sandy loam site there were 8.6 cm of rainfall from July 2 to August 3 and 2.8 cm on September 7. Moisture potential at the 1.3-cm depth was between 0 and 15 bars for 23 days on the area without cover and 40 days on the area with brush cover (Fig. 6).

The effects of dead shrubs on soil temperatures were studied on a fine sandy loam site. A single shrub plant was used for the light plant cover and a layer of three shrub plants for the heavy cover. The average maximum air temperature 10 cm above the ground surface for a summer period was 33°C. The average daily maximum soil temperature at the 1.3-cm depth was

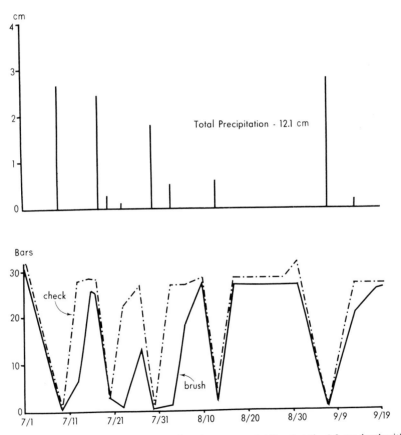

FIG. 6. Daily precipitation (cm) and soil moisture potential (bars) at the 1.3-cm depth without surface cover and under brush cover.

57°C under no cover, 49°C under light cover, and 36°C under heavy brush cover (Fig. 7).

We found that a shrub cover could be utilized to substantially reduce soil temperatures and increase the period of available soil moisture. Therefore, in cooperation with the Agricultural Engineering Department at New Mexico State University, we designed and built equipment for seeding brush-covered rangelands (Fig. 8). The basic part of the equipment was a rootplow with a 2.4-m wide blade. Properly used, the rootplow is very effective in killing the brush and, generally, other competing vegetation. However, the rootplowed seedbed is very loose and fluffy, so we designed a seeder, patterned after the Oregon Press Seeder (Hyder *et al.*, 1961), which firms the surface soil. A brush conveyor was added which picks up the brush behind the rootplow and deposits it behind the seeder. The seeder is only 1-m wide so the brush from a 2.4-m area is concentrated on a strip 1-m wide. In addition there is a hydraulically operated bulldozer blade in front of the seeder which forms basin pits. Thus we were able to concentrate water and provide shade for part of the seeded area. This method was used to seed 12 plots across southern New Mexico in 1967–68. Excellent grass establishment was obtained on nine of these plots. Even on the other three plots with droughty conditions, good grass stands were obtained under some of the brush-covered areas which coincided with slight depressions where water was concentrated.

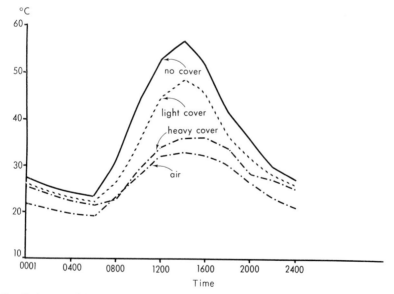

FIG. 7. Average daily soil temperatures at the 1.3-cm depth with light and heavy brush cover and without cover, and air temperatues 10 cm above the soil surface.

Fig. 8. Rootplow, brush conveyor, pitter, and seeder for treating areas infested with brush.

For seeding success on areas with high temperatures and where the surface dries rapidly, some covering for the soil surface is essential. Seeding success on areas where cool temperatures are a problem may be enhanced by the use of black or clear coverings to increase soil temperatures while conserving moisture.

References

Anderson, D., Hamilton, L. P., Reynolds, H. G., and Humphrey, R. R. (1957). Reseeding desert grassland ranges in southern Arizona. *Ariz., Agr. Exp. Sta., Bull.* **249**, 1–32.

Anderson, D. L., and Swanson, A. R. (1948). Machinery for seedbed preparation and seeding on southwestern ranges. *J. Range Manage.* **2**, 64–66.

Anderson, K. L. (1959). Establishing and reseeding grassland in the Great Plains and western Corn Belt. *Proc. Amer. Grassland Counc.* pp. 30–36.

Army, T. J., and Hudspeth, E. B. Jr. (1959). Better grass establishment with plastic covers. *Tex. Agr. Progress*, **5**, (4) 20 and 22–23.

Army, T. J., and Hudspeth, E. B. Jr. (1960). Alteration of the microclimate of the seed zone. *Agron. J.* **52**, 17–22.

Barnes, O K., Anderson, D., and Heerwagen, A. (1958). Pitting for range improvement in the Great Plains and the southwest desert region. *U.S., Dep. Agr., Prod. Res. Rep.* **23**, 1–17.

Bement, R. E., Hervey, D. F., Everson, A. C., and Hylton, L. O. Jr. (1961). Use of asphalt-emulsion mulches to hasten grass-seedling establishment. *J. Range Manage.* **14**, 102–109.

Branson, F. A., Miller, R. F., and McQueen, I. S. (1966). Contour furrowing, pitting, and ripping on rangelands of the western United States. *J. Range Manage.* **19**, 182–190.

Dortignac, E. J., and Hickey, W. C., Jr. (1963). Surface runoff and erosion as affected by soil ripping. *U.S., Dep. Agr., Forest Serv.* pp. 1–13.

Duley, F. L. (1952). Relationship between surface cover and water penetration, runoff, and soil losses. *Proc. 6th. Int. Grassland Cong.*, Vol. 2, pp. 942–946.

Glendening, G. E. (1942). Germination and emergence of some native grasses in relation to litter cover and soil moisture. *J. Amer. Soc. Agron.* **34**, 797–804.

Hanks, R. J., and Woodruff, N. P. (1958). Influence of wind on water vapor transfer through soil, gravel and straw mulches. *Soil Sci.* **86**, 160–164.

Harpaz. Y., Shanan, L., and Tadmor, N. H. (1965). Effects of a synthetic rubber crust mulch on the emergence and early growth of three grasses on sand dunes. *Isr. J. Agr. Res.* **15**, 149–153.

Hudspeth, E. B., Jr., and Taylor, H. M. (1961). Factors affecting seedling emergence of Blackwell switchgrass. *Agron. J.* **53**, 331–335.

Hyder, D. N., and Bement, R. E. (1969). A micro-ridge roller for seedbed modification. *J. Range Manage.* **22**, 54–56.

Hyder, D. N., Booster, D. E., Sneva, F. A., Sawyer, W. A., and Rodgers, J. B. (1961). Wheel-track planting on sagebrush-bunchgrass range. *J. Range Manage.* **14**, 220–224.

Judd, B. I. (1966). Range reseeding success on the Tonto National Forest, Arizona. *J. Range Manage.* **19**, 296–301.

McGinnies, W. J. (1959). The relationship of furrow depth to moisture content of soil and to seedling establishment on a range soil. *Agron. J.* **51**, 13–14.

Mannering, J. V., and Meyer, L. D. (1963). The effects of various rates of surface mulch on infiltration and erosion. *Soil Sci. Soc. Amer., Proc.* **27**, 84–86.

Moldenhauer, W. C. (1959). Establishment of grasses on sandy soil of the southern High Plains of Texas using a mulch and simulated moisture levels. *Agron. J.* **51**, 39–41.

Plummer, A. P., Hull, A. C., Jr., Stewart, G., and Robertson, J. H. (1955). Seeding range-lands in Utah, Nevada, southern Idaho, and western Wyoming. *U.S., Dep. Agr., Agr. Hand.* **71**, 1–73.

U.S. Department of Agriculture, Agricultural Research Service (1962). Study and investigations of use of materials and new designs and methods in public works. U.S. Senate Comm. on Public Work. Print no. 6, 1–71.

Willard, C. J. (1952). Fertilizing and mulching for new grassland seedings. *Proc. 6th Int. Grassland Cong.*, Vol. 1, pp. 695–701.

Chapter 9

The Growth of Leaves and Tillers in *Oryzopsis miliacea*

D. KOLLER AND J. KIGEL

The growth of leaves and tillers in grasses has been reviewed extensively in Barnard (1964) and Milthorpe and Ivins (1966). This chapter will be based on data relating to these subjects, from studies with the perennial *Oryzopsis miliacea* (L.) Asch et Schw., a native of the east Mediterranean phytogeographic region (Koller, *et al.*, 1968).

Oryzopsis miliacea is a qualitative long-day plant with respect to flowering, with a critical photoperiod longer than 8 hr, but shorter than 12 hr. Subcritical photoperiods will be designated SD, and those longer than the critical, LD. In addition to flowering the plant exhibits pronounced morphogenic responses to controlled temperatures and photoperiodic regimes. By far the most dramatic responses shown by the data were to the light environment, to which we shall limit the present discussion. The data referred to deal with plants grown at (a) the optimal temperature (20°) in artificial light from a mixed incandescent and fluorescent source (10^4 lux at plant level), or (b) at the equally optimal alternation of 8 hr at 22°C (0800 to 1600 hr) and 16°C for the remaining 16 hr, in a naturally lit greenhouse (transmitting 85% of incident solar energy), with supplementary low-intensity incandescent light as needed both before sunrise and after sunset. In the green-house, 8-hr photoperiods coincided with the high-temperature part of the cycle, while longer photoperiods extended equally on both sides into the low-temperature part. The plants were grown in gravel–vermiculite substrate, irrigated with a modified Hoagland nutrient solution.

Shoot Growth

Growth of the entire shoot complex combines the activation of axillary buds and their growth and development into branches. In *O. miliacea* buds become active on basal nodes (unelongated internodes) and give rise to basal shoots (tillers), as well as on epigeal nodes (elongated internodes) of elon-gated shoots giving rise to epigeal branches. We shall deal both with the activation of axillary buds, basal and epigeal, and with the growth of the branches that these activated buds give rise to.

In nature, epigeal buds become activated only on the previous years' fertile tillers, on the nodes just below the dead part of the inflorescence. Plants growing in a controlled environment greenhouse, that is, with the main light period in sunlight, failed to activate epigeal buds for about 9 mon. Photoperiodic effects on activation of tiller buds were negligible, at least up to the end of the fourth month, but lowering the level of solar radiation reduced the rate of activation (Fig. 1) (Aspinall and Paleg, 1964). The inhi-bition in activation of tiller buds by lowering the radiation level during the

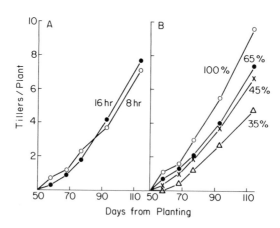

FIG. 1. Kinetics of tillering in *O. miliacea* as affected by photoperiod (A, combined results of 8- and 16-hr photoperiods) and by level of solar radiation (B, combined results at four levels of solar radiation).

main light period was not accompanied by reduced growth of the individual tillers. Analysis of variance of the factorial experiment described above showed that while main effects of radiation level on dry weight of individual tillers were not significant (49, 57, 53, and 55 mg in 100%, 65%, 45%, and 35% relative radiation level), those of photoperiod were highly significant (61 and 46 mg in LD and SD, respectively). Thus radiation level, which determines the availability of photosynthates, affects the number of metabolic sinks in the shoot system without affecting the potential of the individual sinks to draw upon the available photosynthates (Mitchell, 1953). On the other hand LD conditions increase sink potential of the individual shoots, despite the fact that they inhibit leaf expansion (see below) and the reduction they cause in leaf production per tiller (Table 1). This is largely due to the marked stimulation they cause in stem production. As the plants grew older, the activation rate of tillers remained constant in LD and increased continuously with time in SD (Fig. 2). This increase (in SD) was transformed into a linear relationship between the logarithms of the reciprocals of tiller number and of time from the onset of tillering (Fig. 3). There is as yet insufficient data to explain the physiological significance of either of these relationships. Evidently, however, LD conditions eventually inhibit tillering. This inhibition of tillering by LD may be at least partly due to elevation of some of the axillary buds from their basal position by LD-stimulation of internode elongation (as described below). They thus become temporarily dormant epigeal buds. It is not likely that in addition, some of the axillary buds that remain basal are induced to become dormant by being part of a flowering tiller, as in *Hordeum bulbosum* (Ofir, *et al.*, 1967). The photoperiodic responses described above were obtained with plants growing in a greenhouse with natural sunlight for at least part of the daily cycle. When the sole light source was artificial, how-

TABLE 1

EFFECTS OF PHOTOPERIOD ON FLOWERING AND LEAF NUMBER
PER SHOOT IN *O. MILIACEA* AT 20°C

Photo-period (hr)	Flowering shoots per plant	Panicles per plant	Leaves per flowering shoot	Leaver per main shoot
8	0.0	0.0	—	9.2 ± 0.3
12	0.4	0.4	12.1 ± 0.6	13.2 ± 0.3
16	2.8	3.7	7.6 ± 0.1	9.1 ± 0.2
20	3.4	5.7	6.2 ± 0.0	7.1 ± 0.1
24	3.4	5.8	5.9 ± 0.0	6.5 ± 0.1

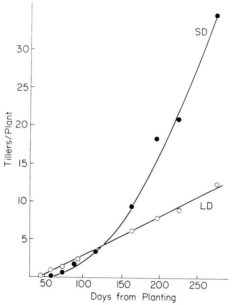

FIG. 2. Long-term kinetics of tillering in *O. miliacea* in a heated greenhouse in 8-hr (SD) and 20-hr (LD) photoperiods.

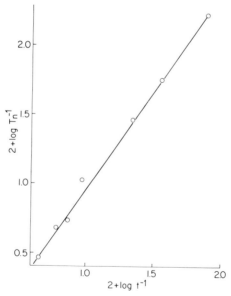

FIG. 3. Long-term kinetics of tillering in *O. miliacea* in a heated greenhouse in 8-hr photoperiods, expressed as log-log relationship between the reciprocals of tiller number and of time from onset of tillering.

ever, the epigeal branching was readily induced. Evidently the artificial light environment was in some way drastically affecting the dormancy of the epigeal buds, either by inhibiting its imposition or by curtailing its duration. The tendency for epigeal branching increased in proportion to the length of the photoperiod but as apparently achieved at the expense of activation of basal tillers (Table 2).

Neither gibberellin (nine applications of 8 or 16 μg GA$_3$ over a period of 28 days), nor CCC (two irrigations with $5 \times 10^{-2} M$ at a 5-day interval) affected activation of the tiller buds on the main shoot in SD or LD. However, development of these buds was reduced by the gibberellin from 40% to 28% in LD and from 33% to 18% in SD, and was increased by CCC to 63% and 54% in LD and SD, respectively. These responses may have resulted from the stimulation of stem elongation of the main shoot by gibberellin and its inhibition by CCC, which affected the competition between the main shoot and its tillers. Both gibberellin and CCC caused activation of epigeal buds, where in the untreated controls they remained dormant (22°/16°C, sunlight), but the nature of the activation was completely different. Prolonged treatment with GA$_3$ (nine applications of 19μg each, over a 28-day period) in SD as well as in LD eventually transformed the main shoot apex into what appeared to be a reproductive state (double ridge), but its axillary meristems grew into vegetative buds and elongated into vegetative epigeal

TABLE 2

EFFECTS OF PHOTOPERIOD ON ACTIVATION OF AXILLARY
BUDS OF *O. MILIACEA*

Photoperiod (hr)	Activated buds per plant (at 20°C)		
	Basal	Epigeal	Total
Experiment I (84 days)			
8	2.8	0.0	2.8
12	5.8	0.0	5.8
16	6.0	0.5	6.5
20	5.2	2.9	8.1
24	4.4	3.2	7.6
Experiment II (95 days)			
8	5.1	0.0	5.1
16	10.5	2.5	13.0
24	8.2	6.7	14.9

branches (Koller *et al.*, 1960; Blondon, 1964). Treatment of CCC (two irrigations with 5×10^{-2}M at a 5-day interval) on the other hand was entirely ineffective in SD, but caused the main shoots of 95% of the plants to branch epigeally in LD (about two branches per shoot), and about half of these epigeal branches were flowering as well as the main shoot. Thus CCC mimicked the artificial light environment in reducing the dormancy of the epigeal buds in LD.

Under photoperiodic conditions that are inductive for flowering in *O. miliacea*, stem elongation starts earlier in longer photoperiods. Thus at 20°C the start in 16-hr photoperiods was made 10 days later than in 24-hr photoperiods (38 and 28 days after planting, respectively). Microdissections showed that internode elongation coincided in time with the first visible change in the shoot apex to the reproductive state ("double ridge"), thus linking onset of stem elongation with flowering. Despite this relationship, stem elongation is not conditionally dependent on flowering, since it also takes place in strictly noninductive photoperiods. It appears that stem elongation may be triggered by a factor which accumulates to its threshold value at a rate dependent on the duration as well as on the number of photoperiods. Nevertheless it is strongly accelerated by the reproductive state. Elongation started above nodes 5–6 in SD and above nodes 3–4 in LD. Furthermore, after elongation had started its rate (at 22°C/16°C) was constant and about 3.5 times as rapid in LD than in SD. It thus appears that when the apex becomes reproductive, it starts to excrete a hormone that promotes stem elongation (Sachs, 1965). Gibberellin promoted stem elongation in SD in a manner similar to that of LD. Elongation in SD started above

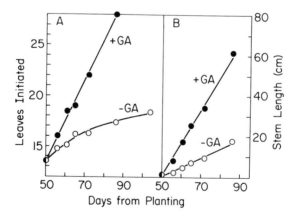

FIG. 4. Effects of gibberellin (6 μ_g GA_3 + GA_4 + GA_7, 10:3:7, daily for five days) on kinetics of leaf primordia initiation (A) and of stem elongation (B) of the main shoot of *O. miliacea* in 8-hr photoperiods at 22°C/16°C.

node 5.3 in the untreated controls and above node 3.2 in the GA-treated plants, and in LD it was unaffected (3.4 and 3.2, respectively). Rate of elongation was also markedly increased (Fig. 4B). Despite the promotive effects of flowering on stem elongation, flowering shoots were shorter in the longer photoperiods (68 vs. 50 cm in 12 and 24-hr photoperiods, respectively). This resulted directly from the progressive acceleration in the transition of the apex to the reproductive state as the photoperiods became more inductive or provided more intercepted light energy (Paleg and Aspinall, 1964), which caused a progressive curtailment in the production of vegetative (that is, leaf-bearing) nodes (Table 1). In plants grown in artificial light, however, the reduction in stem length and leaf number of the individual shoots with increase in length of the photoperiod was apparently compensated for by activation of epigeal buds (Table 2) and their growth. Thus rate of total stem production was a constant 42 mm/day in both 16 and 24-hr photoperiods (correlation coefficients 0.955 to 0.997). Similarly, total leaf number was initially higher in the longer photoperiods but eventually became equal in all inductive photoperiods (Table 3). Rate of leaf appearnce on the main shoot turned out to be initially constant with time (tillers behaved in same manner). In LD, rate of leaf production tapered off and rapidly became zero with the advent of flowering. In SD, leaf production continued for a much longer time, but at a constantly diminishing rate (Fig. 5). Gibberellin (five daily applications of 6μgG A_3 + GA_4 + GA_7 in a 10:3:7 proportion) entirely eliminated this decline in leaf production in SD and maintained rate of leaf production constant (Fig. 4A), possibly by restoring to the apex the capacity to synthesize a substance limiting for leaf production, which was becoming depleted during shoot ontogeny in SD.

TABLE 3

EFFECTS OF PHOTOPERIOD ON TOTAL LEAF PRODUCTION IN *O. MILIACEA*

	Emerged leaves per plant (at 20°C)		
	Experiment I	Experiment II	
Photoperiod	68 days	61 days	84 days
8	9.5	7.9	21.6
12	—	18.2	45.9
16	30.6	27.5	46.5
20	—	28.6	47.0
24	29.3	28.4	42.4

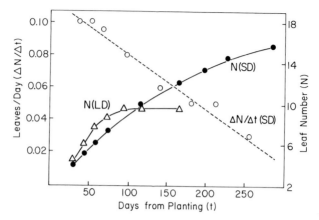

FIG. 5. Kinetics of leaf production on the main shoot of *O. miliacea* in a heated greenhouse in 8-hr (SD) and 20-hr (LD) photoperiods, and changes in rate in SD.

Leaf Growth

The length and width of the leaf blade were maximal at a 12-hr photoperiod and declined sharply in both shorter (8 hr) and longer (up to 24 hr) ones. The same was true for sheath length but to a lesser extent (Fig. 6). The leaves measured were comparable with respect to their developmental stage

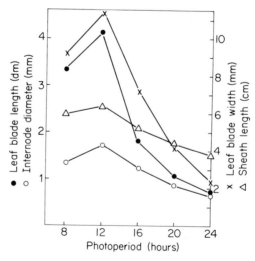

FIG. 6. Effects of photoperiod on dimensions of the last but one fully expanded leaf and diameter of its subtending internode on main shoot of *O. miliacea* at 20°C.

at time of measurement (the last but one fully expanded leaf on the main shoot). They also appeared visibly to represent the leaf population of the entire plant. The relationship between length of the photoperiod (> 12 hr). promotion of flowering (Table 1) and the inhibition of leaf growth (Fig. 6) therefore suggested a causal connection between the quantitative effects of photoperiod on flowering and on leaf growth. The leaves were not comparable with respect to their nodal position, however, since the number of leaves produced on the main shoot by the time of measurement was also dependent on photoperiod (Table 1). For the same reason it is questionable whether comparison of leaves 7-8 in the noninductive 8-hr photoperiods with leaves 11-12 in the inductive 12-hr photoperiods is valid. An additional questionable aspect of these experiments is that level of light energy was constant and equal in all photoperiods, with the result that plants in longer photoperiods were also exposed to an equally greater total dosage of irradiation. Consequently it was impossible to decide on the basis of these data whether the effects on leaf growth were due to direct photoperiodic effects or to total light energy intercepted. Further experiments were made to clarify these points. One approach was to compare simultaneously the effects of level of light energy with those of photoperiod on leaves in identical nodal positions. The data (Fig. 7) show the following with respect to the main shoot (qualitatively the same responses were observed in the first tiller):

(a) Dimensions of the blades as well as number of vascular bundles of leaves in equivalent nodal positions were affected by photoperiod at all levels of solar radiation, being greater in SD than in LD. The reverse response to photoperiod was observed in other species of grasses, but under conditions that prevented the expression of their flowering response to LD, that is, lack of prior vernalization (Ryle, 1966a,b). The effect of photoperiod in *O. miliacea* was least, or even negligible, in the lowest leaves, whose insensitivity to photoperiod was probably symptomatic of their juvenile character.

(b) Dimensions initially increased progressively with advance in nodal position, in both LD and SD. In LD, however, the increase was reversed into a decrease above a certain node. In SD, on the other hand, the increase in blade length with advance in nodal position continued with only slight indications of lessening, while the increase in width leveled off (or was even reversed into a decrease) but at a higher node than in LD.

(c) Decrease in level of solar radiation also progressively increased the length (and therefore also the area) of the blade in comparable leaves. However, it did not affect the qualitative response to photoperiod or to nodal position. As a matter of fact the relative effect of decreasing the level of solar radiation was independent of the positional and photoperiod-related effects on leaf dimensions (Table 4).

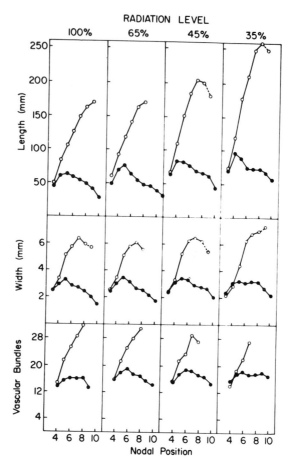

FIG. 7. Effects of nodal position and level of solar radiation on dimensions and vascularization of the leaf blade of the main shoot of *O. miliacea* at 22°C/16°C, in 8-hr (○) and 16-hr
(●) photoperiods.

It thus appears that at least three independent factors control leaf expansion. Two of these are components of the light environment, namely, photoperiod and level of radiation, while the third is ontogenetic and is related to
the nodal position of the leaf on the shoot.

Gibberellin caused an increase in leaf blade area, in both LD and SD, but
its effects were limited to length. Width, vascularization, photoperiodic
effects were unchanged (Fig. 8).

Using leaves cleared by lactic acid treatment, the mean length and width
of cells in the abaxial epidermis and its immediately adjacent layer of chlor-

TABLE 4

RELATIVE EFFECT OF LEVEL OF SOLAR RADIATION ON LEAF
BLADE LENGTH AND AREA ON MAIN SHOOT OF *O. MILIACEA*

Photo-period (hr)	Radiation level (%)	Relative change (percent)[a]	
		Leaf length	Leaf area
	65	110 ± 4	113 ± 5
8	45	135 ± 2	147 ± 4
	35	147 ± 6	161 ± 9
	65	111 ± 3	111 ± 4
16	45	136 ± 4	138 ± 5
	35	160 ± 5	160 ± 12

[a]Means for leaves 3–8, compared with those in 100% radiation.

enchyma was determined. The number of cells in the uppermost layer of the chlorenchyma and in epidermis, respectively, was also determined along the blade and across it at the widest point. By multiplying these values, the surface area of the cells in the plane parallel to the leaf surface could be estimated, as well as the relative number of cells, in each of these tissues. The results (Fig. 9) may be summarized as follows:

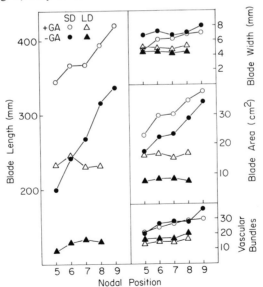

FIG. 8. Effects of gibberellin on blade dimensions and vascularization of leaves in different nodal positions on the main shoot of *O. miliacea* at 22°C/16°C in 8-hr (SD) and 16-hr (LD) photoperiods.

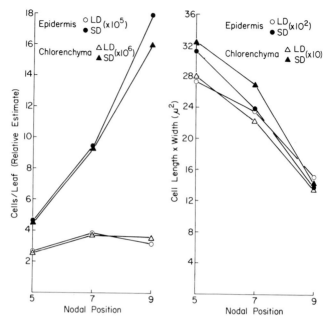

FIG. 9. Effects of nodal position on estimated surface area (right) and relative number of epidermal and adjacent layer of chlorenchyma cells (left) in the plane parallel to the surface of leaves on the main shoot of *O. miliacea* at 22°C/16°C, in 8-hr (SD) and 16-hr (LD) photoperiods.

(a) Cell size (length × width) in both tissues is progressively smaller in leaves on consecutively higher nodes (Ashby and Wangermann, 1950; Humphries, 1967).

(b) Cell size is only slightly affected by photoperiod (Ashby and Wangermann, 1950; Arney, 1954).

(c) Cell number increases in leaves on progressively higher nodes, in plants growing in SD, and is strongly inhibited in LD. These effects were similar on cell numbers along the leaf blade and across it. The positional effects on cell proliferation in the leaf are probably associated with a progressive increase in the dimensions of the shoot apex during its ontogeny. Lateral cell proliferation, which makes the most significant contribution to leaf width, has been related to the circumference of the subapical meristem at the level of inception of the leaf primordium (Abbé *et al.*, 1941; Ledin, 1954; Mitchell and Soper, 1958; Kaufman, 1959).

(d) There is a close relationship between cell size in the epidermis and in the underlying chlorenchyma. The same is true for cell number. These relationships are unaffected by photoperiod or by nodal position.

Leaf dimensions are determined by both number and size of the cells from which they are composed. Therefore in SD leaf dimensions increase progressively on consecutive nodes because the positional tendency for cell proliferation overcomes the positional tendency for cell miniaturization. In LD, on the other hand, inhibition of the positional tendency for cell proliferation gives the upper hand to the positional tendency for cell miniaturization and results in leaves that are smaller than those in SD and that also decrease in size with advance in nodal position.

The striking photoperiodic and positional effects on cell proliferation are further characterized by the close association between leaf width and the number of vascular bundles across the leaf (Fig. 7) in comparable photoperiods, nodal positions, and levels of solar radiation. In other words the number of vascular bundles is controlled by the same factors that are involved in the control of cell proliferation in the leaf in general. This fact is of crucial importance, because it indicates clearly that the photoperiodic and positional controls act on the leaf at a stage in its ontogeny before its vascularization is determined. Similarly, the constant relationship between cell size in the mesophyll and epidermis indicates that their differentiation is either independent of positional and photoperiodic controls or takes place prior to their action.

Another consequence of the relationship between leaf width and the number of vascular bundles across it is that the number of interbundle strands of chlorenchyma is linked with leaf width and consequently with the lateral proliferation of chlorenchyma cells. Thus photoperiodic effects on lateral proliferation of chlorenchyma are at least partly expressed in effects on number of interbundle chlorenchyma strands. It remained to be seen whether and in what manner these strands themselves were affected by photoperiod and by level of solar radiation. To do that comparable strands were studied in transverse sections of comparable leaves of plants grown in SD and LD, respectively, at different levels of solar radiation. To simplify the presentation, Table 5 provides the data for only the highest and lowest radiation levels (100% and 35%). These results may be summarized as follows:

(a) Photoperiod had a marked effect on both width and thickness of the strands, and therefore also on its cross-sectional area. All these dimensions were considerably smaller in LD than in SD. On the other hand spatial organization of the strand (H/V ratio) was hardly affected.

(b) Level of solar radiation had a marked effect on the spatial organization of the strand (H/V ratio). Lower radiation level resulted in increase in width (H) and decrease in thickness (V). On the other hand the cross-sectional area was only slightly, if at all, affected.

(c) Photoperiodic effects on the number of cells along the horizontal and vertical axes of the strand cross section were small and could account for the

TABLE 5

Effects of Photoperiod and Level of Solar Radiation on Cross-Sectional
Structure of Intervascular Chlorenchyma Strands at 22°C/16°C

Photo-period (hr)	Radiation level (%)	Cross-sectional area[a]	Dimensions (μ)			Cell number		
			Horizontal (H)	Vertical (V)	H/V	Horizontal (H)	Vertical (V)	H/V
8	100	8.9 ± 0.4	142 ± 5	118 ± 3	1.20	8.0 ± 0.3	7.4 ± 0.2	1.09
	35	7.8 ± 0.3	174 ± 7	88 ± 10	1.98	8.6 ± 0.3	5.8 ± 0.2	1.49
16	100	5.3 ± 0.5	103 ± 8	98 ± 4	1.05	7.2 ± 0.5	6.9 ± 0.3	1.04
	35	5.0 ± 0.2	131 ± 0	74 ± 2	1.78	6.8 ± 0.3	5.3 ± 0.2	1.29

[a]Arbitrary units.

marked photoperiodic effects on its area only by including the effects on cell size (Fig. 8).

(d) Level of solar radiation changed the spatial organization of the cells in the cross section of the strand, mainly by affecting cell number along its vertical axis. Reduction in radiation level reduced the number of cells in the axis perpendicular to the leaf surface.

These anatomical studies established a clear-cut distinction between the morphogenic effects on leaf area resulting from the daily duration of light on the one hand and those resulting from the level of radiation on the other hand. The former affects cell proliferation, and to a small extent also cell expansion, in the horizontal plane of the leaf. The latter affects the extent of cell division in the chlorenchyma along the vertical axis of the leaf.

Having determined that LD conditions reduce length and width of the blade by inhibiting cell proliferation, we can now turn to the question of whether this effect is direct or is mediated by another photoperiodic response. One indication was obtained from the photoperiodic effects on rate of leaf appearance on the main shoot (Anslow, 1966). Regression analysis of the linear relationship between time and leaf number on the main shoot showed that in artificial illumination the time interval between the appearance of sequential leaves in 8-, 16-, and 24-hr photoperiods was 10.0, 4.0, and 3.6 days, respectively. Emergence of a leaf from the sheath of its predecessor is considered a more or less well-defined stage in its ontogeny (Mitchell, 1953). It was therefore possible that growth in LD conditions, which are inductive to flowering, results in smaller leaves by accelerating rate of leaf appearance (Aspinall and Paleg, 1963, 1964; Langer and Bussell, 1964; Aspinall, 1966; Edwards, 1967a,b) with the resultant shortening of some early developmental stage in leaf ontogeny during which the capacity for cell proliferation is determined (Arney, 1954). More precise information on this point was obtained by periodical microdissections of the shoot apices during which the kinetics of leaf growth could be followed by determination of dry weights of successive leaves throughout their ontogeny. The individual sigmoidal growth curves were analyzed and used to characterize the growth rate by the tangent at maximum slope and to estimate the time of onset of the exponential growth phase of the primordium from the intercept of this tangent with the time axis. The results of this analysis may be summarized as follows:

(a) The time interval between the start of the exponential growth phase of leaves arising from successive primordia was markedly shorter in LD (3.8 ± 0.6 days for leaves 3 through 8) than in SD (6.0 ±0.8 days for leaves 3 through 11). Leaves developing on plants in LD after transfer from SD (42 days after planting) were produced in the same interval as those grown continuously in LD (3.4 ±0.2 days for leaves 6 through 11), despite the fact that some of their primordia had already been initiated in SD (before transfer).

(b) Growth rate of the leaves (tangent of the slope) was considerably greater in SD than in LD, but in plants transferred from SD to LD, primordia that were initiated in SD prior to transfer to LD (numbers 6 through 8) grew at a rate similar to that of leaves growing throughout in SD (Table 6).

(c) The start of the exponential growth phase of any leaf coincided with the period of maximal growth in its predecessor (at the inflexion point in the middle of the sigmoidal growth curve, when the leaf is half expanded) (Fig.

TABLE 6

POSITIONAL AND PHOTOPERIODIC EFFECTS ON GROWTH RATE OF
LEAVES OF *O. MILIACEA*

Nodal	Dry weight accumulation (mg/day)		
Position	8-hr	16-hr	8-hr→16-hr
3	1.2	1.2	—
4	1.6	1.6	—
5	2.7	2.1	—
6	5.2	1.6	5.2
7	4.4	1.6	4.4
8	5.2	2.4	5.0
9	5.9	—	3.7
10	5.7	—	3.3
11	—	—	3.3

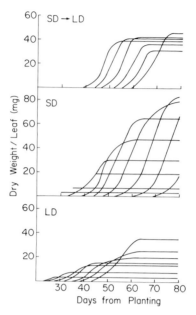

FIG. 10. Kinetics of growth of successive leaves on the main shoot of *O. miliacea* at 22°C/16°C in 16-hr (LD) and 8-hr (SD) photoperiods, and of those transferred from SD to LD 42 days after planting.

10). This suggests a causal relationship between the two developmental events. Either the start of the exponential growth phase in a leaf signals the onset of deceleration in the growth of its predecessor or *vice versa* the attainment of the half-expanded stage in a leaf signals the onset of the exponential growth phase in its follower.

Leaf dimensions are determined by the growth rate and the duration of the growth period of the leaf. These two characteristics exhibit independent physiological responses to the environment, which differ in different species (Williams, 1960; Thomas, 1961). From the analysis of the present data it can be concluded that in *O. miliacea* LD conditions cause a reduction in leaf dimensions by a combined effect on the growth rate and on the duration of an early, though post-initiation, critical phase of leaf growth, slowing down the former and shortening the latter.

Additional information on the process by which photoperiod affects leaf growth was obtained from experiments involving photoperiods with and without a light interruption in the middle of each dark period. Such interruptions induced a considerable degree of flowering (or transformation of the shoot apex to the reproductive state) in otherwise noninductive photoperiods (8hr), provided the light energy during the main light periods was

TABLE 7

EFFECTS OF INTERRUPTED DARK PERIODS ON FLOWERING AND SHOOT
CHARACTERISTICS OF *O. MILIACEA*

Photoperiod	Dark period interrupted[b]	Fraction flowering	Stem length (cm)		Leaf blade area (cm^2)	
			Veg. shoots	Rep. shoots	Veg. shoots	Rep. shoots
8[a]	−	0/14	26	—	14.1	—
	+	6/14	24	50	10.6	7.3
8	−	0/27	23	—	14.1	—
	+	0/28	22	—	13.2	—
12	−	1/28	29	(45)	10.8	(4.1)
	+	21/30	31	46	10.3	4.0
16	−	30/30	—	60	—	2.9
	+	30/30	—	65	—	3.5

[a]Sunlight, 22°C/16°C. In all others, fluorescent 21°C ± 2°C.
[b]30 min (except 15 min in 16 hr) at midpoint.

high. They increased flowering in near-critical photoperiods (12hr) even
when the light energy during the main light period was low. Irrespective of
the continuity or discontinuity of the dark periods, in all cases leaves on
those plants that were induced to flower were markedly smaller than leaves
in comparable nodal positions on plants that had remained vegetative
(Table 7) (cf. Cockshull, 1966). The reverse was true for stem length, which
was considerably greater when the plants were flowering than when they
were vegetative. It thus appears that the photoperiod-dependent changes
in the physiology of leaf growth are directly associated with the consequences that the photoperiod has on the developmental status of the shoot
apex. This has already been suggested by the inverse relationship between
the effects of length of the photoperiod on flowering and on leaf dimensions
(Fig. 4).

One possibility to account for the growth-inhibiting effects of LD on
leaves is that the reproductive apex competes with the young leaves for
growth factors or nutrients (Williams, 1960). Another possibility is that the
change in the apex from the vegetative to the reproductive state extends to
include some of the primordial leaves that had already been initiated. Some
indications were obtained in experiments involving exposure of plants
grown for 42 days in SD to intercalated LD dosages of various lengths, then
observing their development after returning them to SD (Fig. 11). When the
number of intercalated LD was insufficient to induce flowering (5 cycles), no

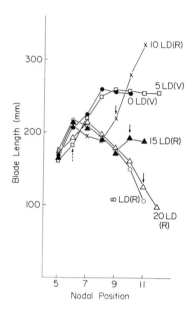

FIG. 11. Effects of number of intercalated 16-hr (LD) photoperiods on leaf dimensions at different nodes on the main shoot of *O. miliacea* growing in 8-hr (SD) photoperiods at 22°C/16°C. (V) apex vegetative; (R) apex reproductive.

reduction occurred in length of any of the leaf blades. When the number of intercalated LD was sufficient to induce flowering ($\geq$ 10 cycles), growth of the leaves formed during the exposure to LD was inhibited. However, if the number of intercalated LD cycles was not too great, for example 10 or even 15, some leaf primordia were evidently not yet fully committed, or may in fact not even have been initiated, when the plant was returned to SD. Their growth was therefore not inhibited and was even stimulated above that of the controls in SD throughout (cf. Thomas, 1961). It thus appears that the stimulus for the transformation of the apical complex into the reproductive state is perceived by the apex itself, as well as by certain leaf primordia that had developed to a receptive stage. The transformation may involve inhibition of leaf growth (*O. miliacea*), or its stimulation, for example, in *Amaranthus amaranticolor* (Thomas, 1961). A similar phenomenon, suggesting transformation of the entire apical complex to a reproductive state, was observed by Ofir (1970) with respect to formation of dormant regeneration buds at the base of flowering tillers in *Hordeum bulbosum*.

References

Abbé, E. C., Randolph, L. F., and Einset, J. (1941). The developmental relationships between shoot spex and growth pattern of leaf blade in diploid maize. *Amer. J. Bot.* **28**, 778–784.

Anslow, R. C. (1966). The rate of appearance of leaves on tillers of the *Gramineae. Herb. Abstr.* **36**, 149–155.

Arney, S. E. (1954). Leaf growth in *Fragaria.* III. The growth of leaves and shoot. *Ann. Bot. (London)* [N.S.] **18**, 349–365.

Ashby, E., and Wangermann, E. (1950). Studies in the morphogenesis of leaves. IV. Further observations on area, cell size and cell number of leaves of *Ipomoea* in relation to their position on the shoot. *New Phytol.* **49**, 23–35.

Aspinall, D. (1966). Effects of daylength and light intensity on growth of barley. IV. Genetically controlled variation in response to photoperiod. *Aust. J. Biol. Sci.* **19**, 517–534.

Aspinall, D., and Paleg, L. G. (1963). Effects of daylength and light intensity on growth of barley. I. Growth and development of apex with fluorescent light source. *Bot. Gaz.* **124**, 429–437.

Aspinall, D., and Paleg, L. G. (1964). Effects of daylength and light intensity on growth of barley. III. Vegetative development. *Aust. J. Biol. Sci.* **17**, 807–822.

Barnard, C., ed. (1964). "Grasses and Grasslands." Macmillan, New York.

Blondon, E. (1964). Contribution à l'étude du développement des graminées fourragères Rye-grass et Dactyle. Thesis No. 768. Fac. Sci., University of Paris.

Cockshull, K. E. (1966). Effects of night-break treatment on leaf area and leaf dry weight in *Callistephus chinensis. Ann. Bot. (London)* [N.S.] **30**, 791–806.

Edwards, K. J. R. (1967a). Developmental genetics of leaf formation in *Lolium.* 1. Basic patterns of leaf development in *L. multiflorum* and *L. perenne. Genet. Res.* **9**, 233–245.

Edwards, K. J. R. (1967b). Developmental genetics of leaf formation in *Lolium.* 2. Analysis of selection lines. *Genet. Res.* **9**, 247–257.

Humphries, E. C. (1967). Leaf growth of *Sinapis alba* in different environments. *Planta* **72**, 223–231.

Kaufman, P. B. (1959). Development of the shoot of *Oryza sativa.* I. The shoot apex. *Phytomorphology* **9**, 228–240.

Koller, D., Highkin, H. R., and Caso, O. H. (1960). Effects of gibberellic acid on stem apices of vernalizable grasses. *Amer. J. Bot.* **47**, 518–524.

Koller, D., Kigel, J, and Keren, N. (1968). Analysis of environmental control of development in *Oryzopsis miliacea. Isr. J. Bot.* **17**, 133–154.

Langer, R. H. M., and Bussell, W. T. (1964). The effect of flower induction on the rate of leaf initiation. *Ann. Bot. (London)* [N.S.] **28**, 163–167.

Ledin, R. B. (1954). The vegetative shoot apex of *Zea mays. Amer. J. Bot.* **41**, 11–12.

Milthorpe, F. L., and Ivins, J. D., eds. (1966). "The growth of Cereals and Grasses." Butterworth, London.

Mitchell, K. J. (1953). Influence of light and temperature on the growth of rye grass (*Lolium* spp.). I. Pattern of vegetative development. *Physiol. Plant.* **6**, 21–46.

Mitchell, K. J., and Soper, K. (1958). Effects of differences in light intensity and temperature on the anatomy and development of leaves of *Lolium perenne* and *Paspalum dilatatum. N. Z. J. Agr. Res.* **1**, 1–16.

Ofir, M. (1970). The physiology of dormancy in *Hordeum bulbosum* L.–a perennial pasture grass. Ph.D. Thesis, Hebrew University of Jerusalem. (Hebrew with English summary).

Ofir, M., Koller, D., and Negbi, M. (1967). Studies on the physiology of regeneration buds of *Hordeum bulbosum* L. *Bot. Gaz.* **128**, 25–34.

Paleg, L. G., and Aspinall, D. (1964). Effects of daylength and light intensity on growth of barley. *Bot. Gaz.* **125**, 149–155.

Ryle, G. J. A. (1966a). Effects of photoperiod in the glasshouse on the growth of leaves and tillers in three perennial grasses. *Ann. Appl. Biol.* **57**, 257–268.

Ryle, G. J. A. (1966b). Effects of photoperiod in growth cabinets on the growth of leaves and tillers of three perennial grasses. *Ann. Appl. Biol.* **57**, 269–279.

Sachs, R. M. (1965). Stem elongation. *Annu. Rev. Plant Physiol.* **16**, 73–96.

Thomas, R. G. (1961). Correlations between growth and flowering in *Chenopodium amaranticolor*. II. Leaf and stem growth. *Ann. Bot. (London)* [N.S.] **25**, 255–269.

Williams, R. F. (1960). The physiology of growth in the wheat plant. I. Seedling growth and the pattern of growth at the shoot apex. *Aust. J. Biol. Sci.* **13**, 401–428.

Chapter 10

Chemical Regulation of Growth in Leaves and Tillers

J. R. GOODIN

Chemical regulation of growth has become familiar to all of biology in recent years, and control of vegetative growth of grasses has many economic implications for agriculture. The basis for these principles is often well documented in research, but the literature is scattered in many fields and often goes unnoticed by workers in a different field.

In order to understand how chemical regulators work at the cellular and molecular level, one must recall the morphological and anatomical patterns which bring about that growth and development.

Anatomy and Morphology

In Gramineae gross recognition is relatively easy because of a particular combination of structural features (Barnard, 1964). These include cylindrical jointed stems with short basal internodes, long narrow leaves with parallel veins and sheathing bases, distichous phyllotaxy, a fibrous root system consisting mainly of adventitious roots arising from nodes of the stem, flowers of an unusual and characteristic structure, albuminous seeds and caryopsis type fruits, and embroys of a characteristic structure. Growth during germination results mainly from elongation of existing embryonic cells and cell division in certain specific groups of cells or meristematic regions, primarily the root and shoot apices. The coleoptile grows first by meristematic activity and cell enlargement, but later cell enlargement alone is almost entirely responsible for its elongation. Elongation of the mesocotyl is similar to that of a stem internode. The first series of adventitious roots arise endogenously from tissue in the vicinity of the scutellar node and the second series from the coleoptilar node. This later series breaks through the base of the coleoptile.

From the time the seedling has become established until the end of the vegetative growth phase there are no basic changes in the plant's structural design and development. The plant grows in size and number of organs, but these arise from meristems in which histogenetic patterns are repeated. New leaves arise in the same manner as the old leaves and tissue organization is similar. All branches originate in cell divisions which follow a well-defined pattern and repeat the structure of the main stem.

The growing point of the stem apex is dome shaped and leaf primordia arise as crescentic ridges alternately on either side of it. Differences in form of the apex are associated with differences in the relative rate of leaf initiation and expansion. The apex may be very elongated with up to 30 distinguishable leaf primordia; in other species only a few leaf primordia may be present, in which case the apices are very short. There is no relation between length of vegetative apex and growth habit, and the apex may differ markedly in related species.

In all grasses there is a two-layered tunica surrounding a central core of cells or corpus. The cells of both the outer tunica (dermatogen) and the inner layer (hypodermis) divide only by anticlinal walls, except where a leaf primordium is being initiated. These layers are thus discrete and maintain their integrity. Cells of the corpus arise from a small group of cells at the tip and no division pattern can be discerned. Divisions just behind the tip are predominantly at right angles to the length of the stem axis and result in longitudinal files of cells. Cells of the corpus become vacuolated early whereas those of the dermatogen and hypodermis do not. Leaf primordia are initiated by periclinal divisions of cells in the hypodermis, and these are immediately followed by periclinal divisions in adjacent cells of the dermatogen. Periclinal divisions occur in hypodermal cells above and below those in which the first divisions took place until a tier of some 3 or 4 cells have so divided. Similar divisions occur in the hypodermis and dermatogen in a horizontal plane extending at least half way around the axis.

Early in the development of a leaf primordium, meristematic activity becomes restricted to a zone of cells at its base, the intercalary meristem (Milthorpe and Ivins, 1966). Initially there is no distinction between lamina and sheath, but in *Lolium perenne*, for example, when the leaf is 1 cm or more in length, the ligule is formed as an outgrowth of the epidermis near the base of the leaf on the adaxial side, and the formation of a band of parenchymatous tissue divides the intercalary meristem into two parts, the upper part responsible for the growth of the lamina and the lower part for that of the sheath. The leaf matures basipetally, the sheath being the last part to do so (Soper and Mitchell, 1956). Once the ligule is exposed, no further elongation of the leaf lamina occurs (Sharman, 1942). It has been demonstrated that elongation of the emerged portion of the lamina has ceased by the time it emerges from the encircling leaf sheaths. On a variety of grasses attempts to stimulate further activity of the intercalary meristem of the lamina, by partially defoliating leaves whose ligules have already emerged, have failed (Begg and Wright, 1962).

The rate of appearance of leaves varies with the environment but remains constant for any given set of conditions (Mitchell, 1953), and it is not affected by a change to the reproductive condition by the stem apex. However, there are marked changes in leaf size (Borrill, 1961); the blades of successive leaves become progressively larger until about the time of inflorescence formation, whereupon laminae up the flowering stem become progressively shorter. This change in length of laminae appears to be more closely correlated with the beginning of stem elongation than with double-ridge formation. In contrast to laminae the length of successive sheaths continues to increase after inflorescence formation; as a result the total area of lamina and sheath increases until inflorescence emergence. Leaf width also increases. Koller and Kigel (this volume) point out that leaf length and width in *Oryzopsis miliacea* is also related to photoperiod.

The continued activity of the intercalary meristem in the sheath, which leads to the increased sheath length, may be closely associated with similar meristematic activity in the extending stem. It appears that the increased sheath length partially compensates for the reduced blade length, so that the photosynthetic surface is not drastically reduced. However, the sheath is only about half as efficient as a photosynthetic organ as the lamina (Thorne, 1959).

Borrill (1961) has shown that before stem extension, the increased blade and sheath lengths of successively older leaves are due to increased cell length, but during stem extension the final rapid increase in sheath length is apparently due to an increase in cell number, although this has not been substantiated. The larger leaves are also wider, the increased width being due to more rows of cells and not to wider cells. The width of the leaf initial itself is related to the circumference of the stem apex.

Regulation of Growth

The question now arises as to how the growth of a particular apex and the subsequent leaves and buds that it produces may be modified experimentally to produce a desired effect in acceleration or retardation. In grasses the kinds of regulation desired run the entire gamut of control. In the case of sugar cane we are interested in producing just as much lamina surface as possible in order to generate a larger photosynthetic surface; in turfgrasses it would be particularly desirable to retard growth rate to reduce maintenance costs, provided quality and esthetic factors can be maintained. In field crops we are concerned with such problems as lodging and photosynthetic efficiency, and in forage crops the concern is with maximizing fresh or dry weight.

Apical Dominance in Grasses

From the vast literature concerned with apical dominance in dicots, it is reasonable to assume that the same type of endogenous growth regulator control might be operating in grasses; that is, the shoot apex may be producing some substance that move basipetally and inhibits lateral bud formation. When apical dominance is destroyed, control over the quiescent axillary buds changes to permit synthesis of deoxyribonucleic acid (DNA), and subsequently ribonucleic acid (RNA) and protein. According to Jacob and Monod (1961), buds under apical dominance may be considered functionally repressed; and when the upper portion of the plant is removed, genetic information in the buds in replicated and active growth begins. Therefore removal of the apex should cause the lateral buds to be activated and begin elongation and growth; replacement of the apex with a new auxin source should keep the lateral buds inhibited. Leopold (1949) has shown that just such a situation does occur in Wintex barley and in Chalco teosinte. When he dissected the shoot apex down to the apical dome and then destroyed a few apical cells with a needle, tiller formation (activation of lateral buds) was dramatically increased. If he replaced the destroyed apical cells with α-naphthaleneacetic acid, tiller formation was not increased (Table 1). Leopold was also able to show that changes in tillering occur not only with season, but also with day length and the addition of auxin. Thus short-day control plants of barley tiller much greater than long-day control plants; and addition of auxin reduces tiller production under both long- and short-day conditions (Fig. 1). He also found that tiller production could be modified chemically by adding TIBA, an auxin antagonist

TABLE 1

TILLERING AS INFLUENCED BY THE APEX IN TEOSINTE AND BARLEY[a]

	Teosinte		Barley	
	Tillering	Not tillering	Tillering	Not tillering
Control	0	10	3	7
Apex destroyed	8	2	9	1
Apex destroyed + NAA	0	10	3	7

[a] α- naphthaleneacetic acid was applied in three weekly applications at the rate of 0.1 ml of 400 mg/1 solution (After Leopold, 1949).

(particularly under long-day conditions) and by other auxin antagonists, such as X-rays and coumarin (Table 2). This was the earliest conclusive study showing that tiller development (although not necessarily tiller initiation) is under at least partial auxin control. Tillering in herbage grasses has been carefully reviewed by Langer (1963).

Growth Regulators

Hormonal regulation in higher plants has recently been reviewed by Galston and Davies (1969). The kinds of physiological response that one

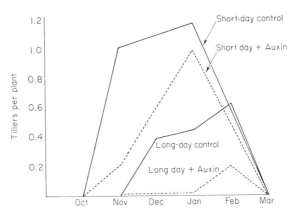

FIG. 1. Changes in tillering of barley with season, day length, and addition of auxin. Day lengths were held constant at 10 and 16 hr (short and long days, respectively) (After Leopold, 1949).

TABLE 2

Auxin Antagonists and Their Influence on Tillering of Barley[a]

	Tillers/plant	
Agent	16 hr	10 hr
Water control (October)	0	0
TIBA (25 mg/1) (October)	0.6	0.1
Water control (November)	0.4	1.0
X-rays (75 R) (November)	1.5	1.3
Water control (January)	0.3	1.2
Coumarin (5 × 10⁻⁵M) (January)	0.6	2.0

[a]Under short- and long-day conditions (After Leopold, 1949)

may expect upon application of a particular growth regulator are complex and varied; under some systems, two regulators may be antagonistic, whereas their presence in other systems may lead to a complete masking effect of one over the other. The broad general classes of regulators now characterized and described are auxins, cytokinins, gibberellins, abscisic acid and other inhibitors, and ethylene. A few other compounds have growth regulating effects on leaves and tillers in grasses.

AUXIN

In addition to the previously mentioned work of Leopold, Cleland (1967) has demonstrated that auxin-induced wall loosening and the subsequent elongation apparently occur in two distinct steps: (1) covalent bonds which render the wall rigid are broken only when the wall is under tension and auxin is present in the tissues, and (2) extension of the wall requires that hydrogen bonding between polymers be broken by a turgor pressure in excess of some critical value. Young, expanding leaves contain relatively large quantities of endogenous auxin, falling to very low levels as the leaf matures. However, senescent leaves of *Avena* again show a dramatic increase in auxin (Sheldrake and Northcote, 1968). Cleland (1965) has studied the site in action of growth retardants in *Avena* leaf sections treated with gibberellin to induce elongation. Although Phosfon D, Amo-1618, CCC, and B9 were all effective in inhibiting growth, the inhibition was not reversed with gibberellin. Addition of IAA will partially reverse the inhibition, leading to the conclusion that retardants act by interfering with auxin metabolism. If this is also true in the dormant bud system, then application of growth retardants should have a dramatic effect on tillering.

Recently Bokhari (1969) has shown that "Uniculm" barley, the single-gene mutant, will respond to CCC by producing tillers that otherwise would not occur. Uniculm seldom produces tillers, although anatomical studies have shown that tiller primordia are present. Concentrations of CCC as low as 10^{-7} M will produce some tillering, and up to 30 tillers may be produced with a 10^{-1} M treatment.

GIBBERELLIC ACID

Gibberelin was first isolated because of the bakanae disease caused by a fungus in rice plants. Unknown at the time, the fungus was producing this regulatory chemical which caused chlorosis and extreme internodal elongation, leading to severe lodging. For the most part the gibberellins can be described as a class of regulators that may give rise to rapid cell elongation and in some instances to cell division. There has been considerable interest in attempting to promote grass growth at times that are unfavorable due to environmental conditions, usually low temperature. Wittwer and Bukovac (1957) induced a pronounced growth of *Poa, Cynodon, Agrositis, Festuca,* and *Lolium* in early spring with foliar applications of Gibberellic acid. Although the temporary effects achieved here and by other workers have been dramatic, the long-term effect results in a higher shoot/root ratio and an eventual depletion of stored reserves in the root system. Thus gibberellin-treated turfs and pastures are often quite inferior to the controls a few months following treatment.

Noting that some slow-growing plant types respond more dramatically than rapid- growing types of the same species, Phinney (1956) demonstrated that single-gene dwarf mutants of corn would respond to gibberellic acid and that the dwarfing effect could be completely overcome. Later, Cooper (1958) achieved the same effect with a genetic dwarf in *Lolium perenne* (Fig. 2). Anatomical studies showed that this dwarf had reduced cell elongation in both leaf blade and sheath. Successive leaves on the shoot remained short and broad, forming a small rosette, whereas rate of leaf appearance was unaffected by the dwarfing. Gibberellic acid applied at 1 ml of 50 mg/liter solution each week resulted in increased cell elongation in the blade and sheath and brought the dwarf within the normal phenotype. He compared lengths of organs and cells under both conditions and demonstrated that even the number of tillers at harvest were similar in the normal control and in the treated dwarf (Table 3).

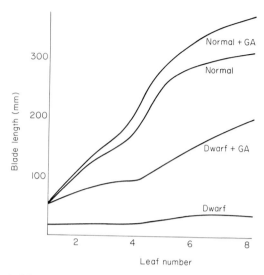

F ɪ ɢ. 2. Effect of gibberellin on normal and dwarf *Lolium perenne* on successive leaf blades (after Cooper, 1958).

R ᴇᴛᴀʀᴅᴀɴᴛs

Among the class of compounds known as "growth inhibitors," maleic hydrazide has received by far the greatest amount of study. In an attempt to reduce maintenance costs of turfgrasses, vegetative inhibition has been demonstrated under many conditions. Similar studies have been performed on roadside grasses in highway maintenance and in field crops. Maleic

TABLE 3

Eғғᴇᴄᴛ ᴏғ Gɪʙʙᴇʀᴇʟʟɪᴄ Aᴄɪᴅ ᴏɴ Nᴏʀᴍᴀʟ ᴀɴᴅ Dᴡᴀʀғ Sᴇᴇᴅʟɪɴɢs ᴏғ *Lᴏʟɪᴜᴍ Pᴇʀᴇɴɴᴇ.*[a]

	Normal		Dwarf	
	Control	Treated	Control	Treated
Length of 7th leaf blade (mm)	226.6	291.0	17.6	199.6
Length of 7th leaf sheath (mm)	51.4	75.2	2.2	42.4
Length of guard cells (μ)	48.5	45.5	37.6	43.9
Length of cells between stomates (μ)	181.6	161.6	58.2	168.5
Number of tillers at harvest	24.8	17.0	9.4	14.8

[a]Each figure represents a mean of five seedlings. All seedlings were sown in February 4 and harvested April 15, 1957 (After Cooper, 1958)

hydrazide shortens and thickens internodes, produces abnormal thickening of all organs, and gives excessive enlargement and vacuolation of cells (Carlson, 1954). In general, maleic hydrazide has been and is being used successfully as an effective grass suppressor for highway roadside maintenance programs, particularly in the eastern United States. The value of maleic hydrazide on regularly mowed turf for growth control is both limited and questionable. The danger of turf discoloration and injury limits the use of maleic hydrazide to those areas where mowing is difficult and where turf discoloration is not an important factor.

CCC (2-chloroethyl) trimethylammonium chloride and related compounds have been studied extensively as retardants under conditions similar to maleic hydrazide. These studies have been particularly successful in field crops, and CCC is now being used commercially in field crops in some European countries. This retardant, being rapidly translocated to all parts of the plant (Ayeke, 1968), causes increased tillering in wheat, shorter and thicker stems, and broader and greener leaves. Similar effects have been shown in barley and oats (Goodin *et al.*, 1966), and the retarding effect can be nullified with gibberellin. Grain yield is usually unaffected or increased slightly, but the shorter and thicker stems give a dramatic resistance to lodging. It has also been reported that treated crops were able to assimilate 15% to 50% more nitrogen than controls (Lhoste, 1967).

CYTOKININS

Thus far most of the work with the cytokinins has been experimental with respect to grasses. This class of compound is identified with cell division and delayed senescence. Rapid decline of protein and RNA in detached rice leaves was suppressed by kinetin (Oritani and Yoshida, 1967). There is considerable evidence that kinetin stimulates protein synthesis essential for the survival of detached or senescing leaves. Such regulatory compounds may have future use in maintaining actively photosynthesizing leaves on grasses for a longer period of time.

MISCELLANEOUS COMPOUNDS

Although 2,4-D and other phenoxy acids would generally fall into the category of auxins since their physiological effect is similar, there have been a number of reports that very low rates of 2, 4-D will increase yields of cereal crops. Recently, Ries and Gast (1965) and Freney (1965) have reported increased growth and nutrient uptake of corn by application of very low concentrations of simazine. Paraquat has been demonstrated as a method for curing of forage grasses while maintaining a high protein content (Agbakoba and Goodin, 1967).

A class of compounds known as morphactins (Fluorene-9-carboxylic acids) is the latest major introduction to the field of growth retardants. They are apparently not readily translocatable, but residual physiological effects seem to outlast maleic hydrazide. These compounds will probably achieve widespread use in extensive landscaping, but their usefulness in chemical mowing of turfgrasses is indeed questionable (Madison *et al.*, 1969).

Although not a very bright prospect for the future, mention must be made of Ordin and Skoe's work (1964) concerning growth inhibition of *Avena* by ozone, a familiar component of West Coast smog. Recent field observations with cereals suggest that smog will become a serious detriment in many grain-producing areas.

References

Agbakoba, S. C. O., and Goodin, J. R. (1967). Effect of paraquat on the nitrogen content and regrowth of Coastal bermudagrass (*Cynodon dactylon* (L.) Pers.) *Agron. J.* **59**; 605–607.

Ayeke, C. A. (1968). The metabolism of (1-2-C^{14} Chloroethyl) trimethylammonium chloride and its nitrogen interaction effects on forage quality in Coastal bermudagrass (*Cynodon dactylon* (L.) Pers.). Ph.D. Dissertation, University of California, Riverside.

Barnard, C., ed. (1964). "Grasses and Grasslands." Macmillan, New York.

Begg, J. E., and Wright, M. J. (1962) Growth and development of leaves from intercalary meristems in *Phalaris arundinacea* L. Nature (*London*) **194**, 1097.

Bokhari, A. (1969). Personal communication.

Borrill, M. (1961). The developmental anatomy of leaves in *Lolium temulentum*. *Ann. Bot.* (*London*) N.S. **25**, 1.

Carlson, J. B. (1954). Cytohistological responses of plant meristems to maleic hydrazide. *Iowa State Coll. J. Sci.* **29**, 105–128.

Cleland, R. (1965). Evidence on the site of action of growth retardants. *Plant Cell Physiol.* **6**, 7–15.

Cleland, R. (1967). A dual role of turgor pressure in auxin-induced cell elongation in *Avena* coleoptiles. *Planta* **77**, 182–191.

Cooper, J. P. (1958). The effect of gibberellic acid on a genetic dwarf in *Lolium perenne*. *New Phytol.* **57**, 235–238.

Freney, J. R. (1965). Increased growth and uptake of nutrients by corn plants treated with low levels of simazine. *Aust. J. Agr. Res.* **16**, 257–263.

Galston, A. W., and Davies P. J. (1969). Hormonal regulation in higher plants. *Science* **163**, 1288–1297.

Goodin, J. R., McKell, C. M., and Webb, F. L. (1966). Influence of CCC on water use and growth characteristics of barley, *Agron. J.* **58**, 453–454.

Jacob, F., and Monod, J. (1961). Enzyme adaptation in microorganisms. *J. Mol. Biol.* **3**, 318.

Langer, R. H. M. (1963). Tillering in herbage grasses. *Her. Abstr.* **33**, 141–148.

Leopold, A. C. (1949). Control of tillering in grasses by auxin. *Amer. J. Bot.* **36**, 437–440.

Lhoste, J. (1967). Les regulateurs de croissance. Emploi du CCC en culture céréalière. *Nucl. Rev. Sci.* **8**, 207–212.

Madison, J. H. Johnson, J. M., Davis, W. B. and Sachs, R. M. (1969). Testing fluorine compounds for chemical mowing of turfgrass. *Calif. Agr.* **23**, 9-10.

Milthorpe, F. L., and Ivins, J. D., eds. (1966). "The Growth of Cereals and Grasses." Butterworth, London.

Mitchell, K. J. (1953). Influence of light and temperature on the growth of ryegrass (*Lolium* spp.). I. Pattern of vegetative development. *Physiol. Plant.* **6**, 21–46.

Ordin, L., and Skoe, B. P. (1964). Ozone effects on cell wall metabolism of *Avena* coleoptile sections. *Plant Physiol.* **39**, 751–755.

Oritani, T., and Yoshida, R. (1967). Studies on nitrogen metabolism in crop plants. II. Effect of kinetin on nitrogen metabolism in detached leaves of rice plant and Italian ryegrass. *Proc. Crop Sci. Soc. Jap.* **36**, 513.

Phinney, B. O. (1956). Growth response of single-gene dwarf mutants in maize to gibberellic acid. *Proc. Nat. Acad. Sci. U.S.* **42**, 185–189.

Ries, S. K., and Gast, A. (1965). The effect of simazine on nitrogenous components of corn. *Weeds* **13**, 272–274.

Sharman, B. C. (1942). Developmental anatomy of the shoot of *Zea mays* L. *Ann. Bot. (London)* [N.S.] **6**, 245–282.

Sheldrake, A. R., and Northcote, D. H. (1968). Production of auxin by detached (*Phaseolus vulgaris, Avena sativa*) leaves. *Nature (London)* **217**, 195.

Soper, K., and Mitchell, K. J. (1956). The developmental anatomy of perennial ryegrass (*Lolium perenne*). *N.Z. J. Sci. Technol., Sect. A*, **37**, 484–504.

Thorne, G. N. (1959). Photosynthesis of lamina and sheath of barley leaves. *Ann. Bot. (London)* [N.S.] **23**, 365–370.

Wittwer, S. H., and Bukovac, M. J. (1957). Gibberellin and higher plants. V. Promotion of growth in grass at low temperatures. *Mich., Agr. Exp. Sta., Quart. Bull.* **39**, 682–686.

Chapter 11

External Factors Affecting Tiller Development

HORTON M. LAUDE

Although the grass plant is an assemblage of shoots, the individual tiller has been considered by many investigators to be the growth unit of grasses. Productivity depends in large measure on the ability of the plant to initiate tillers and on the later development of these shoots. Within the limits set by genotype, growth of the tiller is responsive to the environment. External factors that affect growth and development therefore warrant consideration.

Investigators studying plant response to environmental factors recognize that the effect of any one factor is conditioned by the magnitude or intensity of others. Interpreting the results of various researchers in order to arrive at common relationships and principles requires the utmost care, since experimental conditions and equipment, plant material, and evaluation of results differ. Yet a high measure of agreement can be observed in the considerable amount of research presently available.

The reader is directed to the review by Langer (1963) for a survey of tillering research to that date. The external factors of temperature, light, mineral nutrition, and water supply have received most attention individually or in combination. Stage of development of the plant at the time of observation and management as it alters the plant's environment also deserve consideration.

Temperature as the Principal Variable

Mitchell (1956), using climate cabinets with the same regime of day length and light intensity, determined the growth rate of several species of grass at constant temperatures from 45°F to 95°F. He concluded that the growth rate of the tillers of most species changes little over a comparatively wide range of temperatures, although there are distinct differences among species. In another experiment (Mitchell and Lucanus, 1960) combinations of day temperatures of 60°F, 52.5°F, and 45°F with night temperatures of 45°F, 40°F, or 35°F were employed. Within these ranges, lowering the day temperature reduced the growth of individual tillers more than did lowering the night temperature. The rate of tillering, however, was little affected by reducing the day temperature, whereas with some species the lower night temperature was associated with increased rates of tillering.

Seven species of perennial grass were grown under two temperature regimes in glasshouses at the Grassland Research Institute, Hurley, by Ryle (1964). Growth was from December until April when reproductive development became apparent. Light intensity and day length increased naturally during this period. One glasshouse was unheated, the other was maintained at a minimum of 15°C. Number of tillers per main shoot was increased during the first two months by the warmer temperature (and also by a higher level of nitrogen). The warmer temperature was considered to increase the rate of production of tiller sites by hastening leaf production. Number of tillers per shoot, however, did not relate tillering to the number of leaf axils or potential sites for tiller growth. Ryle expressed his data both in terms of number of tillers per 10 expanded leaves, and in percent of leaf axil sites bearing a tiller. The higher temperatures appeared to inhibit tillering when the number of tillers was related to the number of available leaf axil sites. He also found that lower temperature generally did not affect the node at which tillering began, but did appear to favor more tillers to expand at lower positions on the stem. Varietal differences were evident.

Since the axillary buds from which tillers arise may be positioned at or near the soil surface, it is well to consider soil temperature as well as air temperature. Ketellapper (1960) reported that over a period of four weeks, dry weight of tops and tiller number in *Phalaris tuberosa* were reduced as the soil temperature was increased from 20°C to 30°C. Unfortunately, equipment permitting the control of soil temperature distinct from air temperature is not generally available and research on the soil-temperature factor is meager.

Light as the Principal Variable

From the standpoints of intensity and/or duration light has been studied perhaps more than other factors in relation to tillering. Shading the plant by screens or fabric, thus reducing the natural light, has often been employed to establish a series of intensities for growth. Pritchett and Nelson (1951) were concerned with the effects of oats shading young bromegrass grown with the oats. They grew bromegrass in the greenhouse under full green-house light (2833 ft-c) or under muslin shades which reduced this intensity to 757, 422, 257, or 157 ft-c. The plants experienced no moisture stress and either received no supplemental fertilizer or were given nitrogen at the rate of 80 lb per acre. Top growth and tillering were increased by the higher light intensities. The importance of recognizing the interrelationships of factors was demonstrated in their results. The nitrogen fertilization stimulated tillering only if the light intensity was above the 422 ft-c level, there being no measurable response to nitrogen below that intensity of light.

. In pastures, foliage shades the plant bases. Whether or not shading the base of the plant affected tillering differently than shading the entire plant was considered by Mitchell and Coles (1955) using short-rotation ryegrass. General shading was established by placing layers of fabric above the plants which reduced the incident glasshouse light by 70%. Base shading was obtained by wrapping muslin around the lower portion of the plant to reduce light by the same amount. These two treatments resulted in similar tiller numbers, and it was concluded that the total quantity of light available for photosynthesis was more important than the light intensity at the base of the plant.

Total shoot production in spaced *Bromus mollis* plants grown in the field at Davis, California, was found to be associated with the quantity of natural daylight received. Plastic mesh screens, placed 3 ft above the ground, reduced the natural light to 74%, 45%, 32% or 10%. Shoot production was much greater at the higher light intensities (Davis and Laude, 1964).

Light intensity and photoperiod together have received considerable attention. Aspinall and Paleg (1964) grew young barley plants for six weeks under controlled environments with fluorescent light between 500 and 2000 ft-c and incandescent light ranging up to 300 ft-c. Tiller numbers were reduced by decreasing light intensity, and at low intensities most tillers were primary, arising from the main axis rather than being of higher order. Rate of tillering appeared mainly dependent upon total radiant energy, and changes in photoperiod (independent of light energy) had little effect on tillering.

Orchardgrass responded both to reduced light intensity and to long day by a decline in tillering (Auda *et al.*, 1966). When a 9-hour photoperiod was extended to 18 hours by low-intensity illumination, the rate of tillering was reduced by more than 50% during six weeks of growth. These authors suggest that tillering is more associated with light energy than with photoperiod.

Ryle (1966 a,b) has investigated the effects of photoperiod on growth and tillering using S. 37 cocksfoot, S. 215 meadow fescue, and S. 24 perennial ryegrass grown vegetatively either in the glasshouse or the growth cabinet. In the former, natural light was extended with low intensity artificial illumination whereas in the growth cabinet the amount of daily light was maintained the same for all treatments. In both experimental facilities the results were similar, showing that the number of tillers decreased with increase in photoperiod. Plants under long days tended to have fewer but larger tillers than those under short days. Interrupting a long dark period with one hour of light to achieve the long day photoperiodic effect, however, was relatively ineffective in reducing tiller numbers. Ryle, noting a general relationship between increase in leaf surface expansion and decrease in tillering as photoperiod increased, suggested a correlated effect of photoperiod on growth of the entire plant.

Mineral Nutrition or Water Supply as the Principal Variable

Mineral nutrition must be maintained at an adequate amount for normal tillering. Langer (1959) grew S. 48 timothy at levels of N, P, and K for 21 weeks and noted that the effect of each nutrient was obscured or little evident when the levels of the others were low. Nitrogen was most effective in increasing tiller numbers.

Aspinall (1961) grew barley in vermiculite with applications of complete nutrient solution at periodic stages of development. He was able to obtain increases in tiller numbers throughout the life cycle following nutrient applications. The rate of tillering was nearly constant during growth when nutrients were repeatedly supplied. This was in contrast to the tillering pattern of plants grown in soil that showed rapid tillering during early vegetative growth and a resumption of tillering during the later stages of grain ripening. Both the rate and duration of the tillering period were responsive to nutrient supply in his experiments.

The extent to which periods of drought depress tillering also was demonstrated by Aspinall et al. (1964). Barley watered to field capacity after allowing the soil to reach permanent wilting percentage was observed following one to several cycles of dryness. Although dryness always suppressed tillering, some stimulation often was noted following rewatering especially during the earlier stages of growth. Tillering was most curtailed by stress commencing late in development.

Interaction of Factors

When the influence on tillering of more than one factor is considered, it may be well to reflect on the following conclusion by Mitchell (1953b) based on his studies with ryegrass. He presented evidence to show that a rise in temperature, fall in light quantity, or partial defoliation can induce bud inhibition, and noted that a change in any one factor is conditioned by the level of the other environmental factors and by genotype. This observation is also supported by Mitchell's study (1953a) and is now generally appreciated by other investigators who consider combinations of factors.

Templeton *et al.* (1961) studied the effects of light and temperature on early growth of tall fescue (*Festuca arundinacea*). They found interactions among environmental factors and between environmental and genetic factors. With regard to tillering under the conditions of their experiments, the following interactions were important: photoperiod × temperature, photoperiod × age of plant, photoperiod × plant source, temperature × age of plant, and temperature × duration of treatment.

Number of tillers produced by three orchardgrass varieties under several light and temperature conditions was used by Nittler *et al.* (1963) as a means of identifying differences among varieties. In these experiments light intensity was associated with greater differences in tillering than was temperature. Varietal distinctions were small when light was abundant but were increased under regimes of reduced light obtained either by low intensity or short photoperiod.

Friend (1965) reported extensive experimentation with wheat grown under sand culture with nutrient solution in controlled environment rooms employing temperatures from 10°C to 30°C and light intensities from 200 to 2500 ft-c. He noted that increase in both leaf and tiller number was progressively greater at the higher light intensities at all temperatures used. Friend grew the plants to heading and seed set and observed reduced tillering at heading as well as considerable tiller mortality at this time. It is evident that in studies on tillering the stage of plant development may exert a pronounced effect and must be considered in interpreting results.

Stage of Plant Development and Tiller Senescence

The reproductive stage in plants develops in response to environmental conditions among which the temperature and photoperiod are especially important. Depression of tillering near the onset of heading, therefore, may be construed to be in part a response to external factors. Laude *et al.*

(1968) investigated tillering in hardinggrass (*Phalaris tuberosa var. stenoptera*) in the greenhouse by comparing at one time vegetative and reproductive plants from the same clone. This was possible since the hardinggrass used was long day in photoperiodic response and required some cold preconditioning before floral induction. By adjusting either the vernalization temperature or the photoperiod slightly above or below the threshold for flowering for some of the plants and not for others, simultaneous comparison of vegetative with reproductive plants was possible. Rate of tillering was alike in both lots until two weeks before head emergence. Then for approximately four weeks centering on the time of head emergence, the reproductive plants developed no new tillers whereas the vegetative plants continued to initiate tillers at near the previous rate. Resumption of tillering in headed plants occurred about two weeks after heading. Substantial numbers of tillers died near the onset of heading. These observations are in agreement with studies of seasonal trends in tillering with other species (Lamp, 1952; Langer, 1958; Langer *et al.*, 1964; Taylor and Templeton, 1966). The depression in tillering and tiller mortality in hardinggrass would seem to be associated with the developmental stage of the plant and with the increasing dryness and temperature which usually prevails in California near the time of heading.

Tillering in barley followed the general pattern of hardinggrass near the heading stage although the changes were more pronounced (Laude *et al.*, 1967). During the 10- to 14-day period before awn emergence very few new tillers arose and many tillers died. Mobilization of reserves to the developing caryopsis was thought to be one possible factor in the depression and senescence of tillers. This was explored further by using a near isogenic barley which was segregating for male sterility. However, the male-sterile plants exhibited the same preheading trend in tillering and tiller mortality as did the fertile plants. It was concluded that the depression of tillering in barley was not associated with mobilization of metabolites into the developing fruit, or with the presence of viable pollen or the occurrence of pollination. The triggering mechanism must become operative in very early stages of reproductive development. Further study with barley suggested that these tillering behaviors are associated with early jointing or the commencement of culm elongation (Riveros, 1968).

Management

In the culture and utilization of grasses there is considerable opportunity to influence tillering. Seeding to space the plants in the field certainly affects tillering ability. Kaukis and Reitz (1955), for example, planted oats in

7-in rows at spacings in the row of 2.5 in or 5.0 in. Under their conditions, 75% more grain was produced at the 5-in spacing, and the authors attributed 77% of this increase to greater tillering.

The objective in cultural practice may not, however, always be the stimulation of tillering. Management of some grasses in parts of the world involves ridging or "earthing up" around the plant bases with the objective of suppressing tillering and reducing lodging. Shen and Harrison (1965) discussed this in relation to sugarcane and present experimental data based on sudangrass.

One most important external factor remains to be noted: namely, the effect of the animal on the forage plant. Grazing and defoliation studies have provided much useful information on herbage removal effects. An aspect of grazing which has been less investigated is that of animal treading on the plants. Edmond (1958, 1962, 1963) working in New Zealand studied the effect of driving flocks of mature Romney sheep repeatedly through narrow fenced plots of pasture at different stages of plant growth, levels of soil moisture, and so on. Although his method concentrates the treading normally received over a period of time into a single day, the observations on plant regrowth after treading leave no doubt as to the importance of this factor. Treading was noted to reduce herbage yields in considerable degree by reduced plant vigor and fewer tillers in the trodden areas. Although the damage was greatest when the soil was moist and treading intensity high, some damage was noted under dry soil conditions. Mentioned among the direct effects of treading on the plant were root damage, plant displacement, burial in the mud, and crushing and bruising of leaves and stems.

References

Aspinall, D. (1961). The control of tillering in the barley plant. I. The pattern of tillering and its relation to nutrient supply. *Aust. J. Biol. Sci.* **14**, 493–505.

Aspinall, D. and Paleg, L. G. (1964). Effects of daylength and light intensity on growth of barley. III. Vegetative development. *Aust. J. Biol. Sci.* **17**, 807–822.

Aspinall, D. Nicholls, P. B., and May, L. H. (1964). The effect of soil moisture stress on the growth of barley. I. Vegetative development and grain yield. *Aust. J. Agr. Res.* **15**, 729–745.

Auda, H., Blaser, R. E. and Brown, R. H. (1966). Tillering and carbohydrate contents of orchard grass as influenced by environmental factors. *Crop. Sci.* **6**, 139–143.

Davis, L. A., and Laude, H. M. (1964). The development of tillers in *Bromus mollis* L. *Crop Sci.* **4**, 477–480.

Edmond, D. B. (1958). The influence of treading on pasture a preliminary study. *N.Z. J. Agri. Res.* **1**, 319–328.

Edmond, D. B. (1962). Effects of treading pasture in summer under different soil moisture levels. *N.Z. J. Agri. Res.* **5**, 389–395.

Edmond, D. B. (1963). Effects of treading perennial ryegrass (*Lolium perenne* L.) and white clover (*Trifolium repens* L.) pastures in winter and summer at two soil moisture levels. *N.Z. J. Agri. Res.* **6**, 265–276.

Friend, D. J. C. (1965). Tillering and leaf production in wheat as affected by temperature and light intensity. *Can. J. Bot.* **43**, 1063–1076.

Kaukis, K., and Reitz, L. P. (1965). Tillering and yield of oat plants grown at different spacings. *Agron. J.* **47**, 147.

Ketellapper, H. J. (1960). The effect of soil temperature on the growth of *Phalaris tuberosa* L. *Physiol. Plant.* **13**, 641–647.

Lamp, H. F. (1952). Reproductive activity in *Bromus inermis* in relation to phases of tiller development. *Bot. Gaz.* **113**, 413–438.

Langer, R. H. M. (1958). A study of growth in swards of timothy and meadow fescue. I. Uninterrupted growth. *J. Agr. Sci.* **51**, 347–352.

Langer, R. H. M. (1959). Growth and nutrition of timothy (*Phleum pratense* L.) IV. The effect of nitrogen, phosphorus, and potassium supply on growth during the first year. *Ann. Appl. Biol.* **47**, 211–221.

Langer, R. H. M. (1963). Tillering in herbage grasses. *Herb. Abstr.* **33**, 141–148.

Langer, R. H. M., Ryle, S. M. and Jewiss, O. R. (1964). The changing plant and tiller populations of timothy and meadow fescue swards. I. Plant survival and the pattern of tillering. *J. Appl. Ecol.* **1**, 197–208.

Laude, H. M., Ridley, J. R., and Suneson, C. A. (1967). Tiller senescence and grain development in barley. *Crop Sci.* **7**, 231–233.

Laude, H. M., Riveros, G., Murphy, A. H., and Fox, R. E. (1968). Tillering at the reproductive stage in Hardinggrass. *J. Range Manage.* **21**, 148–151.

Mitchell, K. J. (1953a). Influence of light and temperature on the growth of ryegrass (*Lolium* spp.). I. Pattern of vegetative development. *Physiol. Plant* **6**, 21–46.

Mitchell, K. J. (1953b). Influence of light and temperature on the growth of ryegrass. *Lolium* spp.). II. The control of lateral bud development. *Physiol. Plant.* **6**, 425–443.

Mitchell, K. J. (1956). Growth of pasture species under controlled environment. I. Growth at various levels of constant temperature. *N.Z. J. Sci. Technol., Sect. A* **38**, 203–216.

Mitchell, K. J., and Coles, S. T. J. (1955). Effects of defoliation and shading on short-rotation ryegrass. *N.Z. J. Sci. Technol., Sect. A.* **36**, 586–604.

Mitchell, K. J., and Lucanus, R. (1960). Growth of pasture species under controlled environment. II. Growth at low temperatures. *N.Z. J. Agr. Res.* **3**, 647–655.

Nittler, L. W., Kenny, T. J., and Osborne, E. (1963). Response of seedlings of varieties of orchardgrass, *Dactylis glomerata* L., to photoperiod, light intensity, and temperature. *Crop Sci.* **3**, 125–128.

Pritchett, W. L. and Nelson, L. B. (1951). The effect of light intensity on the growth characteristics of alfalfa and bromegrass. *Agron. J.* **43**, 172–177.

Riveros, G. (1968). Tiller senescence in relation to the reproductive stage in barley. Ph.D. Thesis, University of California, Davis.

Ryle, G. J. A. (1964). A comparsion of leaf and tiller growth in seven perennial grasses as influenced by nitrogen and temperature. *J. Brit. Grassland Soc.* **19**, 281–290.

Ryle, G. J. A. (1966a). Effects of photoperiod in the glasshouse on the growth of leaves and tillers in three perennial grasses. *Ann. Appl. Biol.* **57**, 257–268.

Ryle, G. J. A. (1966b). Effects of photoperiod in growth cabinets on the growth of leaves and tillers in three perennial grasses. *Ann. Appl. Biol.* **57**, 269–279.

Shen, T. C., and Harrison, C. M. (1965). Tillering of sudangrass (*Sorghum vulgare* var. *sudanense*, Hitch.) with special attention to the effects of ridging. *Agron. J.* **57**, 437–441.

Taylor, T. H., and Templeton, W. C., Jr. (1966). Tiller and leaf behavior of orchardgrass (*Dactylis glomerata* L.) in a broadcast planting. *Agron. J.* **58**, 189–192.

Templeton, W. C., Mott, G. O., and Bula, R. J. (1961). Some effects of temperature and light on growth and flowering of tall fescue *Festuca arundinacea* Schreb. I. Vegetative development. *Crop Sci.* **1**, 216–219.

Chapter 12

The Microclimate of Grass Communities

O. T. DENMEAD

The most striking feature of the climate within a community of grass plants is the extent to which it differs from the climate of a weather screen mounted just above it. This difference has for many years intrigued meteorologists and biologists alike. Within the community, gradients (that is, changes with height) for most entities are usually tens and sometimes thousands of times the corresponding gradients at screen height in the free atmosphere, and for some entities such as temperature, there can be a reversal in the sign of the gradient within a few centimeters. Meteorologists have been interested in the physics of the transfer processes that contribute to the development of these profile characteristics, whereas biologists have been concerned with the consequences of climatic differences within the community for such phenomena as evaporation and photosynthesis by plants, tillering by grasses, the temperatures attained by plant parts, and the development and survival of plant pathogens and insects.

Many observations of climatic modification within plant communities have been published. The well-known text of Geiger (1965), for instance, collates hundres of such studies. Typical examples of what is to be found in dense, well-watered, actively growing crops are shown in Fig. 1. The irrigated wheat crop in which the observations were made was 81 cm tall and had a leaf area index of 3.2. Figures 1a and 1b show the changes in temperature T

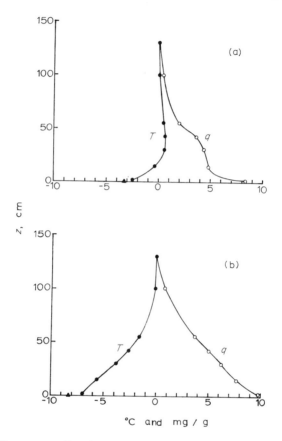

Fig. 1. (a) Temperature T and specific humidity q above and within the canopy of a wheat crop 81 cm tall at Deniliquin, Australia, at 1100 on Oct. 16, 1968. At a height of 130 cm, T was 26.6°C and q was 5.7 mg/g. (b) T and q at 1600 on the same day. At 130 cm, T was 30.6°C and q was 4.9 mg/g. Triangles and temperatures of the ground surface.

and specific humidity q in the canopy at two times of day, 1100 and 1600. A feature common to both occasions is the very large change in humidity. At 1600, for instance, the specific humidity near the ground was three times that at screen level. The temperature distributions exhibit different characteristics. In the observations at 1100 we see the development of a "hotspot" near midcanopy, about 1°C warmer than the air at screen height, and a minimum at the ground surface about 3.5°C less than screen temperature, at 1600 the temperature decreased all the way to the ground reaching a mininum about 8°C less than screen temperature at the ground surface.

The main emphasis of this chapter will be to describe the physics of the development of the canopy microclimate, concentrating particularly on the exchange of energy and its influence on the distributions of temperature and humidity, and to outline a model analysis that attempts to relate the microclimate of the grass canopy to the "screen" climate above it.

Transfer Processes in the Air within the Canopy

The Energy Balance

The main influences of the physical environment on the canopy microclimate are the net input of radiant energy to the community, the extent of mechanical mixing in the air (typified by a height-dependent turbulent or eddy diffusivity), and the supply of soil water both to the plants and at the ground surface.

It is convenient at this point to introduce the energy balance which, through the conservation of energy, relates the net input of energy to the community to the energy loss. The main source of energy for the community is short-wave and long-wave radiation from the sun and the sky. Some of this energy is reflected from the community and some is reradiated to space. The balance is referred to as the "net radiation" and will be designated R.

The chief means of energy dissipation are by evaporation and sensible heat loss (by free and forced convection). The flux density of water vapor (mass of water vapor transported through unit cross-sectional area in the atmosphere in unit time) will be designated as E, and that of sensible heat as H.

Some heat energy is also stored in the community in the vegetation and the ground. In most agricultural crops changes in the heat storage in the vegetation are small and they are neglected in the treatment that follows. The main change in heat storage occurs in the ground. The flux density of heat across the ground surface will be called G. Another sink for short-wave solar energy is fixation as chemical energy in photosynthesis. This too will be ignored because of its (normally) small magnitude in the energy balance—not because of its unimportance to plant growth.

Thus we can write

$$R(z) = LE(z) + H(z) + G \tag{1}$$

In Eq. (1) L is the latent heat of vaporization of water; z denotes height above the ground surface, and the z notation in the equation implies that the energy balance equation is taken to hold at all heights within the canopy.

Net Radiation during Daylight Hours

Net radiation normally decreases with depth in the canopies of crops. The main radiation component of the net radiation is the short-wave radiation from the sun. Measurements have shown that this direct component decreases approximately logarithmically with leaf area index in the canopy and it is not surprising that net radiation exhibits the same trend (Denmead *et al.*, 1962; Allen *et al.*, 1964; Denmead, 1968). Thermal effects resulting from uneven temperature distributions in the canopy can produce important deviations, however, and prediction of the net radiation profile is not a simple task.

Figures 2a and 2b show the change of net radiation with height in the canopy of our example wheat crop. Figure 3 shows the distribution throughout the day of solar and net radiation above the same crop and the distribution of net radiation at three heights within it. It can be seen that whereas the net radiation above the crop is more or less symmetrical about midday, following the course of solar radiation, net radiation within the crop shows a dip in the afternoon. There are also important shifts in the time at which the

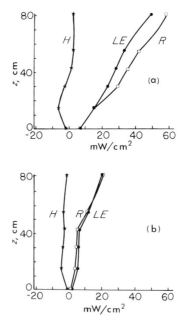

FIG. 2. (a) Measurements of net radiation (R) and calculations of the vertical flux densities of sensible heat (H) and latent heat (LE) in the wheat crop of Fig. 1 at 1100 on Oct. 16, 1968. (b) At 1600 on Oct. 16, 1968.

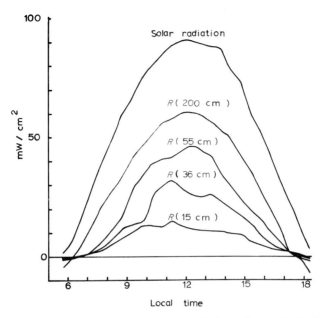

FIG. 3. Distribution throughout the day of solar radiation and net radiation R above and within the canopy of the wheat crop of Fig. 1 on Oct. 16, 1968.

maximum net radiation is reached; the maximum occurs earlier as the ground surface is approached. These phenomena appear to be due to differences in the course of the temperature changes at the ground surface and in the foliage. Ground surface temperature is normally out of phase with foliage temperature; in this instance it was 4°C or 5°C less than the temperature of the foliage immediately above it in the forenoon. In the afternoon, ground surface temperature was only 2°C to 3°C less than that of the foliage and exceeded it just prior to sundown.

GROUND HEAT FLUX AND THE GROUND SURFACE TEMPERATURE

The flux density of heat at the ground surface is determined in the first instance by the net radiation at the ground surface and the soil thermal properties but depends also on the transfers of heat and water vapor at the surface.

The soil thermal properties of importance are the conductivity λ and the volumetric heat capacity C. Both λ and C are functions of soil water content and for a particular soil increase with increasing soil moisture. Heat flow in soil has been fully discussed by van Wijk (1963), and therefore is not pursued here. One consequence of importance for the canopy microclimate is that the ground surface temperature is related to the ground heat flux via the soil thermal properties, so that other things being equal, as the soil dries and λ and C decrease, the ground surface temperature will exhibit more extreme values—that is, a higher maximum and a lower minimum. [The amplitude of the variation of surface temperature about its mean value is inversely proportional to $(\lambda C)^{\frac{1}{2}}$.]

As an example of the range in temperature, Fig. 4 shows observations of ground heat flux and ground surface temperature (the latter made with an infrared thermometer) under the wheat crop on our example day. The surface was "wet" following a heavy irrigation four days previously. Despite the fact that the ground was shaded by the dense wheat crop above it, the prediction Fourier curve fitted to the observations indicates a range from 10°C to 25°C, which is not much less than the range recorded at screen height. An interesting feature of the observations is that the maximum surface temperature occurred about 1445, whereas maximum heat flux into the ground occurred about midday. On the fitted curve, the minimum temperature is at 0600, sunrise.

EVAPORATION AND THE HUMIDITY PROFILE

For most of the daylight hours, when the ground surface is "wet," there will be evaporation from the soil and the flux density of water vapor will increase with height in the canopy due to transpiration from the foliage. The amount of water vapor transported through a unit horizontal area at z in unit

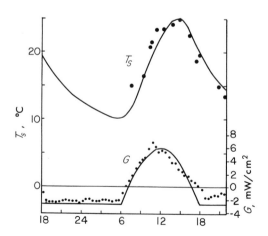

FIG. 4. Observations of ground heat flux density G and ground surface temperature T_s below the wheat crop of Fig. 1 on Oct. 16, 1968.

time will be proportional to the change in water vapor concentration with height. Formally we can write

$$LE(z) = -\rho LK(z)(\partial q/\partial z) \qquad (2)$$

in which ρ is the density of air and K is the turbulent diffusivity. If the flux of water vapor is upward, the gradient of water vapor concentration will be negative; that is, the specific humidity will decrease with height above the soil surface. The magnitude of the humidity change will depend on the extent of mixing in the air in the canopy and so on the magnitude of K and on the strength of the evaporation sources.

In the examples given in Figs. 1 and 2 there is some evaporation from the soil surface, and the flux density of water vapor increases with height due to transpiration. Associated with the transport of water vapor are marked changes in humidity in the canopy.

As indicated earlier the magnitude of the turbulent diffusivity reflects the extent of turbulent mixing and so depends on the wind speed, the aerodynamic roughness of the foliage surfaces in the canopy, and the temperature distribution. On days of high wind speed, K will be large and changes in humidity in the canopy will be relatively small. On calm days, K will be small and changes in humidity will be large. An example of the effect of the magnitude of K on the humidity profile can be seen by comparing the flux densities of water vapor and the humidity gradients in Figs. 1 and 2. At 1600, diffusivities in and above the canopy were less than half those at 1100. Although the amounts of water vapor transported were less at 1600 than at 1100, the humidity gradient was much steeper.

It was indicated earlier that the diffusivity is a function of height. The dependence of K on height within the canopy results from changes in the scale of turbulence as the ground and foliage surfaces are approached, from the absorption of momentum by the foliage, and from uneven temperature distributions. As a rough approximation, K appears to increase approximately logarithmically with height in the canopy.

This description of transfer processes in the canopy has been simplified necessarily. The whole question of the mechanism of transport in the air layers occupied by vegetation is one that is receiving a lot of attention in current research. Its solution will require detailed studies of the structure of turbulence and the associated fluctuations in the concentrations of the transported entities. Further discussion here would be outside the scope of this paper. The subject has been reviewed recently by Lemon (1969).

SENSIBLE HEAT FLUX AND THE TEMPERATURE PROFILE

Following Eq. (2) we can relate the flux density of sensible heat to the temperature gradient,

$$H(z) = -\rho c_p K(z)(\partial T/\partial z) \tag{3}$$

in which c_p is the specific heat of air at constant pressure.

Returning to Figs. 1 and 2, it can be seen in the observations of 11 00 that the heat flux above the "hotspot" is positive (upward) and associated with this is a negative temperature gradient. Below the "hotspot" the heat flux is negative (downward) and this is associated with a positive temperature gradient. The effect of the low diffusivities at 1600 can be seen again in the fact that the temperature gradients are much larger than at 1100, although the amounts of heat transported are generally smaller.

The temperature inversion and the downward movement of sensible heat in the lower part of the canopy are particularly interesting phenomena and have been observed frequently in the canopies of well-watered crops (Denmead, 1964, 1968; Brown and Covey, 1966). This transported heat augments the energy available for evaporation by radiation alone and results in a smoothing of the evaporation load through the canopy. The matter will be discussed further in a later section of the chapter.

LINKING THE TEMPERATURE AND HUMIDITY FIELDS

Returning to the energy balance equation (1) we can substitute for $H(z)$ and $LE(z)$ in terms of Eq. (2) and (3) to give

$$R(z) - G = -\rho c_p K(z) \left[(\partial T/\partial z) + (L/c_p)(\partial q/\partial z) \right] \tag{4}$$

It is convenient to work in terms of the equivalent temperature $\theta \ (= T + Lq/c_p)$. Equation (4) then becomes

$$R(z) - G = -\rho c_p K(z)(\partial \theta/\partial z) \tag{5}$$

As pointed out by Philip (1964), this equation provides a means of relating the temperature and humidity at any height in the canopy to the temperature and humidity at a given reference level. Equation (5) can be integrated to yield

$$\int_{z_1}^{z_2} \frac{R(z) - G}{\rho c_p K(z)} = \theta_1 - \theta_2 \tag{6}$$

Thus if we know the temperature and humidity at the top of the canopy and the ways in which R and K change with height, we can predict the equivalent

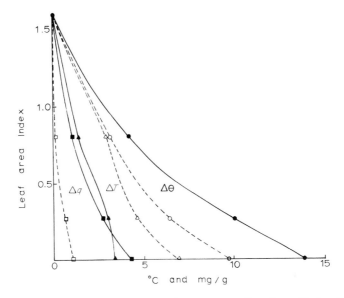

FIG. 5. Changes in equivalent temperature θ, temperature T, and specific humidity q in the canopy of wheat crop of leaf area index 1.6 when the soil surface was "wet" (unbroken lines) and "dry" (dashed lines) [From Denmead (1968)].

temperature distribution within the canopy. The problem still remains to deduce the magnitude of either $T(z)$ or $q(z)$ independently. At the moment it can be pointed out that for given distributions of R and K, the magnitudes of the temperature and humidity changes will depend on the supply of soil water to the canopy as a whole. This is brought out in Fig. 5, from Denmead (1968), which shows changes in θ, T, and q in the canopy of a wheat crop (a different crop from that of Fig. 1) on two occasions when R, G, and K were fairly similar. On one occasion the soil surface was wet and the plants had a plentiful supply of water, and on the other the supply of soil water to both the ground surface and the plants was restricted. We see that changes in the equivalent temperature were about the same on both days, but when the soil was dry, the canopy environment was much hotter and drier.

Transfers at Leaf Surfaces

RADIATION ON THE LEAF

Rewriting Eq. (1) for a leaf in the canopy, we have

$$R_l = H_l + LE_l \tag{7}$$

where the subscript l indicates that the various terms are the fluxes of radiation, heat, and water vapor per unit area of leaf surface.

As for the canopy, the net radiation at leaf surfaces depends on the receipt and reflection of direct and diffuse short-wave radiant energy from the sun and sky, the receipt of long-wave radiation from the sky and the surroundings, and the emission of long-wave radiation from the leaf. Obviously, calculation of the net radiation on an average leaf in the canopy is a difficult problem in geometrical probability. Among other things, it requires a detailed knowledge of canopy structure including leaf area, leaf angle, and leaf orientation; the emissivities and temperatures of the radiating surfaces; and the short- and long-wave radiation from the sun and sky. The subject will not be pursued here. As an indication of the effects of leaf orientation and leaf angle on just one component of the leaf's radiation balance, namely, the receipt of direct sunlight, we refer to Figs. 6 and 7 which are based on the theory of Anderson and Denmead (1969). Figure 6 shows the ratio of the flux density of direct radiation on inclined leaf surfaces to the flux density

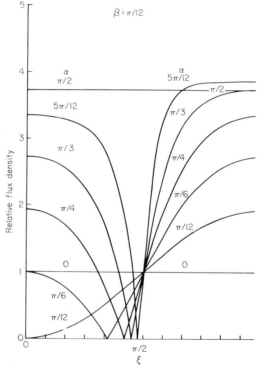

FIG. 6. Ratio of the flux density of direct solar radiation on the surface of leaves to the flux density on a horizontal surface as a function of leaf inclination α and the leaf's orientation with respect to the sun ξ. Calculations for a solar attitude β of 15°.

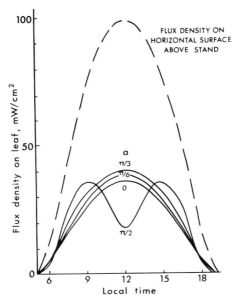

FIG. 7. Distribution throughout the day of the average flux density of direct solar radiation on the surfaces of leaves of different inclination α. Calculations for a leaf area index of 1 and solar altitudes for mid-summer (December 22) at a latitude of 35°S.

on a horizontal surface as leaf orientation changes with respect to the sun. The calculations are for a somewhat extreme case, one in which the solar attitude is only 15°, but they illustrate the point in an exaggerated way. The radiation received by the leaf can be quite different from that on a horizontal surface and changes markedly with the orientation of the leaf.

Figure 7 shows the *average* receipt of direct radiation on leaves in a canopy with a leaf area index of 1. The averaging procedure assumed that the leaves were random in their orientation. In the *average* there are only relatively small differences between canopies of different leaf angle in the flux density of the radiation on the leaves (except for vertical leaves which show a two-peaked distribution throughout the day and a pronounced dip at midday). It will be noticed also that for all leaf angles, with the exception of vertical leaves, the flux density of direct radiation does not change much between 0800 and 1600, that is, for most of the sunlit hours.

TRANSFERS OF SENSIBLE AND LATENT HEAT AND LEAF TEMPERATURE

In considering the transfers of sensible and latent heat at a leaf surface it is convenient to use the electrical analogue,

$$\text{flux} = \text{potential difference/resistance}$$

For sensible heat transfer

$$H_l = \frac{\rho c_p (T_l - T)}{r_a} \qquad (8)$$

where T_l and T are the temperatures of the leaf and the air, respectively, and r_a is an equivalent resistance to transfer between the leaf surface and its surroundings caused by a relatively calm layer of air close to the leaf surface. The magnitude of r_a will depend on such factors as wind speed about the leaf, leaf dimensions, and typical distances between leaves.

For water vapor, transfer is over a path of larger resistance. The vapor must first diffuse through the stomatal cavities and pores (and/or through the leaf cuticle) before it moves away from the leaf surface. Thus

$$LE = \frac{\rho L (q_l - q)}{(r_l + r_a)} \qquad (9)$$

where q_l is the specific humidity at the surfaces of the evaporating cells within the leaf, which we will assume equal to the saturation specific humidity at the leaf temperature T_l, and r_l is the additional resistance associated with the diffusion of water vapor to the leaf surface.

The resistance r_l depends in the first instance on the numbers, shape, and disposition of stomata but it also changes with the age of the leaf and with environmental and physiological factors that affect stomatal aperture. These latter include light intensity, carbon dioxide concentration, and the state of leaf turgor. Maintenance of turgor depends on the ability of the soil and the plant's water-conducting system to supply water to the leaf at a rate fast enough to balance the water lost by transpiration. If the supply rate is insufficient, turgor is lost, stomata close, r_l increases, and transpiration is reduced.

Substitution from Eq. (8) and (9) into Eq. (7) leads to an expression for leaf temperature for a given environment and leaf resistance. The difference in temperature between leaf and air is given by

$$T_l - T = \frac{R_l (r_a + r_l)/\rho L - \delta}{c_p (r_a + r_l)/r_a L + \Delta} \qquad (10)$$

where δ is the specific humidity deficit, that is, $q_{sat}(T) - q$, and Δ is the slope of the curve relating saturation specific humidity to temperature. From Eq. (10) it can be seen that for R_l positive, the leaf can be hotter or cooler than its surroundings depending among other things on the radiation load and the dryness of the air to which the leaf is exposed.

To provide an indication of the range of leaf temperatures likely to be encountered in the field, solutions to Eq. (10) are shown in Fig. 8 from

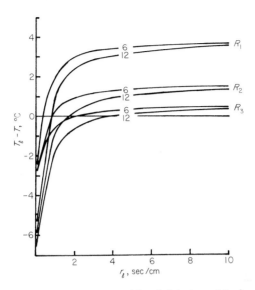

FIG. 8. Effects of radiation load R_l, humidity deficit δ, and leaf resistance r_l on the temperature difference between a leaf and its surroundings $(T_l - T)$. Calculations for R_l of 48,21 and 8 mW/cm^2 (R_1, R_2, and R_3 respectively); δ of 6 and 12 mg/g; T of 28°C; and r_a of 0.1 sec/cm.

Denmead (1968) for various combinations of r_l, R_l, and δ. The values chosen for R_l and δ cover a range representative of many field conditions and the resulting temperature differences are also representative of values reported in the literature. For well-watered corps the leaves are likely to be within 2°C or 3°C of the temperature of their surroundings at most times of day. When the leaf resistance is small, the humidity of the air has a strong influence on whether the leaf is hotter or cooler than the air about it. As stomata close and r_l increases, the humidity of the air has only a weak influence on leaf temperature. When stomata are fully closed, leaf temperatures will rise by a maximum of about 4°C.

Finally, in this connection it is relevant to point out that the lethal effects of plant water stress can often be attributed simply to the attainment of high leaf temperatures. An increase in leaf temperature of 4°C or 5°C above ambient temperature on hot days could kill the leaf. The same remarks apply to possible damage to plants from the use of transpiration suppressants. It is probably undesirable to have them fully effective.

Energy Exchange at the Ground Surface

It was pointed out previously that the wetness of the soil surface has an important moderating influence on the microclimate of the stand. A wet soil surface constitutes a strong heat sink. Associated with the transport of sensible heat to it are marked decreases in temperature and increases in humidity in the bottom of the canopy (see Fig. 1).

The magnitude of the sink strength can be seen in Fig. 9 which shows the net radiation, ground heat flux, and calculations of the sensible and latent heat flux densities at the ground surface in the example wheat crop of Fig. 1. [Sensible and latent heat-flux densities were calculated by the methods described by Denmead (1964, 1968).] The gain of sensible heat at the ground was frequently of the same magnitude as the net radiation so that latent heat consumption was considerably in excess of the available radiant energy for most of the daylight hours. Evaporation from the ground at this time was, in fact, some 17% of the total water loss by the crop.

When the soil surface is dry, evaporation is, of course, negligible and the sensible heat flux at the ground is positive. The return of this heat to the canopy makes for a hotter and drier environment for the foliage than in the case of a wet soil surface (see Fig. 5).

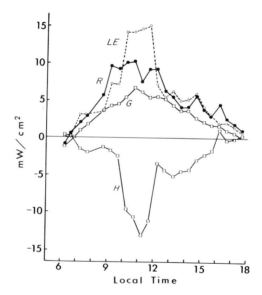

FIG. 9. Energy exchange at the ground surface under the wheat crop of Fig. 1 on Oct. 16, 1968. *R* is net radiation; *G* is ground heat flux density; *LE* is latent heat consumption; and *H* is sensible heat exchange.

Modeling the Microclimate

An important activity in micrometeorological research in recent years has been the development of models whose objective is to link the microclimate within the canopy to relatively simple observations of the climate at screen height Contributions to this field include those of Philip (1964), Waggoner and Reifsnyder (1968), Cowan (1968), and Denmead (1968). Although these analyses differ in some aspects, they all rely on the same basic approach—the energy balance. The formal, physical framework for the modeling process has been outlined in the previous sections.

The energy exchanges at leaf surfaces, Eqs. (7), (8), and (9), can be related to the vertical transfers of heat and water vapor in the bulk air, Eqs. (2), (3), and (6) by the relationships,

$$\frac{dH}{dA} = H_l \tag{11}$$

$$\frac{dE}{dA} = E_l \tag{12}$$

Where A is leaf area index cumulated from the ground. Substitution for H and H_l in Eq. (11) and for E and E_l in Eq. (12) leads to two second-order, differential equations in T and q, viz.,

$$\frac{d}{dz}\left(K\frac{dT}{dz}\right) + \left(\frac{T_l - T}{r_a}\right)\frac{dA}{dz} = 0 \tag{13}$$

and

$$\frac{d}{dz}\left(K\frac{dq}{dz}\right) + \left(\frac{q_l - q}{r_a + r_l}\right)\frac{dA}{dz} = 0 \tag{14}$$

Besides T and q, the other unknown is T_l (which also determines q_l). Equation (6), which links the changes in T and q with the absorption of net radiation and the transport of heat, forms the third equation to the set. Simultaneous solution of Eqs. (13), (14), and (6), with appropriate boundary conditions, yields the profiles of T, q, and T_l in the canopy. From these follow the leaf exchanges of heat and water vapor, Eqs. (8) and (9), and the vertical flux densities, Eqs. (2) and (3). The boundary conditions will usually be a specification of T, q, R, and K (or equivalent parameters) at screen height and conditions on the wetness of the soil surface.

Although the models contain some empiricism, mainly in the specification of r_a and the assumptions of steady-state conditions and one-dimensionality in the transfer processes, they provide a rational, physical basis for extrapolating from screen measurements to the climate within the canopy. Thus they should prove useful in a number of fields such as forecasting the occurrence of extreme climatic conditions in the canopy or climatic conditions favorable for insect or disease development, and predicting the effects of both weather and agronomic practices on evaporation and the energy balance of plant communities.

References

Allen, L. H., Yocum, C. S., and Lemon, E. R. (1964). Photosynthesis under field conditions. VII. Radiant energy exchanges within a corn crop canopy and implications in water use efficiency. *Agron. J.* **56**, 253–259.

Anderson, M. C., and Denmead, O. T. (1969). Short wave radiation on inclined surfaces in model plant communities. *Agron. J.* **61**, 867–872.

Brown, K. W., and Covey, W. (1966). The energy-budget evaluation of the micro-meteorological transfer processes within a cornfield. *Agr. Meteorol.* **3**, 73–96.

Cowan, I. R. (1968). Mass, heat and momentum exchange between stands of plants and their atmospheric environment. *Quart. J. Roy. Meteorol. Soc.* **94**, 523–544.

Denmead, O. T. (1964). Evaporation sources and apparent diffusivities in a forest canopy. *J. Appl. Meteorol.* **3**, 383–389.

Denmead, O. T. (1968). The energy balance of plant communities. *In* "Agricultural Meteorology," Proc. WMO Seminar, p. 71, Bur. Meteorol., Melbourne, Australia.

Denmead, O. T., Fritschen, L. J., and Shaw, R. H. (1962). Spatial distribution of net radiation in a cornfield. *Agron. J.* **54**, 505–510.

Geiger, R. (1965). "The Climate Near the Ground." Harvard Univ. Press, Cambridge, Massachusetts.

Lemon, E. (1969). Gaseous exchange in crop stands. *In* "Physiological Aspects of Crop Yield" (J. D. Eastin *et al.*, eds.), p. 117, Amer. Soc. Agron., Madison, Wisconsin.

Philip, J. R. (1964). Sources and transfer processes in the air layers occupied by vegetation. *J. Appl. Meteorol.* **3**, 390–395.

Waggoner, P. E., and Reifsnyder, W. E. (1968). Simulation of the temperature, humidity and evaporation profiles in a leaf canopy. *J. Appl. Meteorol.* **7**, 400–409.

van Wijk, W. R. (1963). "Physics of Plant Environment." North-Holland Publ. Amsterdam.

Chapter 13

The Turfgrass Community as an Environment for the Development of Facultative Fungal Parasites

R. M. ENDO

Monteith and Dahl (1932) established *Rhizoctonia solani* as the cause of brown patch of bluegrass in 1914. Since then over a hundred fungal pathogens have been identified (Couch, 1962; Howard, 1951) and considerable information has accumulated on the influence of environmental factors such as temperature, pH, soil moisture, and soil fertility on fungal growth and disease development and on control measures based on fungicides and host resistance.

Very little information is available on the interactions that occur between turfgrass plants, fungal parasites, and the varied flora and fauna of the turfgrass community. This is surprising since turfgrass communities possess a unique surface litter consisting of decomposing grass residues that provide an abundant and continuous source of nutrients for the flora and fauna. Whether the activity and survival of fungal pathogens in the litter and soil are suppressed or enhanced by the flora and fauna is determined by numerous interacting abiotic and biotic factors. Very little is known also about the changes in disease resistance that accompany aging and those that are caused by environmental factors, by turf management practices, and by athletic activities.

Erratic Occurrence of Some Turfgrass Diseases

Diseases of most crops worsen with continued monoculture since pathogen populations tend to increase. Turfgrass diseases caused by facultative fungal parasites occur annually but their incidence and severity varies greatly from year to year, and from location to location, bearing little relationship to the age of the planting. The erratic occurrence of disease is attested to by the limited areas that are diseased even under the most favorable conditions, and by the frequent failure of fungicide evaluation trials. In these trials the most susceptible varieties are planted and watering practices are altered to favor disease development. The frequent failure of disease to develop is difficult to explain since even a small lawn consists of millions of ground-hugging plants of similar genotype and disease reaction; the crowded planting and surface litter favor the high humidity and even temperatures required for growth and rapid plant-to-plant spread of the fungal pathogens; and the population of fungal pathogens apparently increase yearly. Turfgrass pathologists rely on natural disease development because most attempts to artificially induce epiphytotics have failed. The factors responsible for this failure and the erratic development of disease are probably biological in origin.

Obligate parasites have evolved life cycles that tend to isolate them from competition. Facultative parasites of turfgrass, on the other hand, are constantly being exposed in the following ways to antagonism and competition from the flora and fauna and therefore are subject to biological influences throughout their lifetime.

(1) The dense plantings and the short, prostrate growth habit place the aerial portions of the plants in contact or in proximity to the microbiologically active surface litter and soil.

(2) The plants are constantly being exposed to microorganisms by means of foot traffic, by maintenance practices such as mowing, fertilization, and irrigation and by the varied activities of the macrofauna such as earthworms, nematodes, birds, and insects.

(3) The grass clippings and the death of lower leaves, stolons, rhizomes, roots, and tillers form the surface litter which is composed of fresh and decaying grass debris in various stages of decomposition. The constant addition of fresh clippings to the litter during the growing season constitutes an effective and continuing source of substrates for the litter-inhabiting microorganisms that actively compete with the fungal parasites for food. The amount of litter that accumulates apparently varies with the plant species, the climate, and other unknown factors. According to Beard (1970), the leaves decompose rapidly, but the lignin-containing plant fractions do not.

(4) Depending on the depth of the litter, a variable amount of the stems and roots will be covered by the biologically active litter.

(5) Because of the exteme root density, the nutrients diffusing from fresh grass clippings may influence the microorganisms of the rhizosphere as well as the litter-inhibiting microorganisms. Thus the total microbiological activity may be very high in the litter and soil and undoubtedly influences the activity and survival of parasitic fungi.

Competitive Saprophytic Ability (CSA)

Although facultative parasites colonize dead tissues as saprophytes, their ability to do so in competition with other microorganisms varies greatly. Of five species of root-infecting fungi that attack turfgrasses as well as cereals, three species—namely, *Fusarium culmorum (F. roseum)*(Sadasivan, 1939), *Pythium ultimum* (Garrett, 1956), and *Rhizoctonia solani* (Blair, 1943)—have been classed as vigorous competitive saprophytes of dead wheat stems; whereas *Helminthosporium sativum* (Butler, 1953 a,b) and *Ophiobolus graminis* (Garrett, 1956) were rated as weak competitive saprophytes. This distinction has proven useful because the competitive saprophytic ability (CSA) of facultative fungal parasites tends to be correlated with their level of pathogenicity, their tolerance to microbial competition, and their length of survival in dead infected tissues and in soil. The root-infecting fungi that are vigorous colonizers of dead host tissue are able to grow as mycelia in soil, but they are generally weak parasites that are restricted in their attacks to immature, wounded, weakened or senescent tissues. Garrett (1956) has referred to this group as saprophytes that occasionally function as parasites. With this group it is possible to obtain considerable disease control by accelerating the maturation of susceptible seedling tissues and by maintaining the vigor of adult plants.

On the other hand, root-infecting fungi that are unable to colonize host debris in competition with other microorganisms tend to be active as hyphae for only short periods in the soil and in infected host debris. They therefore survive in the dormant state as asexual spores, resistant survival structures, or as sexual spores. Some of these fungi are vigorous parasites that are able to cause disease of mature plants (for example, *Ophiobolus graminis*) but others are weak parasites, such as *Helminthosporium sativum* (Garrett, 1956). Most of the remaining facultative fungal parasites of turfgrass that attack the foliage and stems may possess low CSA and tend to be suppressed by the activities of saprophytic microorganisms (Menzies, 1963).

Turfgrass Diseases that Spread by Aerial Hyphae

The above-ground portions of turfgrass are commonly attacked by the hyphae of eight different species of facultative fungal parasites (*Pythium aphanidermatum, P. ultimum, R. solani, Sclerotinia homeocarpa, Corticium fuciforme, F. nivale, Typhula itoana*, and an unidentified sterile basidiomycete species). This clearly indicates that turfgrass plantings constitute an unusually favorable environment for the growth and development of aerial hyphae. Most species of plants are seldom attacked in this manner unless the plants are low growing, densely planted, and heavily canopied. Such conditions occur in any turfgrass planting where, along with the presence of surface litter, they favor the build-up of high humidities and the moderation of air temperatures. Favorable moisture relationships are necessary since most fungal hyphae require relative humidities around 98% (Cochrane, 1958) to prevent hyphal desiccation and temperatures near optimum for rapid hyphal growth.

The eight fungal parasites named above probably start out from centers of infection consisting of one or more infected plants that function as a food base. If temperature and moisture are favorable and nutrients are available, aerial hyphae may grow out rapidly in all directions and infect the above-ground organs of the crowded, uniformly susceptible plants. Since progressive disease development requires nutrients for continual hyphal growth, penetration and infection must follow closely upon the growth of hyphae over the host surfaces. Of the eight fungal species that spread over and infect the host by aerial hyphae, *R. solani* is one of the most successful. This may be related to its ability to translocate materials very rapidly through hyphae in either direction (Wilcoxson and Sudia, 1968), to its ability to cause rapid leakage of electrolytes and amino acids from infected bean tissues (Lai *et al.*, 1968) which may then be utilized for growth by the externally located hyphae, and to its ability to utilize nutrients from guttation water present on the leaf surfaces (Rowell, 1951). Kerr (1958) has shown that hyphae of *R. solani* are able to make extensive saprophytic growth below the turf canopy if a food base is provided by infected plants. Germinating sclerotia also serve as a food base (Menzies, 1963). Garrett (1956) lists the following four factors as being essential for CSA which are probably also essential for aerial growth of hyphae over the host surfaces: (1) very rapid spore germination and hyphal growth rate; (2) good enzyme-producing equipment; (3) production of antibiotics; and (4) tolerance of antibiotics produced by other microorganisms.

Probable Sources of Exogenous Nutrients

Since hyphal growth may be seen frequently on the external surfaces of turfgrass in the absence of apparent infection or an obvious food base, it seems reasonable to suspect that the presence of hyphae indicates the past or present distribution of exogenous substrates. The most likely sources of exogenous nutrients are the following: The first source is senescent tissue. When wet, senescent leaves tend to leak abundant nutrients (Tukey, 1970) which may provide the energy necessary to raise the inoculum potential of the infecting hyphae. Senescent leaves are readily infected and colonized because of their reduced resistance (Garrett, 1956). This has been demonstrated for *S. homeocarpa* attacking the senescent leaves of bentgrass (Endo, 1966) and for *H. sativum* attacking the senescent leaves of bluegrass (Endo, 1965). Following colonization of the senescent tissues, the fungus (for example, *S. homeocarpa* and *C. fuciforme*) may acquire sufficient energy from the food base to grow out of the tissue as hyphae and to infect healthy, vigorously growing leaves. *Sclerotinia homeocarpa* apparently functions in this way, but if host resistance is maintained at optimum levels, infection fails (Endo, 1966). Garrett (1956) has emphasized that if senescent tissues are infected by the primary parasite when resistance is still appreciable, competition from weak secondary parasites and saprophytes is greatly reduced and the parasite enjoys the advantage of being the initial colonizer. It is likely, however, that infection and colonization may fail if the senescent tissues are extensively precolonized by weak secondary parasites and saprophytes. The relation of senescent tissues to the development of turfgrass diseases requires intensive investigation.

The second possible source of exogenous nutrients that may stimulate the germination of dormant fungal structures and sustain the aerial growth of fungal hyphae is guttation fluid. Rowell (1951) first demonstrated that guttation fluid increased hyphal growth and infection of bentgrass by *R. solani*. Suryanarayanam (1958) found that glutamine in guttation fluid induced the germination of conidia of *Piricularia oryzae*, and that the glutamine content of guttation fluid of rice could be increased by nitrogen fertilization. Endo *et al.* (1964) demonstrated that some collections of bentgrass guttation fluid favored the germination, prepenetration, and penetration behavior of conidia of *H. sativum*. Healy and Britton (1968) demonstrated that bentgrass guttation fluid stimulated germ tube growth and infection by conidia of *H. sativum*, but glutamine at 0.01 *M* was more stimulatory than guttation fluid. Endo and Mudd (1970) found that bentgrass guttation fluid contained 780 mg of total solids/liter of which 2.4, 13.0, and 11.0 mg/liter, respectively, were amino acids, carbohydrates, and organic acids. According to Ivanoff (1963) guttation fluid appears to be a very dilute but complete nutrient medium for the growth of microorganisms. Further research is needed on the components of the fluid, the factors that influence its composition, and the ability of various resident microflora (Leben, 1965) that are present on the leaf surfaces to compete with parasites for the nutrients present in the fluid.

The third source of possible nutrients is the organic and inorganic constituents leached from leaves and stems by rain, irrigation water, dew, and mist. Tukey (1970) and associates have demonstrated that material leached include all of the inorganic materials found in plants, large quantities of carbohydrates, 21 amino acids, and 15 organic acids. They also have shown that young tissues leak less than mature tissues, that senescent tissues are very leaky, that wettable leaves leak much more than nonwettable leaves, and that low light intensities, high temperatures, wounding, and prolonged wetting greatly enhanced leaching. When nutrients fell to the soil, some were reabsorbed by the roots. This suggests that microorganisms in the soil and litter could also, on occasion, utilize leached nutrients. Tukey has shown that nutrients are leached from grasses, but the relative importance of this source of nutrients for turfgrass fungal pathogens has not been studied.

The fourth source of possible nutrients is grass clippings, which provides an abundant source of sugars, amino acids, and other readily soluble carbon compounds. Kerr (1958) demonstrated that fresh grass cuttings leaked nutrients that accelerated the growth of *R. solani* hyphae for four days, following which the hyphae lysed. Blair (1943) found that grass cuttings depressed the growth of the same fungus in natural soil.

The fifth possible source of exogenous nutrients is nutrients leaking from injured cells and tissues. Turf may be injured by a wide assortment of factors such as mowing; foot traffic; athletic activity; aerification; vertical mowing; the feeding activities of insects, snails, nematodes, moles, and so on; flooding; pesticides; high soil temperatures; drought; soil compaction; and toxins produced by plants, by the microflora, and by the macrofauna. Drought probably represents the ideal form of injury because (1) increased soil moisture suction inhibits the competing saprophytic bacteria much more than it inhibits the parasitic fungi (D. M. Griffin, 1969); (2) drought injures large areas of cortical root tissue (Russell, 1970); (3) drought probably injures the permeability of the cell membranes which results in the release of nutrients that may stimulate the germination of dormant fungal structure and the growth of hyphae; and (4) the lack of moisture which is needed for hyphal activity is usually applied shortly after the occurrence of drought.

Factors Affecting Fungal Activity

Numerous factors affect the activity of the facultative fungal parasites infecting turfgrasses: some such as nutrients, temperature, and moisture are well known but others such as grass clippings, mowing, soil compaction, and saprophytic microorganisms are not. In order to understand the factors that govern fungal activity, research should distinguish, whenever possible, between effects on spore germination, hyphal growth, infection structure formation (including thallus formation, appressoria formation, and infection peg formation), host penetration, and host colonization.

NUTRITION

Since all fungi and most microorganisms are heterotrophic, competition between microorganisms is mainly for substrates (Alexander, 1961). Saprophytic microorganisms as a tremendously large diverse group are better adapted to compete for nutrients than the small numbers of parasitic fungi and frequently pre-empt the available nutrients and the supply of available oxygen. Not all microorganisms compete for the same substrate, however, since different microorganisms are able to utilize different substrates such as sugars, proteins, cellulose, pectin, hemicellulose, and lignin. (Alexander, 1961.) The main nutritional requirements of parasitic fungi that are likely to be limiting and in short supply are carbon and nitrogen. Macroelements, microelements, growth factors, and vitamins are also required but these are usually obtained in sufficient quantity from the host, from the plant and animal debris, and from the soil solution.

The general nutritional level of the turf litter and soil for microorganisms is undoubtedly higher than in most crops since fresh plant materials are continually being added to the litter. Providing that nitrogen is not limiting, this probably results in a fairly constant, rather high level of microbiological activity. The C/N ratio of turf probably varies over a wider range of values than most crops because mowing may stimulate growth of tillers and stolons. This drain on available soil nitrogen is further aggravated by the immobilization of nitrogen by the saprophytic microorganisms that decompose the turf litter. As a result, soil nitrogen may change from an available to an unavailable state. Experiments on biological control of soil-borne diseases utilizing plant amendments reveal that pathogen activity may be sustained, stimulated, or inhibited depending on the amount of carbon and nitrogen available to the pathogen and to the competing microorganisms. The effects of the C/N ratio on the activity of four facultative fungal parasites show how proper management of the C/N ratio may lead to considerable biological suppression of plant diseases.

Fusarium solani f. phaseoli

The effects of the C/N ratio on *F. solani* (Snyder *et al.*, 1959) may also apply to the three species of *Fusarium* that attack turf. Substrates with C/N ratios above 60 increased survival of *F. solani* but did not favor its parasitic activities; although chlamydospore germination was stimulated and germ tubes formed, the germ tubes lysed without causing infection. Since the germ tubes formed additional chlamydospores before lysis occurred, the population of surviving chlamydospores increased. Substrates with C/N ratios between 20 to 40 contained nitrogen in excess of that required by the competing microorganisms and the excess nitrogen was utilized by the parasite for chlamydospore germination, for growth of hyphae through the rhizosphere, and for the formation of thalli that are required for host penetration (Schroth and Hildebrand, 1964). Disease development was severe under these conditions. The excess nitrogen required by the parasite could also be supplied by fertilization.

High nitrogen fertilization in the fall has been reported to increase the *Fusarium* pink patch disease of turfgrass caused by *F. nivale* during the winter. This has usually been attributed to an increase in host susceptibility (for example, Madison *et al.*, 1960; Goss and Gould, 1968), but the research of Snyder *et al.*, (1959) suggests that the high rate of exogenous nitrogen also favored the germination and parasitic activities of the fungus. The fact that nitrogen availability in soil is increased from two to three times with each 10°C drop in soil temperature (Stevenson, 1965) would also tend to favor the development of snow mold fungus in winter.

Rhizoctonia solani

Crop residues with C/N ratios above 40 tend to suppress the growth and parasitic activity of the bean strains of *R. solani* because the increased microbiological activity results in decreased nitrogen availability and an excess of respiratory carbon dioxide (Davey and Papavizas, 1963). Durbin (1959) has shown that clones of *Rhizoctonia* vary in their sensitivity to carbon dioxide. These findings confirm the earlier conclusions of Blair (1943) who first demonstrated that additions of either dry wheat or grass greatly inhibited the parasitic activities of the wheat strain of this fungus in soil. On the other hand, Papavizas and Davey demonstrated that residues with C/N ratios of less than 20 liberated nitrogen to stimulate the parasitic activity of *Rhizoctonia* hyphae. Weinhold (Weinhold *et al.*, 1969) has recently demonstrated that nitrogen increases the virulence of *Rhizoctonia* clones attacking bean.

The temporary growth suppression of *Rhizoctonia* by C/N amendments above 40 is interesting because the fungus is a soil inhabitant that grows readily through soil and readily colonizes host debris (Blair, 1943). Garrett (1963) suggests that since the primary substrate of the fungus is cellulose, it is temporarily suppressed by microorganisms that utilize the more readily available substrates. In the turfgrass community the effect of clippings on *Rhizoctonia* is unknown, but Kerr (1958) has shown that clippings stimulated growth for four days under laboratory conditions; lysis of hyphae occurred on the fifth day. Attacks of brown patch which sometimes follow overfertilization with nitrogen (Couch, 1962) may result because the excess nitrogen not only favors the parasitic activities of the fungus but also increases host susceptibility through increased succulence of the host (Viets, 1965; Burstrom, 1965).

Ophiobolus graminis

The take-all disease occurs on bentgrass turf in the Pacific northwest, but its occurrence and severity is associated with young plantings; older plantings develop less take-all (Goss, 1969). This may be related to the time required for the accumulation of an appreciable turf litter. Turf sod not only tends to be nitrogen deficient but may also favor the build-up by saprophytic microorganisms of respiratory carbon dioxide. In wheat each of these factors inhibit the survival and activity of hyphae which is the only known means of survival for the fungus. Garrett (1936, 1937, 1967) has shown that (1) the growth and parasitic activity of *O. graminis* hyphae over the root surface of wheat are inhibited by the respiratory carbon dioxide that is formed by the saprophytic microorganisms that decompose wheat debris; (2) that the survival of hyphae in infected host debris depends on a small but constant supply of available nitrogen to nourish the slow-growing hyphae; and that (3) the saprophytic microorganisms decomposing infected wheat debris low in nitrogen usually use up the available nitrogen that is necessary for the survival of *O. graminis* hyphae. The proper management of nitrogen fertilization in relation to the activity of saprophytic microorganisms and to the survival of *Ophiobolus* hyphae would probably also control the take-all disease in turf.

Pythium mammilatum

Although *P. mammilatum* does not occur on turf, the C/N relationships of this fungus probably also apply to the two turfgrass pathogens, *P. ultimum* and *P. aphanidermatum*. Utilizing substrates with different C/N ratios, Barton (1960) demonstrated that only the carbon content influenced saprophytic colonization. If the carbon content was too high, competition from other microorganisms decreased colonization. Success in saprophytic colonization of the carbon substrate depended primarily on the ability of *P. mammilatum* to outstrip its competitors due to its very rapid germination and mycelial growth rate. Sugars also apparently influence the parasitic activity of *Pythium*, because Agnihotri (1969) has demonstrated that sugars stimulate apparent appressoria formation, structures that are required for host penetration.

The fact that *P. aphanidermatum* and *P. ultimum* both attack the above ground portions of turfgrass plants is rather unusual because attacks of most plants by *Pythium* species are confined to the root apices (Mellano *et al.*, 1970). Examination of diseased plants reveals the abundant external development of hyphae on the leaf surfaces. This suggests a food base and/or that carbon is present as an energy source on the turfgrass foliage during periods of rapid disease spread by means of mycelia. The likely source of these sugars is guttation fluid or sugars leached from leaves into drops of water. It is also possible that excess nitrogen fertilization coupled with excess water and excess removal of foliage may result in the formation of thin cell walls that are very susceptible to infection.

Microorganisms

Little information is available on the nature of microflora that develop in and on the roots and aerial organs of turfgrass as they age and become senescent, and on the nature of microflora that develops in the litter, humus, and mineral horizons of the soil. Both beneficial and harmful interactions undoubtedly occur between the members of this flora and pathogenic fungi, but little is known of the participants and of the specific interactions that occur such as competition, predation, biological antagonisms, commensalism, protocooperation, and symbiosis. This is in part due to the lack of suitable techniques to identify the interactants and the basis of their interaction.

Waid (1957) studied the fungi developing on the decomposing cortex of ryegrass roots, and noted that 70% of the initial colonizers were sterile, dark mycelial forms and that *F. culmorum*, a weak facultative parasite, was the dominant secondary colonizer. Boosalis (1956) has shown that green manure amendments in unsterilized soil increased the parasitism of *R. solani* hyphae by the fungi, *Penicillium vermiculatum* and *Trichoderma* sp. Campbell (1956) demonstrated that the addition of *Epicoccum purpurescens* and *Phoma humicola* to unsterilized soil caused a slight reduction in the population of *H. sativum*.

Certain observations suggest that the saprophytic microflora may play a major role in influencing the incidence and severity of facultative fungal parasites that attack common grass hosts, including turfgrasses and cereals:

(1) Experiments (Endo, 1961) were made with ten fungal pathogens which caused more damage to turfgrasses grown in sterile than in normal soil. (2) Pathologists frequently have failed to induce turfgrass diseases in the field. (3) Sanford and Broadfoot (1931) demonstrated that infection of wheat by *O. graminis* in sterile soil was suppressed by each of 80 species of fungi or bacteria. (4) Henry (1932) demonstrated reduced infection of wheat by *O. graminis* over a narrower range of soil temperatures in nonsterile soil than in sterile soil and attributed this to the activity of saprophytic microorganisms. (5) Henry (1931) greatly decreased root infection of wheat seedlings by conidia of *H. sativum* following the addition of a minute quantity of non-sterile soil to sterile soil. (6) The parasitic activities of *R. solani* (Blair, 1943; Davey and Papavizas, 1963) and *O. graminis* (Garrett, 1956), affecting barley and wheat, respectively, were greatly suppressed by the indirect effects of the saprophytic microorganisms that colonized organic amendments of intermediate carbon–nitrogen ratios. Rangaswami and Vidhyasekaren (1966) attributed the failure of *H. sativum* to colonize the rhizosphere of corn to the presence of an antagonistic *Streptomyces* sp.

SOIL REACTION

Hydrogen ion concentration may exert favorable or harmful effects on fungal development by influencing fungal pathogens directly, or indirectly by changes brought about in the saprophytic flora. Most fungi develop over a wide range of hydrogen ion concentrations, usually from pH 4.0 to 9.0; whereas most bacteria develop best near neutrality, and most actinomycetes fail to develop below pH 5.0 (Alexander, 1961).

A few studies have been made on the influence of pH on fungal growth and disease development (Couch *et al.*, 1960, Moore *et al.*, 1963), but these have been carried out with sterile soil or sand. Therefore the differential effects of pH on the competing microflora could not be determined. Weindling and Fawcett (1936) demonstrated that *R. solani* is suppressed by *Trichoderma viride* in sterile soils of acid but not alkaline reaction, evidently because the antibiotic gliotoxin produced by *Trichoderma* is rapidly inactivated in alkaline soils.

Soil pH may regulate carbon dioxide concentrations in soil and thus regulate fungal behavior. Garrett (1937) noted a more extensive development of hyphae of *O. graminis* growing over the roots of wheat in alkaline than in acid soils. Since aeration of acid soils eliminated the inhibition, Garrett attributed inhibition to accumulation of respiratory carbon dioxide produced by the microorganisms, and the lack of inhibition in alkaline soils to the conversion of carbon dioxide to bicarbonate following absorption. Papavizas and Davey (1962) and Blair (1943) have noted this phenomenon in strains of *R. solani* attacking beans and wheat, respectively. Macauley and Griffin (1969) found that 3.5% carbon dioxide reduced mycelial growth of *H. sativum* in culture but attributed this to the bicarbonate ion because growth was affected most at high rather than at low pH values.

TEMPERATURE

It is well known that temperature regulates the rate of physiological and biological processes such as nutrient absorption, spore germination, mycelial growth, sporulation, and host penetration, and that fungi manifest different temperature optima.

When microorganisms compete for the same substrate, temperature helps to select those that are best adapted to multiply in the existing ecosystem; for example, Barton (1960) has demonstrated that *P. mammilatum* is an effective competitor for carbon substrates, primarily because of its rapid spore germination and mycelial growth rate. For turf parasites that spread from plant to plant by aerial hyphae, temperature exerts a very important direct influence because it determines the rate of hyphal growth, the mass of mycelia produced, its inoculum potential, and the amount of disease produced during a finite period of time; aerial temperature, near or at the optimum, obviously favors maximum infection and disease spread.

Fungal diseases with low-temperature optima probably develop in an environment of reduced competition from microorganisms; for example, *T. itoana*, *F. nivale*, and the unidentified, sterile low-temperature basidiomycete (Cormack, 1948) cause the so-called snow mold diseases, developing best below 40°F, and under snow cover. The absence of competition is probably also the determining factor in the low-temperature development of the melting-out diseases caused by *H. vagans* and *H. sativum*, as Burgess and Griffin (1968b) have demonstrated optimum saprophytic activity of *H. sativum* on wheat at soil temperature of 50°F and reduced activity above 50°F. Parasite development in the spring would be greatly favored in regions of fairly severe winters because microbiological activity would virtually cease and would begin slowly during wet, cold springs. On the other hand, *H. sativum* on wheat is also called "dryland foot rot" because it is more damaging during hot weather under dry than wet conditions. This may be similar to the behavior of *F. culmorum* which also causes a dryland foot rot of wheat during hot, dry weather, apparently because the fungus is much less sensitive to reduced moisture tension than the competing bacterial flora (R. J. Cook and Papendick, 1970). The classic demonstration of the indirect effect of temperatures on disease development is the suppression by soil microorganisms of *O. graminis*, the cause of the take-all disease of wheat at temperatures above 18°C; in sterile soil, the disease is severe from 12°C to 28°C (Henry, 1932).

Temperature also exerts a direct effect on the prepenetration activities of root-infecting fungi, but the influence is brief for fungi that are unable to grow through soil as hyphae; *H. sativum* appears to be a fungus of this type. Although the period from germination to infection is short, temperature effects are important because of the sensitivity of *Helminthosporium* to competition (Henry, 1931; Campbell, 1956; Old, 1967), antibiosis (Butler, 1953c; Gilliver, 1946; Simmonds, 1947), and host resistance (Butler, 1948). Ludwig (1957) has shown that conidia of *H. sativum* will seldom infect healthy roots of barley unless they are weakened by a toxin produced by the fungus, and Chinn (Chinn *et al.*, 1953; Chinn and Ledingham, 1961) has shown that conidial germ tubes in soil are readily lysed, apparently by bacteria.

MOISTURE

For sustained fungal activity above ground, either free water or relative humidities above 98% are required for hyphal growth (Cochrane, 1958). That high relative humidities are common in turf is attested to by the large number of facultative fungi that spread by hyphae over the host surfaces. Menzies (1967) concluded that sprinkler irrigation in humid areas increased foliage diseases more than it did in subarid areas because the period of high relative humidities and dew formation was increased more in the former than in the latter. The effect was the greatest in crops with low-growing, dense foliage, and where rains extended the wet period. These relationships probably also apply to foliage diseases of turf that are spread by spores such as gray leaf spot, copper spot, rust and the leaf spot stage of the various *Helminthosporium*-incited diseases. On the other hand, fungi that spread by aerial mycelia do not show a consistent relationship.

Water may exert both direct and indirect effects on the soil fungi, but the problem of soil water has not been adequately studied because of the difficulty of designing suitable experiments and interpreting the data. D. M. Griffin (1969) concluded that fungal growth occurs generally in soils varying from saturation to the permanent wilting point (75% relative humidity), and that some species may grow at relative humidities below 75%. The tolerance of many fungi to reduced relative humidity depends on both temperature and nutrition (D. M. Griffin, 1969) and on temperature and relative humidity (Chen and Griffin, 1966). Burgess and Griffin (1968a) demonstrated that the recovery of *Fusarium graminearum* from infested wheat stems lying on the soil surface at 35°C declined with each increase in relative

humidity from 32.5% to 100% which was attributed to increasing antagonistic activity of microorganisms.

Kerr (1964) concluded that the differences in percentage infection of pea
seedlings by *Pythium ultimum* with different soil moisture treatments resulted
from effects on the rate of diffusion of sugar from pea seeds. R. J. Cook and
Flentje (1967) demonstrated that chlamydospores of *F. solani* f. *phaseoli*
germinated at a moisture content as low as 8.7% if nitrogen and sugars were
present in soils. This fact could be extremely important in turf where fresh
grass clippings may be continually supplying the fungi with substrates. According to D. M. Griffin (1969), the rate of transfer of nonpolarized non-
ionized molecules in soil varies directly with its volumetric water content,
but the rate of transfer of polarized or ionized molecules does not because of
the presence of charged soil surfaces such as clay. Diffusion of exudates
according to Raney (1965) is determined by soil temperature, soil moisture
thickness, and moisture-film continuity. As Pentland (1967) has emphasized,
microhabitats may be more variable in a dry soil than in a wet soil because
there is less movement of water-soluble products in the dry soil.

Couch *et al.*, 1967) and associates (Muse and Couch, 1965; Couch and
Bloom, 1960) have conducted studies on the relation of cyclical water-suction
programs on various turfgrass diseases; that is, whenever the soil water content fell to predetermined suction values, water was added to restore each
treatment to field capacity. Although D. M. Griffin (1969) has emphasized
that cyclical programs are difficult to interpret because of changes in associated factors, such experiments are useful because they simulate field situations. These workers found that *S. homeocarpa* (Couch and Bloom, 1960),
and *Pythium ultimum* (Moore and Couch, 1963) caused increased disease
with increasing matric suction.

Foot rot of wheat caused by *F. roseum* is favored by dry surface soils. R. J.
Cook and Papendick (1970) have attributed this to the fact that the pathogen
escapes microbial antagonism because it can extract and utilize soil water
at higher moisture suctions than its antagonists. This may explain the observation of Bean (1969) who noted a correlation between the occurrence of
Fusarium blight of bluegrass with moisture stress. According to D. M. Griffin
(1969), there is some data available which suggest that bacterial and actinomycetes, which are the usual fungal antagonists, may become attenuated
at smaller moisture suctions than fungi, and that the number of bacteria, but
not fungi, may increase with increasing soil moisture.

The size and shape of soil particles influence the moisture characteristics
of the soil and the forming of moisture films, which is very important for the
development and movement of bacteria (D. M. Griffin, 1969). Movement of
zoospores through soil has always been associated with zoospore motility but
present evidence (Hickman and Ho, 1966) suggests that movement is ac-

complished by the possible transport of zoospores in moving water. Lysis of hyphae is sometimes associated with the build-up of high populations of bacteria and high soil moistures (D. M. Griffin, 1969). This may be related to the dependence of bacteria on water and nutrients for their movement through soils. Blair (1943) noted a reduction in the growth of *R. solani* in soils at high moisture content

D. M. Griffin (1969) hypothesized that the response of fungi to salinity or increased osmotic suctions is very similar to that produced by an equivalent reduction in relative humidity since the water potentials of both are similar.

AERATION

It is virtually impossible to separate the effects of soil aeration from soil moisture because a change in moisture affects aeration by altering the length of the pathways for diffusion through the liquid phase (D. M. Griffin, 1969). In most arable soils the concentration of oxygen is rarely less than 10% and the concentration of carbon dioxide usually varies from 0.2% to 2% but is rarely greater than 10% (D. M. Griffin, 1969). In general, the variation in carbon dioxide and oxygen in cultivated soils is not great enough to affect materially fungal growth except in flooded or flooded-compacted soils (Macauley and Griffin, 1969; Black, 1957). The latter condition is common, however, in turf because foot traffic, athletic activity, and maintenance machinery commonly follow on the irrigation of turfgrass. The ratio of carbon dioxide to oxygen in the soil atmosphere increases because of the low solubility and diffusion rate of oxygen in water (D. M. Griffin, 1963, 1969) and respiratory carbon dioxide accumulates due to the activities of saprophytic microorganisms that decompose the grass litter.

Fungi require oxygen for growth and germination but the required concentration is usually very low: 1% and lower. As a result fungal growth and germination are generally insensitive to changes in oxygen concentration over a wide range (Tabak and Cooke, 1968). However, the optimum amount of oxygen varies with the species, the environment, and nutrient availability; *O. graminis* is unusually sensitive because its growth is reduced at 105 mm of Hg, whereas most fungi grow on agar at oxygen pressures from 10 to 40 mm of Hg (Tabak and Cooke, 1968). Appressoria formation, however, may be very sensitive to oxygen deficits since Suzuki (1939) has demonstrated that appressoria formation by germ tubes of *Piricularia oryzae* requires oxygen concentrations between 10% and 15%, whereas spores germinated between 0% and 5% oxygen.

Waid (1962) has demonstrated an ecological relationship between fungi isolated from the inner and outer cortex of decomposing ryegrass roots and their oxygen tolerances; fungi from the inner cortex are apparently more tolerant to low pO_2 tensions than fungi isolated from the outer cortex. In addition, he has proposed the hypothesis that substrates released from wounded roots may increase the activity of the rhizosphere population to such a high level around the the wound that excess carbon dioxide accumulates and oxygen becomes temporarily deficient. This may inhibit the majority of the microbiological population but favor wound infection by *F. culmorum*, which is tolerant of both excess carbon dioxide and deficient oxygen (Lundegardth, 1923).

In a recent review Tabak and Cooke (1968) concluded that fungi are more sensitive to carbon dioxide than to oxygen, that different genera show considerable variation in their response, and that the response is affected frequently by the oxygen requirement of the species. Low carbon dioxide levels may stimulate spore germination, hyphal growth, and sporulation, whereas high carbon dioxide pressures generally inhibit germination and hyphal growth. The stimulatory or inhibitory level is dependent on the species and other environmental factors such as pH and temperature, the type of nutrients, and the density of the organism.

Since concentrations of carbon dioxide above 10% are generally required to inhibit fungal growth (Macauley and Griffin, 1969), and the usual concentration in soil is 0.2% to 2%, it is probable that carbon dioxide does not usually inhibit fungal growth in soil. However, D. M. Griffin suggests (1963) that concentration of carbon dioxide sufficient to reduce fungal growth may occur in water films containing fungal hyphae and several researchers have noted the sensitivity of certain fungal species to carbon dioxide in compacted soil or to respiratory carbon dioxide accumulated during microbiological breakdown of fresh organic matter.

Lundegardth (1923) demonstrated that 3% to 7% carbon dioxide stimulated the growth of *F. culmorum*, and that infection of wheat seedlings was promoted by high concentrations of carbon dioxide in the soil. The very high tolerance of *Fusarium* to low oxygen and high carbon dioxide may confer a competitive advantage upon *F. nivale, F. roseum*, and *F. tricinctum* within the turfgrass community, because turf is frequently compacted and flooded.

Garrett (1936, 1937) showed that forced aeration of soils overcame the carbon dioxide induced inhibition of *O. graminis* hyphae on wheat roots. Some reduction in the incidence of the take-all disease of wheat has therefore been obtained in compacted soils and following the incorporation of green manures. Papavizas and Davey (1962) noted a considerable suppression of the saprophytic activity of *R. solani* in fresh soil in 10% and 20% carbon dioxide and a strong inhibition at 30%. Of particular significance was the fact that pathogen activity on radish and sugar beet seedlings was more sensitive to carbon dioxide suppression than either its saprophytic or survival phases.

Sclerotinia homeocarpa, the causal fungus of the dollar-spot disease of turf-grass, may be very susceptible to carbon dioxide. Bulit and Louvet (1960) have shown that *S. minor* Jagger is readily inhibited by increasing concentrations of carbon dioxide. Although Durbin (1959) has shown that the root-attacking clones of *Rhizoctonia solani* have a higher tolerance for carbon dioxide than do the hypocotyl- and the leaf-attacking clones, natural selection of clones for increasing tolerance to carbon dioxide does not appear to be occurring in the turf community because most clones are restricted to the foliage. Macauley and Griffin (1969) reported that the mycelial growth of *H. sativum* was reduced by concentrations of oxygen and carbon dioxide of 2% and 3.3%, respectively. Because of the sensitivity of the fungus to carbon dioxide, they postulated that the reduced activity of *H. sativum* in colonizing *Paspalum* stem pieces was due to the direct effect of carbon dioxide on the fungus. The vertical distribution of fungi in soil is determined largely by the tolerance of the different species to increasing concentrations of carbon dioxide which increases with soil depth (Durbin, 1955; Jeffreys *et al.*, 1953).

INFLUENCE OF PESTICIDES

Very little is known about the effects of fungicides, herbicides, nematocides, and insecticides on the soil microflora. It would be surprising, however, if some harmful effects did not occur, especially with compounds that accumulate in the soil environment.

Pesticides may inhibit the saprophytic microorganisms as well as the organisms involved in various biological transformations such as nitrification, organic matter decomposition, humus formation, and various mineralization processes. Inhibition of these processes directly or indirectly affect the growth of plants and fungal pathogens. Chandra (1967) showed that dieldrin and heptachlor inhibited nitrification and microbial numbers in several field soils and that the length of inhibition decreased with increasing time; at optimum temperatures for decomposition there was little or no inhibition. Van Rhee (1967) demonstrated that copper oxychloride sprays used to control scab in apple orchards greatly reduced earthworm populations and Karg (1967) reported that chlorinated hydrocarbons used for insect control decimated some species of collembola and mites, many species of which are fungal feeders.

Pesticides may also affect the development of plant diseases. Richardson (1959, 1960) tested herbicides and insecticides and found that some increased fungal infection of vegetables, some decreased it, and others had no effect. Lindane, aldrin, and dieldrin were the most active in increasing infection by *H. sativum, P. ultimum,* and *R. solani.* The mechanism of increased infection is not clear since Richardson demonstrated that the insecticides inhibited rather than stimulated mycelial growth in agar.

Factors Affecting Host Resistance

Turfgrass is unique because no other cultivated plant is subjected by man to such a wide variety of unnatural conditions: the extremely dense plantings, the regular removal of photosynthetic tissues, the constant exposure of the soil to compaction, the continual accumulation of surface litter, and the numerous stresses and injuries that may result from the improper maintenance of turf. These unnatural man-made conditions are potentially harmful to plants and if the turf is improperly managed, the plants are weakened, their regrowth potential suppressed, and the resistance of mature plants to weak facultative fungal parasites greatly reduced.

Although the concept of lowered host resistance to facultative fungal parasites due to unfavorable environmental and growing conditions is well accepted by turfgrass pathologists, the mechanisms responsible for the apparent change in host reaction are unknown and usually have not been investigated. This is probably because of the impossibility of reproducing in the greenhouse the complex ecological conditions that are associated with field-grown turfgrass plants. Most cases of apparent reduction in disease resistance are based on observations of increased disease in the field and it is usually not known whether decreased host resistance, disease escape, or increased pathogen activity is responsible. Such knowledge is basic to further progress in turfgrass pathology. Some of the more important factors affecting disease resistance in turf follow.

Species Adaptability

Some homeowners plant seeds without regard to their adaptability to the soils and climate and seedsmen often market mixtures that contain unadapted species. Such plants grow poorly, are weak, and are susceptible to facultative fungal parasites. Walker (1965) has emphasized that disease resistance based on multiple genes is more likely to be suppressed than single gene resistance under extremes of environment, such as temperature and host nutrition. Cohen (Cohen *et al.,* 1969) has reported that multigenic resistance in wheat to *H. sativum* is reduced by various environmental factors.

DENSITY OF PLANTING

Planting grass seeds in excess of the amount that the soil can support will result in shading and extreme intraplant and interplant competition for factors that limit growth (Risser, 1969). The resulting plants are weak and spindly, more susceptible than normal to the attack of facultative parasites because of suppressed maturation and growth, and less responsive to renewed shoot, root, and tiller growth. The dense plantings favor the build-up and retention of moisture and high humidities and facilitate the rapid plant-to-plant spread of fungal spores and of aerial and below-ground hyphae. For example, Glynne (Garrett, 1956) found that yield reductions of wheat infected with *O. graminis* dropped from 31% to 12% when the seeding rate was reduced from 3.5 to 1.5 bu per acre. The extremely dense root system also increases the chance that the roots will contact dormant fungal structures in the soil and stimulate their germination by means of root exudates (Schroth and Hildebrand, 1964; Rovira, 1969).

PLANT AGE

In general, turfgrass seedlings are much more susceptible than mature tissues to the attack of facultative parasites. The basis of mature tissue resistance is unknown but barrier tissues and biochemical mechanisms are probably involved. The studies of Dickson and Holbert (1926) mentioned in the previous section are an excellent example of mature leaf sheath resistance that is due to the presence of barrier tissues. The fact that senescent rather than mature leaves were more readily infected and colonized by *S. homeocarpa* (Endo, 1965) *H. sativum* (Endo, 1965) suggests that the resistance of mature leaf tissues to these two pathogens is probably induced and biochemical rather than structural. Clipping grass plants stimulates the initiation and growth of new shoots and tillers that are highly susceptible to infection. The growth and formation of roots, however, are apparently seasonal and are strongly influenced by soil temperatures, light, and nitrogen (Youngner, 1969). Little exact information is available on the life span of individual roots and the factors that influence longevity (Troughton, 1957). The role of immature, mature, and senescent roots in the ecology of root-infecting fungi requires clarification.

Endo (1965) has observed degeneration affecting the root tips of cool season grasses in California. It is more common in hot than in cool weather, affects both young and old roots, and does not yield any consistent fungal or bacterial pathogen upon isolation plates. Although we have shown that *S. homeocarpa* (Endo and Malca, 1965) apparently produces a toxin that causes root-tip degeneration of bentgrass in the laboratory and that D-galactose also causes root-tip degeneration of bentgrass in the laboratory (Endo, 1965), the role of these two factors has not been demonstrated under field condition. Other factors that may be involved in root-tip degeneration are high soil temperatures, excess mowing, and soil phytotoxins (Patrick and Toussoun, 1965).

MOWING

The relation of mowing to foliage and root diseases has not received adequate attention. Interesting exceptions are the *Helminthosporium*-incited diseases of bluegrass; it has consistently been observed that lowering the height of cut of bluegrass plants below 3.75 cm increases the incidence and the severity of diseases (Couch, 1962; Halisky *et al.*, 1966) caused by *H. sativum* and *H. vagans*. Lukens (1970) has suggested that the decrease in resistance may be related to the low sugar content of the foliage which characteristically drops following defoliation. The decrease in sugar is related to the amount of foliage removed because the photosynthates that are required by roots, unemerged leaves, stem apices, and tiller buds are produced solely by the fully expanded mature leaves (Milthorpe and Davidson, 1966). As the height of cut is reduced, a larger percentage of the mature leaves is removed. Lukens (1970) has hypothesized that the decreasing sugar content of the tissues may favor the production of cell wall-macerating enzymes by the *Helminthosporium* fungi and the decreased production by the host of fungitoxic compounds.

Clipping grass plants is an injurious process (Brouwer, 1966; Troughton, 1957) because it also reduces the amount of root growth and root longevity. As far as the author is aware, the relation of root injury caused by improper mowing to a change in disease reaction of the root has not been investigated.

Excess nitrogen fertilization of closely mown turf should be avoided because it may encourage disease (Halisky *et al.*, 1968; Lukens, 1970), probably because nitrogen stimulates the growth of succulent and thin-walled leaf tissue at the expense of the available leaf carbohydrate (Burstrom, 1965; Viets, 1965).

SOIL MOISTURE AND AERATION

When disease resistance of turf is affected by both soil moisture and soil aeration, the pore spaces of the soil usually contain excess water and aeration is greatly reduced. Since soil compaction occurs universally in turf, the reduced size and altered distribution of pores further aggravate the problem.

Under flooded conditions, *P. aphanidermatum* and *P. ultimum* have both caused severe damage, perhaps because the shortage of oxygen and excess carbon dioxide inhibits the following: seedling growth (Bergman, 1959), the maturation of susceptible tissues (Siegel *et al.*, 1962), the suberization and lignification of host cells (Siegel *et al.*, 1962), and the expression of some oxygen-sensitive disease resistant mechanisms such as the production of phytoalexin (Cruickshank and Perrin, 1967) and polyphenol oxidase (Spence, 1961). Rands and Dopp (1938) have reported that salicylic aldehyde, a product of anaerobic oxidation, may accumulate in flooded soils and apparently lowers the resistance of wheat roots to attack by *P. arrhenomanes*. In addition, species of *Pythium*, like species of *Phytophthora* and *Aphanomyces* (Tabak and Cooke, 1968), are probably tolerant of high concentrations of carbon dioxide and low concentrations of oxygen.

SOIL AND AIR TEMPERATURES

That some diseases develop best at temperatures which are unfavorable for host growth but are favorable for fungal growth is sometimes cited as evidence that high temperatures may lower host resistance. For example, Endo (1963) has suggested that an air temperature of 95° F weakens the resistance of bentgrass to *P. aphanidermatum*, but other explanations are possible; high temperature may greatly prolong the susceptible seedling stage and delay the development of the mature resistant stage; or high temperatures may inhibit the growth of competing microorganisms. An example of the former is seedling blight of wheat caused by *Fusarium graminearum*. High soil temperatures favor the development of blight more than cool temperatures because high temperatures inhibit the deposition of lignin and suberin in the susceptible primary cell walls of the leaf sheath which are composed mostly of pectic materials (Dickson and Holbert, 1926).

SHADING

Shading plants generally results in increased disease caused by fungal pathogens (Couch, 1962; Lukens, 1970). This has usually been attributed to longer periods of moisture retention on the shaded plants (Couch, 1962), to increased succulence, and to thin cell walls with reduced mechanical strength (Burstrom, 1965). The change in the quantity of cell wall substances laid down apparently results from the reduced carbohydrate status of the tissues; as a result less carbohydrates are available for wall synthesis. Lukens (1970) found that shading increased the amount of disease caused by *H. vagans*, and attributed this to the decreased sugar content of the tissues.

FERTILIZATION

The evidence for an effect of nitrogen, phosphorus, and potassium on disease resistance is conflicting. Detailed studies have been few and most have been conducted in the field in which reliance is placed on natural infection. Moreover it has been assumed that effects are confined to the host and little attempt has been made to assess the effects of fertilization on the pathogen and on the competing microflora. Two diseases illustrate the possibilities.

Nitrogen fertilization reduces dollar spot caused by *S. homeocarpa* (Couch and Bloom, 1960) but few studies have been made to determine its basis. The efficacy of different forms of nitrogen vary (R. N. Cook *et al.*, 1964; Markland *et al.*, 1969); Markland *et al.* obtained the best control with sewage sludge which contains less than 1% organic nitrogen. Since sewage sludge did not inhibit hyphal growth of *S. homeocarpa*, Markland agreed with Couch and Bloom, (1960) that nitrogen decreased the "disease proneness of plants." The decrease in disease susceptibility may be more apparent than real, however, because plants that are fed adequate nitrogen maintain their resistance whereas nitrogen-starved plants that become weakened or senescent lose it. The fungus is an extremely weak parasite that first attacks the senescent leaves of weakened plants (Endo, 1965). From this food base the fungus obtains sufficient energy to infect other leaves on the same plants. This explanation does not explain why various nitrogen fertilizers give different degrees of control. If the fertilizers vary in the amount of available nitrogen, excess nitrogen probably stimulates the development of both the pathogens and the saprophytic microorganisms whereas low nitrogen stimulates only the competing microorganisms. The form of nitrogen may also be important because different forms may be utilized at different rates by the parasite, the host, or the competing microorganisms. Burstrom (1965) states that a greater amount of carbohydrate is consumed by the plant following ammonium–nitrogen assimilation than with nitrate–nitrogen assimilation because the ammonium ion is converted completely to amide whereas only a part of the nitrate nitrogen is reduced.

Conflicting results have been reported on the effects of nitrogen on melting out, Fusarium patch, Ophiobolus patch, and so on. Garrett's thorough research (1956) on the multiple effects of nitrogen on the fungus, *O. graminis*, its wheat host, the Ophiobolus patch disease, and the soil microflora is therefore instructive. Nitrogen increased the susceptibility of wheat roots, stimulated root formation and elongation, increased hyphal growth over the surface of wheat roots, and stimulated the multiplication of saprophytic microorganisms which produced sufficient respiratory carbon dioxide to inhibit hyphal growth over the surfaces of the roots. Garrett also demonstrated that survival of *Ophiobolus* hyphae in infected wheat debris depended on the availability of a low but constant amount of nitrogen; insufficient nitrogen led to the death of hyphae because apical growth ceased. Complete knowledge of the effects of nitrogen on the ecology of the Ophiobolus patch disease has permitted a rational approach to its control on wheat; these same principles, if carefully applied, should also result in its control on turfgrass. The need for similar knowledge on the effects of each macroelement on the ecology of each turfgrass pathogen and disease is obvious.

Because of the immobilization and mineralization of nitrogen by the soil- and litter-inhabiting microorganisms (Stevenson, 1965) turf tends to be nitrogen deficient. Nitrogen deficiency (Viets, 1965), in general, causes stunted growth of plants, delayed maturity of susceptible seedlings, lack of tillering, premature leaf senescence, and a reduced rate of leaf growth. Such plants may be highly susceptible to the attack of weak facultative parasite such as *S. homeocarpa, R. solani,* and *C. fuciforme,* since affected plants are unable to keep ahead of the disease and are slow to recover because of reduced rates of cell division, tillering, and root formation.

When turfgrass is overfertilized with nitrogen, the response may be similar to that of other plants; leaf size, shoot growth, and tiller formation may be stimulated (Viets, 1965) resulting in rank vegetative growth and a dense canopy of succulent foliage which decreases air movement and increases the relative humidity favorable for fungal development. In bean such cells are highly vacuolated and thin walled (Burstrom, 1965) apparently because nitrogen stimulates the formation of protoplasm and protein at the expense of the available carbohydrates; fewer carbohydrates are then available for incorporation into cell walls. Clipping and shading of turfgrass would probably accentuate these effects.

Phosphorus and potassium are also cited as exerting effects on host resistance (Couch, 1962). Since a deficiency of potassium (Chapman, 1965) generally causes increased susceptibility of plants to infection and invasion and leads to the rapid onset of senescence, the need for adequate potassium is obvious. Evans *et al.* (1964) have observed an increase in leaf-spot diseases in the potassium-deficient sandy soils of Alabama.

Phosphorus appears to conteract the effect of excess nitrogen in increasing disease susceptibility. Vanterpool (1935) has shown that in proper balance with nitrogen, phosphorus favors the formation and elongation of seedling wheat roots, thus allowing the infected plants to keep ahead of the damage caused by the root parasite, *P. arrhenomanes.*

Factors Affecting Fungal Survival

The inoculum concentration is a major factor that determines the amount of disease that may develop during favorable conditions. Consequently, it is important to know the factors that determine the survival of the fungus either as active hyphae, resistant hyphae, or as dormant structures in soil and in dead plant remains. It may then be possible to accelerate the rate of natural decline and affect a reduction in surviving inoculum.

SURVIVAL AS HYPHAE IN DEAD PLANT REMAINS AND IN SOIL

Glynne (1950) demonstrated that the level of resistance is a major factor determining the incidence and extent of infection of wheat by *Cercosporella herpotrichoides*, and that the amount of infection and host colonization largely determines the inoculum level in the crop debris Garrett (1956) demonstrated that live host tissues colonized by increasing amounts of hyphae ahead of competing saprophytes were able to survive longer in the dead host debris.

The ability of a facultative parasite to survive as active hyphae in plant debris in the absence of living host plants depends primarily on its degree of CSA. Fungi which lack CSA disappear rapidly whereas those that are able to colonize plant remains in competition with saprophytic microorganisms grow as hyphae in soil and in dead plant remains. *Helminthosporium sativum* disappears rapidly as hyphae from colonized wheat stems (Butler, 1953b) but *O. graminis* (Garrett, 1956) persists in wheat for a short time as actively growing hyphae because it possesses a low degree of CSA in the presence of available nitrogen. Sod, however, tends to be deficient in nitrogen (Stevenson, 1965) and *O. graminis* probably disappears rapidly from turf debris if the nitrogen required for hyphal growth is not provided by fertilization. In soils planted to wheat, *F. roseum* (Sadasivan, 1939), *P. ultimum* (Garrett, 1956), and *R. solani* (Blair, 1943) have been shown to possess a high degree of CSA and therefore probably manifest this same ability in turf. Other nutritional factors that determine the survival of active hyphae are the availabilty of carbon substrates as well as various macroelements, microelements, and growth factors that are obtained from plant residues or from the soil solution.

Garrett (1956) has stated that environmental conditions that favor maximum biological activity also favor the rapid disappearance of plant residues and fungal hyphae. These conditions are high soil temperatures, abundant soil aeration, moderate soil moisture, and neutral soil reaction.

The effects of the addition of grass clippings on the survival of fungal hyphae are unknown but are likely to be significant because of the increased biological activity. Nitrogen deficiency in turf, or the addition of fertilizer nitrogen in amounts that favor only the competing microorganisms, is likely to shorten the life of fungal mycelia because of the mineralization and immobilization of nitrogen by microorganisms. Since nitrogen may be obtained from dead plant and animal remains, from soluble nitrogen compounds diffusing from fresh grass clippings, and from nitrogen fertilizers, it is difficult to predict the amount of nitrogen available to the fungal parasites.

The effects of competing microorganisms on hyphal persistance have not been studied in turfgrass but the hyphal tips of *R. solani* were observed by Kerr (1958) to lyse four days after feeding on the diffusates from decomposing grass debris, and Blair (1943) noted the suppressing effect of grass debris on *R. solani* hyphae in wheat soils. Chinn *et al.*, (1953) noted that the apices of germ tubes of *H. sativum* lysed rapidly after the conidia were stimulated to germinate by means of soybean residues. Lysis of hyphae may have resulted from the depletion of nutrients or from the activities of competing microorganisms Lockwood (1964). Butler (1953b) showed that a high ratio of nitrogen fertilization hastened the disappearance of *Helminthosporium* hyphae from colonized debris. Butler attributed this to the build-up of antagonistic and competing saprophytic microorganisms, but Garrett (1966) concluded that the primary effect of nitrogen was due to its stimulation of cellulose breakdown by hyphae of the *Helminthosporium* fungus. Since this resulted in the release of surplus glucose, the populations of saprophytic microorganisms increased and the substrate became exhausted.

SURVIVAL AS DORMANT FUNGAL STRUCTURES

Facultative fungal parasites that lack CSA generally survive unfavorable environmental conditions by means of survival structures that remain inactive in the soil or in plant debris until stimulated to germinate by contact with plant roots (Schroth and Hildebrand, 1964; Rovira, 1969). Fungal survival structures normally exist dormant in the soil because of a widespread soil fungistasis (Jackson, 1965; Dobbs and Hinson, 1953). Although soil fungistasis has not been demonstrated in either turf litter or soil, it undoubtedly occurs there also, for Chinn (Chinn *et al.*, 1953) has demonstrated that conidia of *H. sativum* exhibit soil fungistasis in soils planted to wheat. Soil fungistasis (Lockwood, 1964) is attributed to (1) a lack of essential nutrients or metabolities in the dormant structures (Ko and Lockwood, 1967) and/or to (2) inhibition of germination by antibiotics produced by competing microorganisms. Since soil fungistasis may be readily overcome by nutrients obtained from root exudates or from direct root contact (Rovira, 1969; Schroth and

Hildebrand, 1964), the phenomenon obviously reduces wastage of spores. Stimulation or germination of dormant structures by root exudates undoubtedly occurs in turf but stimulation may be due to guttation fluid also or to nutrients leaking from the intact plant or from grass clippings.

Little is known about the factors that determine the survival of dormant structures but they are well adapted to survive in soil for many years in the absence of the host. Survival in soil by asexual spores is rare but species of *Helminthosporium* commonly survive as conidia. Meronuck and Pepper (1968) have reported from field soil the conversion of the cells of the conidia of *H. sativum* into chlamydospores. Since chlamydospores are adapted for long-term survival, their formation in turf needs verification. Survival structures (Garrett, 1956; Menzies, 1963) are insensitive to the extremes of moisture, aeration, temperature, and soil reaction that are encountered normally in soil. According to Garrett (1956), they disappear most rapidly from soil that is maintained at conditions favorable for plant growth and the growth and activity of the flora and fauna, which by their varied activities gradually reduced the populations of survival structures. A recent interesting report is that of Old (1970), who found that the conidial cell walls of *H. sativum* collected from the field exhibited small holes through which species of bacteria entered the spore, apparently causing the death of individual cells of the multicelled spore.

Although some success has been obtained in hastening their destruction by such drastic procedures as flood fallowing (Stover, 1962) and deep plowing (Garrett, 1956), these procedures cannot be employed in turf. The problem of disease control in turfgrass with regard to fungal structures is therefore twofold: (1) To prevent their formation, and (2) to induce their germination in an environment that will tend to inhibit further development. The first approach does not appear possible at the present time; the second appears feasible because mowing may provide the fresh clippings and substrates that may not only stimulate the germination of dormant resting structures but also may stimulate the activities of the competing microorganisms that actively decompose the fresh litter and thereby suppress the further development of plant pathogens.

Conclusions

Because of man's desire to beautify his environment, the turfgrass community represents a truly unique ecosystem. If a plant pathologist set about to establish deliberately the most favorable conditions for disease development, he could scarcely improve upon the present system of planting, establishing, and maintaining turf. There is, however, one additional condition that would greatly favor disease development; the elimination of most members of the flora and fauna, except the plant pathogens. In this chapter, an attempt has been made to present information which suggests that the erratic occurrence of turfgrass diseases caused by facultative fungal parasites is due to the competing and antagonistic activities of the flora and fauna and that disease occurrence usually occurs when disease resistance has been reduced or suppressed and/or when conditions favor the development of the pathogens more than they favor the development of the competing and antagonistic flora and fauna. Future research on turfgrass diseases undoubtedly will place greater emphasis on determining the role of the above factors in disease development.

References

Agnihotri, V. D. (1969). Production and germination of appressoria in *Pythium irregulare.* *Mycologia* **61**, 967–980.

Alexander, M. (1961). "Introduction to Soil Microbiology." Wiley, New York.

Barton, R. (1960). Saprophytic activity of *Pythium mammilatum* in soil. I. Influence of substrate composition and soil environment. *Trans. Brit. Mycol. Soc.* **43**, 529–540.

Bean, G. A. (1969). The role of moisture and crop debris in the development of Fusarium blight of Kentucky bluegrass. *Phytopathology* **59**, 479–481.

Beard, J. B. (1970). Personal communication.

Bergman, H. F. (1959). Oxygen deficiency as a cause of disease in plants. *Bot. Rev.* **25**, 418–585.

Black, C. A. (1957). "Soil-plant Relationships." Wiley, New York.

Blair, I. D. (1943). Behavior of the fungus *Rhizoctonia solani* Kühn in the soil. *Ann. Appl. Biol.* **30**, 118–127.

Boosalis, M. G. (1956). Effect of soil temperature and green-manure amendment of unsterilized soil on parasitism of *Rhizoctonia solani* by *Penicillium vermiculatum* and *Trichoderma* sp. *Phytopathology* **46**, 473–478.

Brouwer, R. (1966). Root growth of cereals and grasses. *In* "The growth of cereals and Grasses" (F. L. Milthorpe and J. D. Ivins, eds.), pp. 153–166. Butterworth, London.

Bulit, J., and Louvet, J. (1960). A technic for the study of the action of carbon dioxide on fungi parasitizing underground plant organs. *Ann. Inst. Pasteur. Paris* **98**, 557–561.

Burgess, L. W., and Griffin, D. M. (1968a). The recovery of *Gibberella zeae* from straw. *Aust. J. Exp. Agr. Anim. Husb.* **8**, 364–370.

Burgess, L. W., and Griffin, D. M. (1968b). The relationship between the spore density of *Cochliobolus sativus* in soil and its saprophytic activity and parasitism. *Aust. J. Exp. Agr. Anim. Husb.* **8**, 371–373.

Burström, H. G. (1965). The Physiology of Plant Roots. *In* "Biology of Soil-borne Plant Pathogens" (K. F. Baker and W. C. Snyder, eds.) pp. 154–166. University of California Press, Berkeley, California.

Butler, F. C. (1948). Frost injury of wheat. *Agr. Gaz. N. S. W.* **59**, 415–418.

Butler, F. C. (1953a). Saprophytic behavior of some cereal root-rot fungi. I. Saprophytic colonization of wheat straw. *Ann. Appl. Biol.* **40**, 284–297.

Butler, F. C. (1953b). Saprophytic behavior of some cereal root-rot fungi. III. Saprophytic survival in wheat straw buried in soil. *Ann. Appl. Biol.* **40**, 305–311.

Butler, F. C. (1953c). Saprophytic behavior of some cereal root-rot fungi. II. Factors influencing saprophytic colonization of wheat straw. *Ann. Appl. Biol.* **40**, 298–304.

Campbell, W. P. (1956). The influence of associated microorganisms on the pathogenicity of *Helminthosporium sativum. Can. J. Bot.* **34**, 865–874.

Chandra, P. (1967). Effect of 2 chlorinated insecticides on soil microflora and nitrification process as influenced by different soil temperatures and textures. *In* "Progress in Soil Biology" (O. Graff and J. E. Satchell, eds.), pp. 320–330. North-Holland Publ., Amsterdam.

Chapman, H. D. (1965). Chemical factors of the soil as they affect microorganisms. *In* "Ecology of Soil-borne Plant Pathogens" (K. F. Baker and W. C. Snyder, eds.), pp. 120–138. Univ. of California Press, Berkeley.

Chen, A. W. C., and Griffin, D. M. (1966). Soil physical factors and the ecology of fungi. VI. Interaction between temperature and soil moisture. *Trans. Brit. Mycol. Soc.* **49**, 551–561.

Chinn, S. H. F., and Ledingham, R. J. (1961). Mechanisms contributing to the eradication of spores of *Helminthosporium sativum* from amended soil. *Can. J. Bot.* **39**, 739–748.

Chinn, S. H. F., Ledingham, R. J., Sallans, B. J., and Simmonds, P. M. (1953). A mechanism for the control of common root rot of wheat. *Phytopathology* **43**, 761.

Cochrane, V. E. (1958). "Physiology of Fungi." Wiley, New York.

Cohen, E., Helgason, S. B., and McDonald, W. C. (1969). A study of factors influencing the genetics of reaction of barely to root rot caused by *Helminthosporium sativum. Can. J. Bot.* **47**, 429–443.

Cook, R. J., and Flentje, N. T. (1967). Chlamydospore germination and germling survival of *Fusarium solani* f. *pisi* in soil as affected by soil-water and pea seed exudation. *Phytopathology* **57**, 178–182.

Cook, R. J., and Papendick, R. I. (1970). Soil water potential as a factor in the ecology of *Fusarium roseum* f. sp. *cerealis* "Culmorum." *Plant Soil* **32**, 131–145.

Cook, R. N., Engel, R. E., and Bachelder, S. (1964). A study of the effect of nitrogen carriers on turfgrass diseases. *Plant Dis. Rep.* **48**, 254–255.

Cormack, M. W. (1948). Winter crown rot or snow mold of alfalfa, clover, and grasses in Alberta. I. Occurrence, parasitism and spread of the pathogen. *Can. J. Res.* **26**, 71–85.

Couch, H. B. (1962). "Diseases of Turfgrass." Reinhold, New York.

Couch, H. B., and Bloom, J. R. (1960). Influence of environment on disease of turfgrasses. II. Effect of nutrition, pH and soil moisture on Sclerotinia dollar spot. *Phytopathology* **50**, 761–763.

Couch, H. B., Purdy, L. H., and Henderson, D. W. (1967). Application of soil moisture principles to the study of plant disease. *Va. Polytech. Inst., Dept. Plant Pathol. Bull.* **4**.

Cruickshank, I. A. M., and Perrin, D. R. (1967). Studies on phytoalexins. Effect of oxygen tension on the biosynthesis of pisatin and phaseolin. *Phytopathol. Z.* **60**, 335–342.

Davey, C. B., and Papavizas, G. C. (1963). Saprophytic activity of *Rhizoctonia* as affected by the carbon-nitrogen balance of certain organic soil amendments. *Soil Sci. Soc. Amer., Proc.* **27**, 164–167.

Dickson, J. G., and Holbert, J. R. (1926). The influence of temperature upon the metabolism and expression of disease resistance in selfed lines of corn. *J. Amer. Soc. Agron.* **18**, 314–322.

Dobbs, C. G., and Hinson, W. H. (1953). A widespread fungistasis in the soil. *Nature (London)* **172**, 197.

Durbin, R. D. (1955). A straight-line function of growth of microorganisms at toxic levels of carbon dioxide. *Science* **121**, 734–735.

Durbin, R. D. (1959). Factors affecting the vertical distribution of *Rhizoctonia solani* with special reference to CO_2 concentrations. *Amer. J. Bot.* **46**, 22–25.

Endo, R. M. (1961). Turfgrass diseases in southern California. *Plant Dis. Rep.* **45**, 869–873.

Endo, R. M. (1963). Influence of temperature on rate of growth of five fungus pathogens of turfgrass and on rate of disease spread. *Phytopathology* **53**, 857–861.

Endo, R. M. (1964). Influence of guttation fluid on infection structures of *Helminthosporium sorokinianum. Phytopathology* **54**, 1327–1334.

Endo, R. M. (1965). Unpublished studies.

Endo, R. M. (1966). Control of dollar spot of turfgrass by nitrogen and its probable bases. *Phytopathology,* **56**, 877.

Endo, R. M., and Malca, I. (1965). Morphological and cytohistological response of primary roots of bentgrass to *Sclerotinia homeocarpa* and D-galactose. *Phytopathology* **55**, 781–789.

Endo, R. M., and Mudd, B. J. (1970). Unpublished studies.

Endo, R. M., Malca, I., and Krausman, E. M. (1964). Degeneration of the apical meristem and apex of bentgrass roots by a fungal toxin. *Phytopathology* **54**, 1175–1176.

Evans, E. M., Rouse, R. D., and Gudauskas, R. T. (1964). Low potassium sets up coastal for leafspot disease. *Highlights Agr. Res.* **11**, 47.

Garrett, S. D. (1936). Soil conditions and the take-all disease of wheat. *Ann. Appl. Biol.* **23**, 667–699.

Garrett, S. D. (1937). Soil conditions and the take-all disease of wheat. II. The relation between soil reaction and soil aeration. *Ann. Appl. Biol.* **24**, 747–751.

Garrett, S. D. (1956). "Biology of Root-infecting Fungi." Cambridge Univ. Press, London and New York.

Garrett, S. D. (1963). "Soil Fungi and Soil Fertility." Pergamon, Oxford.

Garrett, S. D. (1966). Cellulose-decomposing ability of some cereal foot-rot fungi in relation to their saprophytic survival. *Trans. Brit. Mycol. Soc.* **49**, 57–68.

Garrett, S. D. (1967). Effect of nitrogen level on survival of *Ophiobolus graminis* in pure culture on cellulose *Trans. Brit. Mycol. Soc.* **50**, 519–524.

Gilliver, K. (1946). The inhibitory action of antibiotics on plant pathogenic bacteria and fungi. *Ann. Bot. (London)* [N.S.] **10**, 271–282.

Glynne, M. D. (1950). Effect of cultural treatments of wheat on eye spot, lodging, take-all and weeds. *J. Min. Agri. (Gr. Brit.)* **56**, 510–514.

Goss, R. L. (1969). Personal communication.

Goss, R. L., and Gould, C. J. (1968). Some inter-relationships between fertility levels and fusarium patch disease of turf grass. *J. Sports Turf. Res. Inst.* **44**, 19–26.

Griffin, D. M. (1963). Soil moisture and the ecology of soil fungi. *Biol. Rev.* **38**, 141–166.

Griffin, D. M. (1969). Soil water in the ecology of fungi. *Annu. Rev. Phytopathol.* **7**, 289–310.

Halisky, P. M., Funk, C. R., and Engel, R. E. (1966). Melting-out of Kentucky bluegrass varieties by *Helminthosporium vagans* as influenced by turf management practices. *Plant Dis. Rep.* **50**, 703–706.

Healy, M. J., and Britton, M. P. (1968). Infection and development of *Helminthosporium sorokinianum* in *Agrostis palustris. Phytopathology,* **58**, 273–276.

Henry, A. W. (1931). Occurrence and sporulation of *Helminthosporium sativum* in the soil. *Can. J. Res.* **5**, 407–413.

Henry, A. W. (1932). The influence of soil temperature and soil sterilization on the reaction of wheat seedlings to *Ophiobolus graminis. Can. J. Res.* **7**, 198–203.

Hickman, C. J., and Ho, H. H. (1966). Behaviour of zoospores in plant-pathogenic phycomycetes. *Annu. Rev. Phytopathol.* **4**, 195–220.

Howard, F. L. (1951). Fungus diseases of turfgrass. *R. I. Exp. Sta., Bull.* **308**.

Ivanoff, S. S. (1963). Guttation injuries of plants. *Bot. Rev.* **29**, 202–229.

Jackson, R. M. (1965). Antibiosis and fungistasis of soil microorganisms. *In* "Ecology of Soil-borne Plant Pathogens" (K. F. Baker, and W. C. Snyder, eds.), pp. 363–369. Univ. of California Press, Berkeley.

Jeffreys, E. G., Brian, P. W., Hemming, H. G., and Lowe, D. (1953). Antibiotic production by the microfungi of acid heath soils. *J. Gen. Microbiol.* **9**, 314–341.

Karg, W. (1967). Veranderungen in den Bodenlebensgemeinschaften durch die Einwirkung von Pflanzenschutzmitteln. *In* "Progress in Soil Biology", (O. Graff and J. E. Satchell, eds.), pp. 310–319. North-Holland Publ., Amsterdam.

Kerr, A. (1958). The use of cellophane in growth studies on soil fungi. *Trans. Brit. Mycol. Soc.* **41**, 14–16.

Kerr, A. (1964). The influence of soil moisture on infection of peas by *Pythium ultimum. Aust. J. Biol. Sci.* **17**, 676–685.

Ko, W. H., and Lockwood, J. L. (1967). Soil fungistasis: Relation to fungal spore nutrition. *Phytopathology* **57**, 894–901.

Lai, M. T., Weinhold, A. R., and Hancock, J. G. (1968). Permeability changes in *Phaseolus aureus* associated with infection by *Rhizoctonia solani. Phytopathology* **58**, 240–245.

Leben, C. (1965). Epiphytic microorganisms in relation to plant disease. *Annu. Rev. Plant Pathol.* **3**, 209–230.

Lockwood, J. L. (1964). Soil fungistasis. *Annu. Rev. Plant Pathol.* **2**, 341–362.

Ludwig, R. A. (1957). Toxin production by *Helminthosporium sativum* P. K. & B. and its significance in disease development. *Can. J. Bot.* **35**, 291–303.

Lukens, R. J. (1970). Melting out of Kentucky bluegrass, a low sugar disease. *Phytopathology* **60**, 1276–1278.

Lundegardth, H. (1923). Significance of carbon dioxide content and hydrogen ion concentration of the soil for the growth of Fusaria. *Bot. Notis.* 25–52.

Macauley, B. J., and Griffin, D. M. (1969). Effect of carbon dioxide and the bicarbonate ion on the growth of some soil fungi. *Trans. Brit. Mycol. Soc.* **53**, 223–228.

Madison, J. H., Peterson, L. J., and Hodges, T. K. (1960). Pink snow mold on bentgrasses as affected by irrigation and fertilizer. *Agron. J.* **52**, 591–592.

Markland, F. E., Roberts, E. C., and Frederick, L. R. (1969). Influence of nitrogen fertilizers on Washington Creeping bentgrass, *Agrostis palustris* Huds. II. Incidence of dollar spot, *Sclerotinia homeocarpa*, infection. *Agron. J.* **61**, 701–705.

Mellano, H. M., Munnecke, D. E., and Endo, R. M. (1970). Relationship of seedling age of *Pythium ultimum* on roots of *Antirrhinum majus. Phytopathology* **60**, 935–942.

Menzies, J. D. (1963). Survival of microbial plant pathogens in soil. *Bot. Rev.* **29**, 79–122.

Menzies, J. D. (1967). Plant diseases related to irrigation. *In* "Irrigation of Agricultural lands" (R. M. Hagan, H. R. Haise, and T. N. Edminister, eds.), Agron. Monogr. No. 11, pp. 1058–1064. Amer. Soc. Agron., Madison, Wisconsin.

Meronuck, R. A., and Pepper, E. H. (1968). Chlamydospore formation in conidia of *Helminthosporium sativum Phytopathology* **58**, 866–867.

Milthorpe, F. L., and Davidson J. L. (1966) Physiological aspects of regrowth following defoliation. In "The growth of cereals and grasses" (F. L. Milthorpe and J. D. Ivins, eds.) pp. 241–254. Butterworths, London.

Monteith, J., and Dahl, A. S. (1932). Turf diseases and their control. *Bull. U.S. Golf Asso., Green Comm.* **12**, 85–187.

Moore, L. D., and Couch, H. B. (1963). Influence of environment on diseases of turf grasses. III. Effect of nutrition, pH, soil temperature, air temperature and soil moisture on Pythium blight of highland bentgrass. *Phytopathology* **53**, 53–57.

Muse, R. R., and Couch, H. B. (1965). Influence of environment on diseases of turf grasses. IV. Effect of nutrition and soil moisture on Corticium red thread of creeping red fescue. *Phytopathology* 55, 507–510.

Old, K. M. (1967). Effects of natural soil in survival of *Cochliobolus sativus*. *Trans. Brit. Mycol. Soc.* 50, 615–624.

Old, K. M. (1970). Growth of bacterial within lysing fungal conidia in soil. *Trans. Brit. Mycol. Soc.* 54, 337–341.

Papavizas, G. C., and Davey, C. V. (1962). Activity of *Rhizoctonia* in soil as affected by carbon dioxide. *Phytopathology* 52, 759–766.

Patrick, Z. A., and Toussoun, T. A. (1965). Plant residues and organic amendments in relation to biological control. *In* "Ecology of Soil-borne Plant Pathogens" (K. F. Baker and W. C. Snyder, eds.), pp. 440–457. Univ. of California Press, Berkeley.

Pentland, G. D. (1967). The effect of soil moisture on the growth and spread of *Coniophora puteana* under laboratory conditions. *Can. J. Bot.* 45, 1899–1906.

Rands, R. D., and Dopp, E. (1938). The influence of certain harmful soil constituents on severity of Pythium root rot of sugar cane, *J. Agr. Res.* 50, 53–68.

Raney, W. A. (1965). Physical factors of the soil as they affect soil microorganisms. *In* Ecology of Soil-borne Plant Pathogens" (K. F. Baker and W. C. Snyder, eds.), pp. 115–118. Univ. of California Press, Berkeley.

Rangaswami, G., and Vidhyasekaren, P. (1966). Effect of antagonistic microorganisms on the survival of *Helminthosporium sativum*. Pamm, King and Baake in the rhizosphere of maize. *Indian J. Microbiol.* 6. 19–22.

Richardson, L. T. (1959). Effect of insecticides and herbicides applied to soil on the development of plant diseases. II. Early blight and Fusarium wilt of tomato. *Can. J. Plant Sci.* 39, 30–38.

Richardson, L. T. (1960). Effect of insecticide-fungicide combinations on emergence of peas and growth of damping-off fungi. *Plant Dis. Rep.* 44, 104–108.

Risser, P. G. (1969). Competitive relationships among herbaceous grassland plants. *Bot. Rev.* 35, 251–284.

Rovira, A. (1969). Plant root exudates. *Bot. Rev.* 35, 35–58.

Rowell, J. B. (1951), Observations on the pathogenicity of *Rhizoctonia solani* on bentgrasses. *Plant Dis. Rep.* 35, 240–242.

Russell, R. S. (1970). Root systems and plant nutrition. Some new approaches. *Endeavor* 29, 60–66.

Sadasivan, T. S. (1939). Succession of fungi decomposing wheat straw in different soils, with special reference to *Fusarium culmorum*. *Ann. Appl. Biol.* 26, 497–508.

Sanford, G. B., and Broadfoot, W. C. (1931). Studies of the effects of other soil-inhabiting micro-organisms on virulence of *Ophiobolus graminis*. *Sci. Agr.* 11, 512–528.

Schroth, M. N., and Hildebrand, D. C. (1964). Influence of plant exudates on root-infecting fungi. *Annu. Rev. Plant Pathol.* 2, 101–132.

Siegel, S. M., Rosen, L. A., and Renwick, G. (1962). Effect of reduced oxygen tension on vascular plants. Growth and composition of red kidney bean plants in 5% oxygen. *Physiol. Plant.* 15, 304–314.

Simmonds, P. M. (1947). The influence of antibiosis in the pathogenicity of *Helminthosporium sativum*. *Sci. Agr.* 27, 625–632.

Snyder, W. C., Schroth, M. N., and Christou, T. (1959). Effect of plant residues on root rot of bean. *Phytopathology* 49, 755–756.

Spence, J. A. (1961). Black-pod disease of cocoa. II. A study of host-parasite relations. *Ann. Appl. Biol.* 49, 723–734.

Stevenson, F. J. (1965). Origin and distribution of nitrogen in the soil. *In* "Soil Nitrogen"

(W. V. Bartholomew, and F. E. Clark, eds.), Agron. Monogr. No. 10, pp. 1–42. Amer. Soc. Agron. Madison, Wisconsin.

Stover, R. H. (1962). Fusarium wilt (Panama disease) of bananas and other *Musa* species. *Commonw. Mycol. Inst. Phytopathol. Pap.* **4**, 1–117.

Suryanarayanam, S. (1958). Role of nitrogen in host susceptibility to *Piricularia oryzae* Cav. *Curr. Sci.* **27**, 447–448.

Suzuki, H. (1939). Influence of physical and chemical factors upon the formation of appressoria in the conidia of *Piricularia oryzae*. I. Influence of oxygen. *Jap. J. Bot.* **10**, 321–324.

Tabak, H. H., and Cooke, W. B. (1968). The effects of gaseous environments on the growth and metabolism of fungi. *Bot. Rev.* **34**, 126–252.

Troughton, A. (1957). "The Underground Organs of Herbage Grasses," Bull. No. 44. Commonwealth Bureau of Pastures and Field Crops, Hurley Berkshire.

Tukey, H. B., Jr. (1970). The leaching of substances from plants. *Annu. Rev. Plant Physiol.* **21**, 305–324.

Van Rhee, J. A. (1967). Development of earthworm populations in orchard soils. *In* "Progress in Soil Biology" (O. Graff, and J. E. Satchell, eds.), pp. 360–371. North-Holland Publ., Amsterdam.

Vanterpool, T. C. (1935). Studies on browning root rot of cereals. III. Phosphorus-nitrogen relations of infested fields. IV. Effect of fertilizer amendments. V. Preliminary plant analyses. *Can. J. Res., Sect. C* **13**, 220–250.

Viets, F. G., Jr. (1965). The plant's need for and use of nitrogen. *In* "Soil Nitrogen" (W. V. Bartholomew, and F. E. Clark, eds.), Agron. Monogr. No. 10, pp. 508–572. Amer. Soc. Agron., Madison, Wisconsin.

Waid, J. S. (1957). Distribution of fungi within the decomposing tissues of ryegrass roots. *Trans. Brit. Mycol. Soc.* **40**, 391–406.

Waid, J. S. (1962). Influence of oxygen upon growth and respiratory behavior of fresh decomposing ryegrass roots. *Trans. Brit. Mycol. Soc.* **45**, 479–487.

Walker, J. C. (1965). Use of environmental factors in screening for disease resistance. *Annu. Rev. Plant Pathol.* **3**, 197–208.

Weindling, R., and Fawcett, H. S. (1936). Experiments in the control of *Rhizoctonia* damping-off of citrus seedlings. *Hilgardia* **10**, 1–16.

Weinhold, A. R., Bowman, T., and Dodman, R. L. (1969). Virulence of *Rhizoctonia solani* as affected by nutrition of the pathogen. *Phytopathology* **59**, 1601–1605.

Wilcoxson, R. D., and Sudia, T. W. (1968). Translocation in fungi. *Bot. Rev.* **34**, 32–50.

Youngner, V. B. (1969). Physiology of growth and development. *In* "Turfgrass Science" (A. A. Hanson, and F. V. Juska, eds.), Agron. Monogr. No. 14, pp. 187–216. Amer. Soc. Agron., Madison, Wisconsin.

Chapter 14

Effects on Turfgrass of Cultural Practices in Relation to Microclimate

JAMES R. WATSON

Turfgrass is judged by the standards established for its beauty, use, playability, density, freedom from pests, and uniformity of growth and color. A given turfgrass area is the product of the climate, the grass, the soil, and the cultural practices required to maintain it in a manner suitable to the use for which it is grown. All of these factors, plus more, interact to produce the total environment of the grass plant. The microclimate of this environment is dynamic and ever changing. All climatic factors—temperature, light, water, wind movement, and humidity—exert direct and interacting effects on the growth response of the turfgrass. For this reason it is difficult to separate the individual response produced by any one factor. However, there may be an opportunity to alter the microclimate through the application of properly timed cultural practices.

Climate

Climate, especially temperature, is the basic factor that determines the broad adaptation of turfgrasses. Growth response to temperature is generally used to classify turfgrasses as either "cool" or "warm" season; and when

203

either group is grown in marginal zones of adaptation, soil environment and cultural practices become more critical for satisfactory turf growth. Both soil and cultural practices may be modified or adjusted to compensate partially for marginal adaptation; however, neither will alter the broad impact of climate. Thus warm-season grasses grow vigorously in hot weather and slowly during cool weather, whereas cool-season grass growth will slow down and frequently cease when soil temperatures approach 90°F (Beard, 1964; Daniel and Roberts, 1966).

Brown (1943) reported that Kentucky bluegrass made little top growth until the average soil temperature at $\frac{1}{2}$-in. depth rose above 50°F. According to Beard (1969), the optimum temperature for shoot growth of *Poa annua* is 60°F to 70°F and the optimum for root growth is 55°F to 65°F. In his opinion it is more important to maintain an optimum temperature for root growth than for shoot growth. Youngner (1968) indicates that maximum carbohydrate storage for both a warm-season grass (Bermuda) and a cool-season grass (Kentucky bluegrass) occurs at temperatures near the minimum for measurable growth. A high temperature for only a few days may seriously deplete carbohydrate reserves. According to him young Kentucky bluegrass plants are unable to store reserve carbohydrates and may even lose those that may have been stored earlier at a cooler temperature.

LeBeau (1964) has shown that careful control of soil temperature near the surface is effective in reducing snow mold (*Fusarium nivale*) damage. Plots maintained at 3°C and 6°C were severely infected, whereas the unheated plots and plots with controlled minimum temperatures of −3°C were damaged by an unidentified low-temperature basidiomycete. No snow mold was found in plots with minimum controlled temperature of 0°C. Beard (1964) has shown a differential response between Toronto creeping bentgrass, Kentucky bluegrass, and *Poa annua* to various types of ice cover. Under test conditions, Toronto exhibited a high degree and *Poa annua* a low degree of tolerance to all types of covers. Watson *et al.* (1960) and Watson and Wicklund (1962) have shown the effect of various covers on soil temperature at 2-, 4-, and 6-in. depths and discussed their effect on growth and survival of putting green turf. Insulation to prevent wide temperature fluctuations and the retention of moisture are the chief advantages listed. Watson and Wicklund (1962) demonstrated the effects of covers of various colors on growth responses and pointed out the effect of the humid environment they create on the degree of snow mold (*Typhula itoana*) infestation.

Thus any cultural practice that affects even a slight change in the microclimate of a turfgrass area could produce a significant and perhaps vital growth response. The effects may perhaps be temporary and could not be expected to alter the broad impact of climate. Nevertheless they could mean the difference between acceptable and unacceptable turf.

Soil

The soil environment is particularly critical on intensively used turfgrass areas such as golf greens and athletic fields. In addition to its normal role in plant growth, the soil under such areas must provide stability and support for players. And because of the excessive traffic under such conditions, the soil is highly subject to compaction. Modification or adjustment, particularly of textural porosity, will do much to assure a more suitable environment and a more favorable response to cultural practices under such conditions. Ferguson *et al.* (1960) and Madison (1969), among others, have shown the importance of developing and maintaining textural porosity under putting-green conditions. The technique described by Ferguson and associates for construction of a putting green employs the principle of a perched water table to counteract the low water-holding capacity of the sandy soil. Gardner (1962) discusses how this same effect will impede water movement, hence it is important to control the placement of a layer of soil with a more coarse texture. Otherwise the possibility of an overly wet soil with its attendant influence on microclimate may occur.

The trend toward use of marginal land and fill areas for home building and for recreational purposes plays an increasingly significant role in the application of cultural practices and the resulting microclimate of the turf cover. Such is especially true with regard to the drainage characteristics of marginal areas.

Cultural Practices

Cultural practices that influence microclimate of turfgrass may be arbitrarily grouped into two categories: (1) those deemed essential for development of a turf that will meet established quality and use criteria, and (2) those deemed of value in combating adversity or stress resulting from climate and use. The first group would include mowing, watering, fertilizing, cultivating, and programs to control disease, insects, and weeds. The second grouping would include such practices as topdressing, improvement of water and air drainage, mulches, covers, and soil heating.

Essential cultural practices are concerned basically with the development, growth, and maintenance of a *green*, *dense*, and *pest-free* turf. They are the basic cultural techniques required for all types of turf in all locations. The intensity or degree of their application will vary in accordance with the use and quality level expected of the turf site or facility. For example, a successively less-intensive cultural program is required for a putting green clipped at $\frac{3}{16}$ in., a fairway clipped at $\frac{3}{4}$ in., a home lawn clipped at 2 in., a rough at 3 in., an airport or highway right-of-way at 4 in., or, for that matter, a heavily grazed, cultivated pasture which may require only infrequent mowing to assure uniformity of growth.

The basic cultural practices have both direct and interacting effects on the grass plant and the microclimate as well as the turf produced. Because of this, when one or more become limiting, it is possible to overcome partially or to compensate by adjustment or modification of the other factors. Frequently efforts to compensate lead to undue expense and are rewarded by only a very slight improvement in overall turf quality as illustrated by the effects of lowering the height of cut from $1\frac{1}{2}$ in. to $\frac{1}{2}$ in. on a Kentucky bluegrass fairway. A low height is often demanded by today's golfer but Kentucky bluegrass does not produce sufficient leaf mass at a $\frac{1}{2}$-in. cutting height to support the photosynthetic activity required to produce a green, dense, and pest-free turf. Roberts (1965) has shown the deleterious effects of successively lower cutting heights on root growth of Kentucky bluegrass. As a result of lowering the height of cut, fertilizing, watering, and weed control programs must be adjusted to compensate for the reduced root system and the general weakness of the grass. The resulting change in the microclimate of the sward produces an environment conducive to development of disease-producing organisms. In addition, an overly wet soil reduces the oxygen supply and, if heavily trafficked, will become compacted and further complicate the cultural program. Letey *et al.* (1964) discuss a similar compounding or chain-reaction turf deterioration.

Situations in which the acceptable level of quality will permit the neglect, reduction, or omission of one or more of the basic cultural practices may cause turf to lose color, become thin, unthrifty, and weed infested. A marked change in the microclimate of the turf will also result. When water is withheld, the cooling effects of transpiration and evaporation do not exist and an increase in temperature and a decrease in humidity will occur. During a drought, failure to water may produce dormancy or, if prolonged, become lethal with the obvious attendant changes in the microclimate.

Mowing

Mowing is a cultural practice that is necessary for turf production. Proper clipping of adapted grasses stimulates development of tillers and shoots either from the crown or from basal buds on rhizomes or stolons. Mowing is an important grooming technique. Unless it is mowed regularly, a turfgrass area soon becomes overgrown, covered with loose-growing spindly grasses and tall rank weeds which cannot persist under normal mowing practices.

Mowing height must be keyed to the use for which the turfgrass area is being produced. Mowing at the heights necessary to meet use demands severely limits the number of grasses suitable for turf. Musser (1962) estimated less than 40 species are suitable. Davis (1958), Juska *et al.* (1955), Juska and Hanson (1961), Madison (1962), and Roberts (1965), among others, have shown there is a reduction in root growth of turfgrasses as a result of decreasing heights of cut. Root reduction may have a very direct and interacting effect on other cultural practices and therefore on the microclimate. To compensate for the reduction of root growth it becomes necessary to adjust watering practices to suit the more shallow root depth. Unless very careful attention is paid to the watering program, there is a tendency to overwater. The resulting wet soil may produce a more humid microclimate and a reduction in soil oxygen thus encouraging disease development.

Vertical mowing usually removes excess thatch. This thinning operation opens the turf to light and air. If performed when temperature and moisture are also favorable, an ideal microclimate for germination of weeds such as crabgrass or *Poa annua* will be created (Youngner, 1959). However, light vertical mowing to control thatch will aid in maintaining an environment favorable for healthy growth.

Irrigation

Of all the cultural practices, irrigation probably exerts the greatest influence on the microclimate of a turf. Frequency, rate of application, and the amount of water applied at each irrigation are influenced by the kind of soil, rainfall, the depth of root development, and the rate of evapotranspiration. Scheduling irrigation to avoid many of the pitfalls of overwatering is frequently impractical because of interference with play, inadequate distributive systems, or unavailability of labor. Thus many turf areas may be too wet or too dry at any given time.

Water transpired by the leaves serves as a temperature regulator. Van Den Brink and Carolus (1965) and Duff and Beard (1966) have shown that sprinkling will relieve temperature stress. Syringing to maintain turgidity during periods of heat stress is a key factor in golf course maintenance operations. Traffic or pressure on grass leaves when they are under moisture stress will cause severe damage. A light showering of a turf area when the leaf cells begin to lose water will reduce the temperature a few degrees and restore turgidity. Duff and Beard (1966) point out that the application of 0.25 in. of water at 12 noon resulted in only a few degrees drop in temperature in the turf. However, syringing prevented the temperature from reaching the maximum which would have occurred had no water been applied. VanDen Brink and Carolus (1965), on the other hand, found that when irrigation was applied to a tomato field at midday, the temperature at 12 in. was lowered some 18°F and the surface of a muck soil, 22°F.

Water is important in determining the dominant species in a mixed turf. It has been shown (Watson, 1950) that only moderate usage of supplemental irrigation on an intensively managed fairway turf of Kentucky bluegrass, creeping red fescue, and bentgrass caused major shifts in dominance. Within a 2-year period, the irrigated plots were predominately bentgrass, whereas on nonirrigated plots Kentucky bluegrass and red fescue dominated. However, the unwatered plots were not considered satisfactory from a playing standpoint. From these results bentgrass could be expected to dominate a low-cut, irrigated fairway in regions of its adaptation.

Supplemental irrigation is always necessary if turfgrass areas are expected to remain green throughout the growing season. The frequency of irrigation is governed by the water-holding capacity of the soil and the rate at which the available water is depleted. For the most vigorous and healthy growth, watering should begin when approximately 40% to 60% of the available water has been depleted. Most plants show a marked growth response when soil moisture is maintained between these levels. Assuming equal depth of rooting, sandy type soils will have to be watered more frequently than will loams or clays. Climatic conditions, such as high wind movement, intense sunlight, low humidity, and temperature, all contribute to high water-use rates. Such conditions dictate more frequent watering than the reverse set of conditions.

The amount of water to apply at any one time will depend on how much is present in the soil when irrigation is started, the water-holding capacity, and the drainage characteristics of the soil. Enough water should be applied to insure that the entire root zone will be wetted. On natural soils (as opposed to those modified for intensive use) sufficient water should be applied to maintain contact with subsoil moisture and to assure percolation, especially in arid and semiarid regions. Continuous contact between the upper and lower levels of moisture will avoid a dry layer through which roots cannot penetrate. Application of too much water at one time is serious when the soil is poorly drained and the excess cannot be removed within a reasonable period of time. Ponding will cause a marked change in the environment and, under high-temperature conditions, death of the turf.

Fertilization will stimulate growth. When applied in amounts needed by the permanent species and in accordance with their growth response, it will aid in satisfactory development of both roots and leaves. Inadequate amounts, improperly balanced ratios, and incorrect timing of application all contribute to poor turfgrass performance. Soft, succulent turf may result from improper fertilizer application. Such turf is more easily damaged by traffic and requires more frequent watering to prevent collapse under heat or moisture stress. A more humid microclimate is frequently produced by these practices.

Cultivation

Coring, slicing, and spiking operations tend to open the soil and permit movement of water and fertilizer into the root zone. Such practices will assist in drying the surface if it is overly moist and, if excessively dry, will provide a trap for moisture. Thus many greens in northern subhumid and semiarid areas are cored in late fall to trap additional moisture. This aids in combating desiccation during the late winter-early spring when snow cover is absent.

Cultural Practices of Value in Counteracting Adversity of Climate and Use

Wind movement is an effective agent in temperature reduction in the turfgrass microclimate. Carolus (1967) provides calculations showing that at low wind velocities doubling the rate of air movement over a leaf quadruples the rate of potential transpirational water loss. Duff and Beard (1966) reported a 13°F temperature reduction in turf with a wind movement of 4 mph as compared to a restricted 0 mph air movement. Under the study conditions, relative humidity 3 in. above the grass was not influenced by air movement of 4 mph. Thus it seems that removal of obstructions such as mounds, underbrush, and other impediments that restrict air movement aids in controlling temperatures during hot weather.

Topdressing of putting greens is a frequently used technique. The primary purposes of topdressing are to "true" a putting surface and to provide a desirable medium for microbial activity. Because the material usually contains peat or compost, it is dark and amorphous and it will absorb heat. For this reason topdressing of bentgrass greens is usually avoided in the summer months. Conversely, the heating characteristic will produce a favorable response if topdressing or a similar dark material is used during the winter or early spring. The additional warmth is sufficient to stimulate early rapid growth of both bentgrass and bermudagrass greens. Lamp black, activated sewage sludge, and similar materials are often used to assist in the melting of ice sheets in late winter or early spring.

Covers and mulches will substantially alter the microclimate (Watson *et al.*, 1960; Watson and Wicklund, 1962). They insulate against widely fluctuating temperatures and further protect against desiccation. Open-mesh synthetic and wood fibers appear superior to various colors of poly-ethylene.

Soil Heating

In the past few years a number of workers (Daniel and Roberts, 1966) have reported results of soil warming by electric heating cables in turf areas. The investigations have covered several aspects of the engineering, agronomic, and pathological influences on soil and on turfgrass. Installations have been made and are in use in England, Sweden, Missouri, and Wisconsin. The primary prupose of these athletic field installations is to prevent freezing of the soil for late fall and winter games. The electric cables speed the melting of snow although a snow-free turf cannot be assured.

Soil warming may become a useful technique in the maintenance of year-round areas. Further, its use may extend the zone of adaptation of warm season grasses and assure their survival in zones of marginal adaptation.

References

Beard, J. B. (1964). Effects of ice, snow and water covers on Kentucky bluegrass, annual bluegrass and creeping bentgrass. *Crop Sci.* **4**, 638–640.

Beard, J. B. (1969). Environmental stresses of turfgrasses—cause and prevention. *Proc. RCGA Nat. Turfgrass Conf., 20th* pp. 7–10.

Brown, E. M. (1943). Seasonal variations in the growth and chemical composition of certain pasture grasses. *Mo., Agr. Exp. Sta., Res. Bull.* **360**.

Carolus, R. L. (1967). Principles of air-conditioning fruit crops with irrigation. *94th Annu. Meet. Mich. State Hort. Soc. Proc.*

Daniel. W. H., and Roberts, E. C. (1966). Turfgrass management in the United States. *Advan. Agron.* **18**, 259–326.

Davis, R. R. (1958). The effect of other species and mowing heights on persistence of lawn grasses. *Agron. J.* **50**, 671–673.

Duff, D. T., and Beard, J. B. (1966). Effects of air movement and syringing on the micro-climate of bentgrass turf. *Agron. J.* **58**, 495–497.

Ferguson, M. H., Howard, H. L., and Bloodworth, M. E. (1960). Specifications for a method of putting green construction. *USGA (U.S. Gold Asso.) J. Turf Manage.* **8**, No. 5.

Gardner, W. H. (1962). How water moves in the soil. *Crops Soils* **15**, Nos. 1 and 2.

Juska, F. V., and Hanson, A. A. (1961). Effects of interval and height of mowing on growth of Merion and common Kentucky bluegrass (*Poa pratensis* L.). *Agron. J.* **53**, 385–388.

Juska, F. V., Tyson, J., and Harrison, C. M. (1955). The competitive relationship of Merion bluegrass as influenced by various mixtures, cutting heights, and levels of nitrogen. *Agron. J.* **47**, 513–518.

LeBeau, J. B. (1964). Control of snowmold by regulating winter soil temperature. *Phytopathology* **54**, 693–696.

Letey, J., Stolzy, L. H., Lunt, O. R., and Valoras, N. (1964). Soil oxygen and clipping height effects on growth of Newport bluegrass. *Calif. Turfgrass Cult.* **14**, 9–12.

Madison, J. H. (1962). Mowing of turfgrass. II. Responses of three species of grass. *Agron. J.* **54**, 250–252.

Madison, J. H. (1969). Sands used in soil mixes. *Calif. Turfgrass Cult.* **19**, 3–5.

Musser, H. B. (1962). "Turf Management," 2nd ed. McGraw-Hill, New York.

Roberts, E. C. (1965). Getting to the root of turfgrass maintenance problems. *Minn. Turfgrass Conf.* p. 38.

VanDen Brink, C., and Carolus, R. L. (1965). Removal of atmospheric stresses from plants by overhead sprinkler irrigation. *Mich., Agr. Exp. Sta., Quart. Bull.* **47**, 358–363.

Watson, J. R. (1950). Irrigation and compaction on established fairway turf. Ph.D. Thesis, Pennsylvania State University, University Park.

Watson, J. R. and Wicklund, L. (1962). Plastic covers protect greens from winter damage. *Golf Course Rep.* **30**, No. 9, 30–38.

Watson, J. R., Knoll, H., and Wicklund, L. (1960). Protecting golf greens against winterkill. *Gold Course Rep.* **28**, No. 7, 10–13, 16.

Youngner, V. B. (1959). Ecological studies on *Poa annua* in turfgrasses. *J. Brit. Grassl and Soc.* **14**, 233–237.

Youngner, V. B. (1968). The effects of temperature and light on vegetative growth. *Proc. Int. Turfgrass Conf., 39th*, 10–12.

Chapter 15

Population Interactions, Diversity, and Community Structure

S. K. JAIN

Biologists have become increasingly aware of the challenges to mankind in relation to the problems of resource use and the quality of environment. To meet them intelligently an interdisciplinary approach to the ecology and evolution of communities has emerged in recent years to deal with the biology of populations in terms of their genetic and ecological diversity and their evolution. Lewontin (1968) noted at a symposium that "Species are not static entities with fixed relations to the environment, but plastic elements, changing their genetic constitution under the influence of the physical factors of the environment and of the interactions with other species . . . no population ecology can succeed that is not also population genetics." In his classic book *Evolution: The Modern Synthesis*, Huxley (1942) discussed this viewpoint nearly three decades ago. Any modern quantitative analysis of community biology should involve discussions of the structure and diversity of multispecies systems in which the species are treated as heterogeneous, reproductively cohesive, and evolving gene pools. Their total diversity and adaptive strategy is an integrated outcome of the various genetic, ecological, ecogeographical, and demographic parameters. The purpose of this chapter is to discuss briefly the matters of species composition, spatial patterns of distribution, genotypic changes within individual species and certain mea-

212

sures of population interactions; data and examples are drawn from the annual-type grassland community of central California. The species of primary interest currently include the members of genera *Avena, Bromus, Trifolium*, and *Medicago*. To focus our attention on the interactions between the genetic and ecological patterns of community diversity, inquiries in this area might logically be initiated with the following questions: How widespread are genetic polymorphisms (largely used as samples of total genetic variation) in sympatric, congeneric species? In what ways does genotypic variation influence the survival or reproductive strategies? How does the genetic system relate to the regulation of species abundance and distribution? How do population numbers vary over space and time and how do these influence the genetic make-up of a breeding unit, local deme, or the species as a whole?

General Background

The ecology of California grasslands has been discussed by several workers in terms of the climate-soil-plant-animal complex, particularly the role of introduced annuals from the Mediterranean region (Talbot *et al.*, 1939; Biswell, 1956; Burcham, 1957; Heady, 1958; Love, 1956, 1961). The chronological sequence of the dominant species, as noted by Burcham (1957), corresponds to the descending scale of annual plant succession on California ranges, perhaps involving rapid evolutionary changes on a scale unprecedented in human history. Naveh (1967) compared the ecosystems of California and Mediterranean regions emphasizing the preadaptive features of the majority of successful colonizers. Two more recent colonizing episodes of medusahead (McKell *et al.*, 1962) and rose clover (Jain and Shaw, unpublished), on the other hand, illustrate the rapid genetic divergence of their established populations. In a study of old-field succession on Hastings Reservation, California, White (1966) showed that even after 27 years of restricted range use, the annual members of *Bromus* and *Avena* were widespread as dominants in contrast to a slow increase in the pristine species of perennial bunch-grasses. Numerous revegetation studies have involved the changes in species composition during the post-fire conversion of brush to grassland which depend on the relative adaptability and competing ability of various seeded species. In a long-term study at the Tule Springs Range, McKell *et al.* (1965) demonstrated the feasibility of several perennial grasses that can persist with proper management. From the community biology viewpoint, such an "ecological engineering" clearly requires an understanding of the colonization processes in a broad perspective (Baker, 1965). The population dynamics of herbivores, for instance, has been investigated by Fitch and Bentley (1949), Lidicker (1966), Paris (1963), and Taber (1956), among numerous others. Their findings indicate that both structure and energetics of plant community are partially regulated by the herbivores. Harper (1968) further emphasized that "A key to the understanding of niche diversification in grasslands almost certainly lies in the activity of the grazing animal." At the level of primary productivity itself, Williams (1966) and McNaughton (1969) have provided evidence on the role of species diversity, a primary niche dimension being the foliage-configuration types. Several population genetic studies have explored the pattern of variation over space and/or time in the populations of *Avena fatua* and A. *barbata* (Marshall and Jain, 1967; Jain, 1969), *Bromus mollis* (Knowles, 1943; Jain *et al.*, 1971), *Festuca microstachys* (Allard and Kannenberg, 1968), and *Lolium* spp. (Schulke, 1963; Van der Pahlen, 1969). There seem to be a variety of selective mechanisms in all these species to account for the observed large stores of variability locally or over wide areas. To put together these pieces of information, let us turn to the problem of modeling a plant community.

Models of Community Structure

The description and modeling of a community may be approached in various ways depending on the relative emphasis on the flow of nutrients and energy among the trophic levels, the regulation of population numbers, species diversity, or the evolution of niche diversity. Following Levins (1966), several of these approaches are shown in Fig. 1. The clusters of submodels represent the complementary and overlapping nature of the different ways of modeling the structural elements of a community; the experimental analyses may then diverge along the lines of functional versus evolutionary objectives. Based on census data for estimating the components of genetic and species diversity, we are primarily interested in the dynamic nature of species numbers, the strategies of survival and colonization, and the approach to certain equilibrium states. Levins (1965) used the classical Lotka-Volterra equations for two competing species to develop a matrix model for an *n* species community in which a minimum set of parameters include the relative abundance of ith species (x_i), its intrinsic rate of numerical increase (r_i), the carrying capacity measure of an environment (K_i), and the competition coefficients between i^{th} and j^{th} species (a^{ij}). The equilibrium states can be obtained by solving the set of simultaneous equations,

$$\frac{dx_i}{dt} = \frac{r_i x_i (K_i - x_i - a_{ij} x_i)}{K_i} = 0$$

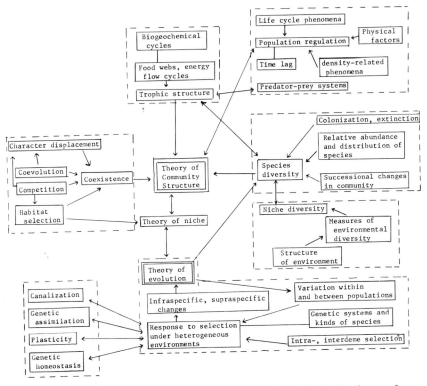

FIG. 1. Chart showing schematically various clusters of models for the theory of community structure (Adapted after Levins, 1968).

Vandermeer (1970) further discussed the use of this model in terms of the effect of competition coefficients (a_{ij}) and the equilibrium species numbers (x_i) to show that a large covariance (cov ax) implies that all abundant species must be good competitors. We expect a larger number of species in the community if this covariance is small, and also if the mean saturation density (K) is large or the variance of K is small. This model emphasizes the role of competitive interactions but ignores higher-order interactions, time lags, and other complicating factors. Experimental methods need to be developed for the estimation of parameters r_i, K_i and a_{ij} under the given limitations. Various features of the community organization such as hierarchy, dominance order, successional change, and the stability over time can also be examined with this model. Recently, McNaughton and Wolf (1970) have attempted to deduce the niche diversity and the role of intra- and interspecies competition in a community from various statistics of relative abundance and dominance. They argued that unequal efficiency or adaptability results in dominance of certain species such that the abundant species have greater genetic diversity and the rarer species are perpetuated through greater genetic uniformity and specialization. However, their arguments for differences in genetic structure are weakened by the lack of evidence for greater phenotypic plasticity of heterozygotes and by ignoring the role of inbreeding, patchiness of distribution, and so on.

Many experimental studies on plant populations provide some basis for the theoretical inputs into the community model of Levins. Harper and his coworkers (Harper, 1961, et seq.) have reported on the plastic and mortal responses to the population numbers approaching the carrying capacity and estimated the frequency, or density, components of the competition coefficients. Palmblad (1968) has initiated a series of similar studies on the weedy species. Marshall and Jain (1969) obtained some evidence for the self-stabilizing properties of the mixed stands of *Avena barbata* and *A. fatua* arising from a negative feedback factor in terms of their relative input proportions. McCown and Williams (1968), on the other hand, investigated the role of competition for sulfur and light in the competitive stands of *Bromus mollis* and *Erodium botrys*, two of the most common annual grassland species in certain areas. They found a net favorable interaction between the two species as judged by the competition index values for the pure versus mixed stands. McKell *et al.* (1969) reported that annual ryegrass has marked inhibitory effects on several other species tested but also exhibited self-interference when grown in various highly competitive situations. Clearly the modeling of multispecies competition requires a critical and cumulative use of many such studies although Vandermeer's analysis provides some good deductive generalizations. Perhaps a greater insight is gained by the stage-by-stage census of various populations, as illustrated by our preliminary studies in *Avena* (Marshall and Jain, 1967). Here the estimates of species abundance were obtained during the seed, seedling, and adult stages over two seasons that relate directly to the mechanism of population regulation. Harper (1968) has reviewed similar work on *Rumex* species in analyzing the niche width during the seedling establishment period.

By sacrificing mathematical generality, larger system models of a community can be built for computer analysis along the lines discussed by Watt (1966), Paulik (1965), Van Dyne (1968), and others. Large amounts of real data can be input through a formal flow chart of information among a set of variables and certain preassigned transfer functions and controls. Individual species populations can be thought of as subsystems with their genetic and ecological properties prescribed and these subsystems interconnected by another set of relationships. Simulation is used to study the relative importance of different parameters and their interactions and to analyze the behavior of system as a whole, in both deterministic and probabilistic terms. Among the simulation studies of continuous systems in biology,

Garfinkel (1965) and Loomis *et al.* (1967) may be cited. Van Dyne has provided a detailed plan for modeling the grassland ecosystem, formulated in terms of the flow of energy and nutrients. Evolutionarily speaking, our modeling efforts are directed toward the analyses and prediction of changes in the patterns of diversity observed at the levels of local deme, species, or the community.

Patterns of Diversity

A focal issue in the biology of populations is organic diversity in space and time. The species diversity of a community depends on the number of species (variety), their relative abundance (equitability), and stratification resulting in spatial heterogeneity, life form, and so on (MacArthur, 1965; Odum, 1968). Accordingly, a variety of statistical measures of species diversity have now been developed (Pielou, 1969) and used in numerous recent studies. Similarly, measures of genetic diversity within individual species are based on a variety of features such as the proportion of loci with widespread polymorphisms, multiple allelism, heterozygosis, gene frequency variances among populations, and the presence of identifiable races and subspecies (Table 1). The ecological and genetic diversity must have interactions through such verifiable items as the correlation between species abundance and amount of variation (Ford, 1964), character displacement in cohabiting species (Brown and Wilson, 1956), reduced genetic variation in the mixed cultures of related species (Jain, 1969), and nonrandom distribution of genotypes and species (Goodall, 1952; Hairston, 1964). The increasing variety of coexisting species or genotypes must subdivide the available niches in somewhat similar and complementary ways with one notable exception: the genetic polymorphisms are likely to be further reinforced by the reproductive unity of a species. McNaughton and Wolf (1970) have argued that species occurring in climax communities evolve toward more individual heterozygosity and population homogeneity, whereas successional stages have more species with a greater interpopulational differentiation and less heterozygosis. Many of the grassland annuals mentioned earlier are characterized by a predominantly inbreeding system and with population structures varying in the levels of genetic variation within and between populations (Allard, 1965; Allard *et al.*, 1968; Jain *et al.*, 1971). This point will be discussed further in the following section. If successional gradients can be defined within a series of similar habitats, the McNaughton-Wolf hypothesis certainly deserves a careful examination.

In California grassland communities there are many examples on record

TABLE 1

MEASURES OF DIVERSITY IN A COMMUNITY

Genetic–phenotypic	Ecological
1. Mendelian characters: Gene and genotypic frequencies Proportion of polymorphic loci Amount of heterozygosity per locus Polymorphism index Variances and covariances of gene frequencies among populations	1. Number of species in an area
2. Continuously inherited characters: Total phenotypic variance or coefficient of variation Genetic components of variance Mean and variance of fitness-related traits Limits of response to selection Environment-induced variation Genotype–environment interactions	2. Species-abundance curves: Equitability Dominance Information theory measure
3. Adaptive surface: presence of multiple peaks and ridginess	3. Stratification: trophic diversity habitat and pattern diversity geographical gradients
4. Taxonomic divergence: numerical, biochemical (local races, ecotypes, subspecies)	4. Environmental components: niche diversity limiting similarity of coexisting species

describing the nonrandom distribution of species, often attributed to the habitat preferences. The results of soil-vegetation surveys may reflect this in many instances (Love and Begg, 1966). Our data based on several quadrats located within a nearly 500 sq ft area, chosen visually for species patchiness, gave clear evidence for small neighborhoods abounding with different species and stable over successive years. Furthermore in one study of the allelic distribution among populations of *Avena barbata* the patchiness of genotypic distribution was also found to be correlated with the relative abundance of three *Bromus* species within neighboring patches. Such heterogeneity may result from habitat selection, history of natural selection, common (familial) origin through inbreeding and reduced gene flow, or mere accidents of sampling. Patchy distributions of genotypes are far more frequent in populations of *A. barbata* and *Medicago polymorpha* than in *A. fatua* and *Bromus mollis*. Such differences in the pattern of diversity might well be related to the strategies of population regulation and competition coefficients. Localized differences in species composition also provide an opportunity to test the relationship postulated between abundance and variability. A series of samples were analyzed for the relative proportions of two *Avena* species and three *Bromus* species, and for estimating total phenotypic variation within each species the coefficients of variation were estimated for two quantitative traits. In addition, for the simply inherited markers polymorphism indices were calculated from the allelic frequency estimates. In *Bromus mollis* the values of the coefficients of variation were highest for the subsites where it was most abundant. In *Avena* the data indicated reduction in variability in their mixed stands as compared with the pure stand values. A similar relationship can be tested in the *Festuca microstachys* complex based on the studies by Allard and Kannenberg (1968). Thus joint analyses of these patterns of diversity in coexisting species would provide the first clues to the evolutionary processes at the level of communities.

Genetic Variability in Related Species

The subject of genetic variation and natural selection has been reviewed by many biologists. Population genetics largely deals with the questions on the origin, maintenance, and utilization of variability within populations in adaptive responses to the environmental changes. In plants there exists a great variety of breeding systems involving devices favoring inbreeding or outbreeding, which in combination with numerous other features of the genetic system may be used to describe the different kinds of species (Mayr, 1963). The variation pattern in predominantly self-fertilizing species has been recently re-examined in some detail (Allard *et al.*, 1968). Several questions were raised on the genetic polymorphisms.

How widespread are genetic polymorphisms in related groups of species? There are now extensive data available on polymorphisms in *Avena* species for four morphological markers and several isoenzymatic markers (scored by the starch gel electrophoresis method). Almost all samples of *A. fatua* were found to be polymorphic for one or more loci; in contrast, *A. barbata* samples from a rather wide region in the Central Valley were monomorphic for the same set of alleles. In the San Francisco Bay region and vicinity, *A. barbata* populations showed a low degree of polymorphism at a majority of sites and high polymorphism at a few sites. The presence and absence of variation were found to be highly correlated between the two sets of markers, morphological and isoenzymatic, and on a geographical scale variation seemed to coincide with the regions of warm and cool summer

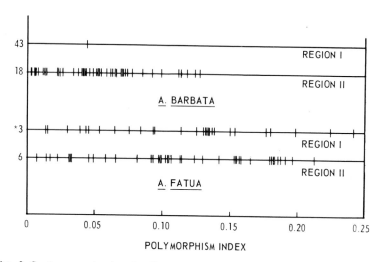

FIG. 2. Scattergram showing the distribution of values of polymorphism index in populations of *Avena fatua* and *A. barbata* for regions of Central Valley and vicinity (I) and San Francisco Bay (II).

Mediterranean climate. Quantitatively, the variation in the two species and two regions was compared by defining the polymorphism index as the product of allelic frequencies averaged over loci, a measure linearly related to the genetic variance per additive locus. Figure 2 shows the scatter of values along a linear range of 0 to 0.25, from which *A. fatua* is far more polymorphic than *A. barbata*. A similar survey of variability in *Avena barbata* and *A. hirtula* samples from the Mediterranean region showed a similar localized presence of few polymorphic sites (Singh and Jain, 1971). The comparative results from these *Avena* studies are summarized in Table 2 showing a variety of the contrasting features of the ecogenetic system. A point to note is the postulated difference in the adaptive strategy of two similar, coexisting species, at least with regard to the genetic polymorphisms versus phenotypic plasticity. Several recent papers in plant population biology have emphasized this aspect (Bradshaw, 1965; Cook and Johnson, 1968). Baker (1965) reported on the comparisons of phenotypic plasticity between several pairs of weedy and nonweedy relatives which need to be supplemented with some information on the genetic variation. Carson (1965) provided some interesting comparisons of chromosomal polymorphisms among several groups of ecologically similar *Drosophila* species. Several parallel studies have been initiated in bromes, clovers, and other introduced grasses. The omparative studies of *Bromus mollis* and *B. rigidus* populations so far suggest that the pattern might resemble in some ways the one described for *Avena* species. Most populations of *B. mollis* were found to

TABLE 2

SUMMARY TO COMPARE SOME FEATURES OF THE ECOGENETIC SYSTEM OF *AVENA FATUA* AND *AVENA BARBATA*

Characteristic	Quantity	Comparison
1. Mating system	% outcrossing rate	2%–3% in *A. fatua*; nearly 2% in *A. barbata* (higher under optimal growth conditions)
2. Pollen and seed dispersal	Rate and mean distance	Small in both species; most probably leptokurtic; larger seed in *A. fatua* may have lower dispersal
3. Genetic polymorphism (marker loci)	Morph-ratios or gene frequencies	*A. fatua*—high in feral populations, perhaps lower in peripheral areas; *A. barbata*—low, often monomorphic
3a. Heterozygosity levels	Genotypic frequencies and selective values	Higher in *A. fatua*; heterozygote advantage in some *A. fatua* populations
4. Genetic components of variation (quantitative)	Between- and within-family variability	Higher in *A. fatua*
5. Phenotypic plasticity	Environment-induced variability	High in both; higher in *A. barbata* for most characters
6. Total phenotypic variability	Coefficients of variability	High in both; higher in *A. barbata*
7. Response to within-family selection	Changes in means of high, low selection lines	Perhaps lower in *A. barbata* (evidence inconclusive)
8. Clines (geographical and micro-geographical	Morph-ratio or gene frequency	Regional and localized patterns in both species; greater patchiness in *A. barbata*
9. Dormancy and overlapping generations	Seed carry over and germination rates	Low in both; perhaps greater site to site differentiation in *A. barbata*
10. Early seedling growth and interference	Total dry matter output and seedling survival	More rapid in *A. fatua*; greater self-thinning in *A. barbata*
11. Flowering time	Days to flowering and distribution of range	Earlier in *A. fatua*; greater canalization in *A. barbata*
12. Reproductive capacity	Mean fertility and fecundity	Often Higher in *A. barbata*; greater response to density

be polymorphic, with rather low levels of heterozygosis in relation to the estimates of outcrossing rates (Jain *et al.*, 1971). The overall picture of highly differentiated populations from each other in many of these introduced species suggests that perhaps within a short post-colonizing period rather rapid evolutionary changes have occurred and are likely to continue in this process of genetic divergence.

What are the factors maintaining genetic variation? Based on a review of the better known examples in literature, we can list the following main factors: (1) identical or nearly identical net selective values of two or more alleles at a locus. Mukai (1969) discussed the evidence on recurrent mutation rates as a major factor in maintaining polygenic and isoallelic variation. This view does not necessarily assume totally nonadaptive variation as implied by some authors. (2) Heterozygote advantage arising from true or marginal overdominance. This includes a wide variety of selective forces including those arising from epistatic gene interactions and genetic homeostasis (Lerner, 1954). (3) Ecological mosaicism resulting either from stable niches differentiated in space (coarse-grained environment, Levins, 1968), or cyclic, periodic, and random variation in selective values over time. (4) Disassortative mating, with or without frequency dependency in the mating frequencies among unlike genotypes or phenotypes. (5) Other behavioral, mimicry related, or coadaptational factors that favor intraspecific variation. The various elements of a genetic system as well as a balance among the forces of selection, migration, mutation, recombination, and drift yield a vast array of theoretical models allowing the maintenance of genetic variation. In fact, it seems that the lack of genetic variation as noted in the case of *A. barbata* now raises more interesting questions on the ecological significance of variation.

What is the role of genetic variation in the ecology of a species? It has often been tacitly assumed that a species responds to varying environments through natural selection sorting out more favorable genotypes. Several lines of evidence have been reported: correlation with some environmental factors (for example, altitude, humidity), higher buffering capacity as tested under varying environments, relationship with higher productivity, expansion in the area of distribution, and in some cases direct evidence for selective premium on variation (for example, cryptic coloration, mimicry, sex recognition). Adaptedness, defined in terms of long-term persistence versus ecological efficiency, and adaptability, defined in terms of ability to respond to new ecological needs both require long-term studies at the level of individual organism as well as population.

Levins (1968) developed his theory of adaptive strategies taking environmental heterogeneity as a key point of departure from the classical theory of population genetics. He showed that fitness or adaptive value measure-

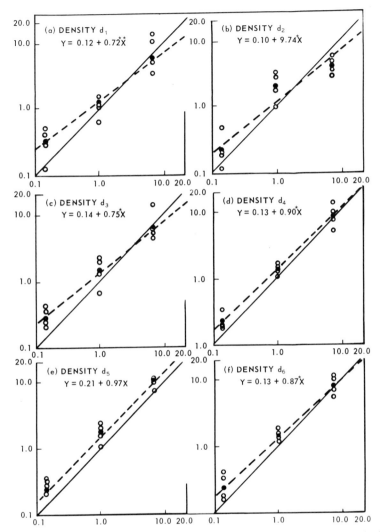

FIG. 3. Ratio diagrams showing the regression of input ratio of *Avena fatua* to *A. barbata* (number of seeds sown) and the output ratio of the numbers of seed produced (dotted line, observed; solid line, expected with no interference). After Marshall and Jain (1969).

ments can be used in niche theory in analyzing the role of genetic parameters in a species' strategies. Different populations of a species may adopt different strategies ranging from monomorphic specialization to environmental tracking, depending on the adaptive function and grain of environment. Independent niche analyses could begin with the investigation of tolerance range and optima such as done by Maguire (1967), the usual grist of physiological ecology. These same studies could further describe the response in terms of survival as well as reproductive fitness. For further discussions of the recent developments of niche theory, see MacArthur (1968), Schoener (1968), and McNaughton and Wolf (1970). The biology of colonizing species was discussed in these terms by MacArthur and Wilson (1967) and Harper (1965).

Population Interactions

Earlier the role of interspecies competition was mentioned in relation to a model of community structure. The ecological literature has reports of many examples and theoretical models of the ways in which populations of animals and plants living in the same area interact, ranging from mutualism and commensalism to allelopathy, predation, or parasitism. These interactions regulate the species composition of a community as well as the relative spatial distribution of different species and therefore deserve wide attention in both natural and experimental communities. Harper and his coworkers (1961) and others (Risser, 1968) have discussed the mechanisms of competition in plants largely in terms of their regulation through mortal or plastic responses. The general principle as stated by several authors is that two species can coexist only if each inhibits its own population more than others. Risser reviewed the pertinent grassland literature on competition emphasizing the variety of plant adaptations and the role of population structure in the outcome. However, genetic variation has rarely been considered in interspecies competition. The work of Park (1954, et seq.) and Lerner and Dempster (1962) on *Tribolium* species is a classic example of how the apparent indeterminacy in the outcome was based on the presence of genetic variability within each competitor species. Pimentel (1964) pointed out the role of genetic feedback in the numerical oscillations of a two-species system. Avoidance through character displacement, evolution of superior competing ability, and other forms of coevolutionary changes are all relevant to the diversity patterns discussed earlier.

Population Regulation

By regulation we refer to the general implication that a species has ecologically or evolutionarily acquired some means of avoiding underpopulation or overpopulation so that its population numbers, either locally or as a whole, may fluctuate within certain limits. Most theories on population regulation discuss the relative importance of weather, natural enemies, and direct density related factors of competition. The key point at issue seems to be whether competition occurs frequently in nature as related to some resource in limiting supply. Experimental studies on density related changes show that decrease in population numbers could involve emigration, deterioration of genetic quality, behavioral interference, and so on. In order to emphasize some of the genetic aspects of regulation, a diagrammatic cycle is given in Scheme 1, based on a recent essay by Carson (1968). Many of the links in this scheme are still in somewhat speculative phase; however, the role of interdeme gene flow and the resulting hybridization or introgressive transfer of new genes has been particularly recognized in plant populations. In many of the colonizing episodes in the California vegetation, the Mediterranean species were presumably favored through preadaption as well as with high reproductive rates. Thus one should distinguish between the colonization of home-like territories and newly arising niches. Another crucial issue is the intensity of selective forces during the flush and crash periods. Within the range of distribution of a species, some populations may undergo regular fluctuations, whereas in other parts there might be continual process of extinction and recolonization. Weather fluctuations from year to year seem to be highly correlated with the annual fluctuations in California grassland vegetation (Talbot *et al.*, 1939; Heady, 1958). With the help of genetic polymorphisms the role of intraspecies competition in regulation can be analyzed in terms of the relative sizes of random and nonrandom com-

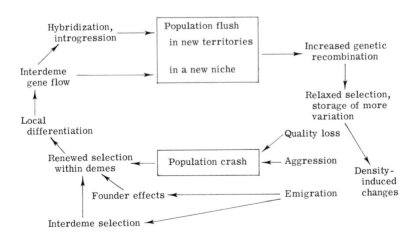

SCHEME 1. Genetic aspects of population regulation (Carson, 1968).

TABLE 3[a]

SOME EVOLUTIONARY PROPERTIES OF AN ECOSYSTEM

Ecosystem attribute	Developmental stages	Mature stages
Species diversity:	Low	High
Variety	Low	High
Equitability	Low	High
Stratification	Low	High
Spatial heterogeneity	Low	High
Biochemical	Low	High
Niche specialization	Broad	Narrow
Life cycles	Short, simple	Long, complex
Growth form	Rapid growth	Feedback
Production	(r selection)	(k selection)
Stability (resistance to external perturbations)	Quality poor	Quality good

[a]Adapted after Odum (1968)

ponents. Dormancy, seed depredation by herbivores, seedling deaths, and losses through migration might be associated with the presence of genetic differences (Marshall and Jain, 1971).

To summarize, the structure of grassland communities may be analyzed from diverse approaches combining the genetic, ecological, mathematical, and biogeographical treatments. In the future, population biology should play a key role in our analytic and quantitative researches on some of the questions posed here. The current ideas on the nature of ecosystems and succession as stated by Odum (1968) and given in part in Table 3 should be evaluated experimentally for their relevance to the current problems of resource use and management.

References

Allard, R. W. (1965). Genetic systems associated with colonizing ability in predominantly self-pollinated species. *In* "The Genetics of Colonizing Species" (H. G. Baker and G. L. Stebbins, eds.), pp. 50–78. Academic Press, New York.

Allard, R. W., and Kannenberg, L. W. (1968). Population studies in predominantly self-pollinating species. XI. Genetic divergence among the members of the *Festuca microstachys* complex. *Evolution* **22**, 517–528.

Allard, R. W., Jain, S. K., and Workman, P. L. (1968). The genetics of inbreeding populations. *Advan. Genet.* **14**, 55–131.

Baker, H. G. (1965). Characteristics and modes of origin of weeds. *In* "The Genetics of Colonizing Species" (H. G. Baker and G. L. Stebbins, eds.), pp. 147–172. Academic Press, New York.

Biswell, H. H. (1956). Ecology of California grasslands. *J. Range Manage.* **9**, 19–24.

Bradshaw, A. D. (1965). Evolutionary significance of phenotypic plasticity in plants. *Advan. Genet.* **13**, 115–155.

Brown, W. L., and Wilson, E. O. (1956). Character displacement. *Syst. Zool.* **5**, 49–64.

Burcham, L. T. (1957). "California Range Land." Division of Forestry, Department of Natural Resources, State of California.

Carson, H. L. (1965). Chromosomal morphism in geographically widespread species of *Drosophila*. *In* "The Genetics of Colonizing Species" (H. G. Baker and G. L. Stebbins, eds.), pp. 503–531. Academic Press, New York.

Carson, H. L. (1968). The population flush and its consequences. *In* "Population Biology and Evolution" (R. C. Lewontin, ed.), pp. 123–138. Syracuse Univ. Press, Syracuse.

Cook, S. A., and Johnson, M. P. (1968). Adaptation to heterogeneous environments. I. Variation in heterophylly in *Ranunculus flammula* L. *Evolution* **22**, 496–516.

Fitch, H. S., and Bentley, J. R. (1949). Use of California annual plant forage by range rodents. *Ecology* **30**, 306–321.

Ford, E. B. (1964). "Ecological Genetics." Methuen, London.

Garfinkel, D. (1965). Computer simulation in biochemistry and ecology. *In* "Theoretical and Mathematical Biology" (T. H. Waterman, and M. J. Morowitz, eds.), pp. 292–310. Ginn (Blaisdell), Boston, Massachusetts.

Goodall, D. W. (1952). Quantitative aspects of plant distribution. *Biol. Rev.* **27**, 194–245.

Hairston, N. G. (1964). Studies on the organization of animal communities. *J. Anim. Ecol.* **33**, 227–239.

Harper, J. L. (1961). Approaches to the study of plant competition. *Symp. Soc. Exp. Biol.* **15**, 1–39.

Harper, J. L. (1965). Establishment, aggression and cohabitation in weedy species. *In* "The Genetics of Colonizing Species" (H. G. Baker and G. L. Stebbins, eds.), pp. 245–267. Academic Press, New York.

Harper, J. L. (1968). The regulation of numbers and mass in plant populations. *In* "Population Biology and Evolution" (R. C. Lewontin, ed.), pp. 139–158. Syracuse Univ. Press, Syracuse.

Harper, J. L., Clatworthy, J. N., McNaughton, I. H., and Sagar, G. R. (1961). The evolution and ecology of closely related species living in the same area. *Evolution* **15**, 209–227.

Heady, H. F. (1958). Vegetational changes in the California annual type. *Ecology* **39**, 402–416.

Huxley, J. (1942). "Evolution. The Modern Synthesis." Allen & Unwin, London.

Jain, S. K. (1969). Comparative ecogenetics of two *Avena* species occurring in Central California. *Evol. Biol.* **3**, 73–118.

Jain, S. K., and Shaw, M. Unpublished data.

Jain, S. K., Marshall, D. R., and Wu, K. K. (1971). Genetic variation in *Bromus mollis* populations. *Evolution* (in press).

Knowles, P. F. (1943). Improving an annual bromegrass, *Bromus mollis* L., for range purposes. *J. Amer. Soc. Agron.* **35**, 484–594.

Lerner, I. M. (1954). "Genetic Homeostasis." Wiley, New York.

Lerner, I. M., and Dempster, E. R. (1962). Indeterminism in interspecific competition. *Proc. Nat. Acad. Sci. U.S.* **48**, 821–826.

Levins, R. (1965). Genetic consequences of natural selection. *In* "Theoretical and Mathematical Biology," (T. H. Waterman, and H. J. Morowitz, eds.), p. 371–386. Ginn (Blaisdell), Boston, Massachusetts.

Levins, R. (1966). Strategy of model building in population biology. *Amer. Sci.* **54**, 421–431.

Levins, R. (1968). "Evolution in Changing Environments." Princeton Univ. Press, Princeton.

Lewontin, R. C. (1968). Introduction. *In* "Population Biology and Evolution" (R. C. Lewontin, ed.), pp. 1–4. Syracuse Univ. Press, Syracuse.

Lidicker, W. Z. (1966). Ecological observations on a feral house mouse population declining to extinction. *Ecol. Monogr.* **36**, 27–50.

Loomis, R. S., Williams, W. A., and Duncan, W. G. (1967). Community architecture and the productivity of terrestrial plant communities. *In* "Harvesting the Sun: Photosynthesis in Plant Life" (A. San Pietro, F. A. Greer, and T. J. Army, eds.), Academic Press, New York.

Love, R. M. (1956). Better adaptation of plants to arid conditions. *In* "The Future of Arid Lands" Publ. No. 73, pp. 343–367. *Amer. Ass. Advance. Sci.*, Washington, D.C.

Love, R. M. (1961). The range—natural plant communities or modified ecosystems. *J. Brit. Grassland Soc.* **16**, 89–99.

Love, R. M., and Begg, E. L. (1966). Use of the soil-vegetation survey in predicting success of establishment of improved grassland species. *Proc. Int. Grassland Congr., 10th, 1966* pp. 893–896.

MacArthur, R. H. (1965). Patterns of species diversity. *Biol. Rev.* **40**, 510–533.

MacArthur, R. H. (1968). The theory of the niche. *In* "Population Biology and Evolution" (R. C. Lewontin, ed.), pp. 159–176. Syracuse Univ. Press, Syracuse.

MacArthur, R. H., and Wilson, E. O. (1967). "The Theory of Island Biogeography." Princeton Univ. Press, Princeton.

McCown, R. L., and Williams, W. A. (1968). Competition for nutrients and light between the annual grassland species *Bromus mollis* and *Erodium botrys*. *Ecology* **49**, 981–990.

McKell, C. M., Robinson, J. P., and Major, J. (1962). Ecotypic variation in medusahead, an introduced annual grass. *Ecology* **43**, 686–699.

McKell, C. M., and Brown, V. W., Walker, C. F., and Love, R. M. (1965). Species composition changes in seeded grasslands converted from chaparral. *J. Range Manage.* **18**, 321–326.

McKell, C. M., Duncan, C., and Muller, C. H. (1969). Competitive relationships of annual ryegrass (*Lolium multiflorum* Lam.) *Ecology* **50**, 653–658.

McNaughton, S. J. (1969). Structure and function in California grasslands. *Ecology* **49**, 962–972.

McNaughton, S. J., and Wolf, L. L. (1970). Dominance and the niche in ecological systems. *Science* **167**, 131–139.

Maguire, B., Jr. (1967). A partial analysis of the niche. *Amer. Natur.* **101**, 515–523.

Marshall, D. R., and Jain, S. K. (1967). Cohabitation and relative abundance of two species of wild oats. *Ecology* **48**, 656–659.

Marshall, D. R., and Jain, S. K. (1969). Interference in pure and mixed populations of *Avena fatua* and *A. barbata*. *J. Ecol.* **57**, 251–270.

Marshall, D. R., and Jain, S. K. (1971). The role of seed depredation and dormancy in the regulation of *Avena* populations. *Ecology* (in press).

Mayr, E. (1963). "Animal Species and Evolution." Belknap Press, Harvard.

Mukai, T. (1969). Maintenance of polygenic and isoallelic variation in populations. *Proc. Int. Genet. Congr., 12th, 1968* vol. 3, pp. 293–308.

Naveh, Z. (1967). Mediterranean ecosystems and vegetation types in California and Israel. *Ecology* **48**, 445–459.

Odum, E. P. (1968). The strategy of ecosystem development. *Science* **164**, 262–270.

Palmblad, I. G. (1968). Competition in experimental populations of weeds with emphasis on the regulation of population size. *Ecology* **49**, 26–33.

Paris, O. H. (1963). The ecology of *Armadillidium vulgare* (Isopoda: Oniscoidea) in California grassland. *Ecol. Monogr.* **33**, 1–22.

Park, T. (1954). Competition: An experimental and statistical study. *In* "Statistics and Mathematics and Biology" (O., Kempthorne, *et al.*, eds.), pp. 175–196. Iowa State Coll. Press, Ames.

Paulik, G. J. (1965). Digital simulation of natural animal communities. *In* "Marine and Pollution Ecology," pp. 67–85. (eds. T. A. Alson and F. J. Burgers).

Pielou, E. C. (1969). "An Introduction to Mathematical Ecology." Wiley, New York.

Pimentel, D. (1964). Population ecology and the genetic feedback mechanism. *Proc. Int. Genet. Congr., 11th, 1963* pp. 483–487.

Risser, P. G. (1968). Competitive relationships among herbaceous plants and their influence on the ecosystem function in grasslands. IBP-Grassland Synthesis Project Workshop, Halsey, Nebraska.

Schoener, T. W. (1968). Size of feeding territories among birds. *Ecology* **49**, 123–141.

Schulke, J. D. (1963). Genetic variability in natural populations of *Lolium multiflorum*. Ph.D. Dissertation, University of California Davis.

Singh, R. S., and Jain, S. K. (1971). Isozyme polymorphisms in natural populations of *Avena. Theor. Appl. Genet.* (in press).

Taber, R. D. (1956). Deer nutrition and population dynamics in the North Coast range of California. *Trans. N. Amer. Wildl. Cong.* **21**, 159–172.

Talbot, M. W., Biswell, H. H., and Hormay, A. L. (1939). Fluctuation in the annual vegetation at California. *Ecology* **20**, 394–402.

Vandermeer, J. H. (1970). The community matrix and the number of species in a community. *Amer Natur.* **104**, 73–84.

Vander Pahlen, A. (1969). The genetics of isozyme polymorphisms in natural populations of *Lolium multiflorum* Lam. Ph.D. Dissertation, University of California, Davis.

Van Dyne, G. M. (1968). Some mathematical models of grassland ecosystems. IBP-Grassland Synthesis Project Workshop, Centennial, Wyoming.

Watt, K. E. F., ed. (1966) "Systems Analysis in Ecology." Academic Press, New York.

White, K. L. (1966). Old-field succession on Hastings Reservation, California. *Ecology* **47**, 865–868.

Williams, W. A. (1966). Range improvement as related to net productivity, energy flow, and foliage configuration. *J. Range Manage.* **19**, 29–34.

Chapter 16

Competition within the Grass Community

RAYMOND A. EVANS and JAMES A. YOUNG

Competition determines the ecological structure of seral grassland communities; it controls shifts in floristic composition in response to environmental manipulations; and its action constitutes a major deterrent in establishing replacement vegetation. A basis for better understanding of the role of competition within plant communities must include a knowledge of species assemblages with genetic variability among and within the component species, the nature of environmental complexes with man's interferences, and interrelations among all of these in the ecosystem.

On assessing the effects of competition, one must be cognizant of an interplay of limiting factors that are presented by the many variables occurring in the complex of edaphic factors, climatic parameters, and cultural practices.

Introduction and Dominance of Species in the Community

Millions of acres of rangeland in the intermountain area are dominated by either of two highly competitive alien annual grasses, *Bromus tectorum* L. or *Taeniatherum asperum* (Sim.) Nevski. Such dominance is the culmination of succession through lower seral stages represented by broadleaf species. The most common broadleaf species are *Sisymbrium altissimum* L., *Descurainia pinnata* (Walt.) Britt., *Lepidium perfoliatum* L., *Erodium cicutarium* L'Her, and *Salsola kali* L. var. *tenuifolia* Tausch.

This highly competitive alien annual complex began to dominate these rangelands in the late 1800's after severe depletion of native, perennial grass-dominated communities by grazing of domestic livestock.

Before the introduction of concentrations of domestic livestock, little of the intermountain area of western North America was subjected to grazing by large gregarious herbivores. The vegetation of much of this area, which is suitable for grazing, was dominated by shrubby species of *Artemisia* with a perennial grass understory. Differentiation of numerous species of *Artemisia* occurred in response to various climatic and edaphic situations within this vegetation formation (Beetle, 1960). The bunchgrass understory was composed of a number of genera and species with floristic composition which varied in its apparent response to differing environmental potentials. These native communities evolved to a precarious equilibrium with an extremely erratic climate. The perennial habit of the components of these native communities made annual re-establishment unnecessary. Seedling establishment during the irregularly occurring maximal years of precipitation (Antevs, 1948) may have been sufficient to maintain stand density. Harris (1967) has shown that seedlings of the once extensively dominant bunchgrass, *Agropyron spicatum* (Pursh) Scribn. and Smith, naturally survive competition only in the summers of above average precipitation.

Before Europeans settled western North America, the stand renewal process was not conducive to creating and maintaining large areas at a low seral status. The woody portions of native communities were at times undoubtedly destroyed by wildfire (O. C. Stewart, 1955, 1963). But the perennial grass portion of the native communities probably benefited by the reduced competition (Blaisdell, 1953). A number of short-lived perennial grasses and root-sprouting shrubs, *Chrysothamnus nauseosus* (Pall.) Britt., *C. viscidiflorus* (Hook.) Nutt., *Tetradymia glabrata* A. Gray, *Prunus andersonii* Gray, and *Gutierrezia sarothrae* (Pursh) Britt. and Rusby, rapidly colonize burned *Artemisia* communities (McKell and Chilcote, 1957; Robertson and Cords, 1957).

Apparently no highly competitive native annual species evolved in western North America to play a successional role in low seral communities. The number of individual native species occurring in these communities can be moderately large; but rarely if ever do native annuals dominate low seral communities in this vegetation type. We might ask the question, "Is the lack of competitive native annual species in the grassland of the intermountain area a reflection of the conditions under which the communities evolved?"

The only other area of the world with vegetation similar to the *Artemisia* formation of western North America is the *Artemisia* steppe of central Asia (Mirov, 1951). The highly competitive annual species which now play such a dominant role in the succession of shrub grasslands in the intermountain area of western North America fulfill a similar role in seral communities of the *Artemisia* steppe of central Asia (Lavrenko and Soczava, 1956; Sin'Kowskii, 1959; Telwar, 1961). The annual colonizing species may have originated elsewhere, but if so, they must have found the condition in central Asia conducive to the selection of highly competitive genotypes. The *Artemisia* steppes of central Asia have been subjected to centuries of intensive grazing by a wide spectrum of herbivores, wild and domestic, including horses, asses, cattle, sheep, goats, camels, and wild gazelle and antelopes (Ensminger, 1951; Larin, 1963). In Turkestan, bones of domestic sheep have been found in strata dating from 8250 B.C. (Hilzheimer, 1936). Animal husbandry in these regions has always been of nomadic nature (Larin, 1947). The movements of nomadic tribes and the restricted distribution of stock water produced concentrations of grazing livestock which tended to create and maintain low seral plant communities (Kashkarov and Kurbatov, 1930). The ancient migratory routes of the "people who are no more," could be identified in the Bet-Pak-Dala Desert by the predominance of weedy annuals (Kubanskaja, 1956). We ask, "Has this continued grazing pressure on plant communities for centuries provided the environment necessary for the selection of highly competitive annual species?" Even if the weedy seral species of the *Artemisia* communities of central Asia were introduced to western North America by way of Australia, North Africa, or Chile, they lost little of their inherent competitive ability in passing through some of the most intensely grazed portions of the world (Lavrenko, 1962).

During 75 years of investigations, scientists have gradually comprehended the magnitude of the inherent competitive ability of alien annuals. Peimeisel (1951) observed that alien annuals only passively enter voids in perennial communities created by disturbance. Pickford (1932) reported *Bromus tectorum* made up less than 1% of the natural vegetation of ungrazed and unburned ranges in Utah. Where disturbance has created voids in perennial vegetation, G. Stewart and Hull (1949) counted 1080 to 15,000 *B. tectorum* seedlings per sq m.

Biologic competition may be slight on sites denuded to bare mineral soil, but the physical environment is extremely harsh and the alien annuals occupy the voids with dense and often monospecific communities.

In southeastern Washington, Daubenmire (1940, 1952), Poulton (1955), and Harris (1967) observed that *B. tectorum* has inserted itself successfully into climax bunchgrass stands that have been protected from grazing or fire for as long as 50 years.

These extremes in successional level illustrate the amplitude of the competitive ability of *B. tectorum* and many of the other alien weeds. At low seral levels the aliens occupy the multitude of available niches to the exclusion of perennial grass seedlings. This heterogeneous environment offers havens for a number of slightly different genotypes or requires phenotypic plasticity to occupy completely the site potential. The high seral community presents an extremely homogeneous environment to the alien. Site potential is largely pre-empted by native perennials that have evolved in place to provide vegetation assemblages in equilibrium with their environment. The alien must out compete the perennials or exist on environmental potential remaining after the demands of the assemblages of native perennial species have been met. If the latter is true, apparently there is a lack of native species that can fully utilize the site. The environment may have lacked the selection pressure to fix this level of competitiveness in the native populations, or basic genetic material was not available from which these kinds of competitive species could evolve.

After a tour in 1901 of western Nevada ranges, which had been greatly depleted by concentrated sheep grazing, Kennedy and Doten (1901) noted the need for selecting desirable native species to revegetate the range. They doubted the wisdom of importing alien species to revegetate these areas, because the native species had become perfectly adapted to the soil and the climate of the region. Since 1900, attempts to revegetate these rangelands with native perennial grass species have usually failed. By contrast millions of acres have been revegetated with perennial wheatgrasses from central Asia (L. D. Love and Hanson, 1932; Hull and Klomp, 1966, 1967). Apparently the spheres of competitiveness under which the native vegetation had evolved were irreversibly destroyed by alien introduction, or at least by the conditions conducive to the alien introduction.

The introduction of a host of new highly competitive genotypes did not simply elevate competitiveness in the vegetation to a different level from which succession could proceed to a new equilibrium. The amount and types of disturbance in the grasslands of western North America have not stabilized since the introduction of aliens. In one century the stand renewal process in the vegetation of western North America has successively operated (1) at pristine levels, (2) with uncontrolled burning and grazing by domestic livestock, and (3) under attempted complete suppression of fires with continued attrition by grazing. The process of stand renewal is an important factor in establishing the initial level of competition (Daubenmire, 1961; Young *et al.*, 1967). The net result of this century of turmoil has been decline and suppression of native perennial grasses and unlimited opportunity for the spread and establishment of alien annuals.

Given time and complete freedom from disturbance, native perennial grasses can suppress the highly competitive alien grasses *B. tectorum* and *Taeniatherum asperum* (Hironaka and Tisdale, 1963). Disturbance from native rodents is sufficient to impede or induce regression in the succession (Piemeisel, 1945). Grazing by domestic livestock in the intermountain area results in a virtually closed community to invasion and establishment of native perennial grasses (Robertson and Pearse, 1945).

Alien annual species compete with perennial grasses, not only as individuals, but as vegetation assemblages. This may appear to be in opposition to the monospecific structure of many alien grass communities; but once invasion has produced a *B. tectorum* community on depleted intermountain rangelands, a reserve of seeds of species of the lower successional levels is present in the litter and soil (Young *et al.*, 1969). Portions of the seed supply of several of these species have been induced to a dormat condition which helps maintain this reserve. These reserves provide "potential" competitive communities in case the seral status of the site is depressed by excessive grazing or severe drought. This continuum of competitive alien communities keeps the sites closed to invasion and establishment by seedlings of perennial grasses. Eckert and Evans (1967) and Evans *et al.* (1967) demonstrated this principle through the use of herbicides to fracture annual communities.

A series of investigations has been conducted to determine the characteristic that allows the alien annual species to compete so successfully. The investigations have shown dramatic advantages for individual alien species, but failed to show any single over-riding competitive advantage shared by all of the aliens.

McKell *et al.* (1962) proposed that the inherent plasticity of the aliens was the answer to their consistent competitive advantage. In the terminology of Levins (1968), the aliens have a superior strategy of adaptation in response to changing environments.

The habitats occupied by alien annuals consist of a mosaic of specific microenvironments. These include microrelief, litter, and microchemical variations. Harper *et al.* (1965) and Palmblad (1968) have stressed the physical characteristics of the seed bed as the factor determining population size and species composition of colonizing communities. Varying efficiency in moisture imbibition and germination in relation to substrates has been demonstrated among various colonizing species (Harper and Benton, 1966; Young *et al.*, 1970). Probably the simplest and most effective system for the efficient occupation of such mosaic environments would be the development of an all-purpose genotype with infinite plasticity (Allard, 1965). *Bromus tectorum* has sufficient plasticity in reproductive potential to dynamically respond to annual shifts in environmental potential (Young *et al.*, 1969). It is perhaps impossible, however, owing to the limitation of biological processes, for a plant to achieve the necessary degree of adaptation by a system of plasticity alone (Allard, 1965). To occupy the habitat with the greatest competitive efficiency, a plant species should assume a mosaic pattern corresponding to the mosaic of microenvironments within the habitat. Stebbins (1957) proposes that the genetic system associated with predominant self-pollination is admirably suited to success in colonizing such complex habitats. This allows for continued repatterning of the gene pool, differing only in degree from outbreeding populations. This breeding system provides for perpetuation of superior genotypes along the pattern postulated for self-pollinated populations (Allard, 1965).

Introduction and dominance of alien annual species on rangelands of cismontane California have also recently occurred. These alien species were first introduced in 1769 with the coming of Spanish Mission days (Robbins, 1940). This introduction continued through Gold Rush days, and even more recently, as witnessed by the startling invasion of such species as *T. asperum* and *Aegilops triuncialis* L. Alien annual species have replaced either native perennial grasses or native annuals and now constitute at least 50%, and in many instances often account for 90% of the plant cover (Biswell, 1956). Of the almost 400 species of alien plants, some are well adapted, aggressive, and found widespread throughout California rangelands. Others are more restricted in site selection, but as a whole they represent an almost complete domination of this rangeland type.

In California as in the intermountain area, introduction of annuals has been largely determined by the movement of people and their domesticated animals. Of these species 72% have their origin in either Europe or western Asia with 15% coming from the Mediterranean areas (Robbins, 1940). Davy (1902) in describing the stock ranges of northwestern California, emphasized the role of livestock overgrazing in the replacement of bunchgrasses of the native grasslands by the alien annuals. In the San Joaquin Valley, the original vegetation was markedly modified by man through overgrazing and cultivation and thus, once again, allowed invasion of these aliens (Piemeisel and Lawson, 1937).

These seral communities of California are characterized by annual species having tremendous and diverse reproductive capacities, high density populations, and genetic variability within and among species to most efficiently utilize the diverse environment (Heady, 1956; McKell *et al.*, 1962).

Fertilizer Studies

Changes in floristic composition of seral rangeland communities in response to man-induced manipulations other than grazing aid in our understanding of the functioning of competition among species of the community and with replacement species. Composition changes result from differential responses of species to the added nutrients and from competition for various factors of the environment among the associated plants. Experiments to ascertain the mechanism of and factors involved in competition that produce these floristic changes have also been reported. Evans (1956) indicated that *Bromus mollis* L. dominated the community with increasing nitrogen in the presence of adequate phosphorus (Fig. 1). *Erodium botrys* (Cav.) Bertol and *Bromus rigidus* Roth. also increased but with an accompanying decrease by such species as *Festuca megalura* Nutt., *Aira caryophyllea* L., *Gastridium ventricosum* (Govan) Schinz and Thell., and *Briza minor* L. These dramatic shifts did not occur without adequate phosphorus.

A greenhouse study involving *B. mollis*, *F. megalura*, and *E. botrys* indicated that competition among these species was effective through differences in nitrogen uptake (Evans, 1960). These differences were expressed in growth with sufficient phosphorus and as changes in nitrogen content of the plants with minimal growth responses when phosphorus was limiting. Differential ability to take up and utilize soil nitrogen was postulated to be the effective mechanism in competition between grasses and differential shading of plants between grasses and the broadleaf species, *E. botrys*.

McCown and Williams (1968) showed that competition between *B. mollis* and *E. botrys* differed in relation to the sulfur status of the soil and plant density. They indicated that *E. botrys* acquired a greater share of sulfur because of more rapid root extension under a low soil-sulfur regime. However, at high sulfur levels *B. mollis* became increasingly competitive as its population density was increased. Leaf area and illumination profiles revealed that *B. mollis* became the superior competitor for light because of its greater stature and more erect leaf habit when exposed to favorable nutrition and population density.

Complex interplay of factors often affect the outcome of competition among species of this community when nutrient status of the soil is altered. Jones and Evans (1960) showed from a three-year study that floristic changes resulting from application of nitrogen and phosphorus were altered by sheep grazing, by year-to-year weather differences, and from the interaction between grazing and yearly variation of precipitation and temperature.

Botanical changes resulting from added soil nutrients in the alien annual communities of the intermountain area are not as complex as those found in the California annual range. An impoverished flora and an almost overwhelming lack of available soil moisture during the growing period are perhaps the important factors limiting floristic expression. Kay (1966a) showed virtually a two-species community (*Bromus tectorum* and *Descurainia pinnata*) in fertilizer trials conducted in northeastern California with *B.*

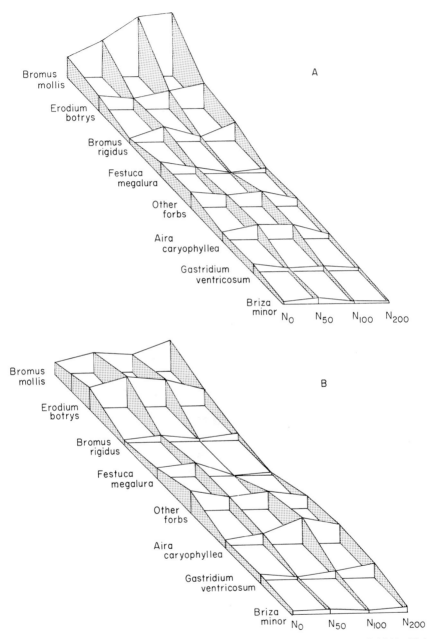

FIG. 1. Floristic changes in response to applied nitrogen at 0 to 200 lb/A (0-224 kg/Ha) (A) with applied phosphorus at 200 lb/A (224 Kg/Ha) and (B) without added phosphorus in an annual rangeland community of California (Evans, 1956).

tectorum gaining significantly from nitrogen applied in almost all years except in the three driest of the 11-year study. In these three years, fertilization either did not increase yields or produced all *D. pinnata*.

Significant reductions in stand of *Agropyron intermedium* (Host) Beauv. resulted from the increased competition of *B. tectorum* induced by applied nitrogen in a study conducted in northeastern California (Kay and Evans, 1965). With grazing, combined with the increased growth of *B. tectorum*, the perennial grass was almost eliminated. This study was conducted in years of below average precipitation, so that rapid depletion of soil moisture resulting from increased growth of *B. tectorum* was thought to be the principle factor that reduced the perennial grass.

Weed Control and Revegetation Studies

Plant competition becomes most apparent and can be studied in detail when attempting to establish replacement vegetation in rangelands.

In *B. tectorum*-dominated communities of the intermountain area, chances for establishment of perennial grasses without weed control are very low because of intense competition of these alien annuals (G. Stewart and Hull, 1949; Hull and Pechanec, 1947; Evans *et al.*, 1967).

Most perennial grasses are particularly susceptible in the seedling stage to competition because of relatively low seedling vigor and slow, early growth in comparison with *B. tectorum* and other annual species. Timing of germination and early growth is also a vitally important factor. When seedlings of the annuals are given an initial advantage, they quickly pre-empt the environmental potential.

Competition between *B. tectorum* and seedlings of perennial grasses has been demonstrated by experiments utilizing controlled populations growing in the greenhouse. Rummell (1946) showed that *B. tectorum* adversely affected establishment of seedlings of *Agropyron cristatum* (L.) Gaertn. and *A. smithii* Rydb. His studies indicated that reduction in numbers of seedlings and of tillers, and weight of tops and roots of both perennial species resulted from *B. tectorum* competition.

Evans (1961) assessed the relative effects of different densities of *B. tectorum* on growth and survival of *A. desertorum* (Fisch.) Schult. during germination, emergence, and growth of seedlings in a greenhouse experiment. Results of this study showed that competitive effects increased markedly with increasing density of *B. tectorum* and with a density normally associated with field populations, seedlings of *A. desertorum* did not survive (Fig. 2). Soil moisture was depleted from saturation to 15 bars of tension in

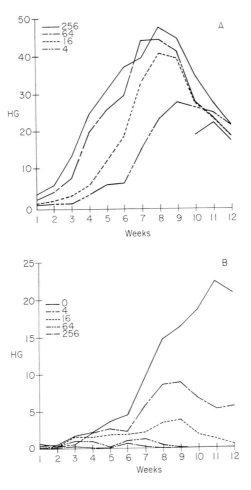

FIG. 2. (A) Shoot growth through the growing period of *Bromus tectorum* planted at densities of 4, 16, 64, and 256 plants per sq ft (42, 170, 690, and 2760 per sq meter); (B) shoot growth of *Agropyron desertorum* grown alone (0) and with *Bromus tectorum* at these densities (Evans, 1961).

13 weeks when *A. desertorum* was grown alone in a soil column 1 m deep. When grown with *B. tectorum* at a density of 2760 plants per sq m, soil moisture depletion from this column of soil occurred in nine weeks (Fig. 3).

Much has been learned concerning competition in these seral communities by experimenting with methods of weed control and seeding replacement vegetation in field studies.

A field study evaluating methods of weed control and reseeding in *B.*

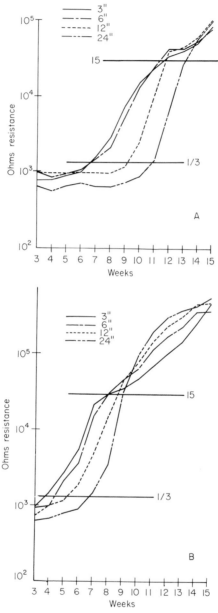

FIG. 3. (A) Soil moisture depletion at four depths, 3, 6, 12, and 24 in. (7.5, 15, 30, and 60 cm) with *Agropyron desertorum* grown alone; and (B) soil moisture depletion with *Agropyron desertorum* and *Bromus tectorum* at 2760 plants per sq meter. Horizontal lines indicate $^1/_3$ and 15 bars of tension. (Evans, 1961).

tectorum communities of Nevada reflected an inverse relation between yield of *B. tectorum* and first-year density of seedlings of *Agropyron intermedium* (Fig. 4) (Evans *et al.*, 1967). It also exemplified fracturing of the community by using a herbicide 1,1'-dimethyl-4,4'-bipyridinium salts (paraquat) that controlled the dominant species, *Bromus tectorum*, thus permitting the lower seral species, *Sisymbrium altissimum* and *Salsola kali*, to express themselves in the community. When other species in the community were allowed to grow without competition from *B. tectorum*, they immediately formed a closed stand and excluded establishment of the perennial grass.

For replacement of annual species with perennial grasses, the suppression of the dominant grass species and release of subordinate broadleaf plants is often the key to success because the broadleaf plants can be controlled by low rates of phenoxy herbicides, usually (2,4-dichlorophenoxy) acetic acid (2,4-D), that have little or no adverse effect on seedlings of perennial grasses. So by releasing subordinate species of the community by spraying

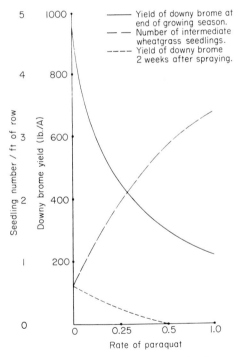

FIG. 4. Average first-year yields of *Bromus tectorum* 2 weeks after spraying paraquat at 0 to 1.0 lb/A (0 − 1.12 Kg/Ha) and at end of growing season and numbers of seedlings of *Agropyron intermedium* for 3 years (1963–1965) exhibiting an inverse relation resulting from competition (Evans *et al.*, 1967).

selective herbicides or by providing environmental conditions for growth of these species during the time of establishment of replacement vegetation, the problems of weed control are much reduced.

Evans and Young (1970) have demonstrated that plant litter alters temperature and moisture conditions of both air and soil and thus provides suitable microsites for the germination and establishment of *B. tectorum*. In contrast *S. altissimum* can become established without the protection of litter. So by baring the ground with a weed-control reseeding treatment such as chemical fallow, the weed-control problem is changed from removing an annual grass to removing an annual broadleaf plant from a seedling perennial grass stand, with the latter being infinitely easier to accomplish.

In the annual grasslands of California many studies have shown the severe competitiveness of this community in attempting revegetation. *Phalaris tuberosa* var. *stenoptera* (Hack.) Hitchc., the most common perennial grass used as a revegetation species, has a weak seedling which compounds the problem of establishment in a community of vigorous growing annual species. Other common replacement species are the annual legumes *Trifolium hirtum* All. and *T. subterranean* L. These plants have different nutritional requirements from most of the species in the community and exhibit vigorous growth with adequate phosphorus.

Cultivation for initial control of the annual species combined with grazing for continued control during the seedling stage of the replacement vegetation have resulted in good establishment of *P. tuberosa* and *Trifolium* species in many instances (R. M. Love, 1952). More recently the combination of chemical control and grazing has extended the practicability of reseeding in this community (Kay, 1966b).

Optimum temperatures and precipitation for plant growth do not necessarily occur concurrently in either the annual rangelands of California or in intermountain rangelands, since both are areas of predominantly winter precipitation. In most years the early spring growing period is characterized by precipitation but as temperatures rise and plant growth accelerates, chances of rainfall quickly diminish. This inbalance of moisture and temperature becomes more demanding on plant growth in the drier areas of California and in the intermountain areas. In the fall this moisture–temperature inbalance is even more critical for plant growth and only in the mesic parts of California can seedling growth of replacement species be expected regularly in this season.

When competition, is viewed in context with moisture-temperature relations, in limiting establishment of replacement vegetation it becomes apparent that moisture will become an effective parameter in this competition.

In Nevada, Evans *et al.* (1970) monitored biologic and microenvironmental parameters of *B. tectorum* communities during the spring establishment period of seedlings of *Agropyron intermedium*. These measurements were made in relation to weed control and seeding treatments. Results indicated that growth of annual species and establishment of replacement vegetation were directly related to available soil moisture and favorable temperatures in the immediate environment of growing plants. Lack of available soil moisture during critical periods of the growing season was the major deterrent to seeding success. The limited precipitation was stored as soil moisture and in most years was available to perennial grass seedlings where the annual species were controlled. Without weed control, growth of *B. tectorum* and associated species pre-empted the effective precipitation, and moisture became limiting for growth of perennial grass seedlings. So even in favorable moisture years in the intermountain area, competition from annual species can prevent establishment of perennial grass by limiting soil moisture during critical periods of seedling growth.

From a recent weed-control seeding study done in the California annual type, Kay and Owen (1970) postulated that a two-phase competition was operative between annuals of the community and seedlings of replacement vegetation. Early in the growing period competition for light was effective in reducing vigor of seedlings and later the effect of competition made soil moisture nonavailable to the seedlings. This type of competition probably prevails under most California conditions when reseeding is attempted.

Summary and Conclusions

The aggressive nature of alien annual species and their high competitive potential is expressed first by their ability to invade and dominate many different plant communities under the changed conditions brought about by grazing pressure. Second, their vigorous response, especially by the dominant species, to fertilization portrays their competitiveness. Third, the extreme difficulty by which replacement species are introduced without controlling all fractions of these communities attests for the competitive ability of not only individual species but the community as a whole.

References

Allard R. W. (1965). Genetic systems associated with colonizing ability in predominantly self-pollinated species. *In* "The Genetics of Colonizing Species" (H. G. Baker and G. L. Stebbins, eds.), 49–76. Academic Press, New York.

Antevs, E. (1948). The Great Basin III—Climatic changes and pre-white man. *Bull. Univ. Utah* **38**, 168–191.

Beetle, A. A. (1960). A study of sagebrush, the section *Tridentatae* of *Artemisia. Wyo, Univ., Agr. Exp. Sta., Bull.* **368**, 1–83.

Biswell. H. H. (1956). Ecology of California grasslands. *J. Range Manage.* **9**, 19–24.

Blaisdell, J. P. (1953). Ecological effects of planned burning of sagebrush-grass range on the Upper Snake River Plains. *U.S., Dep. Agr., Tech. Bull.* **1075**, 1–39.

Daubenmire, R. F. (1940). Plant succession due to over-grazing in the *Agropyron* bunchgrass prairie of southeastern Washington. *J. Ecol.* **26**, 59–64.

Daubenmire, R. F. (1952). Forest vegetation of northern Idaho and adjacent Washington and its bearing on concepts of vegetation classification. *Ecol. Monogr.* **22**, 301–330.

Daubenmire,. R. F. (1961). Vegetation indicators of rate of height growth in ponderosa pine. *Forest Sci.* **7**, 23–24.

Davy, J. B. (1902). Stock ranges of northwestern California. *U.S. Bur. Plant Ind., Bull.* **12**, 1–81.

Eckert, R. E., Jr., and Evans, R. A. (1967). A chemical-fallow technique for control of downy brome and establishment of perennial grasses on rangeland, *J. Range Manage.* **20**, 35–41.

Ensminger, M. E. (1951). "Horse Husbandry." Interstate Printers and Publishers, Danville, Illinois.

Evans, R. A. (1956). Reaction systems among species and their environments in range populations. Ph.D. Dissertation, University of California, Berkeley.

Evans, R. A. (1960). Differential responses of three species of the annual grassland type to plant competition and mineral nutrition. *Ecology* **41**, 305–310.

Evans, R. A. (1961). Effects of different densities of downy brome (*Bromus tectorum*) on growth and survival of crested wheatgrass (*Agropyron desertorum*) in the greenhouse. *Weeds* **9**, 216–223.

Evans, R. A., and Young, J. A. (1970). Plant litter and establishment of alien annual weed species in rangeland communities. *Weed Sci.* **18**, 697–703.

Evans, R. A., Eckert, R. E., Jr., and Kay, B. L. (1967). Wheatgrass establishment with paraquat and tillage on downy brome ranges. *Weeds* **15**, 50–55.

Evans, R. A., Holbo, H. R., Eckert, R. E., Jr., and Young, J. A. (1970). Functional environment of downy brome communities in relation to weed control and revegetation. *Weed Sci.* **18**, 154–162.

Harper, J. L., and Benton, R. A. (1966). The behavior of seeds in the soil. II. The germination of seeds on the surface of a water supplying substrate. *J. Ecol.* **54**, 151–166.

Harper, J. L., Williams, J. T., and Sagar, G. R. (1965). The behavior of seeds in soil. I. The heterogeneity of soil surfaces and its role in determining the establishment of plants. *J. Ecol.* **53**, 273–286.

Harris, G. A. (1967). Some competitive relationships between *Agropyron spicatum* and *Bromus tectorum. Ecol. Monogr.* **37**, 89–111.

Heady, H. F. (1956). Evaluation and measurement of the California annual type. *J. Range Manage.* **9**, 25–27.

Hilzheimer, M. (1936). Sheep. *Antiquity* **10**, 199.

Hironaka, M., and Tisdale, E. W. (1963). Secondary succession in annual vegetation in southern Idaho. *Ecology.* **4**, 810–812.

Hull, A. C., Jr., and Klomp, G. J. (1966). Longevity of crested wheatgrass in the sagebrush-grass type of southern Idaho. *J. Range Manage.* **19**, 5–11.

Hull, A. C., Jr., and Klomp, G. J. (1967). Thickening and spread of crested wheatgrass stands on southern Idaho ranges, *J. Range Manage.* **20**, 222–227.

Hull, A. C., Jr., and Pechanec, J. F. (1947). Cheatgrass—A challenge to range research. *J. Forest.* **45**, 555–564.

Jones, M. B., and Evans, R. A. (1960). Botanical composition changes in annual grassland as affected by fertilization and grazing. *Agron. J.* **52**, 459–461.

Kashkarov. D., and Kurbatov, V. (1930). Preliminary ecological survey of the vertebrate fauna of the central Kara-Kum desert in west Turkestan. *Ecology*, **11**, 35–60.

Kay, B. L. (1966a). Fertilization of cheatgrass ranges in California. *J. Range Manage.* **19**, 217–220.

Kay, B. L. (1966b). Paraquat for range seeding without cultivation. *Calif. Agr.* **20**, 2–4.

Kay, B. L., and Evans, R. A. (1965). Effects of fertilization on a mixed stand of cheatgrass and intermediate wheatgrass. *J. Range Manage.* **18**, 7–11.

Kay, B. L., and Owen, R. E. (1970). Paraquat for range seeding in cismontane California. *Weed Sci.* **18**, 238–243.

Kennedy, P. B., and Doten, B. S. (1901). A preliminary report on the summer ranges of western Nevada sheep. *Nev., Agr. Exp. Sta, Bull.* **51**, 1–54.

Kubanskaja, Z. V. (1956). "The Vegetation and Fodder Resources of the Bet-Pak-Dala Desert." Alma-Alta Acad. Sur. Kazah, USSR.

Larin, I. V. (1947). U.S.S.R. (In) The use and misuse of shrubs and trees as fodder. *Imp. Agr. Bur., Joint Publ.* **10**, 129–156.

Larin, I. V. (1963). "Natural Meadows and Pastures." State Publ. Agr. Lit. and J., Moscow.

Lavrenko, E. M. (1962). "Basic Features of the Phytogeography of the Deserts of Eurasia and North Africa." Acad. Sur. USSR, Leningrad.

Lavrenko, E. M., and Soczava, U. B. (1956). "Vegetation Cover USSR." Acad. Sci. USSR, Moscow.

Levins, R. (1968). "Evolution in Changing Environments." Princeton Univ. Press. Princeton.

Love, L. D., and Hanson, H. C. (1932). Life history and habits of crested wheatgrass. *J. Agr. Res.* **45**, 371–383.

Love, R. M. (1952). Range Improvement experiments at the Arthur Brown Ranch, California. *J. Range Manage.* **53**, 120–123.

McCown, R. L., and Williams, W. A. (1968). Competition for nutrients and light between the annual grassland species (*Bromus mollis and Erodium botrys.*) *Ecology.* **49**, 981–990.

McKell, C. M., and Chilcote, W. W. (1957). Response of rabbitbrush following removal of competing vegetation. *J. Range Manage.* **10**, 228–230.

McKell, C. M., Robinson, J. P., and Major, J. (1962). Ecotypic variation in medusahead, an introduced annual grass. *Ecology.* **43**, 686–699.

Mirov, N. T. (1951). "Geography of Russia." Wiley, New York.

Palmblad, I. G. (1968). Competition in experimental populations of weeds with emphasis on the regulation of population size. *Ecology* **49**, 26–34.

Pickford, G. D. (1932). The influence of continued heavy grazing and of promiscuous burning on spring-fall ranges in Utah. *Ecology* **13**, 159–171.

Piemeisel, R. L. (1945). Natural replacement of weed hosts of the beet leafhopper as affected by rodents. *U.S., Dep. Agr.,* Cir. **739**.

Piemeisel, R. L. (1951). Causes affecting change and rate of change in a vegetation of annuals in Idaho. *Ecology* **32**, 53–72.

Piemeisel, R. L., and Lawson, R. F. (1937). Types of vegetation in the San Joaquin Valley of California and their relationship to the beet leafhopper. *U.S., Dep. Agr., Tech. Bull.* **557**, 1–29.

Poulton, C. E. (1955). Ecology of the non-forested vegetation in Umatilla and Morrow counties, Oregon. Ph.D. Dissertation, Washington State University, Pullman.

Robbins, W. W. (1940). Alien plants growing without cultivation in California. *Calif., Agr. Exp. Sta., Bull.* **637**, 1–128.

Robertson, J. H., and Cords, H. P. (1957). Survival of rabbitbrush, *Chrysothamnus* spp., following chemical, burning, and mechanical treatments. *J. Range Manage.* **10**, 83–89.

Robertson, J. H. and Pearse, C. K. (1945) Artificial reseeding and the closed community. *Northwest Sci.* **19**, 58–66.

Rummell, R. S. (1946). Some effects of competition from cheatgrass brome on crested wheatgrass and bluestem wheatgrass. *Ecology* **27**, 159–167.

Sin'Kowskii, L. P. (1959). *Artemisia* spp. from the sub-genus *Seriphidium* as fodder plants, and test for their cultivation in Soviet Central Asia. Paper Trudy Turkmen, Sci. Res. Inst. Anim. Prod. and Vet. Sur., USSR.

Stebbins, G. L., Jr. (1957). Self-fertilization and population variability in the higher plants. *Amer. Natur.* **9**, 332–354.

Stewart, G., and Hull, A. C. (1949). Cheatgrass (*Bromus tectorum*)—An ecological intruder in southern Idaho. *Ecology* **30**, 58–74.

Stewart, O. C. (1955). Forest and grass burning in the mountain west. *Southwest. Lore* **21**, 5–8.

Stewart, O. C. (1963). Barriers to understanding the influence of use of fire by aborigines on vegetation. *Proc. Tall Timbers Fire Ecol. Conf., 2nd, 1963*, pp. 117–126.

Telwar, G. M. (1961). "Grasses of Afghanistan," Lab. Manual No. 1. Kabul Univ., Kabul, Afghanistan.

Young, J. A., Hedrick, D. W., and Keniston, R. F. (1967). Forest cover and logging—herbage and browse production in the mixed coniferous forest of Northeastern Oregon. *J. Forest.* **65**, 807–813.

Young, J. A., Evans, R. A., and Eckert, R. E., Jr. (1969). Population dynamics of downy brome. *Weed Sci.* **17**, 20–26.

Young, J. A., Evans, R. A., Gifford, R. O., and Eckert, R. E., Jr. (1970). Germination characteristics of three species of Cruciferae. *Weed Sci.* **18**, 41–47.

Chapter 17 _____

Soil Aeration and Gas Exchange in Relation to Grasses

LEWIS H. STOLZY

The atmosphere and the soil are the environment in which plants live and grow. It is unlikely that man will control the entire environment of plants. However, an understanding of soil–plant relations in terms of important physical processes will contribute to a better understanding of the cultural and ecological distribution of plants.

Respiration is an important process in most living cells in providing energy for growth and metabolism. Beevers (1961) reviewed the respiratory metabolism in plants and showed how respiration is coupled directly or indirectly to many plant functions, including salt uptake, cell expansion, cell division, and growth regulation effects. Cells of plants consume oxygen during oxidative phosphorylation; a process in which oxygen is enzymically reduced to water. As a result of this, an oxygen concentration gradient exists between the atmosphere and the cells of plants. Roots of plants growing in soil may receive oxygen by diffusion through the soil and root wall (soil aeration) or by diffusion from the atmosphere by gas spaces that exist between cells within the plant (plant aeration). For most field crops soil aeration is considered the dominant process (Russell, 1952), whereas for paddy rice, plant aeration is the dominant pathway (van Raalte, 1940).

Oxygen supply to plant roots through different external media has been the subject of a great amount of past research. A review of the early literature on aeration of plants was prepared by Clements in 1921. A review by Russell (1952) covered the three decades following Clements' survey. In the last 12 years several reviews covering specific aspects of soil and plant aeration have been written (Bergman, 1959; Domsch, 1962; Erickson, 1966; Kramer, 1965; Letey, 1965; Letey *et al.*, 1967; Stiles, 1960; Stolzy and Letey, 1964a, Stotzky, 1965; Wesseling and van Wijk, 1957; Zentmyer, 1965). The most complete review dealing with many aspects of soil aeration and plant growth was recently prepared by Grable (1966).

Much of the recent research in soil aeration has been possible because of the polarographic methods for measuring oxygen. The development of the platinum microelectrode technique for measuring oxygen diffusion rates in soil by Lemon and Erickson (1952, 1955) has provided a method for characterizing the oxygen status in soil. The membrane-covered oxygen cathode (Clark electrode) has also been a useful tool in studies of soil aeration (McIntyre and Philip, 1964; Papendick and Runkles, 1965; Willey and Tanner, 1963).

Past research on oxygen and plant growth has emphasized measuring minimum demands of root systems upon external soil environments for oxygen. However, a few of the early reports suggested or showed the internal transport of oxygen from tops to roots for certain plant species (Conway, 1940; Coult and Vallance, 1958; Laing, 1940; van Raalte, 1940, 1941, 1943; Sifton, 1957; Zimmerman, 1930). More recently by means of oxygen-15 tracing, the rapid, internal diffusion of oxygen from the foliage to the roots has been directly demonstrated in broad bean (*Vicia faba*) seedlings by Evans and Ebert (1960) and in barley and rice seedlings by Barber *et al.* (1962). Furthermore they showed that the movement of oxygen within the root could be described by a theoretical model consisting of gaseous diffusion down a hollow tube.

That oxygen may diffuse out of roots into the surrounding medium has been demonstrated for rice by van Raalte (1940, 1941), for the bogbean (*Menyanthes trifoliata* L.) by Coult and Vallance (1958), for corn (*Zea mays* L.) by Jensen *et al.* (1964), for barley by van der Heide *et al.* (1963), and for the bog plants *Eriophorum angustifolium* Honch., *Menyanthes trifoliata* L., and *Molinea coerulea* L. Moench., by Armstrong (1964). Several factors appear to govern the concentration of oxygen within the root and its movement through the root and exchange with the rhizosphere: (1) the amount and tortuosity of the intercellular air space within the root, (2) oxygen permeability of the root epidermis and rhizoplane, (3) the respiratory consumption of the oxygen in the root and rhizoplane, and (4) oxygen gradients extending longitudinally within the root and radially out from within the root.

The main emphasis in this chapter will be measurement of soil aeration in the soil-liquid phase and the relationships of this measurement to the response of grasses. Also considered will be the other source of oxygen to plant root via the plant system. The relative importance of the two pathways will be discussed. Even though the main attention is given to oxygen exchange in this paper the principles apply also to carbon dioxide.

Three general procedures for directly evaluating soil air are (1) composition of the gas in soil pores. (2) diffusion of oxygen in the gas phase of soil pores, and (3) diffusion of oxygen through the gas–liquid–solid medium. The last method is currently being used and evaluated by the author as well as by other workers. The principle is that when a certain electric potential is applied between a platinum microelectrode inserted in the soil solution and a reference electrode, oxygen is reduced at the platinum surface. An electric current flows between the two electrodes and is proportional to the rate of oxygen reduction. The rate of oxygen reduction is, in turn, related to the rate at which it diffuses through the soil solution to the electrode (Stolzy and Letey, 1964a; Stolzy and Van Gundy, 1968). The assumption is that the platinum wire is in a soil environment similar to that of a root. A measured oxygen diffussion rate (ODR) to the platinum microelectrode indicates that a root in the same position can receive oxygen at the same rate. Experiments for measuring the oxygen diffusion rate and determining plant response are generally of two types. In the first, the oxygen diffusion rate measurements are made and plant growth observed under existing soil conditions either in the field or the greenhouse. In the second, soil environments are purposely modified so different ODR's are obtained in soil columns. A complete description of the apparatus is shown by Stolzy and Letey (1964b). A special soil column for grass studies is shown in Fig. 1, and is described by Letey *et al.* (1962). Briefly, the container is constructed from plexiglas tubing. The gas mixture with a given oxygen percentage flows around the upper 5 cm of the soil column through the space D. The upper 5 cm of soil is retained by plastic screening (E), and a hole (C) is used for watering. The platinum electrodes are inserted through 10 portholes (F) for oxygen diffusion measurements. The holes are covered with black plastic tape between measurements.

A study of plant aeration requires that several plant characteristics be defined (Luxmoore *et al.* 1970a). One important plant characteristic for internal aeration is a measurement of the gas-space fraction or porosity of plant roots (Woolley, 1965). Jensen *et al.* (1969) developed a pycnometer method for measuring gas spaces in roots. This method involves weighing roots in a pycnometer bottle before and after they have been homogenized. The percentage of gas-filled pores in roots is used as indication of the degree of plant aeration.

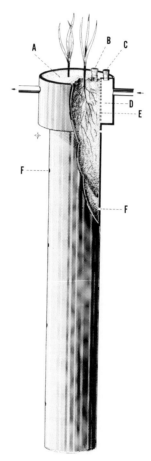

FIG. 1. Apparatus used to modify the rhizosphere oxygen concentration in grass studies. (A) latex–sand seal, (B) opening for salt bridge, (C) opening for water, (D) space for gas flow around the soil, (E) screen to retain the soil, and (F) portholes for insertion of the electrodes. (From Letey *et al.*, 1962.)

Soil Aeration

Two recent reviews by Stolzy and Letey (1964a,b) showed that different investigators are in substantial agreement on the relationship between oxygen diffusion rate and root growth. The critical oxygen diffusion rate value of soils in which roots of many plants will not grow is $0.20 \ \mu g \ cm^{-2} \ min^{-1}$. Oxygen diffusion between $0.20 \ \mu g$ and $0.30 \ \mu g \ cm^{-2} \ min^{-1}$ retard root growth. Letey *et al.* (1962, 1964, 1965, 1966) and Valoras and Letey (1966) conducted a number of experiments on grassplants. They found that an oxygen diffusion rate of 0.20 µg or higher was required for root growth of Newport bluegrass and that an optimum rate was above 0.40 µg (Letey *et al.*, 1964). However, in a study with common bermudagrass (*Cynodon dactylon*) their general conclusion was that root growth was reduced or stopped by an oxygen diffusion rate of less than 0.15 µg cm^{-2} min^{-1} (Letey *et al.*, 1966). In a study with barley it was found that an oxygen diffusion rate of 0.15 µg was limiting root growth (Letey *et al.*, 1962), although with corn oxygen diffusion rate greater than 0.10 µg was necessary for growth, for maximum root growth a rate of 0.40 µg or above was needed. Rice roots can grow at an ODR as low as 0.07 µg cm^{-2} min^{-1} (Valores and Letey, 1966).

For other types of plant responses such as wheat seedling emergence, it was necessary to have an oxygen diffusion rate of 0.50 to 0.70 µg cm^{-2} min^{-1} (Hanks and Thorp, 1956), whereas in vegetative growth of plant tops a diffusion rate greater than 0.40 µg has little or no effect (Stolzy and Letey, 1964a,b). The above studies on soil aeration and root growth would indicate plant tolerance to poor aeration woul be in the following order: rice > corn > bermudagrass > barley > Newport Kentucky bluegrass. These results were determined independently of the oxygen concentration in gas-filled pores in the soil.

Letey and Stolzy (1967) considered the limiting distance between a root and the gas phase for adequate oxygen supply. Using the correlation between oxygen diffusion rate and adequate plant growth of 0.20 to 0.40 µg cm^{-2} min^{-1} a relationship between water film thickness and adequate oxygen was obtained for various soil porosities. At a soil porosity of 40% the limiting water film thicknesses were in the range of 0.01 to 0.025 cm.

Luxmoore (1969) in his studies chose four water film thicknesses to give a range of soil aeration conditions: 0.005, 0.01, 0.05 and 0.10 cm. He calculated oxygen diffusion rates equivalent to these water film thicknesses for a platinum electrode from the Letey and Stolzy equation (1967). For an electrode radius of 0.023 cm, a liquid porosity factor of 40%, and a soil oxygen concentration of 18%, the oxygen diffusion rates for the water films are as shown in the following tabulation:

Water film thickness (cm):	0.005	0.01	0.05	0.10
ODR (µg cm^{-2} min^{-1}):	1.66	0.77	0.11	0.06

These values indicate that the two large oxygen diffusion rates represent a well-aerated soil and the two smaller values are limiting for plant growth, according to the correlation given by Stolzy and Letey (1964a).

A mistake often made is to compare data obtained by bubbling gases with different oxygen concentrations through solution cultures to determine at what level oxygen is limiting for plant growth. Gases with relatively low oxygen content can be bubbled through solutions and cause no reduction in plant growth. If, for example, the solution is in equilibrium with 2% oxygen, a diffusion layer around the root of 0.0007 cm is necessary to lower the oxygen diffusion rate to 0.20 μg cm^{-2}min^{-1}. In a solution with vigorous bubbling it is unlikely that a diffusion layer of this magnitude would develop. Letey and Stolzy (1967) contended that a root would not be able to grow into the center of a water-saturated soil aggregate if its porosity was 30% and its diameter was greater than 0.60 mm. Past theories on diffusion were based on the assumption that soils were homogeneous with respect to random distribution of pores; this may be true for soils high in silt and sand content but not for aggregated soils. Currie (1961) pointed out that the pores between the aggregates (noncapillary) will drain first, and the more complex aggregate pores (capillary) will be full. He assumed a spherical aggregate model and from this predicted the percentage of the aggregate center that will be anaerobic. This depends on the size, pore space, and water content of the aggregate. Under the conditions of Currie's study, 1 mm aggregates are fully aerobic over the whole range of available water (6 cb to 15 bars), whereas the larger aggregates become partly anaerobic as field capacity is approached.

Plant Aeration

The air space of plant roots is important for their internal aeration. The extent of air spaces in roots varies with both the species, variety, and type of root, a fact of considerable ecological significance. Measurements of root porosities for different plant species were in the following ranges: bean 4.2%, tomato 6.0%, pea 4.3%, corn 7.6%, rice 26.5%. Luxmoore and Stolzy (1969) compared primary and adventitious roots of rice and corn. After 38 days of growth, primary roots of rice were 13.6% and adventitious roots were 33.2%, whereas with corn, after 34 days, the primary roots were 9.0% and adventitious roots were 16.3%. Root porosities of two dwarf high-yielding varieties of wheat developed in Mexico were compared. The Inia variety had 11.3% root porosity while the Ciano variety had 6.9%. Several climatic and soil environmental factors are also responsible for differences in percentage of air space of plant roots (Luxmoore and Stolzy, 1969; Yu *et al.*, 1969).

Jensen *et al.* (1964) showed that $^{18}O_2$ moved through corn roots. The amount of oxygen transported across wax membranes was a linear function of the number of corn roots penetrating the membrane. Three separate experiments showed that the amount of oxygen transported per root penetrating the membrane differed, indicating different transport characteristics of roots grown in the experiments. These differences could be related to variation in root porosity, root radius, root-wall permeability to oxygen, and root length. In a later study Jensen *et al.* (1966) applied diffusion theory to oxygen tracer movements in plants and defined an index of plant tolerance to low partial pressures of oxygen in the root environment. Tolerance increased with increase in root radius and root porosity and decreased with increase in root-wall permeability to oxygen. It was also predicted by them that tolerance would decrease with longer roots due to surface available for leakage. He predicted from this work the following order of tolerances of three plant species to low soil aeration: rice > corn > barley. The same order of tolerance to low soil aeration for these three plant species was shown in early studies when soil aeration was measured with the platinum microelectrode.

It is likely that not all gas spaces measured by the pycnometer method form a continuous network. The porosity effective in gas transport would be less than the total porosity. Jensen *et al.* (1966) used data of Evans and Ebert (1960) and Barber *et al.* (1962), and estimated that the tortuosity factor for broad bean roots was 0.433. If cells and spaces can be assumed to follow a random packing, then the model of Millington and Quirk (1964) indicated that tortuosity is equal to the porosity to the third power.

Soil-Plant Aeration

Luxmoore *et al.* (1970a) proposed a model for steady-state, isothermal oxygen diffusion into a cylindrical root surrounded by a water film of uniform thickness. Equations were developed which accounted for longitudinal oxygen flux through the intercellular gas spaces, radial flux through the water film, and a respiratory oxygen sink which was defined as a function of oxygen concentration.

They considered a root described by a cylinder of radius r, length L, and terminated by a hemispherical root tip of radius r. This model is surrounded by a uniform water film to thickness w and contains a fixed proportion of soil particles. The top of the cylinder is open to the atmosphere with an oxygen concentration of 0.208 ml/ml. The soil oxygen concentration in the gas phase is considered to be uniform and constant. This approximation is valid because the flux rate in air is 10,000 times greater than in water. The main barrier to diffusion is at the water film adjacent to the root surface, where large diffusion gradients may occur (Lemon, 1962).

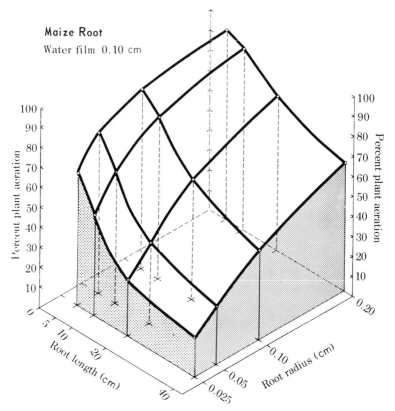

FIG. 2. Percentage plant aeration as a function of length and radius of a maize root surrounded by 0.1 cm water film. (From Luxmoore, 1969.)

The cylinder is considered to be a porous medium with a gas-phase porosity that varies along the cylinder length in some known form. The cylinder
wall is characterized by its permeability to oxygen, which varies with position
along the cylinder. Similarly, the maximum respiration rate of a tissue section changes with distance along the cylinder. The model allows consideration of the following root characteristics: (1) root length, (2) root radius, (3)
gas-phase porosity as a function of porosity along the root, (4) root-wall
permeability as a function of porosity along the root, (5) maximum respiration rate as a function of porosity along the root, and (6) oxygen concentration at which respiration is half maximum. Characteristics (5) and (6)
are used to calculate a respiration rate that is concentration dependent
following Michaelis-Menten enzyme kinetic function. The soil characteristics that can be considered are (1) oxygen partial pressure, (2) water film
thickness, (3) soil temperature, (4) tortuosity and liquid-phase porosity
factor within the water film (Luxmoore *et al.*, 1970a).

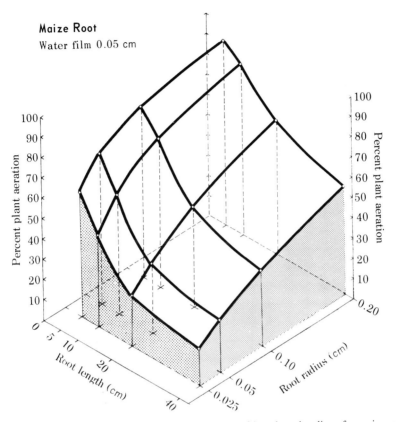

FIG. 3. Percentage of plant aeration as a function of length and radius of a maize root surrounded by 0.05 cm water film (Luxmoore, 1969).

A method of computer analysis is outlined whereby the law of continuity is applied sequentially to small sections of root such that the amount of oxygen diffusing into a section is equated with the oxygen diffusing out plus the respiratory consumption. The solution for the model defines a series of oxygen concentrations along the root length. From these data the amount of oxygen consumed in respiration that diffuses into the top of the root (plant aeration) and the amount diffusing radially from the soil (soil aeration) may be calculated. Effects of soil and plant characteristics are examined.

Oxygen concentration profiles, mean respiration rates, and the percentage of plant aeration were obtained from an analysis of steady-state oxygen diffusion in maize root models under simulated field conditions (Luxmoore *et al.*, 1970c). An increase in root radius and in water film thickness as occurs after rainfall or irrigation induced a decrease in oxygen concentration within the root, a decrease in mean respiration rate, and an increase in percentage of plant aeration (Figs. 2 and 3). An increase in root length reduced the percentage of plant aeration. In the growth of adventitious roots of maize (0.05 cm root radius and 20 cm root length), percentage of plant aeration was 34% for a well-aerated soil (0.1 cm water film), and 42% for a soil that is oxygen deficient (0.05 cm water film). Plant aeration is a significant factor in the oxygen relations of maize roots. For a given root system, the gas-filled porosity and the thickness of the water film around the root have the greatest influence on this process. Plant aeration is estimated to supply as much as 30% to 74% of the respired oxygen, depending on the root radius. These values increase as water film thickness increases.

Valoras and Letey (1966) found rice roots grown under flooded conditions were larger in diameter, straighter, and had fewer root hairs than roots developing under nonflooded conditions. The model analysis indicates that a larger root radius has an oxygen environment that favors a higher mean respiration rate. Under aerated soil conditions, thinner roots are associated with a more favorable soil oxygen environment for respiration. This was shown in the maize analysis (Luxmoore *et al.*, 1970c). The direction of the radial oxygen flux for rice is a leakage out of the root which is opposite to that for the maize model (Luxmoore *et al.*, 1970d). An increase in tolerance to anaerobic conditions was predicted by Jensen *et al.* (1966) with an increase in both root radius and apparent diffusion coefficient of oxygen in the root and with a decrease in root permeability. These same responses were obtained in the model study of rice. A 20-cm rice root with a 0.05-cm radius is predicted to radially lose about 5% to 7% of the oxygen diffusing into the top of the root. This has considerable ecological significance for roots growing in an anaerobic medium.

References

Armstrong, W. (1964). Oxygen diffusion from the roots of some British bog plants. *Nature* (*London*) **204**, 801–802.
Barber, D. A., Ebert, M., and Evans, N. T. S. (1962). The movement of O^{15} through barley and rice plants. *J. Exp. Bot.* **13**, 397–403.
Beevers, H. (1961). "Respiratory Metabolism in Plants." Harper, New York.
Bergman, H. F. (1959). Oxygen deficiency as a cause of disease in plants. *Bot. Rev.* **25**, 417–485.
Clements, F. E. (1921). Aeration and air content. The role of oxygen in root activity. *Carnegie Inst. Wash. Publ.* **315**, 1–183.
Conway, V. M. (1940). Aeration and plant growth in wet soils. *Bot. Rev.* **6**, 149–163.
Coult, D. A., and Vallance, K. B. (1958). Observations on the gaseous exchanges which take place between *Menyanthes trifoliata* L. and its environment. *J. Exp. Bot.* **9**, 384–402.
Currie, J. A. (1961). Gaseous diffusion in the aeration of aggregated soils. *Soil Sci.* **92**, 40–45.
Domsch, K. H. (1962). Bodenatmung, Sammelbericht über Methoden und Ergebnisse. *Zentralbl. Bakterial., Parasitenk., Infektionskr. Hyg.* **116**, 1–78.
Erickson, A. E. (1965). Short term oxygen deficiencies and plant response. *In* "Drainage for Efficient Crop Production Conference Proceedings." pp. 11, 12, and 23, American Society of Agricultural Engineers, St. Joseph, Michigan.

Evans, N. T. S., and Ebert, M. (1960). Radioactive oxygen in the study of gas transport down the root of *Vicia faba. J. Exp. Bot.* **11**, 246–257.

Grable, A. R. (1966). Soil aeration and plant growth. *Adv. Agron.* **18**, 57–106.

Hanks, R. J., and Thorp, F. C. (1956). Seedling emergence of wheat as related to soil moisture content, bulk density, oxygen diffusion rate, and crust strength. *Soil Sci. Soc. Amer., Proc.* **20**, 307–310.

Jensen, C. R., Letey, J., and Stolzy, L. H. (1964). Labeled oxygen: Transport through growing corn roots. *Science* **144**, 550–552.

Jensen, C. R., Stolzy, L. H., and Letey, J. (1966). Tracer studies of oxygen diffusion through roots of barley, corn and rice. *Soil Sci.* **103**, 23–29.

Jensen, C. R., Luxmoore, R. J., Van Gundy, S. D., and Stolzy, L. H. (1969). Root air space measurements by a pycnometer method. *Agron. J.* **61**, 474–475.

Kramer, P. J. (1965). Effects of deficient aeration on the roots of plants, *In* "Drainage for Efficient Crop Production Conference Proceedings." pp. 13, 14, and 23, American Society of Agricultural Engineers, St. Joseph, Michigan.

Laing, H. E. (1940). The composition of the internal atmosphere of *Nuphar advenum* and other water plants. *Amer. J. Bot.* **27**, 861–868.

Lemon, E. R. (1962). Soil aeration and plant root relations. I. Theory. *Agron. J.* **54**, 167–170.

Lemon, E. R., and Erickson, A. E. (1962). The measurement of oxygen diffusion in the soil with a platinum microelectrode. *Soil Sci. Soc. Amer., Proc.* **16**, 160–163.

Lemon, E. R., and Erickson, A. E. (1955). Principle of the platinum microelectrode as a method of characterizing soil aeration. *Soil Sci.* **79**, 383–392.

Letey, J. (1965). Measuring aeration in drainage. *In* "Drainage for Efficient Crop Production Conference Proceedings." pp. 6–10, American Society of Agricultural Engineers, St. Joseph, Michigan.

Letey, J., and Stolzy, L. H. (1967). Limiting distances between root and gas phase for adequate oxygen supply. *Soil Sci.* **103**, 404–409.

Letey, J., Stolzy, L. H., Valoras, N., and Szuszkiewicz, T. E. (1962). Influence of soil oxygen on growth and mineral concentration of barley. *Agron J.* **54**, 538–540.

Letey, J., Stolzy, L. H., Lunt, O. R., and Youngner, V. B. (1964). Growth and nutrient uptake of Newport bluegrass as affected by soil oxygen. *Plant Soil* **20**, 143–148.

Letey, J., Stolzy, L. H., and Valoras, N. (1965). Relationships between oxygen diffusion rate and corn growth. *Agron. J.* **57**, 91–92.

Letey, J., Morgan, W. C., Richards, S. J., and Valoras, N. (1966). Physical soil amendments, soil compaction, irrigation, and wetting agents in turfgrass management. III. Effects on oxygen diffusion rate and root growth. *Agron. J.* **58**, 531–535.

Letey, J., Stolzy, L. H., and Kemper, W. D. (1967). Soil aeration. *In* "Irrigation of Agricultural Lands." (R. M. Hagan, H. R. Haise, and T. W. Edminister, eds.), Chapter 47, pp. 941–945. Amer. Soc. Agron., Madison, Wisconsin.

Luxmoore, R. J. (1969). Oxygen diffusion in the soil-plant system. An assessment of the significance of plant aeration. Ph.D. Dissertation, University of California, Riverside.

Luxmoore, R. J., and Stolzy, L. H. (1969). Root porosity and growth responses of rice and maize to oxygen supply. *Agron. J.* **61**, 202–204.

Luxmoore, R. J., Stolzy, L. H., and Letey, J. (1970a). Oxygen diffusion in the soil–plant system. I. A model. *Agron. J.* **62**, 317–322.

Luxmoore, R. J., Stolzy, L. H., and Letey, J. (1970b). Oxygen diffusion in the soil–plant system. II. Respiration rate, permeability, and porosity of consecutive excised segments of maize and rice roots. *Agron. J.* **62**, 322–324.

Luxmoore, R. J., Stolzy, L. H., and Letey, J. (1970c). Oxygen diffusion in the soil–plant system. III. Oxygen concentration profiles, respiration rates, and the significance of plant aeration predicted for maize roots. *Agron. J.* **62**, 325–329.

Luxmoore, R. J., Stolzy, L. H., and Letey, J. (1970d). Oxygen diffusion in the soil–plant system. IV. Oxygen concentration profiles, respiration rates and radial oxygen losses predicted for rice roots. *Agron. J.* **62**, 329–332.

McIntyre, D. S., and Philip, J. R. (1964). A field method for measurement of gas diffusion into soils. *Aust. J. Soil Res.* **2**, 133–145.

Millington, R. J., and Quirk, J. P. (1964). Formation factor and permeability equations. *Nature (London)* **202**, 143–145.

Papendick, R. I., and Runkles, J. R. (1965). Transient-state oxygen diffusion in soil. I. The case when rate of oxygen consumption is constant. *Soil Sci.* **100**, 251–261.

Russell, M. B. (1952). Soil aeration and plant growth. *In* "Soil Physical Conditions and Plant Growth" (B. T. Shaw, ed., Chapter 4, pp. 253–301. Academic Press, New York.

Sifton, H. B. (1957). Air space tissues in plants. II. *Bot. Rev.* **23**, 303–312.

Stiles, W. (1960). The composition of the atmosphere (oxygen content of air, water, soil, intercellular spaces, diffusion, carbon dioxide, and oxygen tension). *In* "Handuch der Pflanzenphysiologie" (W. Ruhland, ed.). Vol. 12, Part 2, pp. 114–146. Springer Verlaz, Berlin and New York.

Stolzy, L. H., and Letey, J. (1964a). Characterizing soil oxygen conditions with a platinum microelectrode. *Advan. Agron.* **16**, 249–279.

Stolzy, L. H., and Letey, J. (1964b). Measurement of oxygen diffusion rates with the platinum microelectrode. III. Correlation of plant response to soil oxygen diffusion rates. *Hilgardia* **35**, 567–576.

Stolzy, L. H., and Van Gundy, S. D. (1968). Physical factors affecting soil microflora and microfauna. *Phytopathology* **58**, 889–899.

Stotzky, G. (1965). Microbial respiration. *In* "Methods of Soil Analysis" (C. A. Black, ed.)," Part 2, Chapter 13, pp. 1550–1572. Amer. Soc. Agron., Madison. Wisconsin.

Valoras, N., and Letey, J. (1966). Soil oxygen and water relationships to rice growth. *Soil Sci.* **101**, 210–215.

van der Heide, H., de Boer-Bolt, B. M., and van Raalte, M. H. (1963). The effect of a low oxygen content of the medium on the roots of barley seedlings. *Acta Bot. Neer.* **12**, 231–247.

van Raalte, M. H. (1940). On the oxygen supply of rice roots. *Ann. Jard. Bot. Buitenzorg* **50**, 99–113.

van Raalte, M. H. (1941). On the oxygen supply of rice roots. *Ann. Jard. Bot. Buitenzorg* **51**, 43–57.

van Raalte, M. H. (1943). On the oxidation of the environment by the roots of rice (*Oryza sativa* L.). Hortus Botanicus, Bogariensis, Java. *Syokubutu-Iho* **1**, 15–34.

Wesseling, J., and van Wijk, W. R. (1957). Land drainage in relation to soils and crops. *In* "Drainage of Agriculture Lands" J. N. Luthin, ed., Chapter 5, pp. 461–578. Amer. Soc. Agron., Madison, Wisconsin.

Willey, C. R., and Tanner, C. B. (1963). Membrane-covered electrode for measurement of oxygen concentration in soil. *Soil Sci. Soc. Amer., Proc.* **27**, 511–515.

Woolley, J. T. (1965). Drainage requirements of plants. *In* "Drainage for Efficient Crop Production Conference Proceedings." pp. 2–5, American Society of Agricultural Engineers, St. Joseph, Michigan.

Yu, P. T., Stolzy, L. H., and Letey, J. (1969). Survival of plants under prolonged flooded conditions. *Agron. J.* **61**, 844–847.

Zentmyer, G. A. (1965). Soil aeration and plant disease. *In* "Drainage for Efficient Crop Production Conference Proceedings." pp. 15, 16, and 36, American Society of Agricultural Engineers, St. Joseph, Michigan.

Zimmerman, P. W. (1930). Oxygen requirements for root growth of cuttings in water. *Amer. J. Bot.* **17**, 842–861.

Chapter 18

Soil Moisture Control for Maximum Grass Response

DANIEL HILLEL

It is a truism that in arid and semiarid habitats water generally constitutes the primary limiting factor in plant growth. Hence the major tasks of management under such conditions are to ensure the maximal supply and to conserve and efficiently utilize water in the field. Numerous methods have been proposed, yet the results are often baffling. Such is the complex nature of the soil–water–plant–atmosphere system and such is its variability that no single method can be expected a priori to apply equally or even similarly at different times and locations. It is altogether too tempting and easy for field experimenters and even theorists to fall into the trap of ascribing universal truth to an approximation that fits a specific set of conditions. Our best hope is not to find universal prescriptions but to understand the physical processes taking place in the habitat, and to learn how to modify these processes to best advantage in particular circumstances.

The purpose of this chapter is to elucidate the principles of soil water conservation in the field with reference to grass production in arid and semi-arid conditions. Special emphasis will be given the most critical and vulnerable stage of grass production—namely, the germination and seedling establishment stage.

259

The Field Water Balance

It is appropriate to begin a discussion of soil water conservation and water use efficiency with a consideration of the field water balance, which is a convenient way to evaluate the field water cycle as a whole and the relative magnitude of the various processes comprising it. Just as a businessman regularly summarizes the financial balance of his business (including an itemized listing of all income sources, expenditures, inventory, and change in net worth), so the agricultural physicist must attempt to account for all of the water entering, leaving, and remaining in the soil during any period of time.

The field water balance is intimately connected with the energy balance (Lemon, 1963; Tanner, 1960), since the various processes comprising the water balance also require energy. The content of water in the soil affects the way in which the solar radiation reaching the field is partitioned and utilized. Likewise the energy flux affects the state and movement of soil water.

In its simplest form the water balance is merely a statement that in a given body of soil the difference between the amount of water supplied (W_{in}) and the amount of water withdrawn (W_{out}) during a. certain period is equal to the change in total water content (ΔW).

$$W_{in} - W_{out} = \Delta W$$

When supply exceeds withdrawal, the water content change is positive and, conversely, when withdrawal exceeds supply, ΔW is negative.

In order to itemize these additions and subtractions, we should ponder the fate of rain or irrigation water reaching the soil surface during a given period of time. Some of this water infiltrates into the soil and some may accumulate in puddles over the surface or trickle downslope as surface run-off. Of the water entering the soil, some evaporates directly from the soil surface, some is extracted by plants for their growth or for transpiration to the atmosphere, some may drain beyond the root zone, and some may accumulate and remain (for a time) within the root zone. Additional water can also reach an area, either by runoff from an adjacent area or by capillary rise from a water table or wet layers present at some depth. The pertinent soil depth for which the water balance is computed is determined arbitrarily. From an agricultural or plant ecological point of view it is generally most appropriate to consider the rooting depth (or root zone) of the crop or plant community growing in the field.

The total water balance is (Hillel, 1971)

$$P + I = R + D + (E + T) + \Delta W$$

where P is precipitation; I is irrigation; R is runoff (which generally involves a loss of water by the field but may constitute a gain if runoff enters the field from some higher area); D is the movement below the root zone (which, if downward, is termed "drainage," and if upward is termed "capillary rise"); E is the direct evaporation from the soil surface; T is the transpiration from the plant canopies; and therefore $(E + T)$ is the evapotranspiration.

Simple and readily understandable as the field water balance may seem in principle, it is still rather difficult to measure (and even more difficult to control) in actual practice. Generally the largest component of the field water balance is the evapotranspiration, which is difficult to measure directly. To be able to compute it from the water balance, accurate measurements of all other terms of the equation are needed. It is relatively easy to measure the amount of water added to the field by precipitation and irrigation, even though it is necessary to consider possible nonuniformities in the areal distribution. The amount of runoff is generally small in agricultural fields, so that it can sometimes be taken as zero.

For a long period, such as a whole season, the change in water content of the root zone is likely to be small in relation to the total water balance. In this case the sum of the rain and irrigation is approximately equal to the sum of evapotranspiration and drainage. For shorter periods the change in soil water content can be relatively large and must be measured, either by sampling periodically or by the use of such instruments as neutron or gamma-ray monitors.

Common practice is to measure the total water content of the root zone just prior to an irrigation and to supply the amount of water necessary to replenish the deficit which has developed since the last irrigation. It is often assumed that this deficit is due to evapotranspiration only, thus disregarding the amount of water that may flow through the bottom of the root zone, either downward or upward. This flow is not always negligible, and can sometimes constitute a tenth or more of the total water balance (Rose and Stern, 1967). The measurement of root-zone or subsoil water content by itself cannot give the rate and direction of soil water movement. Even if the water content at a given depth remains constant, we cannot conclude that the water there is immobile, since it might be moving steadily through without causing any moisture changes in the conduction layer itself. Tensiometric measurements can, however, indicate the directions and magnitudes of the hydraulic gradients through the profile (Richards, 1965), and allow us to compute the fluxes on the basis of the hydraulic conductivity versus water content function, if it is known for the particular soil (Rose et al., 1965). More direct measurements of the deep percolation component of the field water balance will become possible with the development of water flux meters (Cary, 1968). Such devices are still in the preliminary development stage, however.

"Efficiency" of Water use

Several indices have been proposed to characterize the relative efficiency of water use in the field. One way is to calculate the ratio of the amount of dry matter produced to the total amount of water supplied. Another way is to calculate the ratio between dry-matter production and the amount of water used in evapotranspiration or in transpiration alone. The latter index is the inverse of the classical "transpiration ratio," which depends greatly on the climate and may be in the order of 500:1 or even 1000:1 in an arid region, where the evaporative demand of the atmosphere can be extremely high. For a given climate the value of this index depends primarily on the productivity of the crop and the fertility of the soil (Viets, 1962, 1966).

Still another way is to disregard plant response and to calculate the ratio of evapotranspiration to the total supply of water. This index can approach 100% when the water movement below the root zone is negligible. Such a high "efficiency" is seldom desirable, however, as it might result in the progressive salinization of the soil, especially in arid regions. Plants normally extract water while leaving behind much of the soluble salt originally present in the soil solution. Some excess supply of water over the amount of evapotranspiration is therefore needed in order to prevent the accumulation of salts in the root zone. On the other hand too large an excess may involve waste of water, leaching of nutrients, and impeded aeration.

In general, maximal plant response in yield and quality is commensurate with maximal transpiration—that is, with the provision of sufficient water for plants to transpire at the rate dictated by the effective climate. There appears to be little possibility for reduction of transpiration in the open field without an accompanying reduction in plant growth. Probably the best opportunity for water saving lies in the removal of extraneous losses (as by weeds, soil water evaporation, excessive downward seepage as well as all other factors inhibiting plant growth (e.g. lack of nutrients), thus ensuring the maximum possible yield for the amount of water supplied.

Infiltration Management

Effective utilization of precipitation depends in the first place on the capability of the soil to absorb the water as it arrives—namely, on the infiltration process. In attempting to increase infiltration several factors are important. The first is to maintain a high infiltration rate by "opening" the soil surface (as by tillage, aggregation, and turf aerification), or by protecting it against slaking and crusting (as by the use of mulches). The second factor is to provide time to permit complete infiltration even where the rain intensity might temporarily exceed the infiltration rate. This can be accomplished either by leveling, contour furrowing, or pitting the land surface in order to impound and hold the excess precipitation water in place until it can infiltrate. Some soils are naturally water repellent and respond to treatment with wetting agents (Letey *et al.*, 1962).

Runoff Inducement and Utilization

In many arid regions large tracts of land remain unused owing to insufficient or unstable rainfall, poor soils (shallow, stony, or saline), or irregular topography. The possibility of controlling and increasing the amount of surface runoff obtainable from such lands can be of great importance, particularly where water is scarce and the runoff thus obtained can augment the water supply for crops or livestock (Myers, 1963; Hillel, 1968b; Hillel and Rawitz, 1968).

Where rainfall is insufficient but the soil is otherwise arable, it may be possible to utilize the land in a system of "runoff farming" for example, (Mickelson *et al.*, 1965) in which alternate "runoff strips" are treated (surface-sealed and stabilized) so as to contribute their share of the rainfall as runoff to adjacent "runon strips" in which crops can be grown (Hauser and Cox, 1962; Hillel, 1968b).

Runoff farming is in fact a very old art, practiced in the Middle East as well as in North America by ancient farmers. Even at best, however, the farmers of old were able to collect no more than about 20% of the annual rainfall, while the greater part of the precipitation soaked into the ground. In desert areas the latter amount can be considered a complete loss, as it soon evaporates either directly or through uneconomic vegetation. The ancient runoff farmers therefore needed a runoff-to-runon area ratio of 20:1 or more in order to supply their fields with enough water.

Modern technology holds the promise of more effective runoff inducement. By means of mechanical treatments (stone clearing, smoothing, and compaction) as well as by a variety of chemical treatment to seal and stabilize the surface, it is possible to increase runoff severalfold, thus reducing the runoff-to-runon area ratios and increasing the cropped land area.

As the need increases for expanding production in arid regions, artificial methods for runoff inducement and utilization will surely deserve more attention.

Evapotranspiration

Evapotranspiration is a process largely dictated by climatic factors, notably incident solar radiation and advected heat, which provide energy for the process, and atmospheric vapor content and wind movement, which control vapor and heat flow phenomena (Tanner, 1960). Plant factors influence transpiration and radiation utilization in photosynthesis; soil factors, especially water content and transmission properties, influence storage and conduction of water and thus influence the partitioning of radiation and advected energy. The proportion of plant cover affects the relative magnitude of evaporation and transpiration (Peters, 1960). These factors alter, within limits, the proportion of total energy consumed in the evapotranspiration process. This complex of interrelated and as yet incompletely understood factors suggests a number of possible control measures—climatic, soil, and plant—that may be exercised to alter evapotranspiration.

One means of controlling incident radiation is by shading or by selective absorption (filtering) of incident light. This is generally impractical in the open field. A more feasible means is by modifying the reflectivity of the soil or of plant canopies.

When growing plants are present, both transpiration by plants and evaporation from the soil may be appreciable. The relative magnitude of these two processes depends in each case on the soil water content distribution as well as on the characteristic density and areal cover of the vegetative canopy (which are affected by the plant species, age, and planting pattern). When plant cover is more or less complete, the effect of soil surface on energy absorption and evapotranspiration is largely overshadowed by the plant effects. With plants the source of water being evaporated may extend throughout the entire root zone. Furthermore the absorption of solar radiation, the production or consumption of sensible heat, and the profile of the vapor gradients above the soil surface are greatly altered (Lemon, 1963).

An important climatic factor subject to alteration is the flow and transport characteristics of the lower atmospheric layer. The generally turbulent air is largely responsible for transmission of water vapor and sensible heat from the earth's surface to the upper air layers and for carrying CO_2 from the open atmosphere to plant leaves. Where the wind velocity above the vegetation is reduced, turbulent transfer becomes less important and diffusion becomes the dominant transfer mechanism with the rate of water loss thereby decreasing. The chief means of altering wind velocity near the surface is through wind barriers, both artificial and vegetative. The reduction of evaporative potential downwind from a shelterbelt can be as great as 20% to 30% in the zone up to 10 times the barrier height (Bates, 1944). However, vegetative windbreaks themselves use water and, therefore, partially offset any moisture saving that they produce in the crop, unless the water needs of the shelterbelt are satisfied from a water table at some depth below the ground surface. Furthermore, the heat-trapping effect of windbreaks party offsets their effectiveness in reduction of advection.

Generally, the presence of a water table nearer the soil surface than about 100 cm in the case of coarse-textured soils, or nearer than about 200 cm in fine-textured ones, will affect evapotranspiration. This can have the beneficial effect of supplying plant water requirements, but can also result in the gradual salinization of the soil through capillary rise and restricted leaching. A too-shallow water table can also limit aeration in the soil above it (Luthin, 1966).

Limiting Bare Soil Evaporation

In the absence of plants or in exposed bare spots between plants evaporation from the soil surface constitutes an important water-loss mechanism.

Soil water evaporation is controlled either by atmospheric evaporativity or by the profile's own transmission properties. Typically, following a wetting, the initial evaporation rate (while the soil is relatively moist and its water transmission rate is not limiting) is constant and dictated by the external evaporativity acting on the soil surface. Sooner or later, however, if evaporation persists and the soil surface dries, the ability of the soil profile to transmit water to the surface falls below the evaporative demand of the atmosphere, and the actual evaporation rate drops—sometimes quite abruptly and drastically (Lemon, 1956).

The length of time the initial stage of drying can persist depends on the intensity of the meteorological factors that determine atmospheric evaporativity as well as on the conductive properties of the soil itself. When external evaporativity is relatively slight, the initial constant-rate stage of drying is slower and can persist longer. Under similar external conditions, the first stage of drying will be sustained longer in a clayey than in a sandy soil, since the clayey soil retains a higher conductivity as suction develops in the surface zone of the profile (Hillel, 1968a).

The choice of means for the reduction of evaporation depends on the stage of the process one wishes to regulate: whether it be the first stage, in which the effect of meteorological conditions on the soil surface dominates the process; or the second stage in which the rate of water supply to the surface, determined by the transmitting properties of the profile, becomes the rate-limiting factor. Methods designed to affect the first stage cannot a priori be expected to serve during the second stage, and vice versa.

Covering or mulching the surface with residues or with reflective materials can reduce the intensity with which external factors, such as radiation and wind, act on the surface (Hanks *et al.*, 1961). Thus such surface treatments can retard evaporation during the initial stage of drying. A similar effect can result from the application of materials that lower the vapor pressure of water (Law, 1964; Olsen *et al.*, 1964), or from shallow cultivations designed to produce a "soil mulch" or "dust mulch" at the surface (Army *et al.*, 1961). Retardation of evaporation during the first stage can provide the plants with a greater opportunity to utilize the moisture of the uppermost soil layers, an effect that can be vital during the germination and establishment phases of plant growth. The retardation of initial evaporation can also enhance the process of redistribution and internal drainage, and thus allow more water to migrate downward into the deeper parts of the profile where it is conserved longer and is less likely to be lost by evaporation.

During the second stage of drying, the effect of surface treatments is likely to be only slight, and reduction of the evaporation rate and of water loss in the long run will depend on decreasing the diffusivity or conductivity of the soil profile in depth.

A too-frequent irrigation regime can cause the soil surface to remain wet and the first stage of evaporation to persist most of the time, resulting in a maximal rate of water loss. The water loss by evaporation from a single deep irrigation will often tend to be smaller than from two shallow ones with the same amount of water.

Tillage for seedbed preparation, weed control, or other purposes is perhaps the most ubiquitous of soil management practices. Soil disturbance by tillage implements generally results in loosening of the tilled layer. This generally increases evaporation from the tilled layer, but may also result in a marked decrease of water movement from the layers below. These mechanisms produce offsetting results and the net effect depends on the duration of the process, as well as on the depth, degree, and frequency of tillage and on the effect of rainfall on reconsolidating the tilled layer.

In general, the deeper the water is stored in the soil, the more slowly will it be removed by evapotranspiration. Thus depth of water storage is an important consideration in the potential reduction of evaporation losses. (Hillel *et al.*, 1971). Soil texture and profile stratification are the principal properties controlling the distribution of water storage in the soil. Coarse-textured soils usually drain more rapidly than fine-textured soils and thus retain less water for plant use per unit volume of soil at equal times. This may be an advantage in arid regions, where the small amount of precipitation water is transmitted to greater depth from which it is less subject to evaporation (provided this depth is not below the rooting zone of the plants). Under such conditions, coarse-textured soils constitute a moister habitat than fine-textured ones (Hillel and Tadmor, 1962). Under higher rainfall regimes, however, it is the finer-textured soils that hold more water in the root zone for a longer time and can provide more moisture for plant growth.

A stratified profile usually retains a higher moisture content above the discontinuity for some time following infiltration than does a uniform profile. It depends, however, on the depth of this discontinuity whether the increased retention actually benefits the plants or merely increases evaporation from the soil.

In principle the best condition from the standpoint of both evaporation and infiltration control is to have a coarse layer of large pores at the surface. Such a layer would conduct the water readily at saturation during infiltration, but would restrict liquid flow at unsaturation during evaporation. Since vapor diffusion is relatively slow compared to liquid flow in moist soils, rapid drying of a few millimeters of the surface can materially reduce evaporation.

The effectiveness of vegetative mulches may be limited unless they are sufficiently thick, because their high porosity permits rapid diffusion and air currents (Hanks and Woodruff, 1958). The initial evaporation rate under a mulch is usually reduced, but for extended periods a mulch may keep the soil surface much more moist and thus produce no net saving of water. Since mulches of crop residues tend to be more reflective than most soils, they usually result in cooler surface temperatures. Consequently, early plant growth under mulches is often retarded.

Since evaporation is an energy consuming process, treatments designed to decrease the energy flux to the soil might reduce evaporation, particularly during its initial stage. Color, slope, aspect, and surface roughness may alter the energy absorption of the soil surface (Hanks *et al.*, 1961). Soils of light color reflect a higher percentage of incident radiation than do darker colored ones. As soil organic matter and water content increase, colors darken and reflectance decreases. Artificial treatments, such as the application of chalk powder over dark soils, are sometimes effective in reducing direct soil water evaporation (Hillel, 1968a).

Specific Aspects of Soil Water Conservation during Germination and Seedling Establishment

The problem of ensuring proper germination of planted seeds and subsequent establishment of seedlings is of general importance in agriculture. The germination, emergence, and establishment phase is critical in the growth cycle of plants, as it determines the density of the stand obtained, influences the degree of weed infestation, and limits the eventual yield. Un-

less the success of this early phase is assured, the entire planting may be doomed from the outset. The problem of germination and establishment is especially acute under arid zone conditions, where the soil surface is wetted only infrequently and the rate of evaporation is high. In such circumstances a seedling must compete with the process of atmospheric drying for the rapidly diminishing moisture of the surface layers. Often these layers dry out too rapidly for the seedling to extend its roots downward into the deeper layers where available moisture can be found. Partially germinated seeds may fail to survive, even though overall conditions may be favorable for the mature plants (Tadmor, *et al.*, 1969).

Still another hindrance to germination is the tendency of certain soils to slake when wetted (particularly under the beating action of raindrops) and to form a hard crust upon drying. Tender seedlings, unable to emerge through the crust, may lie smothered only a few millimeters below the surface. Where the crust is kept moist and prevented from hardening, it may nevertheless hinder germination by limiting aeration. The extreme temperature fluctuations that take place at the bare soil surface may further limit the chances of a seed to germinate and of a seedling to survive. Arid zone soils may also contain soluble salts that may tend to accumulate and form excessive concentrations at the soil surface as a consequence of evaporation.

Especially sensitive and susceptible to adverse soil conditions are range plants with small seeds and tender seedlings. Even where overall ecological conditions are favorable for a given species, the difficulty of obtaining an adequate stand may decide at the outset against successful seeding operations.

Depth of sowing is an important consideration in seeding practice. The deeper the seeds are placed, the longer they are assured of the soil moisture content remaining in the favorable range.

As a first approximation the evaporation rate beyond the initial, constant-rate stage of the drying process can be taken as inversely proportional to the square root of time. The duration of the water content remaining above a certain value can thus be assumed to be proportional to the depth squared, so that a doubling of the seeding depth quadruples the effective duration of favorable soil moisture for germination. However, as range plant seeds tend to be small and their seedlings delicate in comparison with most of the cultivated field crops, excessively deep placement might prevent emergence. For this reason research is necessary to determine the optimal depth of placement for given species under given soil and climatic conditions.

Seed-bed compaction is usually considered to have an adverse effect on germination and seedling emergence, as it increases the mechanical resistance of the soil and often results in retardation of root development and in restricted aeration. On the other hand under marginal soil moisture conditions, a certain degree of compaction may improve germination (Dasberg *et al.*, 1966). In fact limited compaction over the seeding row is a common agronomic practice and most seeding implements have attachments for re-compacting the excessively loose soil that falls over the seeds. Seed-bed compaction can improve the seed-to-soil contact (thus decreasing the contact resistance to water flow from soil to seed) and can enhance the hydraulic conductivity of the unsaturated soil itself. The optimal degree and mode of compaction, however, must be determined experimentally for each specific set of conditions.

A very promising method to promote germination and seedling growth is to coat the soil surface with a thin film of either plastic materials or of petroleum-derived asphalt or wax. Such a coating can prevent crusting, conserve moisture, and warm the seed bed. Because of their higher costs, the use of plastic materials for mulching is necessarily limited to plants of a high potential return per unit area. Range grasses do not generally fit this category. However, sprayable oil mulches may be feasible for crops of moderate value, and possibly for the initial establishment of perennial turf grasses.

References

Army, T. J., Wise, A. F., and Hanks, R. J. (1961). Effect of tillage and chemical weed control practices on soil moisture losses during the fallow period. *Soil Sci. Soc. Amer. Proc.* **25**, 410–413.

Bates, C. G. (1944). The windbreak as a farm asset. *U.S. Dep. Agr. Farmer's Bull.* **1405**.

Cary, J. W. (1968). An instrument for *in situ* measurement of soil moisture flow and suction. *Soil Sci. Soc. Amer. Proc.* **32**, 3–5.

Dasberg, S., Hillel, D., Arnon, I. (1966). The response of grain sorghum to seedbed compaction. *Agron. J.* **58**, 199–201.

Hanks, R. J., and Woodruff, N. P. (1958). Influence of wind on water vapor transfer through soil, gravel and straw mulches. *Soil Sci.* **86**, 160–164.

Hanks, R. J., Bowers, S. A., and Bark, L. D. (1961). Influence of soil surface conditions on net radiation, soil temperature and evaporation. *Soil Sci.* **91**, 233–238.

Hauser, V. L., and Cox, M. B. (1962). Evaluation of Zingg conservation bench terraces. *Agr. Eng.* **43**, 462–464, 467.

Hillel, D. (1968a). "Soil water evaporation and means of minimizing it" Spec. Publ. Fac. Agr. Hebrew University of Jerusalem.

Hillel, D. (1968b) "Runoff inducement in arid lands," Spec. Publ. Fac. Agr. Hebrew University of Jerusalem.

Hillel, D. (1971). "Soil and Water: Physical Principles and Processes." Academic Press, New York.

Hillel, D., and Rawitz, E. (1968). A field study of soil surface treatments for runoff inducement. *Trans. Int Congr. Soil Sci., 9th, 1968* Vol. I, pp. 303–312.

Hillel, D., and Tadmor, N. (1962). Water regime and vegetation of principal plant habitats in the Negev Highlands of Israel. *Ecology* **43**, 33–41.

Hillel, D., Gardner, W. R., and Benyamini, Y. (1971). Post-irrigation movement of soil water. II. Simultaneous redistribution and evaporation. *Water Resour. Res.* **6**, 1148–1153.

Law, J. P. (1964). The effect of fatty alcohol and non-ionic surfactant on soil moisture evaporation in a controlled environment. *Soil Sci. Soc. Amer. Proc.* **28**, 695–699.

Lemon, E. R. (1956). The potentialities for decreasing soil moisture evaporation loss. *Soil Sci. Soc. Amer. Proc.* **20**, 120–125.

Lemon, E. R. (1963). Energy and water balance of plant communities. *In* "Environmental Control of Plant Growth" (C. T. Evans, ed.), pp. 55–78. Academic Press, New York.

Letey, J., Welch, N., Pelishek, R. E., Osborn, J. (1962). Wetting agents in irrigation of water repellent soils. *Calif. Agr.*, **16**, 12–13.

Luthin, J. N. (1966) "Drainage Engineering." Wiley, New York.

Mickelson, R. H., Cox, M. B., and Musick, J. (1965). Runoff water spreading on leveled cropland. *J. Soil Water Conserv. India* **20**, 57–60.

Myers, L. E. (1963). Water harvesting. *Agr. Res.* **12**, 10–11.

Olsen, S. R., Watanabe, F. S., Clark, F. E., and Kemper, W. D. (1964). Effect of hexadecanol on evaporation of water from soil. *Soil Sci.* **97**, 13–18.

Peters, D. B. (1960). Relative magnitude of evaporation and transpiration. *Agron. J.* **52**, 236–238.

Richards, S. J. (1965). Soil suction measurements with tensiometers. *In* "Methods of Soil Analysis," *Amer. Soc. Agron. Monogr.* **9**, 153–163.

Rose, C. W., and Stern, W. R. (1967). The drainage component of the water balance equation. *Aust. J. Soil Res.* **3**, 95–100.

Rose, C. W., Stern, W. R., and Drummond, J. E. (1965). Determination of hydraulic conductivity as a function of depth and water content for soil *in situ. Aust. J. Soil Res.* **3**, 1–9.

Tadmor, N., Hillel, D., and Cohen, Y. (1969). Establishment and maintenance of seeded dryland range under semiarid conditions. *Volcani Inst. Agr. Res., Spec. Publ.* pp. 1–69.

Tanner, C. B. (1960). Energy balance approach to evapotranspiration from crops. *Soil Sci. Soc. Amer. Proc.* **24**, 1–9.

Viets, F. G. (1962). Fertilizers and the efficient use of water. *Advan. Agron.* **14**, 223–264.

Viets, F. G. (1966). Increasing water use efficiency by soil management. *In* "Plant Environment and Efficient Water Use," (W. H. Pierre, *et al.*, eds.) pp. 259–274. Amer. Soc. Agron., Madison, Wisconsin.

Chapter 19

Problems in Nutrient Availability and Toxicity

O. R. LUNT

An extensive literature attests to the complexity of managing mixed populations of grasses, particularly with legumes, so as to maintain populations within desired limitations. Nutritional parameters may, of course, markedly influence population characteristics. Much nutritional research has focused on the requirements of legumes in mixtures since it is a rather general observation that when the nutrient requirements of legumes are met, associated grasses usually do not respond to additional nutrients other than nitrogen. Where it is the intent to maintain a relatively pure stand of grass, fertility management is substantially simplified. For a general discussion of the nutrition of grasslands see Loneragan's review (1964).

Grasses establish successfully on an extremely wide range of soil conditions and even within a given species considerable genetic variability may exist permitting the grass to tolerate unusual conditions.

Mineral Toxicities

Much empirical data exist relative to the tolerance of grasses to unusually high mineral concentrations in soils that normally result in toxic response. Within the last 20 years it has become clear that much phenotypic plasticity exists in a number of grass species, which allows the emergence of strains tolerant to unusually high concentrations of heavy metals such as lead, zinc, nickel, and copper.

Illustrative of this variability is the data of Jowett (1958) in which root growth as a percentage of that in the control solution not containing the toxic ion is compared for two strains of *Agrostis tenuis*. (Table 1). One strain was collected from a high nickel site whereas the other was considered to be normal.

It is apparent that the nickel-tolerant strain also exhibited marked copper and zinc tolerance.

The rapidity with which tolerant populations may emerge when confronted with edaphic conditions highly toxic to "normal" populations is also striking. Bradshaw *et al.* (1965) suggest that by breeding and selecting for individuals of *A. tenuis* tolerant to lead, for example, very high tolerance to lead toxicity may be achieved in about five generations. Thus practical solutions to specific toxic problems may be achieved in some cases. British

TABLE 1

ROOT GROWTH AS A PERCENTAGE OF THAT IN CONTROL SOLUTIONS, FREE OF HEAVY METAL FOR TWO STRAINS OF *AGROSTIS TENUIS* (from Jowett, 1958).

Metal (μmole/liter)		Nickel tolerant *A. tenuis*	Normal *A. tenuis*
Copper	5	66	4
	10	51	0
	15	29	0
Nickel	5	103	30
	10	84	9
	15	20	0
Lead	75	27	28
	125	22	12
Zinc	20	65	34
	40	42	21
	60	23	13

workers have made notable contributions on the tolerance of various grass species to specific metal toxicities. Reference is made, to the reviews of Bradshaw *et al*. (1965), Gregory and Bradshaw (1965), Bradshaw (1965), and Bollard and Butler (1966).

As a worldwide problem, the toxicity associated with acid soils far outstrips in importance the toxicities due to specific heavy metals. The soil chemistry and plant physiology considerations of this problem are complex. Reviews of the current status of the problem have been prepared by Coleman and Thomas (1967) on soil chemistry and by Jackson (1967) on physiological aspects. In general, infertility on acid soils is attributed to aluminum toxicity, manganese toxicity, phosphorus deficiency, molybdenum deficiency, and magnesium and calcium deficiencies. A number of investigators have suggested that variation in sensitivity to a toxic element such as aluminum is related to the plant's ability to chelate the ion and thus detoxify it (Jones, 1961). Others have stressed that sensitivity is related to translocation of the toxic ions to the shoot. Ouellette and Dessureaux (1958) showed that a number of clones of alfalfa, differing in sensitivity to aluminum and manganese, adsorbed about equal amounts of aluminum and manganese and that translocation to the shoots correlated with sensitivity to the ion. Phosphorus accumulation is reduced by high aluminum levels (Clarkson, 1969). Likewise, high phosphorus levels will reduce aluminum toxicity (Wright, 1937). Poor growth of roots of species at toxic levels of aluminum appears to be due to the inhibition of cell division in the root apices (Levan, 1945). Clarkson's review (1969) of metabolic aspects of aluminum toxicity implicates aluminum interference with DNA synthesis in the "S" period of the mitotic cycle and a separate important effect of depressing respiratory metabolism through its effects on phosphorylated intermediates. Mechanisms which impart tolerance to aluminum or other toxic elements are poorly understood. Clarkson (1969) suggests that in the case of aluminum some plants may have sites within the cell where the element may be harmlessly accumulated. An alternative or additional method may involve precipitation at the cell surface. Foy *et al*. 1965) have attributed differential aluminum tolerance among some varieties of wheat to plant-induced pH changes around their roots. Turner's review (1969) of heavy metal tolerance in plants stresses the possible role of the cell wall as a site for inactivation of toxic ions within the plants. Cell walls or woody parts of the plant deserve more attention as a site of precipitation of toxic elements. Lunt and Kofranek (1971) using an acid tolerant *Ericacae* species exceptionally tolerant to both aluminum and manganese showed marked differences in the distribution of these elements. Aluminum was largely confined to the roots whereas manganese accumulated in woody parts of the plant.

Considerable differences in tolerance to aluminum among four species of

Agrostis was demonstrated by Clarkson (1966) with *A. setacea* being most tolerant and *A. stolonifera* being least tolerant. However, in striking contrast to the variability in tolerance to several heavy elements displayed by certain species of *Agrostis*, differential resistance to aluminum toxicity in populations of *Agrostis* species was not demonstrated.

The extensive investigations of Hewitt and his associates on a large number of economic plants showed a tendency among many species for aluminum and manganese to moderate the influence of each other. With many species sensitive to aluminium, the addition of manganese increased yields. However, adding aluminum to manganese-sensitive crops aggravated manganese toxicity as did making the solutions more acid (Hewitt, 1948).

Interaction between aluminum and calcium in relation to aluminum toxicity is known to exist in some plants. Foy *et al.* (1969) showed that an "aluminum-sensitive" variety of soybean was more adversely affected by decreasing levels of calcium at a given level of aluminum than was an "aluminum-tolerant" variety. These observations are consistent with speculations that aluminum reacts with membranes, enzymes, and so on, in ways that are detrimental to their function, and that calcium as a competitive ion in such adsorptions is largely innocuous and therefore protective against the effects of some toxic ions as proposed by Wallace *et al.* (1966).

Salinity Tolerance

Variability among genera of grasses in tolerance to excessive levels of soluble salts or to sodic soils is likewise notable. *Puccinellia distans* showed only about a 25% reduction in yield when the substrate contained a salt solution of 330 m.e./liter of soluble salts—more than half the concentration of sea water (Lunt *et al.*, 1961). Bermudagrass also tended to be highly tolerant while *A. tenuis* was relatively sensitive. Youngner and Lunt (1967) showed a sensitivity range of about twofold to exist among nine varieties of bermudagrass. Several of these varieties showed a positive response in root growth to moderate levels of salinity.

Many grasses exhibit excellent tolerance to sodic soil conditions—notable examples being tall wheatgrass, dallisgrass, sudangrass, seaside bentgrass, and *Puccinellia distans* (Lunt *et al.*, 1964). The writer is not aware that efforts have been made to examine variability in alkali tolerance within a given species.

Sensitivity to boron injury appears to correlate well with the rate of uptake. Oertli *et al.* (1961) observed boron accumulated in the tips of blades and was thereby substantially removed by mowing. Under these conditions growth was not inhibited by high levels of boron in the substrate.

Nutrient Availability

As with tolerance to toxic conditions in the soil, grasses show great variability in their response to nutrient supply. Nutritional parameters may strongly influence populations and distributions of species. In an examination of seven grass species, Bradshaw *et al.* (1964) found marked differences in the response to NO_3 nitrogen. *Lolium perenne* and *Agrostis stolonifera* showed greatest response at the highest levels, that is, 243 ppm nitrogen. However, *Agrostis canina* showed no further response above 27 ppm nitrogen supplied, and *Nardus stricta* showed a reduction in yield at nitrogen levels higher than this. The economic grasses are, by and large, very responsive to nitrogen supply and it is a common observation that when mixed pastures are fertilized with nitrogen, grass growth is greatly stimulated at the expense of legumes. Bradshaw *et al.* (1964) consider that larger differences exist between species in response to nitrogen than to either calcium or phosphorous. They support a considerable body of opinion that nitrogen is a major ecological factor determining the distribution of species.

Except for nitrogen introduced by fertilization or biological fixation, nitrogen supply in soils is largely dependent on mineralization of organic matter. In temperate regions nitrogen is mineralized from humus at the rate of about 1% or 2% per year. Numerous reviews have dealt with nitrogen transformations and the conditions affecting them—for example, the review by Harmsen and Van Schreven (1955). In turfgrass culture some success has been achieved in developing nitrogen fertilizers of controlled availability. The objective here has been to have available nitrogen sources that supply nitrogen over extended periods and reduce flushes of growth. The success achieved for this objective is shown in Fig. 1 taken from Kaempffe and Lunt (1967) for urea formaldehyde. In these studies growth correlated closely with nitrogen recovery. Other materials such as 1.1-diureidoisobutane and coated fertilizers may achieve this objective.

Detailed field work by Sonneveld *et al.* (1959) on the distribution of pasture species as related to the availability of phosphorus has shown that phosphorus supply may be an important parameter affecting botanical composition of pastures. Bradshaw *et al.* (1960) have shown modest differences among grasses in their response to phosphorous levels in sand culture. It seems clear that these relatively modest differences which can be measured in noncompetitive situations may, along with other factors, exert powerful effects on population distributions in competitive communities. Lunt *et al.* (1966) were not able to demonstrate substantial differences among five grass species in their ability to extract phosphorus from low phosphorus soils. All grasses were deficient on the same soils or showed similar responses on soils moderately deficient in phosphorus.

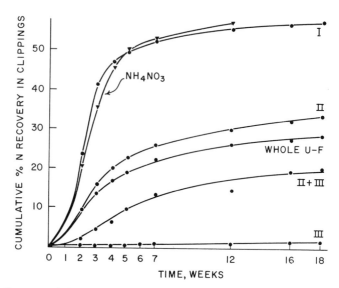

FIG. 1. Recovery of nitrogen by *Alta Fescue* from NH_4NO_3 and urea formaldehyde. Fraction I from U–F is soluble in cold water, II is soluble in hot water, and fraction III insoluble in hot water. (From Kaempffe and Lunt, 1967.)

References

Bollard, E. G., and Butler, G. W. (1966). Mineral nutrition off plants. *Annu. Rev. Plant Physiol.* **17**, 77–105.

Bradshaw, A. D. (1965). Evolutionary significance of phenotypic plasticity in plants. *Advan. Genet.* **13**, 115–155.

Bradshaw, A. D., Chadwick, J. J., Jowett, D., Lodge, R. W., and Snaydon, R. W. (1960). Experimental investigations into the mineral nutrition of several grass species. III. Phosphate level. *J. Ecolol.* **48**, 631–637.

Bradshaw, A. D., Chadwick, J. J., Jowett, D., and Snaydon, R. W. (1964). Experimental investigations into the mineral nutrition of several grass species. IV. Nitrogen level. *J. Ecolol.* **52**, 665–676.

Bradshaw, A. D., McNeilly, T. S., and Gregory, R. P. G. (1965). Industrialization, evolution and the development of heavy metal tolerance in plants. *In* "Ecology and the Industrial Society" (G. T. Goodman, R. W. Edwards, and J. M. Lambert, eds.), pp. 327–343. Oxford Univ. Press, London and New York.

Clarkson, D. T. (1966). Aluminum tolerance in species within the genus *Agrostis*. *J. Ecol.* **54**, 167–178.

Clarkson, D . T. (1969). Metabolic aspects of aluminum toxicity and some possible mechanisms for resistance. *Brit. Ecol. Soc. Symp.* **9**, 381–397.

Coleman, N. T., and Thomas, G. W. (1967). The basic chemistry of soil acidity. *In* "Soil Acidity and Liming" (R. W. Pearson and F. Adams, eds.), pp. 1–41. Amer. Soc. Agron., Madison, Wisconsin.

Foy, C. D., Burns, G. R., Brown, J. C., and Fleming, A. L. (1965). Differential Al tolerance of two wheat varieties associated with plant induced pH changes around their roots. *Soil Sci. Soc. Amer., Proc.* **29**, 64–67.

Foy, C. D., Fleming, A. L., and Armiger, W. H. (1969). Aluminum tolerance of soybeam varieties in relation to calcium nutrition. *Agron. J.* **61**, 505–511.

Gregory, R. P. G., and Bradshaw, A. D. (1965). Heavy metal tolerance in populations of *Agrostis tenuis* Sibth. and other grasses. *New Phytol.* **64**, 131–143.

Harmsen, G. W., and Van Schreven, D. A. (1955). Mineralization of organic nitrogen in soil. *Advan. Agron.* **7**, 299–398.

Hewitt, E. J. (1948). The resolution of the factors in soil acidity. IV. The relative effects of aluminum and manganese toxicities on some farm and market garden crops (cont.). *Long Ashton Hort. Res. Sta.* [*Univ. Bristol*], *Annu. Rep.* pp. 58–65.

Jackson, W. A. (1967). Physiological effects of soil acidity. *In* "Soil Acidity and Liming" (R. W. Pearson and F. Adams, eds.), pp. 43–124. Amer. Soc. Agron., Madison, Wisconsin.

Jones, L. H. P. (1961). Aluminum uptake and toxicity in plants. *Plant Soil* **13**, 297–310.

Jowett, D. (1958). Populations of *Agrostis spp.* Tolerant of heavy metals. *Nature* (*London*) **182**, 816–817.

Kaempffe, G. C., and Lunt, O. R. (1967). Availability of various fractions of urea-formaldehyde. *J. Agr. Food Chem.* **15**, 967–971.

Levan, A. (1945). Cytological reactions induced by inorganic salt solutions. *Nature* (*London*) **156**, 751–752.

Loneragan, J. F. (1964). The nutrition of grasslands. *In* "Grasses and Grasslands" (C. Bernard, ed.), p. 206–220. Macmillan, New York.

Lunt, O. R., and Kofranek, A. M. (1971). Manganese and aluminum tolerance of azalea, CV. "Sweetheart Supreme." *Proc. Hort. Cong., 18th, 1970* (in press).

Lunt, O. R., Youngner, V. B., and Oertli. J. J. (1961). Salinity tolerance of five turfgrass varieties. *Agron. J.* **53**, 247–249.

Lunt, O. R., Kaempffe, C., and Youngner, V. B. (1964). Tolerance of five turfgrass species to soil alkali. *Agron. J.* **56**, 481–483.

Lunt, O. R., Branson, R. L., and Clark, S. B. (1966). Response of five grass species to phosphorus on six soils. *Proc. Int. Grassland Congr., 9th, 1965* Vol. 1, pp. 1687–1701.

Oertli, J. J., Lunt, O. R., and Youngner, V. B. (1961). Boron toxicity in several turfgrass species. *Agron. J.* **53**, 262–265.

Ouellette, G. J., and Dessureaux, L. (1958). Chemical composition of alfalfa as related to degree of tolerance to manganese and aluminum. *Cana. J. Plant Sci.* **38**, 206–214.

Sonneveld, F., Kruijne, A. A., and de Vries, D. M. (1959). Influence of phosphate on the botanical composition and on the grade of quality of herbage. *Neth. J. Agr. Sci.* **7**, 40–50.

Turner, R. G. (1969). Heavy metal tolerance in plants. *Brit. Ecol. Soc. Symp.* **9**, 399–410.

Wallace, A., Frolich, E., and Lunt, O. R. (1966). Calcium requirements of higher plants. *Nature* (*London*) **209**, 634.

Wright, K. E. (1937). The effects of phosphorus and lime in reducing the toxicity of aluminum in acid soils. *Plant Physiol.* **12**, 173–181.

Youngner, V. B., and Lunt, O. R. (1967). Salinity effects of roots and tops of bermuda grass. *J. Brit. Grassland Soc.* **22**, 257–259.

Chapter 20

Nutrient Uptake and Assimilation for Quality Turf versus Maximum Vegetative Growth

ROY L. GOSS

Nutrient Availability and Uptake

According to Meyer *et al.* (1960) a clear distinction should be drawn between the absorption of a salt and the subsequent utilization of it or its component ions. Absorption of the ions or molecules of salts does not necessarily mean that they will be utilized. Some remain for more or less indefinite periods in the ionic state in the cells. These ions may eventually be incorporated into the structure of more complex but unassimilated molecules synthesized by the plant such as storage proteins, calcium oxalate, glycosides, or into the protoplasm of the cell walls. Utilization therefore implies the incorporation of mineral elements into the relatively permanent constituents of the cell walls and protoplasm or for their participation in fundamental metabolic reactions.

Absorption or uptake of plant nutrients occurs principally from two mechanisms: (1) the salt accumulation mechanism and (2) the ionic exchange mechanism. Limited quantities of mineral salts do pass into some cells under certain conditions, but this is considered relatively unimportant.

NUTRIENT AVAILABILITY

Nutrient availability is influenced by (1) level and form of the nutrient in the soil, (2) the degree of fixation of the nutrient, (3) rooting characteristics of the plant, and (4) environmental factors such as moisture, oxygen, temperature, and the presence of soil microorganisms. Robinson *et al.* (1962) working with orchardgrass found that potassium applications on soils with low residual levels produced greater yield and maintained better stands than the untreated checks. Summer applications, providing potassium when critically needed by the plant, tended to maintain adequate percentages of potassium in the tissue throughout the growing season. Miller and Ohlrogge (1958) found from fertilizer banding experiments on corn that nitrogen placed with phosphorus in a localized band increased the relative feeding power of the corn plant on the band-placed phosphorus at soil-phosphorus levels ranging from 0 to over 887 kg/ha. When nitrogen and phosphorus bands were separated, nitrogen increased the root feeding power on phosphorus only at low soil-phosphorus levels. Development of a root mass in the area of nitrogen and phosphorus placement appeared to be the most important mechanism responsible for these effects. Doll *et al.* (1959) reported increased uptake of potassium by orchardgrass—alta fescue—Ladino clover herbage when applications ranged from 22 to 88 kg/ha annual applications. They reported potassium uptake of over 249 kg/ha from the highest rate applied after four years' treatment. Hylton *et al.* (1965) reported that the growth and absorption of phosphorus by ryegrass was affected by the available supply. Distribution and accumulation of phosphorus within the plant were related to kind and age of tissue.

EFFECT OF OXYGEN ON NUTRIENT UPTAKE

Oxygen levels in the soil greatly influence both nutrient uptake and growth of most plants. Letey *et al.* (1962) found that low oxygen concentrations caused a decrease in phosphorus and potassium concentration in barley shoots, whereas sodium, calcium, and magnesium were not greatly modified. Later work by Letey *et al.* (1965) showed that soil aeration influenced the concentration of many minerals in barley plant shoots. Nitrogen, phosphorus, and potassium were increased and sodium decreased with increased oxygen supply. When excised roots of barley were immersed in dilute salt solutions, accumulation of salts within the root cells occurred readily if air was bubbled through the system, but little or no accumulation occurred if nitrogen was bubbled through the solution (Hoagland and Broyer, 1936). In the absence of oxygen, aerobic respiration was checked and the accumulation of electrolytes in the root cells virtually ceased. This seemed to be especially true with potassium. A similar relation between aerobic respiration and accumulation of salts has also been demonstrated in other plant tissues. It is pertinent to recall in this connection that absorption of water by many plant species also requires adequate aeration of the roots.

EFFECT OF SOIL TEMPERATURE ON NUTRIENT UPTAKE

Knoll *et al.* (1964) present evidence that soil temperature affects nutrient uptake, especially phosphorus. In greenhouse studies with corn, phosphorus uptake and yield increased as temperatures were increased from 15°C to 25°C. When phosphorus at 39 and 78 kg/ha was mixed with the soil as compared to layered in the soil, the uptake of phosphorus was less at the lower temperatures but generally higher at the highest soil temperature.

Nielsen *et al.* (1961) found that phosphorus uptake and yield of both tops and roots of corn increased with increasing root zone temperatures. Nightingale (1933) also pointed out the role of low soil temperature in reducing the uptake, translocation, and assimilation of nitrogen in tomato plants. Temperature exerted a marked effect on the nitrate-reducing capacity. Although nitrates were quickly absorbed, their reduction and the synthesis of organic nitrogen compounds occurred very slowly at 13°C. At 21°C both absorption and reduction of nitrate ions occurred very rapidly.

Nutrients for Quality versus Growth in Turfgrass

Quality in turfgrasses, unlike that in forage grass, is somewhat nebulous. In the writer's opinion, turfgrass quality is composed of the following individual components:

1. Color: The deeper the green, the better the acceptability, generally.

2. Optimum growth rate for the intended use: Grasses subjected to heavy wear should grow at a faster rate than those for esthetic purposes only.

3. Density of stems and leaves: The greatest number of plants per unit area is desirable in most turfgrass areas, especially golf course putting greens and athletic fields.

4. Disease resistance: Many turfgrasses are not resistant to diseases, hence are dependent on fungicidal programs for their success.

5. Ability to withstand close and frequent mowing.

6. Ability to recover from injury caused by excessive wear and other causes.

7. Other factors including shade tolerance, insect and nematode resistance, ability to withstand saline or alkali soils, winter hardiness, ability to withstand wet soils and drought.

Nutrient uptake and assimilation have an important relationship to most of these factors.

Madison and Anderson (1963) in an attempt to assess a quality factor to turfgrass that could be repeated employed a chlorophyll index to measure the response of Seaside and Highland bentgrass to mowing, irrigation, and fertility treatments. They found that only variations in nitrogen fertility levels produced significant differences in chlorophyll index. Madison (1962) proposed the term "verdure" for the green leaves and stems remaining in the turf after mowing, which is the product of turfgrass culture. He found that the most verdure and the greatest yield were produced with high nitrogen treatments; but mowing and irrigation treatments that increased yield decreased verdure. This indicates that yield may be inappropriate for accurate evaluations of turfgrasses.

Goss and Law (1967) investigated effects of mowing heights and nitrogen levels on shoot and root production of bluegrass varieties. They reported significantly higher shoot yields at high compared to low fertility at two cutting heights. Lower yield of shoots by Merion bluegrass at both nitrogen levels is one quality factor that makes it an outstanding bluegrass variety.

Waddington *et al.* (1964) studying various rates and sources of nitrogen on bluegrass turf demonstrated that the factors that produce yield were also most important in producing turf quality. Highest turf color ratings and relative chlorophyll content were usually obtained from plots yielding the most clippings.

EFFECT OF NITROGEN ON ROOT PRODUCTION

In contrast to shoot yield, Goss and Law (1967) showed that mean root production was reduced significantly by high rates of nitrogen for all varieties. This agrees with the report of Madison (1962) that an inverse relationship exists between nitrogen supply and root development.

Powell *et al.* (1967) found that bentgrass root-growth rate was highest during fall and spring and lowest in winter. In each of these seasons nitrogen additions reduced the immediate rate of root growth but enhanced future root growth. They suggested that root-growth reduction with high rates of nitrogen fertilization could be associated with low carbohydrates. Sugars needed for root growth were probably utilized in increased rates of nitrogen metabolism.

TISSUE NUTRIENT CONTENT AND NUTRIENT RECOVERY

Goss and Law (1967) also reported that tissue nitrogen was higher from the higher nitrogen application among all varieties tested at two cutting heights as shown in Table 1. Significantly higher percentages of nitrogen were recovered from low nitrogen applications than from high.

Investigations by Goss (1965) on putting green bentgrass turf revealed relationships between the uptake of nitrogen and potassium and the subsequent recovery of these elements in the clippings. Fertility treatments consisted of 292, 584, and 974 kg N/ha from urea; 0 and 86 kg P/ha from treble superphosphate; and 0, 162, and 325 kg K/ha from KCl/yr. These treatments were applied in a factorial arrangement every two weeks beginning in March until the season total was applied. After the treatments had been carried out for five years, plots were sampled weekly for dry matter yield and nutrient content. These yields were extrapolated to annual totals for dry matter, nitrogen, phosphorus, and potassum. Six from a total of nineteen treatments were thus sampled. Only one treatment from the highest levels was selected for analysis since it was felt that these levels were not practical for bentgrass turf. None were selected from the lower levels since visual observations indicated substandard turf quality, color, density, and growth. Table 2 shows the treatments and recovery of nitrogen and potassium for the selected treatments. From applications of 974 kg N/ha, only 26% was recovered in the tissue as compared to 43% recovery from applications of 584 kg/ha. High amounts of nitrogen were not taken up in either case, but extreme waste was evident at the higher rate.

When potassium was applied at 325 kg/ha, recovery was 47%, but in-

TABLE 1

MEAN PERCENT TISSUE NITROGEN AND PERCENT NITROGEN
RECOVERY FOR FOUR SELECTED BLUEGRASS VARIETIES FOR TWO
CUTTING HEIGHTS AND TWO NITROGEN LEVELS FOR 1957 AND 1958

	Year	High nitrogen		Low nitrogen	
		High cut	Low cut	High cut	Low cut
Tissue Nitrogen, %	1957	3.8	4.1	3.2	3.4
	1958	4.0	4.3	3.6	3.7
Nitrogen recovery, %	1957	44	41	79	75
	1958	31	43	74	89

TABLE 2

YIELD OF NITROGEN AND POTASSIUM PER HECTARE RECOVERED
FROM TURFGRASS CLIPPINGS

Application	Rate/ha	in kg	Recovery of Nitrogen	Recovery of Potassium in kg/ha
Nitrogen	Phosphorus	Potassium	in kg/ha	
974	86	325	251	142
584	86	325	251	153
584	86	162	248	151
584	0	325	199	124
584	0	162	214	120
584	0	0	226	118

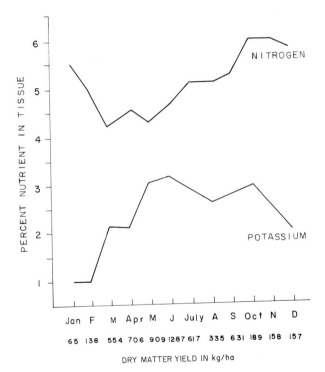

FIG. 1. Mean dry matter yield in kilogram per hectare per month and percent nitrogen and potassium in tissue for the highest level nutritional treatment on putting green bentgrass. Treatment: N, 974 kg/ha/yr; P, 86 kg/ha/yr; K, 325 kg/ha/yr.

creased to 93% when 162 kg/ha were applied. Goss (1965) has shown a depletion of exchangeable potassium in the latter case and that part of this recovery must be due to mineralized potassium. These investigations were conducted on a Puyallup fine sandy loam soil that usually exhibits both high potassium fixation and supplying power. Figure 1 shows the percentage of nutrient in the tissue by month, and the monthly clipping yield for the highest nutrient treatment. Figure 2 shows nutrient removal in kg/ha by the month as related to monthly yields. Treatment 584–86–325 produced higher clipping yields, percent nitrogen in tissue, and total nitrogen than the 974–86–325 treatment. Continued high nitrogen applications during July and August caused some injury and reduced clipping yields, which in turn caused reduced nitrogen recovery.

Tissue nitrogen was generally lower during the maximum growth period than during the late fall period. Tissue potassium conversely was highest during the peak growth period and lower the remainder of the year. It is

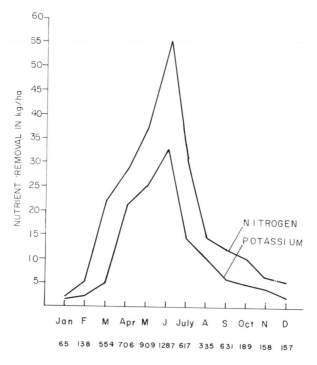

FIG. 2. Mean dry matter yield in kilogram per hectare per month and kilograms of nitrogen and potassium removed per month for the highest nutritional level on putting green bentgrass. Treatment: N, 974 kg/ha/yr; P, 86 kg/ha/yr; K, 325 kg/ha/yr.

probable that potassium stimulates greater growth provided there are no other limiting factors. Although maximum vegetative growth is not necessarily desirable, plots with higher potassium levels exhibited the best turf quality.

In the 584–0–0 treatment tissue nitrogen content increased and tissue potassium decreased during the maximum growth period of May through July. This probably reflects the importance of potassium in the reduction of nitrates and the synthesis of amino acids and their eventual synthesis of plant protein. Griffith *et al*. (1964) working with orchardgrass pointed out that asparagine accumulated abnormally in the second and third harvest when potassium fell below 1.6% of the dry weight. McNew (1953) has pointed out that "Unlike other essential nutrients, potassium does not become a structural part of the plant cell. It is the immobile regulator of cell activity and promotes the reduction of nitrates and the synthesis of amino acids from carbohydrate and inorganic nitrogen." He further states that "A deficiency of potassium enforces the accumulation of carbohydrates and inorganic nitrogen in the plant. Eventually it retards photosynthesis and the production of new tissues."

Nutrient Uptake and their Effect on Turfgrass Diseases

The quality of turfgrasses is severely affected by diseases. Diseased spots and patches cause poor appearance and serviceability on nearly any turfgrass area. Areas killed by turf diseases are most often invaded by undesirable plants, composed of broadleafed weeds, *Poa annua*, and other weedy grasses.

FUSARIUM PATCH DISEASE

Goss and Gould (1968) found that the number of Fusarium spots caused by *Fusarium nivale* decreased as nitrogen applications were reduced from 974 to 292 kg/ha/yr without regard to phosphorus and potassium. There were 48 spots per plot for the 974 kg N rate as compared to 27 for 584 kg N, and only 13 spots for the 292 kg N rate. Figures 3 and 4 show the effects of 0 and 86 kg P/ha with all combinations of nitrogen and potassium. Less disease was encountered at the two lower nitrogen levels when phosphorus was applied; however, at the highest nitrogen rate, neither phosphorus nor potassium had much effect on the number of disease spots. Potassium exerted its greatest effect in reducing disease at the lower nitrogen levels in the presence of phosphorus. Gould (1965) pointed out that high nitrogen

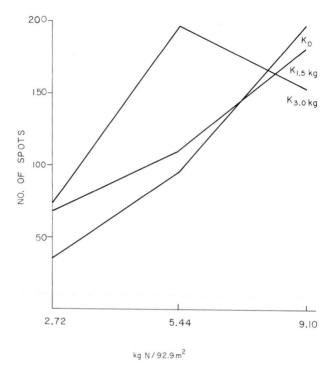

kg N / 92.9 m^2

FIG. 3. The effects of various rates of nitrogen and potassium on the number of Fusarium spots (*Fusarium nivale*) on putting green turf when P = 0.

levels resulted in more loss from Fusarium patch than lower levels. Smith (1953) reported that management which produces succulent growth may stimulate infection by *Fusarium nivale*.

OPHIOBOLUS PATCH DISEASE

This disease is caused by the fungus *Ophiobolus graminis* Sacc. var. *avenae* and is particularly destructive on *Agrostis spp.* This pathogen also causes the take-all disease in cereal crops. Stumbo *et al.* (1942) were able to eliminate *O. graminis* infection by heavy applications of phosphatic fertilizers when nitrogen levels were maintained slightly in excess of that required for good wheat growth. This work correlates closely with that of Goss and Gould (1967). Nitrogen levels as high as 974 kg/ha/yr helped reduce the severity of this disease. The beneficial effect of nitrogen in increasing new root production on mature plants may have outweighed its adverse effect in increasing susceptibility of individual roots to infection, according to

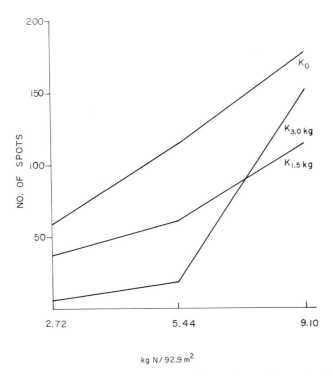

Fig. 4. The effects of various rates of nitrogen and potassium on the number of Fusarium spots (*Fusarium nivale*) on putting green turf when P = 0.80.

Garrett (1937). The application of 974 kg N/ha did not hold the disease down in 1961, but was very effective in 1964, when the plots were older. Both phosphorus and potassium were important in controlling this disease.

RED THREAD DISEASE

Red thread disease is caused by *Corticium fuciforme* and is strongly affected by nitrogen levels and to a lesser degree by phosphorus and potassium. Goss and Gould (1961) demonstrated that nitrogen levels interact with phosphorus and potassium to reduce the severity of infection from this disease on *Agrostis spp.* and *Festuca spp.* managed as lawns. Figures 5 and 6 show the relationship of nitrogen, phosphorus, and potassium to this disease. Ultimately, nitrogen is the major factor, but 3.0 kg K/92.9 m^2 produced the least red thread disease at both levels of phosphorus. Erwin (1941) stated that ammonium or sodium nitrate at rates of 1725 kg/ha would check the red thread causing pathogen.

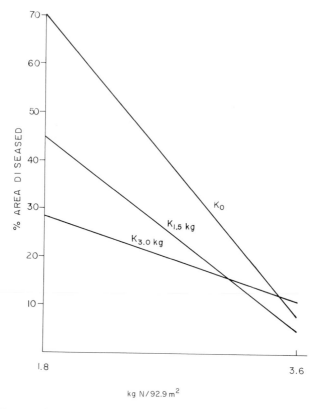

FIG. 5. Degree of red thread infection (*Corticium fuciforme*) with various rates of both nitrogen and potassium when P = 0 and mowing height of 1.8 cm.

OTHER DISEASES

A leaf spot disease on Coastal bermudagrass caused by two undisclosed fungi was reported by Evans *et al.* (1964). This disease is more severe when potassium levels are low. Severe attacks were incited with zero levels of potassium and high nitrogen treatments.

Pritchett and Horn (1966) reported significant differences among seven different potassium sources in their ability to control dollar spot disease, caused by *Sclerotinia homeocarpa*, on Tifway bermudagrass. They reported that 0.91 kg K/92.9 m²/season from KCL, K_2CO_3, K_2SO_4, and FN 519 (frit) were significant in yield and in control of dollar spot.

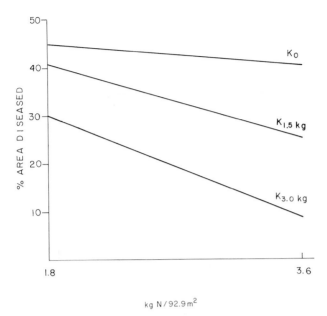

F$_{\text{IG}}$. 6. Decrease in red thread infection (*Corticium fulciforme*) with increasing rates of both nitrogen and potassium when P $=$ 0.80 kg and mowing height of 1.8 cm.

Conclusions

There is little doubt that if no other factors are limiting, nitrogen is the factor regulating growth in grasses and is a major factor controlling quality in turfgrasses. Kaempffe and Lunt (1967) state that "The objective of good turf culture is not high yield production, but maintenance of an adequately dense turf and acceptable color." This latter leaves a great deal to individual taste, or the degree of quality desired. Their work with urea formaldehyde nitrogen points out the importance of slow or controlled nitrogen release which provides the plants with a smaller, though probably adequate, amount of available nitrogen during the growing season at any one time. This results in less leaching, less "explosive" growth, and usually acceptable color for most conditions.

Finally, ratio of plant nutrients for maximum quality must be considered. Quality, here, is implied as color, density, and freedom from diseases and weeds. Fisher and Caldwell (1959) produced 29,120 kg/ha of Coastal bermudagrass hay with 1120 kg N/ha annually. Plant and soil analyses suggested a 5.0 to 0.44 to 1.66 ratio of nitrogen, phosphorus and potassium should be applied to obtain high production. The data of Goss (1965) indicates a ratio of approximately 3 to 0.44 to 1.66 of nitrogen, phosphorus, and potassium. It is the writer's conclusion that the ratio of plant nutrients more nearly equates to quality whereas intensity of application equates to maximum vegetative growth.

References

Doll, E. C., Hatfield, A. L., and Todd, J. R. (1959). Effect of rate and frequency of potash additions on pasture yield and potassium uptake. *Agron. J.* **51**, 27.

Erwin, L. E. (1941). Pathogenicity and Control of *Corticium fuciforme*. *R.I., Agr. Exp. Sta., Bull.* **278**.

Evans, E. M., Rouse, R. D., and Gudauskas, R. T. (1964). Low soil potassium sets up coastal for leaf spot disease. *Highlights Agr. Res.* **11**, No. 2.

Fisher, F. L., and Caldwell, A. G. (1959). The effects of continued use of heavy rates of fertilizers on forage production and quality of coastal bermudagrass. *Agron. J.* **51**, 99.

Garrett, S. D. (1937). Soil conditions and the take-all disease of wheat II. The relation between soil reaction and soil aeration. *Ann. Appl. Biol.* **24**, 747–751.

Goss, R. L. (1965). Nitrogen-potassium team on turfgrasses. *Better Crops Plant Food.* **49**, 34.

Goss, R. L., and Gould, C. J. (1967). Some interrelationships between fertility levels and ophiobolus patch disease in turfgrasses. *Agron. J.* **59**, 149.

Goss, R. L., and Gould C. J. (1968). Some interrelationships between fertility levels and *Fusarium* patch disease of turfgrasses.

Goss, R. L., (1965). Unpublished data.

Goss, R. L., and Gould, C. J. (1961). Unpublished data.

Goss, R. L., and Law, A. G. (1967). Performance of bluegrass varieties at two cutting heights and two nitrogen levels. *Agron. J.* **59**, 516.

Gould, C. J. (1965). Research progress on controlling turf diseases. *Proc. Northwest Turfgrass Conf., 19th*, pp. 13–15.

Griffith, W. K., Teel, M. R., and Parker, H. E. (1964). Influence of nitrogen and potassium on the yield and chemical composition of orchardgrass. *Agron. J.* **56**, 473–475.

Hoagland, D. R., and Broyer, T. C. (1936). General nature of the process of salt accumulation by roots with description of experimental methods. *Plant Physiol.* **11**, 471–507.

Hylton, L. O. Jr., Ulrich, A., Cornelius, D. R., and Okhi, K. (1965). Phosphorus content of Italian ryegrass relative to growth, moisture content and mineral constituents. *Agron. J.* **57**, 505.

Kaempffe, G. C., and Lunt, O. R. (1967). Availability of various fractions of urea-formaldehyde. *Agr. Food Chem.* **15**, 967.

Knoll, H. A., Brady, N. C., and Lathwell, D. J. (1964). Effect of soil temperature and phosphorus fertilization on the growth and phosphorus content of corn. *Agron. J.* **56**, 145.

Letey, J., Stolzy, L. H., Valoras, N., and Szuszkiewicz, T. E. (1962). Influence of soil oxygen of growth and mineral concentration of barley. *Agron. J.* **54**, 538.

Letey, J., Richardson, W. F., and Valoras, N. (1965). Barley growth, water use, and mineral composition as influenced by oxygen exclusion from specific regions of the root system. *Agron. J.* **57**, 629.

McNew, G. L. (1953). Plant diseases. *Yearbo. Agri.* pp. 100–114.

Madison J. H. (1962). Turfgrass ecology. Effects of mowing, irrigation, and nitrogen treatments of *Agrostis palustris* Huds. "Seaside" and *Agrostis tenuis* Sibth; "Highland" on population, yield, rooting , and cover. *Agron. J.* **54**, 407.

Madison, J. H., and Anderson, A. H. (1963). A chlorophyll index to measure turfgrass response. *Agron. J.* **55**, 461.

Meyer, B. S., Anderson, D. B., and Bohning, R. H. (1960). "Introduction to Plant Physiology," p. 296–332.

Miller, M. H., and Ohlpogge, A. J. (1958). Principles of nutrient uptake from fertilizer bands. I. Effect of placement of nitrogen fertilizer on the uptake of band-placed phosphorus at different soil phosphorus levels. *Agron. J.* **50**, 95.

Nielsen, K. F., Holstead, R. L., MacLean, A. J., Bourget, S. J., and Holmes, R. M. (1961). The influence of soil temperature on the growth and mineral composition of corn, bromegrass, and potatoes. *Soil Sci. Soc. Amer., Proc.* **25**, 369–372.

Nightingale, G. T. (1933). Effects of temperature on metabolism in tomato. *Bot. Gaz.* **95**, 35–58.

Powell, A. J., Blaser, R. E., and Schmidt, R. E. (1967). Effect of nitrogen on winter root growth of bentgrass. *Agron. J.* **59**, 529.

Pritchett, W. L., and Horn, G. C. (1966). Fertilization fights turf disorders. *Better Crops Plant Food.* **50**, 22–25.

Robinson, R. R., Rhykerd, C. L., and Cross, C. F. (1962). Potassium uptake by orchardgrass as affected by time, frequency and rate of potassium fertilization. *Agron. J.* **54**, 351.

Smith, J. D. (1953). Fusarium patch disease. *J. Sports Turf Res. Inst.* **8**, 29 and 230.

Stumbo, C. R., Gainey, P. L., and Clark, F. E. (1942). Microbiological and nutritional factors in the take-all diseases of wheat. *J. Agron. Res.* **64**, 653–655.

Waddington, D. V., Troll, J., and Hawes, D. (1964). Effect of various fertilizers on turfgrass yield, color, and composition. *Agron. J.* **56**, 221.

Zhurbitskii, A. I., and Shtrausberg, D. V. (1958). The effect of temperature on the mineral nutrition of plants. *Radioisotopes Sci. Res., Proc. Int. Conf., 1957,* Vol. 4, pp. 270–285.

Chapter 21

Physiology of Defoliation and Regrowth

V. B. YOUNGNER

The varied and pronounced effects of defoliation on the grass plant must be considered in any discussion of the physiology of grasses used for forage, hay, or turf. Defoliation in these instances means removal of varying amounts of top growth frequently including portions of stem as well as leaves. Growth and development of all tissues and organs are effected by this practice.

Clipping Effects on Top and Root Growth

Agriculturists have recognized for many years that grazing or mowing practices will determine in part the yield and quality of forage obtained. Dry matter production will be effected by both frequency and height of cutting (Holscher, 1945; Thaine, 1954; Madison, 1962). Close or frequent clipping will generally reduce total dry matter production of individual plants or stands of single species whereas percentage of digestible dry matter may be increased by increasing cutting frequency (Burton et al., 1963). Prine and Burton (1956) reported that crude protein percentage of coastal bermuda-grass, Cynodon dactylon, decreased with increasing clipping frequency. These responses to defoliation may be modified by other factors such as soil, climate, nutrients, light, and time of clipping (Alberda, 1957).

Root growth of most species is reduced by defoliation, a direct result of the reduction in amount of photosynthetically active tissue. The few contradictory reports may be the result of unusual experimental circumstances or unique growth characteristics of a species not adequately accounted for in the experimental procedure. Numerous studies on many species reviewed by Troughton (1957) show that the lower the cutting height or the more frequent the cutting interval, the greater is the reduction in root weight. Clipping frequency and clipping height are complimentary; a reduced severity of one will offset an increased severity of the other as they affect the root system.

Jacques and Edmond (1952) working with orchardgrass, *Dactylis glomerata*, and perennial ryegrass, *Lolium perenne*, observed that clipping reduced the number of new roots initiated in direct proportion to the severity of defoliation. Also the closer the clipping, the greater was the tendency for the plant to produce new leaves before root growth resumed.

Crider (1955) removed top growth of several grass species in increments of 10% from 0% to 90%. Removal of more than 40% of the top in a single clipping stopped root elongation of all species; the larger the percentage removed, the longer the period of root growth stoppage. As the severity of clipping increased, the larger became the number of roots not resuming growth. Tillers behaved as individual units in their reaction to clipping. Root growth of unclipped tillers was unaffected even though all the remainder of the plant was severely clipped.

Degeneration of the root tip and often general die-back of the root system may result from severe defoliation (Robertson, 1933; Endo, 1967). Under field conditions not favorable to immediate root rejuvination, plant mortality may be high.

Weinman and Goldsmith (1948) reported a high tolerance of close and frequent clipping with little reduction in root growth in bermudagrass, *Cynodon dactylon*. There were no significant differences in root weights of plant clipped "high" or "low" at monthly, biweekly, or weekly intervals. However, in a later study plants almost completely defoliated at weekly intervals for 25 weeks had significantly lower root weights compared to the control. The prostrate growth habit and closely overlapping leaves characteristic of the species permitted a large portion of green leaves to remain after the low clipping of the earlier experiment. Thus a high level of photosynthesis and an adequate level of carbohydrates for root growth were maintained.

Defoliation also restricts rhizome growth of most species but the rhizomes of *C. dactylon* like the root system are affected only by very close clipping (Weinmann and Goldsmith, 1948). Harrison and Hodgson (1939) noted that in *Poa pratensis* the number of rhizomes initiated as well as their weight were reduced by clipping. However, E. M. Brown (1943) reported that plots of *Poa pratensis* clipped to 1 in (2.5 cm) biweekly had lower rhizome weights during the summer but higher weights in the fall than plots clipped at $2\frac{1}{2}$ in (6.25 cm).

Tillering Rates

Conflicting reports on the effects of defoliation on tillering appear in the literature. Much of the confusion might be removed if differences in experimental conditions and defoliation treatments were considered. Troughton (1957) reviewed the older studies stating that they showed that the number of tillers produced by a plant was reduced by defoliation. The greater the severity of defoliation, the greater was the decrease in tiller number. Apparently only leaf tissue was removed in these studies although this is not always clearly specified in the original papers.

If defoliation includes removal of apexes of elongating stems, results opposite from those cited above are obtained (Cook and Stoddart, 1953). Maeda and Ehara (1962) found that by clipping Italian ryegrass to 2 cm most of the growing points were removed. This severe defoliation caused death of many tillers and an initial decrease in number of new tillers followed by a large increase compared to the unclipped control. A 6-cm clipping height removed few apexes; tillers multipled slowly and at the conclusion of the experiment they were fewer in number than in the unclipped control.

Jameson and Huss (1959) studied tillering following clipping of elongated and unelongated culms of little bluestem, *Andropogon scoparius*. Tillering was stimulated by clipping of elongated culms at both midsummer (July 30) or late summer (August 23) compared to that in the unclipped control. No increase in tillering resulted from the midsummer clipping of unelongated culms but there was a slight increase from the late summer clipping.

Kikuyugrass, *Pennisetum clandestinum*, presents an interesting example of the effects of removal of stem apexes. In the unclipped condition the long stolons produce few lateral branches and flowering is rare. Clipping or grazing to remove the stolon apexes stimulates development of short lateral shoots terminating in very simple panicles. In a closely clipped turf eight or more flowering laterals per 10 cm of stolon are not unusual (Youngner, 1961).

Reasons for these differences in tillering response to clipping may not be simple but they surely relate to photosynthate supply and to apical dominance. Cutting of stem apexes stimulates tillering by removing the major source of auxin which inhibits lateral bud development. Inactive lateral buds are then free to develop (Leopold, 1949).

Defoliation to remove leaves only retards tillering through a reduction of photosynthetically active tissue with a resulting reduction in carbon assimilation. Available carbohydrate supplies may be used for renewal of the leafage first, and only after this need has been met are they used for tiller growth. With no further defoliation as new leaves develop the normal tillering rate is resumed. Mitchell (1953) proposed an interaction between auxin and carbohydrate supplies to explain tiller reduction after leaf removal. Before defoliation larger amounts of carbohydrate are produced and more auxin is required to inhibit bud development. Following defoliation carbohydrate supplies are limited and less auxin is needed for inhibition. After leaf regrowth higher carbohydrate levels again tend to overcome some of the auxin effect and the tillering rate is again normal.

Mitchell (1954, 1955) reported that leaf emergence rates as well as tillering rates were retarded by defoliation. However, Youngner and Nudge (1969), by removing leaf blades of *Poa pratensis* at the time of full expansion, showed that leaf emergence rates of individual shoots were not affected by defoliation. Although the total number of leaves produced on a plant per unit of time was reduced, this resulted from retardation of tiller development. Within a cultivar the mean number of days between emergence of successive leaves of a tiller was the same on both clipped and unclipped tillers. At the same time the mean number of days between emergence of successive tillers was significantly reduced by clipping on one cultivar but not on the other. As the proportion of leaf surface removed was the same for both cultivars, the difference in tillering response cannot be easily explained by a simple difference in growth habit. However, these results could come from genetic differences in photosynthetic activity of the leaf, especially of the sheath since it remained intact. Differences in auxin production might be another explanation if we consider the auxin–carbohydrate interaction theory.

Defoliation of grasses in closed stands under field conditions may stimulate tillering even though stem apexes remain intact (Lambert, 1962). McKee *et al.* (1967) reported that frequent defoliation of a three-year-old stand of tall fescue stimulated tillering regardless of nitrogen fertility level.

Compared to no defoliation, stimulation of tillering in these cases could result from creation of a more favorable light environment for tillering. Tillering is reduced by low light intensity (Davis and Laude, 1964; Auda *et al.*, 1966) and shading of only the leaf bases reduced tillering of ryegrass in studies by Mitchell and Coles (1955). Thus as growth accumulates, tillering may be reduced because of shading of the basal part of the plants or of young tillers by older shoots. Removal of part of the top growth at regular intervals would maintain satisfactory light conditions.

Carbohydrate Reserves

Carbohydrate reserves, nonstructural carbohydrates that accumulate in leaf bases, roots, rhizomes and other grass structures, are lowered by defoliation (Sullivan and Sprague, 1943; McCarty, 1935). Reduction of carbohydrate reserves is in direct proportion to the severity and frequency of defoliation (McCarty and Price, 1942; Weinmann, 1944). Weinmann and Goldsmith (1948) reported little effect of clipping on carbohydrate reserves of *Cynodon dactylon* unless clipping was extremely close, a result of the species' prostrate and creeping growth habit. Clipping of *C. dactylon* removes apexes of stolons stimulating lateral stem development to produce a dense prostrate stand capable of maintaining a high rate of photosynthesis and a resulting high level of reserve carbohydrates under continued frequent clipping.

Interaction of Clipping with Environmental Factors

Environmental factors may interact with defoliation treatments to intensify the effects. Sullivan and Sprague (1949) observed that as temperature increased from 50°F to 90°F, reduction in root weight following defoliation became greater. Increased nitrogen fertilization intensified the root growth retardation that resulted from clipping (Harrison, 1934). Both increasing temperature and increasing nitrogen fertility levels stimulate leaf and stem growth resulting in increased severity of defoliation effects.

Intense defoliation may prevent the effects of other environmental factor from being expressed (Youngner and Nudge, 1969). Plants of *Cynodon dactylon*, "Santa Ana," were grown in nutrient solution cultures with salinity levels, produced by the addition of equal amounts of sodium and calcium chlorides, ranging from 20 to 340 me/liter. Two clipping treatments, weekly clipping to 1 in. and a single clipping at the end of eight weeks, were imposed on all salt treatments. Total top growth decreased sharply with increasing salinity on the plants clipped only once, the usual effect of salinity. The plants clipped weekly produced significantly less total top growth than the plants clipped once and showed no reduction with increased salinity. Root weights increased with moderate increases in salinity on plants clipped once (a response to salinity observed only on *Cynodon* species). Root weights were markedly reduced by the clipping but there was no effect of the salinity within the clipped treatment. Reserve carbohydrate levels were lowered by the clipping treatment but were unchanged by salinity within either clipping treatment.

Selection of Ecotypes

Natural selection of grass ecotypes by grazing or mowing practices has been reported by a number of workers. Gregor and Sansome (1927) reported selection of prostrate ecotypes of perennial ryegrass by severe grazing for many years. Brougham *et al.* (1960) studied natural selection by frequency and intensity of grazing on stands of short-rotation ryegrass (*Lolium perenne* × *L. multiflorum*). There was a selection toward perennial types under frequent and heavy grazing and a selection toward the Italian (annual) types under the less severe grazing.

Studies of *Poa annua* collections from various environments showed that under the close (5 mm) and frequent (five times weekly) mowing practices on golf greens there was a natural selection for prostrate, dense perennial, shy flowering, frequently sterile types (Hovin, 1957; Youngner, 1959). Selections of these types have been vegetatively propagated and maintained under golf green conditions for five years. The contrasting ecotypes from fields and waste areas were upright in growth habit, open, annual, free flowering, and highly fertile. A dense, prostrate, and perennial growth habit gives a competitive advantage to the plant under golf green conditions with the low fertility being a relatively minor disadvantage compared to what it would be in a field environment. On the other hand the open, upright growth habit of the field types almost certainly assures their elimination under the putting green environment.

Relationship of Carbohydrate Reserves to Regrowth

The accumulation and utilization of carbohydrate reserves have been assigned important roles in the grass plant's responses to defoliation and its subsequent recovery. Much of the support for this view is based on the fact that levels of soluble carbohydrates fluctuate with defoliation treatments and regrowth patterns (Graber *et al.*, 1927). More recently the primacy of reserve carbohydrates in regrowth has been questioned (May, 1960). At the same time the importance of leaf area and current photosynthate to regrowth has received greater recognition (Donald and Black, 1958). Present evidence indicates that both leaf area and reserves determine regrowth potential.

Carbohydrate reserves accumulate during periods of temperature that are favorable for photosynthesis but suboptimum for foliage growth. Accumulation of reserves is generally highest when grasses are maturing, a stage that may never be truly reached under some turf and pasture management programs. Many climatic, edaphic, and cultural factors influence the rate and level of carbohydrate accumulation. These have been reviewed by Troughton (1957), May (1960), and McIlroy (1967).

Reduction of the root system of grasses by defoliation is usually attributed to a shortage of carbohydrates for root growth. The shoot is thought to have priority over other plant parts for the utilization of carbohydrates from both reserves and current photosynthate. According to this theory, with frequent defoliation reserves are translocated from roots, rhizomes, and leaf bases to the shoot for the development of new top growth, thus filling the deficiency of current photosynthate created by defoliation. Although loss of carbohydrates from the root system following defoliation has been shown by many studies (Sampson and McCarty, 1930; Aldous, 1930; Sullivan and Sprague, 1943), the relative amounts used for regrowth and respiration have not been determined. Sullivan and Sprague (1953) concluded that regrowth of *Dactylis glomerata* was dependent on reserves from roots and leaf bases for approximately the first four days following defoliation.

Ehara *et al.* (1967) grew *Pasplum notatum*, Pensacola bahiagrass, in an atmosphere containing $^{14}CO_2$ prior to clipping. As regrowth tissue contained ^{14}C it was concluded that reserve carbohydrate from roots or stubble was utilized for development of new leaves directly as well as for respiration. Plants grown in the dark following defoliation made no further increase in dry weight of new leaves after the sixth day, whereas those grown in light continued to increase in dry weight of leaves.

May (1960), reviewing the role of reserve carbohydrates, suggested that there was no evidence of benefit from reserves in excess of that needed to support the early regrowth of tops and to meet the respiratory requirement of the underground organs while tops were missing.

Davidson and Milthorpe (1966) studying *Dactylis glomerata* suggested that soluble carbohydrates in the bases of expanding leaves were important to the growth of those leaves only during the first two days following defoliation. Carbohydrates in old expanded leaves made little if any contribution to regrowth but were thought to be utilized for root and tiller development. They stated that after severe defoliation, regrowth is limited first by the concentration of carbohydrates in bases of expanding leaves, next by the rate of photosynthesis, and last by the rate of nutrient uptake by the roots that had been restricted in growth by the defoliation.

Ward and Blaser (1961) showed that both carbohydrate reserves in the stubble and the leaf area remaining influenced the rate of regrowth of *Dactylis glomerata* following defoliation. They measured the recovery response of individual orchardgrass tillers containing different levels of carbohydrate reserves and subjected to different degrees of defoliation during a 35-day period. Tillers with high carbohydrate reserves produced more dry matter during the first 25 days than did low reserve tillers. Regardless of the amount of reserves, tillers with two leaf blades remaining produced more dry matter than did plants with all blades removed throughout the 35-day period.

Leaf Area, Light, and Regrowth Relationships

Numerous research workers have stressed the importance of the inter-relationships of light and leaf area for rapid regrowth and high yields of forage plants (Black, 1957; Donald and Black, 1958; Donald, 1963). According to this reasoning when water and nutrients are in adequate supply, light usually becomes the factor limiting growth or dry matter production. As Donald (1963) has pointed out, competition for light exists whenever one plant shades another or when one leaf shades another leaf on the same plant. Even when another factor—for example, water—is in short supply, competition for light remains an important factor. Maximum forage yields can thus be obtained only through cultural practices that permit the highest possible utilization of the incident light throughout the growing period.

A young sward with well-spaced plants may use only a small part of the total light falling on it. As the sward grows, an increasing amount of the light is intercepted by the leaf canopy until eventually the amount of light reaching the soil beneath is reduced to almost zero. However, if all leaves receive adequate light and no other factor becomes limiting, the sward will be growing at its maximum possible rate. As density of the leaf canopy increases, lower leaves receive insufficient light and their contribution to the growth of the sward decreases and the growth rate of the sward declines. Eventually old leaves die and a time is reached when leaf death rate equals leaf emergence rate. At this point maximum sward yield is reached.

Defoliation as cutting or grazing will change these light relationships and thus the growth rates. Forage yields can be greatly increased through grazing or mowing practices that maintain growth rates as near the maximum as possible.

Interest in these relationships was stimulated when Watson (1947) placed them on a quantitative bases with his introduction of the idea of the leaf area index (LAI), defined as the ratio of leaf area (one surface) to a unit area of the soil occupied by the plants. The LAI for nearly complete light interception, termed the "critical" or "optimum" LAI, varies with species and varieties because of different forms of growth.

Evidence supporting these concepts is illustrated by the studies of Brougham (1955, 1957) on a mixed clover short-rotation ryegrass sward cut at 1, 3, and 5 in. During recovery, maximum growth rate was reached at a specific LAI regardless of the intensity of the previous defoliation. The time maximum rate of growth was reached coincided with the time of nearly complete (95%) light interception. The more severe the defoliation, the longer was the time required for this point to be reached.

In the same studies Brougham measured the effects of cutting height on net assimilation rate (NAR); the rate of dry matter increase per unit area of leaf. The maximum NAR was reached at the point of nearly complete light interception in the 3- and 5-in. defoliation treatments but before the point of complete light interception in the 1-in. cutting treatment. The NAR values immediately following cutting were directely related to the severity of defoliation, the lowest value being for the 1-in. cutting height. Beyond the point of complete light interception, the NAR gradually declined.

Brougham attributed the low initial NAR for the 1-in. cutting height to a higher ratio of respiration to assimilation because of a high proportion of leaf sheath and meristem tissue. However, a higher maximum NAR was reached for this treatment because most of the leaves were then of an optimum physiological age for maximum photosynthesis. After the point of complete light interception was reached, the NAR declined due to shading of lower leaves and an increased number of old leaves with a reduced photosynthetic efficiency.

Studies by Alexander and McCloud (1962) on *Cynodon dactylon* illustrate the effects of cutting height on light saturation and net photosynthetic rate as measured by CO_2 uptake. To reach the compensation point of an individual leaf at least 300 ft-c of light were required and from 2500 to 3000 ft-c were required to reach the level of light saturation.

Swards cut daily at 8 in. required about 5000 ft-c for saturation and those cut at 1 and 2 in. were not saturated at 7000 ft-c. As the LAI for the three swards was approximately the same, the difference in light requirement was attributed to differences in leaf arrangement. Leafage under the 1-in. cut was composed of closely overlapping broad stubs which required high levels of light intensity to illuminate the underlying leaves. At the 2-in. cut, leaf orientation was largely vertical resulting in inefficient light absorption. At the 8-in. cut, light saturation was obtained because of a vertical dispersal of horizontally oriented leaves which permitted light intensity to be brought to the saturation level for nearly all leaves.

Net photosynthesis in uncut swards at heights of 20 and 26 in. was reduced by lodging and intense competition for light leading to death of the lower leaves from shading. Following their being cut to 8 in., few green leaves remained and CO_2 uptake or net photosynthesis fell sharply. Swards cut to 8 in. from a height of 14 in. showed a less extreme reduction in net photosynthesis since there had been better light penetration into the sward prior to cutting, thus permitting more functional leaf tissue at the lower levels.

Thus net photosynthesis in a sward is affected not only by the cutting height but by the light and leaf area relationships that existed in the sward prior to cutting.

From these and similar studies the proposal has been put forward that for maximum yield a sward should be so managed as to maintain it close as possible at the optimum LAI (Donald and Black, 1958). In theory the objective is to bring it quickly to this level and then to maintain it there through frequent cutting or grazing, removing leaf tissue as rapidly as it is produced. In practice this ideal can only be approached. Too early grazing or mowing of a sward before complete light interception is reached must be avoided. On the other hand, delayed utilization allowing the sward to become overgrown may be as harmful.

Agreement on these propositions is by no means complete. Recently R. H. Brown and Blaser (1968) stated that the use of the LAI concept has been oversimplified and interception of light has been overemphasized. They argued that absorption of light by old leaves and stem bases is wasteful and that tiller production may be hindered by these structures shading the soil. Higher yield in some cases might be obtained by complete defoliation followed by initiation of new tillers and young leaves. Low LAI values may be desirable at times because they favor tiller production. Values of LAI above the optimum may be desirable at other times when regrowth may be dependent on stored reserves.

References

Alberda, T. H. (1957). The effect of cutting, light intensity, and temperature on growth and carbohydrate content of perennial ryegrass. *Plant Soil* **8**, 190–230.

Aldous, A. E. (1930). Relation of organic food reserves to the growth of some Kansas pasture plants. *J. Amer. Soc. Agron.* **22**, 385–392.

Alexander, C. W., and McCloud, D. E. (1962). CO_2 uptake (net photosynthesis) as influenced by light intensity of isolated bermudagrass leaves contrasted to that of swards under various clipping regimes. *Crop Sci.* **2**, 132–135.

Auda, H., Blaser, R. E., and Brown, R. H. (1966). Tillering and carbohydrate content of orchardgrass as influenced by environmental factors. *Crop Sci.* **6**, 139–143.

Black, J. N. (1957). The influence of varying light intensity on the growth of herbage plants. *Herb. Abstr.* **27**, 89–98.

Brougham, R. W. (1955). A study in rate of pasture growth. *Aust. J. Agr. Res.* **6**, 804–812.

Brougham, R. W. (1957). Some factors that influence the rate of growth of pasture. *19th Conf. N. Z. Grasslands Ass.* pp. 109–116.

Brougham, R. W., Glenday, A. C., and Fejer, S. O. (1960). The effects of frequency and intensity of grazing on the genotypic structure of a ryegrass population. *N. Z. J. Agr. Res.* **3**, 442–453.

Brown, E. M. (1943). Seasonal variations in the growth and chemical composition of Kentucky bluegrass. *Mo., Agr. Exp. Sta., Res. Bull.* **360**, 1–56.

Brown, R. H., and Blaser, R. E. (1968). Leaf area index in pasture growth. *Herb. Abstr.* **38**, 1–9.

Burton, G. W., Jackson, J. E., and Hart, R. H. (1963). Effect of cutting frequency and nitrogen on yield, in vitro digestibility, and protein, fiber, and carotene content of coastal bermudagrass. *Agron. J.* **55**, 500–502.

Cook, C. W., and Stoddart, L. A. (1953). Some growth responses of crested wheatgrass following herbage removal. *J. Range Manage.* **6**, 267–270.

Crider, R. J. (1955). Root growth stoppage resulting from defoliation of grass. *U.S., Dep. Agr., Tech. Bull.* **1102**.

Davidson, J. L., and Milthorpe, F. L. (1966). Leaf growth in *Dactylis glomerata* following defoliation. *Ann. Bot. (London)* [N. S.] **30**, 173–184.

Davis, L. D., and Laude, H. M. (1964). The development of tillers in *Bromus mollis*. *Crop Sci.* **4**, 477–480.

Donald, C. M. (1963). Competition among crop and pasture plants. *Advan. Agron.* **15**, 1–118.

Donald, C. M., and Black, J. N. (1958). The significance of leaf area in pasture growth. *Herb. Abstr.* **28**, 1–6.

Endo, R. M. (1967). Root tip degeneration of turf grasses, natural and induced. *Calif. Turf Cult.* **17**, 17–18.

Ehara, K., Yamada, Y., and Maeno, N. (1967). Physiological and ecological studies on the regrowth of herbage plants. IV. The evidence of utilization of food reserves during the early stage of regrowth in bahiagrass. *J. Jap. Soc. Grassland Sci.* **12**, 1–4.

Graber, L. F., Nelson, N. T., Lenkel, W. A., and Albert, W. B. (1927). Organic food reserves in relation to the growth of alfalfa and other perennial herbaceous plants. *Wis., Agr. Exp. Sta., Bull.* **80**, 1–128.

Gregor, J. W., and Sansome, F. W. (1927). Experiments on the genetic of wild populations. I. Grasses. *J. Genet.* **17**, 349–364.

Harrison, C. M. (1934). Responses of Kentucky bluegrass to variations in temperature, light cutting and fertilizing *Plant Physiol.* **9**, 83–106.

Harrison, C. M., and Hodgson, C. W. (1939). Response of certain perennial grasses to cutting treatments. *Agron. J.* **31**, 418–430.

Holscher, C. E. (1945). The effects of clipping bluestem, wheatgrass and blue grama at different heights and frequencies. *Ecology* **26**, 148–156.

Hovin, A. W. (1957). Variation in annual bluegrass. *Golf Course Rep.* **25**, 7–18.

Jacques, W. A., and Edmond, D. B. (1952). Root development in some common New Zealand pasture plants. V. the effects of defoliation and root pruning on cocksfoot (*Dactylis glomerata*) and perennial ryegrass (*Lolium perenne*). *N. Z. J. Sci. Technol.* **34**, 231–248.

Jameson, D. A., and Huss, D. L. (1959). The effect of clipping leaves and stems on number of tillers, herbage weights, root weights and food reserves of little bluestem. *J. Range Manage.* **12**, 122–126.

Lambert, D. A. (1962). A study of growth in swards of timothy and meadow fescue. III. The effect of two levels of nitrogen under two cutting treatments. *J. Agr. Sci.* **59**, 25–32.

Leopold, A. C. (1949). The control of tillering in grasses by auxin. *Amer. J. Bot.* **36**, 437–440.

McCarthy, E. C. (1935). Seasonal march of carbohydrates in *Elymus ambiguus* and *Muhlinbergia gracilis* and their reaction under moderate grazing. *Plant Physiol.* **10**, 727–751.

McCarty, E. C., and Price, R. (1942). Growth and carbohydrate content of important mountain forage plants in central Utah as affected by clipping and grazing. *U.S., Dep. Agr., Tech. Bull.*, **818**, 1–51.

McIlroy, R. J. (1967). Carbohydrates of grassland herbage. *Herb. Abstr.* **37**, 79–87.

McKee, W. H., Jr., Brown, R. H. and Blaser, R. E. (1967). Effect of clipping and nitrogen fertilization on yield and stands of tall fescue. *Crop Sci.* **7**, 567–570.

Madison, J. H. (1962). The mowing of turfgrass. II. Responses of three species of grass. *Agron. J.* **54**, 250–253.

Maeda, S., and Ehara, K. (1962). Physiological and ecological studies on clipping of herbage plants. *Proc. Crop Sci. Soc. Jap.* **30**, 313–317.

May, L. H. (1960). The utilization of carbohydrate reserves in pasture plants after defoliation. *Herb. Abstr.* **30**, 239–245.

Mitchell, K. J. (1953). Influence of light and temperature on the growth of ryegrass (*Lolium spp.*). II. Control of lateral bud development. *Physiol. Plant.* **6**, 425–443.

Mitchell, K. J. (1954). Growth of pasture species. I. perennial and short rotation ryegrass. *N. Z. J. Sci. Technol., Sect. A* **36** 193–206.

Mitchell, K. J. (1955). Growth of pasture species. II. Perennial ryegrass (*Lolium perenne*), cocksfoot (*Dactylis glomerata*) and paspalum (*Paspalum dilatatum*). *N. Z. J. Sci. Technol., Sect. A* **37** 8–26.

Mitchell, K. J., and Coles, S. T. J. (1955). Effects of defoliation and shading on short rotation ryegrass. *N. Z. J. Sci. Technol., Sect. A.* **37**, 586–604.

Prine, G. M., and Burton, G. W. (1956). The effect of nitrogen rate and clipping frequency upon the yield, protein content and certain morphological characteristics of coastal burmudagrass. *Agron. J.* **48**, 296–301.

Robertson, J. H. (1933). The effect of frequent clipping on the development of certain grass seedlings. *Plant Physiol.* **8**, 425–427.

Sampson, A. W., and McCarty, E. C. (1930). The carbohydrate metabolism of *Stipa pulchra*. *Hilgardia* **5**, 61–100.

Sullivan, J. T., and Sprague, V. G. (1943). Composition of the roots and the stubble of perennial ryegrass following partial defoliation. *Plant Physiol.* **18**, 556–670.

Sullivan, J. T., and Sprague, V. G. (1949). The effect of temperature on the growth and composition of the stubble and roots of perennial ryegrass. *Plant Physiol.* **24**, 706–719.

Sullivan, J. T., and Sprague, V. G. (1953). Reserve carbohydrates in orchardgrass cut for hay. *Plant Physiol.* **28**, 304–313.

Thaine, R. (1954). The effect of clipping frequency on the productivity and root development of Russian wild rye in the field. *Sci. Agr.* **34**, 299–304.

Troughton, A. (1957). "The Underground Organs of Herbage Grasses," Bull. No. 44. Commonwealth Bureau of Pastures and Field Crops, Hurley, Berkshire.

Ward, C. Y., and Blaser, R. E. (1961). Carbohydrate food reserves and leaf area in regrowth of orchardgrass. *Crop Sci.* **1**, 366–370.

Watson, D. J. (1947). Comparative physiological studies on the growth of field crops. *Ann. Bot. (London)* [N.S.] **11**, 41–76.

Weinmann, H. (1944). Root reserves of South African high veld grasses in relation to fertilizing and frequency of cutting. *J. S. Afr. Bot.* **10**, 37–53.

Weinmann, H., and Goldsmith, E. P. (1948). Underground reserves of *Cynodon dactylon*. *In* "Better Turf Through Research," pp. 56–75. African Explosives and Chemical Industries, Ltd., Frankenwald.

Youngner, V. B. (1959). Ecological studies on *Poa annua* in turfgrasses. *J. Brit. Grassland Soc.* **14**, 233–237.

Youngner, V. B. (1961). Observations on the ecology and morphology of *Pennisetum clandestinum*. *Phyton* **16**, 77–84.

Youngner, V. B., and Nudge, F. J. (1969). Unpublished data.

Chapter 22

Defoliation in Relation to Vegetative Growth

D. N. HYDER

If other elements are equal, plant growth is a function of the amount of leaf tissue exposed to sunlight (Watson, 1952; Donald and Black, 1958). Nevertheless we tend to ignore the morphological details of leaf expansion and leaf replacement. Since better management can be attained by matching the harvest to the growth of plants, this chapter emphasizes the morphological aspects of vegetative growth as related to defoliation.

Organization of the subject matter of developmental morphology to emphasize the effects of defoliation is largely new to the literature. A new concept of leaf replacement potential is an important factor in the determination of resistance to grazing. When the rhythm of growth of a plant is understood, the same concept is a key to appropriate grazing management, especially on semiarid grasslands. Terminology is conventional, except for descriptive phrases such as "culmed vegetative shoots" and "culmless vegetative shoots" (Hyder and Sneva, 1963b).

304

Adaptational Variation in Morphological Types

Some grasses exhibit morphological adaptations that permit them to endure repeated partial defoliation. However, such adaptations are not exclusive to the grasses. A brief review of morphological variation among plants can begin with the type of herbage growth exhibited by most varieties of alfalfa (*Medicago sativa* L.). The apical meristem, the source of new leaves, is elevated by stem elongation. Removal of or damage to the apical meristem stops stem elongation and leaf expansion from that axis. Subsequent growth and leaf replacement is delayed until a new stem arises from dormant basal buds because alfalfa does not exhibit free branching. Harvest is best scheduled to coincide with declining vegetative activity and the initiation of a new set of stems. Otherwise plants with this type of terminal growth are susceptible to extreme reductions in herbage production. A tiny nibble can remove an apical meristem and stop growth. The effect can be especially serious to some deciduous shrubs, such as fourwing saltbush (*Atriplex canescens* (Pursh) Nutt.) and bitterbrush (*Purshia tridentata* (Pursh) DC.). Thus the time and rate of grazing must be adjusted to retain most of the apical meristems throughout a season or a rhythm of growth.

A modification to prolific branching provides better adaptation to endure grazing. Russian thistle (*Salsola kali* L.) is a good example (Stevens, 1943). Numerous branches (some of them quite decumbent) tend to assure that some apical meristems will escape removal by grazing animals. Furthermore, grazing tends to increase the number of branches. However, the replacement of shoot apices by branching often is slow. Since the leaves and leaf primordia of such plants are elevated, this type of growth is better adapted to periodic harvest by machine or animal than by continuous grazing.

Some forbs, such as dandelion (*Taraxacum officinale* Wiggars), have basal leaf primordia that are never elevated. This characteristic provides a protected potential for leaf replacement. On the other hand leaf meristems are elevated at an early time. An immature leaf lamina can be removed completely.

Further adaptations, as by some monocotyledons, provide protection for leaf intercalary meristems as well as for new leaf primordia. In this case the intercalary meristem remains in a basal position so that the elevated part of a leaf blade can be removed without stopping growth. This structural adaptation has sometimes been attributed to all grasses. On the contrary, a great diversity in form is found among grass species. Although all grasses presumably have intercalary meristems at the base of blades, the entire leaf may be greatly elevated as in most bamboo (*Bambuseae*).

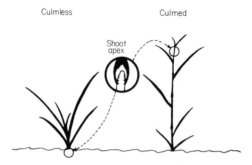

FIG. 1. Grasses with culmed or culmless vegetative shoots. The extent and time of shoot apex elevation by culmed shoots affects the leaf replacement potential.

Culmless Vegetative Shoots

Grasses have culmed or culmless vegetative shoots (Fig. 1). Lawn and turf grasses, such as Kentucky bluegrass (*Poa pratensis* L.) and many native semiarid grasses such as blue grama (*Bouteloua gracilis* (H. B. K.) Lag. ex Steud.), squirreltail (*Sitanion hystrix* (Nutt.) J. G. Smith), and big bluegrass (*Poa ampla* Merr.) have culmless vegetative shoots (Fig. 2). The basal position of apical meristems and leaf primordia protect the sources of further leaf expansion and of leaf replacement after defoliation. Furthermore, most grazing animals cannot graze so closely as to remove all of the leaf tissue. If the proportion of shoots that differentiate to reproductive status is small, a single apical meristem may remain vegetatively active for several years. Growth stops in quiescent periods; but cell division and expansion resume in both apical and intercalary meristems when growing conditions again become favorable. Consequently dead leaf tips are common on spring growth and may be exhibited with any new surge of growth when exerted portions of immature leaves die back during the quiescent period (Fig. 3). A

FIG. 2. Big bluegrass (left) and squirreltail (right) with culmless vegetative shoots. A small to intermediate percentage of shoots become reproductive.

FIG. 3. Dead leaf tips common on spring growth from culmless vegetative shoots. Blue grama is shown as an example. (Photo by Dr. W. J. McGinnies.)

grass blade intercalary meristem apparently ceases activity by the time of leaf collar exsertion (Sharman, 1947; Cook *et al.*, 1958).

Culmless vegetative shoots do not always preclude the elevation of shoot apices. For example, Russian wildrye (*Elymus junceus* Fisch.) exhibits an elevation due to elongation of a stolonlike structure called a "mesocotyl" by Lawrence and Ashford (1964). (The term "mesocotyl" applies more specifically to a structure of a grass seedling.) This elevation exposes the shoot apices and rudimentary inflorescences to winter damage or removal by grazing. However, close grazing at the proper time prevents the elevation. In other species large proaxes (basal parts of stems in which the internodes remain indistinct) may elevate the sites of origin of new tillers and nodal roots. In effect, such plants "grow themselves out of the ground," eventually leaving dead centers that later may be reoccupied.

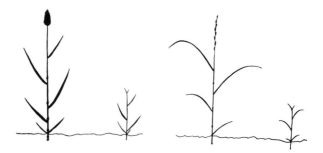

FIG. 4. Crested wheatgrass (left) and beardless wheatgrass (right) with culmed vegetative shoots. An intermediate to large percentage of shoots become reproductive.

Culmed Vegetative Shoots

Some grasses, such as crested wheatgrass (*Agropyron desertorum* (Fisch.) Schult.) and beardless wheatgrass (*Agropyron inerme* (Scribn. and Smith) Rydb.), have culmed vegetative shoots (Hyder and Sneva, 1963a, b) (Figure 4). A number of leaves arise and reach maturity before the initiation of internode elongation. Thus the form of growth is at first equivalent to that of culmless vegetative shoots. Culm elongation in culmless vegetative shoots proceeds only after floral induction. When floral induction is not a prerequisite of internode elongation, culm growth may be linked enzymatically to day length and energetically to leaf maturation. For example, crested wheatgrass grown in the greenhouse in winter failed to exhibit either culm elongation or floral differentiation until the light period was lengthened artificially (Hyder, 1960).

Before internode elongation begins, exserted leaves can be removed without stopping leaf expansion or the differentiation of new leaf primordia. Subsequently internode elongation elevates the shoot apex and culm leaves. Shoot apices thus elevated soon become susceptible to removal by grazing (Branson, 1953, 1956). In this event leaf expansion and shoot growth are stopped. Leaf replacement and additional growth then require the initiation of activity in axillary buds and the appearance of new shoots (even as for alfalfa). Culmless vegetative shoots may continue growth for two or more years. Grasses with culmed vegetative shoots have an annual turnover of tillers except in near-tropical environments.

Reproductive Shoots

Depending on genetic and environmental congruity, some shoot apices differentiate to reproductive status. This differentiation is preceded by a fast elongation of the shoot apex (Cooper, 1954). Spikelet primordia often appear first at about the middle of the elongated apex (Evans and Grover, 1940), and further differentiation proceeds upward and downward. When a spikelet primordia appears at the lowermost leaf primordium, there is no further potential for the initiation of new leaves. Thus vegetative growth becomes determinate regardless of the status of inflorescence development.

With slight culm elongation all leaves can be removed by cutting just above or through the rudimentary inflorescence (Rechenthin, 1956). Subsequently the culm remains morphologically obliged to grow, even though it will remain leafless (Cook and Stoddart, 1953). Leafless reproductive shoots, of course, are of slight value either to the plant or an animal looking for forage. Some types of regrowth exhibited by grass shoots are illustrated in Fig. 5. A harvest that cuts below the inflorescence and peduncle stops further growth. Thus regrowth requires the initiation of new tillers. Although a new set of tillers cannot arise promptly after the removal of immature reproductive shoots, they will eventually grow and produce leaves for benefit to plants and herbivores. This is the principle that permits the development of one-crop and multiple-crop systems of grazing (Hyder and Sneva, 1963a).

Strongly awned grasses such as squirreltail and needle and thread (*Stipa comata* Trin. & Rupr.) cause mechanical injury to animals and confound the problem of grazing uniformity. The inflorescences of these grasses can be removed safely while in the boot stage of development. Thereafter leaf growth by culmless vegetative shoots is advantageous to both plants and animals. Eventually we should be able to treat grasses with hormone compounds at the time of floral induction to prevent reproductive development.

Reproductive shoots are adapted for seed production rather than for tolerance to defoliation. Consequently the percentage of shoots becoming

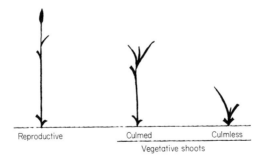

FIG. 5. The nature of regrowth after defoliation by culmless and culmed vegetative shoots and reproductive shoots. By proper timing and height of defoliation, culmed shoots can be stopped to force tillering from basal axillary buds.

TABLE 1
THE PERCENTAGE OF GRASS SHOOTS BECOMING REPRODUCTIVE AS
AFFECTED BY ROW SPACING AND NITROGEN FERTILIZATION

Affect	Agropyron desertorum	Poa ampla
Row spacing		
6 in.	24	18
12 in.	40	23
18 in.	59	34
Fertilization		
None	58	9
30 lb N/A	88	30

[a](From Hyder and Sneva, 1963b.)

reproductive is relevant to grass management. The reproductive-shoot percentage varies greatly among species, and from year to year and place to place within a species (Branson, 1953; Hyder and Sneva, 1963b). For many grasses a thin stand has a higher reproductive-shoot percentage than a thick stand; and nitrogen fertilization generally increases that percentage (Table 1).

Aborted reproductive shoots, those in which the peduncle and rudimentary inflorescence have been killed, soon reach maximum development and will not provide further growth (Fig. 6). However, they often lose apical dominance over basal axillary buds and contribute new tillers at an earlier time than exhibited in an unaltered rhythm of growth.

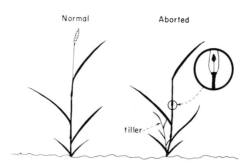

Fig. 6. Aborted reproductive shoots soon reach maximum development, but often lose apical dominance over axillary buds and contribute new tillers.

Resistance to Grazing

Resistance to grazing tends to increase with a decrease or delay in height and erectness of growth, growth rate, leaf elevation, shoot apex elevation, time of floral differentiation, and proportion of reproductive shoots (Cooper, 1951; Branson, 1953; Neiland and Curtis, 1956; Peterson, 1962; Scott, 1957). A single concept encompasses all of these characteristics. Resistance to grazing increases with an improvement or advantage in leaf replacement potential, which varies with stage of growth as well as among species.

Overemphasis of resistance to grazing is unwise, because this characteristic is inversely related to herbage productivity. Buffalo grass (*Buchloe dactyloides* (Nutt.) Engelm.) is greatly resistant to grazing, but is not favored as a species for improved pastures. At the other extreme, corn (*Zea mays* L.) is poorly adapted for pasturing but exhibits great productivity under favorable growing conditions. Forage quality, also, is involved in structural phenomena. Leaves are more nutritious than mature culms. Harvesting, so as to stop the later stages of culm maturation, promotes a second crop of shoots that may be less affected by "summer slump" (Heppner, 1961) or may provide a palatable and nutritious crop for late season grazing (Hyder and Sneva, 1963a).

Regrowth after clipping arises from existing active meristematic tissues (usually fast) or from previously quiescent axillary buds (usually slow). Residual active meristematic tissues, including those of an immature inflorescence, are obliged to continue growth. Thus we can find great variation in growth forms and rapidity of leaf replacement among types of shoots. Leaf replacement is most favorable from culmless vegetative shoots, intermediate from culmed vegetative shoots clipped above the apical meristem, and least from reproductive shoots clipped above or through the rudimentary inflorescence. With the latter two types clipping removes leaves and subsequently results in leafless culms or portions thereof. Consequently the most favorable leaf replacement can be attained by scheduling the time and height of defoliation to stop the culms and promote new tillers (Humphreys, 1966). Machine harvest or rotational grazing is indicated for culmed shoots. Continuous grazing is more appropriate for grasses with culmless vegetative shoots than for those with culmed shoots. Grasses with different types of growth and regrowth after defoliation can be integrated in rotational pasturing sequences to gain advantages in forage quantity and quality (Hyder and Sneva, 1963b).

The Grass Phytomer

A phytomer includes the sequence of structures produced by the meriste-matic tissue contiguous to a leaf primordium (Evans, 1958). From top to bottom, a phytomer consists of blade, sheath, internode (even though not visibly elongated), axillary bud (or potential thereof), and node (Fig. 7). Since the bottom of a leaf sheath tightly encloses the node of the next higher phytomer, its anatomical unity with the internode below can be obscure. Cell division in the leaf primordium appears at one side of the apical cone and alternates from side to side in adjacent primordia to produce the two-ranked arrangement of leaves. From the initiation center, cell divisions propagate to both sides until they encircle the apical cone and overlap without becoming attached. This growth is at first apical and marginal in kind; but the duration of apical and marginal growth is very short. Cell division is restricted to the base of the tissue at an early time. Before the blade attains much length, a collar develops and demarcates the intercalary meristems of blade and sheath. Sheath development lags considerably behind that of the blade. Meristematic specialization proceeds into the interior of the apical cone, below the sheath meristem, where the intercalary meristem of the culm internode may develop. The growth of blade, sheath, and internode overlaps somewhat, but appears predominantly as a one, two, three sequence. However, internode elongation may not occur, depending on species, shoot status, phytomer position, and environmental conditions. On the other hand there is much overlap in activity among adjacent phy-tomers. One leaf blade follows closely and is enclosed by the one arising immediately below it.

Growth by a vegetative shoot is described as vegetatively indeterminate because there is a potential for continuous formation of leaf primordia. An individual phytomer exhibits a determinate type of vegetative growth. If the blade is cut when immature, the undamaged intercalary meristem at the base

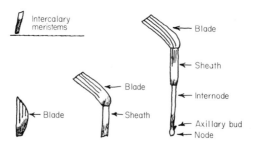

Fig. 7. The grass phytomer as a unit growth of grass shoots.

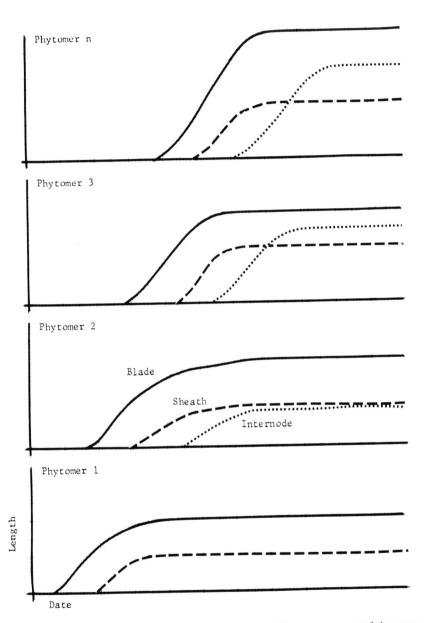

FIG. 8. A model of the growth of phytomers in a grass shoot. The measurements of phytomers can be carried through defoliation treatments to define the leaf replacement potential.

continues to differentiate blade tissue. The leaf tip cannot be rejuvenated. The individual phytomer has no potential for leaf replacement other than by the initiation of growth by the tiller bud. The lowermost part of a phytomer is identified as the node. Axillary buds arise from the upper part of the node, which also may give rise to nodal roots. The movement of assimilates from leaves to the central axis, and thence to other plant parts, is affected by the location and activity of intercalary meristems. An immature grass leaf has two sites of meristematic activity. One is located at the base of the blade, the other is located at the base of the sheath. This structural arrangement provides competitive advantage to the leaf intercalary meristems for photosynthates produced in an exserted part of an immature leaf. In fact it has been shown that immature grass leaves do not export assimilates to other plant parts (Williams, 1964).

The rhythm of growth in grass shoots is defined phytomer by phytomer (Ayuko, 1968; Lang' at, 1968). The graphing of rhythm of growth within and among phytomers is illustrated in Fig. 8. Total shoot elongation is plotted as the totals of leaf, sheath, and internode parts. Further definition, however, requires a separate record for exserted and total lengths, as illustrated in Fig. 9. Records of this kind are needed for each type of shoot. Vegetative and reproductive shoots exhibit different sequences of growth and should be depicted separately after the appearance of distinguishing features. Furthermore the segregation of culmless vegetative shoots by time of origin two or more years previous, one year previous, or current season can lead to functional interpretations. Older shoots are likely to produce larger leaves and

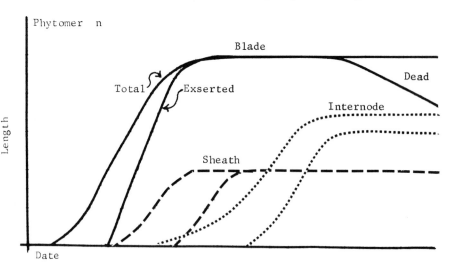

FIG. 9. A model of total and exserted growth in a phytomer.

FIG. 10. Clipping crested wheatgrass on May 15 at 2 in. above the soil resulted in the growth of leafless reproductive stems (center), and clipping at 1 in. resulted in a second crop of leafy vegetative shoots (right). An unclipped plant is shown at left.

are more likely to differentiate to reproductive status. Since different shoot types can exhibit different responses to defoliation, the rhythm of growth by phytomers can be plotted through clipping at different times and heights. Such evaluation will quantify the effects that later result in leafless culms (Cook and Stoddart, 1953; Hyder and Sneva, 1963a) or in complete shoot stoppage (Fig. 10). The primary difficulty is the enumeration of phytomers consistently from one time to another. Mower strips cut closely at weekly intervals during the growing season demonstrate regrowth types and leaf replacement potential.

Tiller Dynamics

Tiller dynamics are elucidated by the percentage of shoots of each type and age class, and by the seasonal change in numbers per unit area. At any given time the potential for tillering generally exceeds that exhibited. Nevertheless tiller survival is small in a thick stand (Langer *et al.*, 1964). New tillers generally do not appear until more than two leaves have exserted above the node of tiller origin (Ryle, 1964). More specifically an axillary bud initiates growth after termination of meristematic activity in the blade and sheath of the same phytomer. The lack of translocation of assimilates from immature leaves (Williams, 1964) presumably restricts tiller development from that phytomer by competitive advantage of leaf meristems for assimilates. Apical dominance and direct chemical inhibition also may be involved. Tillering increases with an increase in temperature and nitrogen fertility (Ryle, 1964; Paulsen and Smith, 1968), but can be either increased or decreased by defoliation. Defoliation at an early stage of growth can reduce tillering (Jameson, 1963). At later stages of growth, defoliation, or even the plucking of heads (Stapledon and Milton, 1930), generally increases tillering (Heidemann and Van Riper, 1967). Reproductive shoots, especially, often maintain apical dominance and suppress tiller formation (Jameson and Huss, 1959).

Modification to horizontal stem growth from axillary buds, to produce rhizomes or stolons, generally occurs about midseason. Defoliation after the initiation of growth by terminal rhizomes of switchgrass (*Panicum virgatum* L.) and sideoats grama (*Bouteloua curtipendula* (Michx.) Torr.) causes the rhizomes to turn upward and produce aerial shoots, which otherwise would not arise until autumn or even the next year (Ayuko, 1968). Nitrogen fertilization decreases late-season rhizome initiation and increases tillering in Kentucky bluegrass (Harrison, 1934). Thus when applied at suitable stages of growth, defoliation and fertilization can contribute to stand management.

References

Ayuko, L. J. (1968). The developmental morphology of sideoats grama and switchgrass in northeastern Colorado. M.S. Thesis, Colorado State University, Fort Collins.
Branson, F. A. (1953). Two factors affecting resistance of grasses to grazing. *J. Range Manage.* **6**, 165–171.
Branson, F. A. (1956). Quantitative effects of clipping treatments on five range grasses. *J. Range Manage.* **9**, 86–88.
Cook, C. W. and Stoddart, L. A. (1953). Some growth responses of crested wheatgrass following herbage removal. *J. Range Manage.* **6**, 267–270.
Cook, C. W., Stoddart, L. A., and Kinsinger, F. E. (1958). Responses of crested wheatgrass to various clipping treatments. *Ecol. Monogr.* **28**, 237–272.
Cooper, J. P. (1951). Studies on growth and development in *Lolium*. II. Pattern of bud development of the shoot apex and its ecological significance. *J. Ecol.* **39**, 228–270.
Cooper, J. P. (1954). Studies on growth and development in *Lolium*. IV. Genetic control of heading responses in local populations. *J. Ecol.* **42**, 521–556.
Donald, C. M., and Black, J. N. (1958). The significance of leaf area in pasture growth. *Herb. Abstr.* **28**, 1–6.

Evans, M. W. (1958). Growth and development in certain economic grasses. *Ohio, Agr. Exp. Sta., Agron. Ser.* **147**, 1–123.

Evans, M. W., and Grover, F. O. (1940). Developmental morphology of the growing point of the shoot and the inflorescences in grasses. *J. Agr. Res.* **61**, 481–520.

Harrison, C. M. (1934). Responses of Kentucky bluegrass to variations in temperature, light, cutting, and fertilizing. *Plant Physiol.* **9**, 83–106.

Heidemann, G. S., and Van Riper, G. E. (1967). Bud activity in the stem, crown, and rhizome tissue of switchgrass. *J. Range Manage.* **20**, 236–241.

Heppner, M. B. (1961). No summer dormancy. *Farm Quart.* Summer Issue, p. 61 +.

Humphreys, L. R. (1966). Pasture defoliation practice: A review. *J. Aust. Inst. Agr. Sci.* **32**, 93–105.

Hyder, D. N. (1960). Unpublished observation.

Hyder, D. N., and Sneva, F. A. (1963a). Morphological and physiological factors affecting the grazing management of crested wheatgrass. *Crop Sci.* **3**, 267–271.

Hyder, D. N., and Sneva, F. A. (1963b). Studies of six grasses seeded on sagebrush-bunchgrass range. *Oreg., Agr. Exp. Sta., Tech. Bull.* **71**, 1–19.

Jameson, D. A. (1963). Responses of individual plants to harvesting. *Bot. Rev.* **29**, 532–594.

Jameson, D. A., and Huss, D. L. (1959). The effect of clipping leaves and stems on number of tillers, herbage weights, root weights, and food reserves of little bluestem. *J. Range Manage.* **12**, 122–126.

Lang'at, R. K. (1968). Developmental morphology of the shoots of *Bouteloua gracilis* and *Andropogon hallii* in relation to grazing. M. S. Thesis, Colorado State University, Fort Collins.

Langer, R. H. M., Ryle, S. M., and Jewiss, O. R. (1964). The changing plant and tiller populations of timothy and meadow fescue swards. 1. Plant survival and the pattern of tillering. *J. Appl. Ecol.* **1**, 197–208.

Lawrence, T., and Ashford, R. (1964). Seed yield and morphological development of Russian wild ryegrass as influenced by grazing. *Can. J. Plant Sci.* **44**, 311–317.

Neiland, B. M., and Curtis, J. T. (1956). Differential responses to clipping of six prairie grasses in Wisconsin. *Ecology* **37**, 355–365.

Paulsen, G. M., and Smith, D. (1968). Influence of several management practices on growth characteristics and available carbohydrate content of smooth bromegrass. *Agron. J.* **60**, 375–379.

Peterson, R. A. (1962). Factors affecting resistance to heavy grazing in needle-and-thread grass. *J. Range Manage.* **15**, 183–189.

Rechenthin, C. A. (1956). Elementary morphology of grass growth and how it affects utilization. *J. Range Manage.* **9**, 167–170.

Ryle, G. J. A. (1964). A comparison of leaf and tiller growth in seven perennial grasses as influenced by nitrogen and temperature. *J. Brit. Grassland Soc.* **19**, 281–290.

Scott, J. D. (1957). The study of primordial buds and the reaction of roots to defoliation as the basis of grassland management. *Proc. Int. Grassland Congr., 7th, 1956* pp. 479–487. New Zealand.

Sharman, B. C. (1947). The biology and developmental morphology of the shoot apex in the Gramineae. *New Phytol.* **46**, 20–34.

Stapledon, R. G., and Milton, W. E. J. (1930). The effect of different cutting and manurial treatments on tiller and root development of cocksfoot. *Welsh J. Agr.* **6**, 166–174.

Stevens, O. A. (1943). Russian thistle life history and growth. *N. Dak., Agr. Exp. Sta., Bull.* **326**, 1–20.

Watson, D. J. (1952). The physiological basis of variation in yield. *Advan. Agron.* **4**, 101–145.

Williams, R. D. (1964). Assimilation and translocation in perennial grasses. *Ann. Bot. (London)* [N.S.] **28**, 419–429.

Chapter 23

Carbohydrate Reserves of Grasses

DALE SMITH

The primary sources of reserve energy for the growth of perennial grasses are the nonstructural carbohydrates stored in the vegetative organs. Carbohydrate reserves are essential for survival and for the production of new tissues during periods when carbohydrate utilization exceeds the supply from photosynthesis. A knowledge of the kinds and trends of energy-providing carbohydrates in the stem bases and/or roots is important to cutting and grazing management studies. Estimating the status of the carbohydrate reserve will indicate the periods of storage and utilization and the potential of plants to regrow following cutting or grazing.

Carbohydrate Changes in the Stem Bases with Advance in Maturity

The percentages of nonstructural carbohydrates in the stem bases of perennial grasses typically decrease with the initiation of growth in spring and after cutting, and increase with advance in maturity to flowering and seed formation (Aldous, 1930; Lindahl *et al.*, 1949; Sonneveld, 1962; Sprague and Sullivan, 1950; Sullivan and Sprague, 1943; Weinmann, 1948, 1961). Studies with timothy (*Phleum pratense* L.) and bromegrass (*Bromus inermis*

318

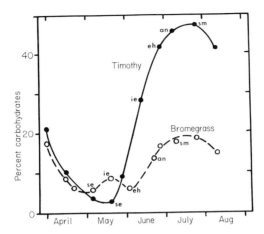

Fig. 1. Changes in percentage (dry weight) of total nonstructural carbohydrates in the stem bases of timothy and bromegrass from early spring to seed maturity at Madison, Wis.; se, beginning of stem elongation; ie, inflorescence emergence; eh, early heading; an, early anthesis; sm, seed mature.

Leyss) have shown the lowest percentages during early stages of stem elongation and the highest at near seed maturity (Eastin *et al.*, 1964; Okajima and Smith, 1964; Paulsen and Smith, 1968; Reynolds and Smith, 1962). This is shown for timothy and bromegrass in Fig. 1. However, all species may not have their low and high concentrations at these particular growth stages. McCarty (1938; McCarty and Price, 1942), for example, found mountain bromegrass (*Bromus carinatus* Hook. and Arn.) to be lowest in carbohydrate reserves when the flower stalks became evident and a high level did not occur until after the seeds were ripe. This is an appropriate example that the responses of one species cannot always be used without specific data to explain the responses of another species.

The trend of total nonstructural carbohydrates in stem bases provides information needed in management studies, but it is physiologically of interest to know something about the carbohydrates that make up the nonstructural fraction. Those most often involved are the monosaccharide glucose and fructose sugars, the disaccharide sucrose and maltose sugars, and the starch and fructosan polysaccharides (Table 1). It is the utilization and accumulation of the nonstructural polysaccharides that cause the fluctuations found in the carbohydrate reserves of the stem bases, as shown in Fig. 2 for the fructosans in the stem bases of timothy. The sugars are largely metabolic intermediates, and their concentrations change little in the timothy stem bases as compared with the fructosans.

TABLE 1

THE MOST COMMON NONSTRUCTURAL CARBOHYDRATES FOUND IN
THE VEGETATIVE PARTS OF GRASSES

Monosaccharides, $C_6H_{12}O_6$
    Glucose
    Fructose
Disaccharides, $C_{12}H_{22}O_{11}$
    Sucrose
    Maltose
Polysaccharides
    Glucosans, $(C_6H_{10}O_5)n$
        Starches – glucose polymers
    Fructosans, $(C_6H_{10}O_5)n$
        Fructosans – fructose polymers

Starch Accumulators

Perennial forage grasses fall into two groups based on the type of non-structural polysaccharide accumulated in their vegetative parts. Grasses of tropical and subtropical origin accumulate starch, but grasses of temperate origin accumulate fructosans. This separation of species was first proposed

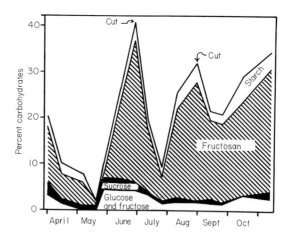

FIG. 2. Trends of nonstructural carbohydrate fractions (percent dry weight) in the stem bases of timothy at successive stages of growth during 1960 with two cuttings for hay (June 27 at early heading and August 29 at inflorescence emergence) at Madison, Wis. [From Okajima and Smith (1964).]

by De Cugnac in 1931 and has been supported by the work of other investigators (Ojima and Isawa, 1968; Smith, 1968b; Weinmann and Reinhold, 1946).

Starch is a pure glucose polymer, $G-G-(G)_n$, that occurs in two forms, amylose and amylopectin (Akazawa, 1965; Davies *et al.*, 1964; McIlroy, 1967). Amylose is essentially a linear molecule of $\alpha 1-4$ linked glucose units of low molecular weight (50 to 1500 glucose units). It is highly water soluble, especially in hot water. In contrast amylopectin is a highly branched molecule; the linkage at the branch points being $\alpha 1-6$. It is of high molecular weight (2000 to 220,000 glucose units) and is not soluble in water. The relative proportions of the two components are likely to vary with species, plant parts, and stages of maturity. Akazawa (1965) states that the amylose content of most starches ranges from 10% to 30%, whereas the amylopectin content varies from 70% to 90%. However, amylose is the predominant starch found in the vegetative parts of corn (*Zea mays* L.). Starches are the primary nonstructural polysaccharides accumulated in most of the native perennial grasses found in the United States (Smith, 1968b).

Fructosan Accumulators

Fructosans are the primary nonstructural polysaccharides accumulated in the vegetative parts of species in the *Aveneae, Festuceae,* and *Hordeae* (*Triticeae*) tribes (De Cugnac, 1931; Ojima and Isawa, 1968; Smith, 1968b; Weinmann and Reinhold, 1946). Fructosans are fructose polymers, $G-F-(F)_n$, that contain a terminal glucose (Akazawa, 1965; Bacon, 1960; Bhatia, 1955; Edelman, 1960; Hirst, 1957; McIlroy, 1967). They appear to be formed by the addition of fructose units to a sucrose (G-F) molecule. Fructosans occur in two forms, inulins and levans.

Inulins are $\beta 2-1$ linked fructose polymers and are found primarily in certain species in the *Compositae* (that is, *Helianthus tuberosum* L., *Cichorium intybus* L., *Taraxacum officinale* Haller). Much of our present knowledge of fructosans has come from a considerable amount of work on the inulins of the Jerusalem artichoke (*Helianthus tuberosum* L.) (Edelman and Jefford, 1968).

Fructosans found in the forage grasses are levans because they are $\beta 2-6$ linked fructose polymers. The grass fructosans have a low degree of polymerization (DP), as compared with the starches, and are more similar in degree of polymerization to the shortest-chain amyloses. The largest fructosan molecules in the stem bases of grasses vary from a degree of polymerization of ca. 26, as found in bromegrass, to ca. 260, as found in timothy

(Grotelueschen and Smith, 1968). Levans in the forage grasses appear to be linear molecules. They are very water soluble and cold water is the usual method of extraction.

Differential Solubility of Levans

Fructosans occur in a homologous series in plant tissue with the degree of polymerization of the longest fructosan molecule varying with the species. Fractional separation of the fructosans is therefore difficult. They are, however, differentially soluble in ethanol; and the relative amount of fructosans of different chain length in grass tissue can be obtained by extraction with a series of ethanol concentrations and water. Short-chain fructosans are extracted with high ethanol concentrations, and longer-chain fructosans are extracted with each successively lower concentration of ethanol. Using this system on the stem base tissue of several temperate-origin grass species, Smith and Grotelueschen (1966) found that bromegrass, tall fescue (*Festuca arundinacea* Schreb.), perennial ryegrass (*Lolium perenne* L.), and quackgrass (*Agropyron repens* (L.) Beauv.) yielded no additional carbohydrate with ethanol concentrations lower than 65% to 50%, indicating that the fructosans present were all relatively short-chain polymers. On the other hand timothy, reed canarygrass (*Phalaris arundinacea* L.), orchardgrass (*Dactylis*

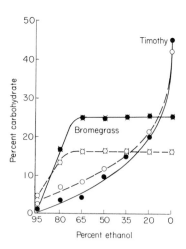

FIG. 3. Percentages (dry weight) of total carbohydrate extracted from two bromegrass and two timothy stem base tissue samples (plants near seed maturity) with decreasing concentrations of ethanol and water. [Adapted from Smith and Grotelueschen (1966).]

glomerata L.), Kentucky bluegrass (*Poa pratensis* L.), and redtop (*Agrostis alba* L.) yielded increasing percentages of carbohydrate with ethanol concentrations from 95% to 0%, indicating a series of fructosans of increasing chain length, predominated by those of long chain length. This is shown in Fig. 3 for bromegrass and timothy. Later work by Grotelueschen and Smith (1968) indicated that timothy contained a fructosan with a maximum degree of polymerization of ca. 260 as compared with only ca. 26 for bromegrass.

Separation of Fructosans from the Total Sugars

The presence of high percentages of short-chain fructosans, as found in the stem base tissue of bromegrass (Fig. 3), tall fescue, ryegrass, and quackgrass (Smith and Grotelueschen, 1966), raises the question of the ethanol concentration that should be used in routine analyses to separate free sugars from low molecular weight fructosans. Most fractionation methods are based on experience with plants that store starches. Thus the use of 80% ethanol to extract total sugars is a widely accepted practice (Association of official Agricultural Chemists, 1955; Whistler and Wolfrom, 1962), leaving the insoluble starches to be removed with takadiastase enzyme or other means. However, low molecular weight fructosans can be extracted in 80% ethanol along with the free sugar, as was pointed out by Wylam (1954) in work with ryegrass. The proper ethanol strength to use, therefore, can be established only by determination of the exact amount of free sugars in the tissue by a method such as chromatography.

Smith and Grotelueschen (1966) analyzed the stem base tissue of several fructosan-accumulating grasses for individual sugars by thin-layer chromatography and compared these results with those from ethanol extractions (Table 2). Thin-layer chromatography indicated that 85% ethanol was the most suitable concentration with which to separate the free sugars from the fructosans in those species containing predominantly long-chain fructosans (that is, timothy, orchardgrass, reed canarygrass, and redtop). Ethanol at 90% was found to be most suitable for species containing predominantly short-chain fructosans (that is, bromegrass, tall fescue, quackgrass, and ryegrass). Recent work with the roots of *Asparagus officinalis* L., a monocot in the *Liliaceae* family, has indicated that even higher concentrations than 90% ethanol are needed to separate the fructosans from the free sugars (Smith, 1970). The roots appear to accumulate extremely short-chain fructosans.

TABLE 2

Percentages (Dry Weight) of Carbohydrate Extracted from Stem Base
Tissue of Several Grasses with 95% to 80% Ethanol and with Thin-Layer
Chromatography[a]

Species	Ethanol concentration (%)					Total sugars by TLC[b]
	95	92½	90	85	80	
	Long-chain fructosan accumulators					
Timothy	0.6	—	2.1	3.2	3.7	3.2
Orchardgrass	1.7	—	4.3	5.7	6.5	5.3
Reed canarygrass	1.2	—	3.1	4.1	4.5	3.5
Redtop	1.5	—	3.7	4.6	5.4	4.4
	Short-chain fructosan accumulators					
Bromegrass	1.4	3.4	7.0	12.8	16.6	4.1
Tall fescue	1.7	—	4.9	7.4	10.2	5.8
Quackgrass	1.3	—	4.7	8.8	16.4	5.6
Ryegrass	5.9	—	10.3	12.2	13.2	10.6

[a]Adapted from Smith and Grotelueschen (1966).
[b]Total of sucrose, glucose, and fructose.

Molecular-Size Distribution of Fructosans in Stem Bases at Various Growth Stages

The nonstructural carbohydrate concentrations in the stem bases of timothy and bromegrass (Fig. 1, and insets of Fig. 4) decrease with the initiation of growth, but later increase to high levels at near seed maturity. This is due largely to changes in the amount of fructosans (Fig. 2). The question arises as to whether the predominant fructosan (short or long chain) may be different at one growth stage than at another. Using a graded-ethanol series, Smith (1967) found only short-chain fructosans in the stem bases of bromegrass at all growth stages (Fig. 4). The predominant fructosans in the stem bases of timothy varied with growth stage. At the mature growth stage when

FIG. 4. Carbohydrates (percent dry weight) extracted with decreasing ethanol concentrations and water from the stem bases of timothy (upper graph) and bromegrass (lower graph) at successive stages of development during the spring growth. Timothy: A, growth beginning; B, tillering; C, stem elongation beginning; D, stem elongation 13 cm; E, boot; F, early heading; G, seeds in dough. Bromegrass: A, B, and C, tillering; D, stem elongation beginning; E, early boot; F, anthesis; G, green seeds. [From Smith (1967).]

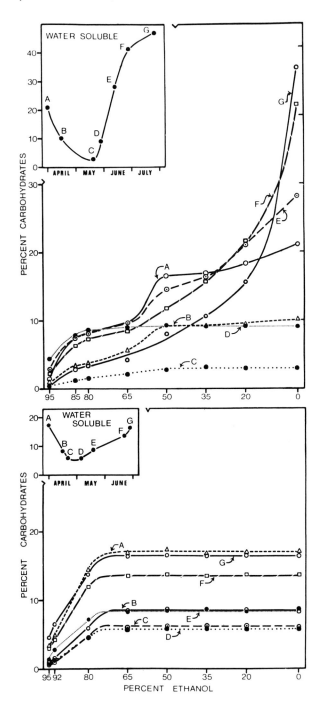

Fig. 4

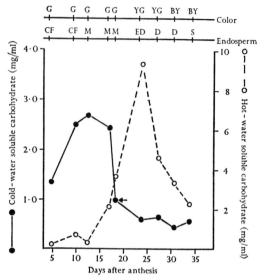

FIG. 5. Changes in cold-water soluble and hot-water soluble carbohydrates during ripening of seeds of *Lolium temulentum* L.; G, green seed coat; YG, yellow-green seed coat; BY, brown-yellow seed coat; CF, clear fluid endosperm; M, milk-stage endosperm; ED, early dough-stage endosperm; D, dough-stage endosperm; S, granular endosperm; ←, point of maximum seed viability. [From Stoddart (1966).]

carbohydrate concentration was high, a series of fructosans were present and they were predominantly of long-chain length. However, only short-chain fructosans were found when carbohydrate concentration was low.

No comparable work appears to have been done to show the changes in molecular-size distribution of the starches in the stem bases of starch-accumulating grasses at different growth stages. However, Stoddart (1966) made such a study during the ripening of *Lolium temulentum* L. seeds (Fig. 5). Successive extractions of the 80% ethanol residue (free sugars removed) showed that cold-water extractable carbohydrate predominated during the early stages of seed development and that hot-water extractable carbohydrate predominated at later stages. However, he did not treat the hot-water residues with takadiastase enzyme to obtain values for the water-insoluble, amylopectin starches.

Molecular-Size Distribution of Fructosans in Various Plant Parts

Because long-chain fructosans predominate in the stem bases of timothy at near maturity does not mean that this need also be true in other parts of the plant. Hirst (1957) states that different enzymes can be present in various plant parts so that fructosans of totally different structure may occur in different regions of the same plant. Analysis of plant parts of timothy at near anthesis (Smith, 1967) has shown this to be the case (Fig. 6). Using a graded-ethanol series, timothy at near anthesis contained only short-chain fructosans in the inflorescences, leaf blades, and in the upper sheaths and internodes. However, the lower sheaths and internodes and the roots contained predominantly long-chain fructosans. Fructosans were of short-chain length in all comparable samples of bromegrass.

The ability of a plant to form long-chain fructosans is dependent on the presence of the necessary enzymes. It seems quite possible that bromegrass does not have an enzyme system that can extend the fructosan molecule beyond a short-chain length [degree of polymerization of ca. 26 based on Grotelueschen and Smith (1968)]. This may also be the case in the leaves and upper plant parts of timothy where only short-chain fructosans are found. This was borne out in a study with timothy leaf blades from plants grown at warm and cool temperatures (Fig. 7) (Smith, 1968a). Little carbohydrate occurred in the warm-origin blades, and the small concentration of fructosans present was of very short-chain length. In contrast the cool-origin

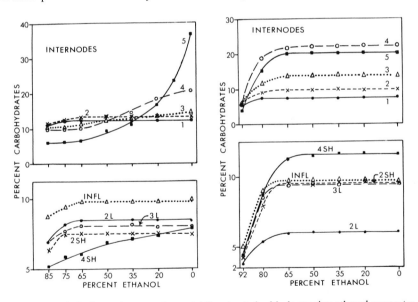

FIG. 6. Carbohydrates (percent dry weight) extracted with decreasing ethanol concentrations and water from various plant parts of timothy (left graphs) and bromegrass (right graphs) at early anthesis. Numbers refer to plant parts counting from top to bottom of shoot. Internode 5 is the stem base; INFL, inflorescence; L, leaf blade; and SH, sheath. [From Smith (1967).]

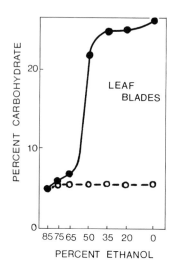

Fig. 7. Carbohydrates (percent dry weight) extracted with decreasing ethanol concentrations and water from leaf blades of timothy grown to early anthesis in cool (●————●, 18.5/10°C day/night temperatures) and warm (○————○, 29.5/21°C) temperatures. [From Smith (1968a).]

blades accumulated ca. 21% fructosans. The greatest proportion of this was extracted between 65% and 50% ethanol, indicating that the fructosans were of short-chain length [a degree of polymerization of ca. 30 to 60 based on the timothy results of Grotelueschen and Smith (1968)] even though a high concentration had accumulated.

Carbohydrate Reserves in Relation to Taxonomy

The fact that temperate-origin grasses can be separated into those that accumulate only short-chain fructosans and those that can accumulate long-chain fructosans in their stem bases (Smith and Grotelueschen, 1966) can be used to extend the taxonomic findings of De Cugnac (1931) that species of tropical origin accumulate starch as their principal nonstructural polysaccharide and that those of temperate origin accumulate fructosans. Thus Smith (1968b) analyzed the stem bases of 28 native and 16 introduced perennial grass species that occur in Canada and in the northern areas of the United States. Stem base tissue was used, rather than the herbage as was done by Ojima and Isawa (1968), because this is the plant part where high concentrations of nonstructural polysaccharides accumulate when photosynthesis exceeds the carbohydrate needs of growth. Smith (1968b) found that species in the *Aveneae, Hordeae,* and *Festuceae* (*Triticeae*) tribes accumulated fructosans in their stem bases whether native or introduced (Table 3). In addition they also accumulated small amounts of starch (1% to 6% of the dry weight). Species in the *Hordeae* tribe accumulated only short-

TABLE 3

CLASSIFICATION OF PERENNIAL FORAGE GRASSES AS STARCH OR FRUCTOSAN
ACCUMULATORS IN THEIR STEM BASES BASED ON WORK BY SMITH (1968b) WITH
NATIVE AND INTRODUCED SPECIES.[a]

Subfamily	Tribe	Genus	No. of species analyzed	Predominant nonstructural polymer	Predominant fructosans[b]
Festucoideae	Aveneae	Arrhenatherum	1	Fructosans	LC
		Agrostis	1	Fructosans	LC
		Alopecurus	1	Fructosans	LC
		Calamagrostis	1	Fructosans	LC
		Phalaris	1	Fructosans	LC
		Phleum	1	Fructosans	LC
	Festuceae	Bromus	3	Fructosans	SC
		Festuca	3	Fructosans	SC
		Lolium	1	Fructosans	SC
		Dactylis	1	Fructosans	LC
		Poa	2	Fructosans	LC
	Hordeae	Agropyron	5	Fructosans	SC
		Elymus	2	Fructosans	SC
		Hordeum	1	Fructosans	SC
	Stipeae	Oryzopsis	1	Starch	
		Stipa	3	Starch	
Arundinoideae	Arundineae	Phragmites	1	Starch	
Eragrostoideae	Aeluropideae	Distichlis	1	Starch	
	Spartineae	Spartina	1	Starch	
	Eragrosteae	Eragrostis	1	Starch	
		Muhlenbergia	1	Starch	
		Sporobolus	2	Starch	
	Chlorideae	Bouteloua	2	Starch	
		Buchlöe	1	Starch	
Panicoideae	Paniceae	Leptoloma	1	Starch	
		Panicum	2	Starch	
	Andropogoneae	Andropogon	2	Starch	
		Sorghastrum	1	Starch	

[a]Perennial grasses placed in a taxonomic system formulated by Stebbins and Crampton as outlined by Booth (1964). Also see Gould (1968).

[b]SC, predominantly short-chain fructosans, and LC, predominantly long-chain fructosans based on extraction with a graded ethanol series and water.

chain fructosans, species in the *Aveneae* tribe accumulated a series of fructosans predominated by those of long-chain length, and both types of accumulators were found in the *Festuceae* tribe. In the *Festuceae* tribe the *Bromus*, *Festuca*, and *Lolium* species accumulated only short-chain fructosans, whereas the *Poa* and *Dactylis* species accumulated long-chain fructosans.

Most of the species native to the United States were found to accumulate starches, possibly indicating a tropical origin. Ecotypes that can survive in the north apparently have developed by natural selection, but they have retained the carbohydrate storage characteristics of their tropical counterparts.

Analyzing for Total Nonstructural Carbohydrates

An estimate of the concentration of total nonstructural carbohydrates is usually desired in most management studies, rather than an estimate of each individual fraction (sugars, fructosans, and starches). The selection of a method can be complicated when one wishes to study both a starch and a fructosan accumulator.

The most common methods for such comparative studies have been those using takadiastase or acid solutions (Grotelueschen and Smith, 1967; Smith *et al.*, 1964; Webster *et al.*, 1963; Weinmann, 1961). In the takadiastase method the enzyme preparation hydrolyzes the disaccharides and starches to monomers when it contains invertase, maltase, and amylase enzymes. The fructosans extracted in the solution are then hydrolyzed to monomers with acid, since these enzymes do not hydrolyze fructosans. In the acid methods acid solutions are used to hydrolyze the sugars and nonstructural polysaccharides to monomers. However, an acid solution may hydrolyze some structural carbohydrates when the solution is too concentrated or may not hydrolyze all of the starch when the solution is too weak in concentration (Burris *et al.*, 1967; Grotelueschen and Smith, 1967). Fructosans are readily hydrolyzed to monomers by weak acid solutions, but high acid concentrations can destroy fructose (Grotelueschen and Smith, 1967).

Removal of the nonstructural carbohydrates from fructosan accumulators has been accomplished by many investigators with only water (Grotelueschen and Smith, 1967; Smith *et al.*, 1964; Waite and Boyd, 1953), since the sugars and fructosans are readily soluble in water. However, fructosan accumulators also contain small concentrations of starches [1 to 6% (Smith, 1968b)], and as a result water will not remove all of the total nonstructural carbohydrates.

In light of the above considerations the most accurate overall method for removal of the total nonstructural carbohydrates appears to be one that employs a takadiastase enzyme solution followed by acid hydrolysis of the extract. A very suitable enzyme method has been described by Weinmann (1947), modified by Lindahl et al. (1949), and further modified by Smith (1969).

References

Akazawa, T. (1965). Starch, inulin, and other reserve polysaccharides. In "Plant Biochemistry" (J. Bonner and J. E. Varner, eds.), 2nd ed., pp. 258–297. Academic Press, New York.

Aldous, A. E. (1930). Relation of organic food reserves to the growth of some Kansas pasture plants. J. Amer. Soc. Agron. 22, 385–392.

Association of Official Agricultural Chemists. (1955). "Official Methods of Analysis," 8th ed., AOAC, Washington, D.C.

Bacon, J. S. D. (1960). The oligofructosides. Bull. Soc. Chim. Biol. 42, 1441–1449.

Bhatia, I. S. (1955). Fructosans. J. Sci. Ind. Res., Sect. A 14, 522–530.

Booth, W. E. (1964). "Agrostology," pp. 168–169. Endowment and Research Foundation, Montana State College, Bozeman, Montana.

Burris, J. S., Brown, R. H., and Blaser, R. E. (1967). Evaluation of reserve carbohydrates in Midland bermudagrass (Cynodon dactylon L.). Crop Sci. 7, 22–24.

Davies, D. D., Giovanelli, J., and ap Rees, T. (1964). "Plant Biochemistry." Blackwell, Oxford.

De Cugnac, A. (1931). Recherches sur les glucides des graminées. Ann. Sci. Natur.: Bot Biol. Veg. 13, 1–129.

Eastin, J. D., Teel, M. R., and Langston, R. (1964). Growth and development of six varieties of smooth bromegrass (Bromus inermis Leyss.) with observations on seasonal variation of fructosan and growth regulators. Crop Sci. 4, 555–559.

Edelman, J. (1960). Transfructosylation in plants, and especially in Helianthus tuberosus L. Bull. Soc. Chim. Biol. 42, 1737–1744.

Edelman, J., and Jefford, T. G. (1968). The mechanism of fructosan metabolism in higher plants as exemplified in Helianthus tuberosus. New Phytol. 67, 517–531.

Gould, F. W. (1968). "Grass Systematics." McGraw-Hill, New York.

Grotelueschen, R. D., and Smith, D. (1967). Determination and identification of nonstructural carbohydrates removed from grass and legume tissue by various sulfuric acid concentrations, takadiastase, and water. J. Agr. Food Chem. 15, 1048–1051.

Grotelueschen, R. D., and Smith, D. (1968). Carbohydrates in grasses. III. Estimations of the degree of polymerization of the fructosans in the stem bases of timothy and bromegrass near seed maturity. Crop Sci. 8, 210–212.

Hirst, E. L. (1957). Some aspects of the chemistry of the fructosans. Proc. Chem. Soc., London pp. 193–204.

Lindahl, I., Davis, R. E., and Shepherd, W. O. (1949). The application of the total available carbohydrate method to the study of carbohydrate reserves in switch cane (Arundinaria tecta). Plant Physiol. 24, 285–294.

McCarty, E. C. (1938). The relation of growth to the varying carbohydrate content in mountain brome. U.S., Dep. Agr., Tech. Bull. 598, 1–24.

McCarty, E. C., and Price, R. (1942). Growth and carbohydrate content of important mountain forage plants in central Utah as affected by clipping and grazing. *U.S., Dep. Agr., Tech. Bull.* **818**. 1—51.

McIlroy, R. J. (1967). Carbohydrates of grassland herbage. *Herb. Abstr.* **37**, 79–87.

Ojima, K., and Isawa, T. (1968). The variation of carbohydrates in various species of grasses and legumes. *Can. J. Bot.* **46**, 1507–1511.

Okajima, H. and Smith, D. (1964). Available carbohydrate fractions in the stem bases and seed of timothy, smooth bromegrass, and several other northern grasses. *Crop Sci.* **4**, 317–320.

Paulsen, G. M., and Smith, D. (1968). Influences of several management practices on growth characteristics and available carbohydrate content of smooth bromegrass. *Agron. J.* **60**, 375–379.

Reynolds, J. H., and Smith, D. (1962). Trend of carbohydrate reserves in alfalfa, smooth bromegrass, and timothy grown under various cutting schedules. *Crop Sci.* **2**, 333–336.

Smith, D. (1967). Carbohydrates in grasses. II. Sugar and fructosan composition of the stem bases of bromegrass and timothy at several growth stages and in different plant parts at anthesis. *Crop Sci.* **7**, 62–67.

Smith, D. (1968a). Carbohydrates in grasses. IV. Influence of temperature on the sugar and fructosan composition of timothy plant parts at anthesis. *Crop Sci.* **8**, 331–334.

Smith, D. (1968b). Classification of several native North American grasses as starch or fructosan accumulators in relation to taxonomy. *J. Brit. Grassland Soc.* **23**, 306–309.

Smith, D. (1969). Removing and analyzing total nonstructural carbohydrates from plant tissue. *Wis. Agr. Exp. Sta., Res. Rep.* **41**, 1–11.

Smith, D. (1970). Unpublished data.

Smith, D., and Grotelueschen, R. D. (1966). Carbohydrates in grasses. I. Sugar and fructosan composition of the stem bases of several northern-adapted grasses at seed maturity. *Crop Sci.* **6**, 263–266.

Smith, D., Paulsen, G. M., and Raguse, C. A. (1964). Extraction of total available carbohydrates from grass and legume tissue. *Plant Physiol.* **39**, 960–962.

Sonneveld, A. (1962). Distribution and redistribution of dry matter in perennial forage crops. *Neth. J. Agr. Sci.* **10**, 427–444.

Sprague, V. G., and Sullivan, J. T. (1950). Reserve carbohydrates in orchardgrass clipped periodically. *Plant Physiol.* **25**, 92–102.

Stoddart, J. L. (1966). Changes in the molecular-size distribution of carbohydrates during ripening in attached and detached seeds of *Lolium temulentum* L. *Ann. Bot. (London)* [N.S.] **30**, 311–319.

Sullivan, J. T., and Sprague, V. G. (1943). Composition of the roots and stubble of perennial ryegrass following partial defoliation. *Plant Physiol.* **18**, 656–670.

Waite, R., and Boyd, J. (1953). The water-soluble carbohydrates of grasses. 1. Changes occurring during the normal life-cycle. *J. Sci. Food Agr.* **4**, 197–204.

Webster, J. E., Shryock, G., and Cox, P. (1963). The carbohydrate composition of two species of grama grasses. *Okla., Agr. Exp. Sta., Tech. Bull.* **104**, 1–16.

Weinmann, H. (1947). Determination of total available carbohydrates in plants. *Plant Physiol.* **22**, 279–290.

Weinmann, H. (1948). Underground development and reserves of grasses—a review. *J. Brit. Grassland Soc.* **3**, 115–140.

Weinmann, H. (1961). Total available carbohydrates in grasses and legumes. *Herb. Abstr.* **31**, 255–261.

Weinmann, H., and Reinhold, L. (1946). Reserve carbohydrates in South African grasses. *J. S. Afr. Bot.* **12**, 57–73.

Whistler, R. L., and Wolfrom, M. L., Eds. (1962). "Methods in Carbohydrate Chemistry," Vol. 1. Academic Press, New York.

Wylam, C. B. (1954). Analytical studies on the carbohydrates of grasses and clovers. IV. Further developments on the methods of estimation of mono-, di-, and oligo-saccharides and fructosan. *J. Sci. Food Agr.* **5**, 167–172.

Chapter 24

Grass Reproduction

ARTHUR R. BERG

Species of the grass family have a characteristic morphology and anatomy of the vegetative and floral organs. The differences that are observable between the 130-ft bamboo forests and the $\frac{1}{2}$- to 3-in. species such as *Coleanthus subtilis* Scid. (Arber, 1934, p. 209) or the rapidly spreading prostate grasses, such as Bermudagrass, are a result of variations on a basic theme. This basic theme is a jointed stem of phytomer units made up of node, bud, internode, and leaf, with root formation only at the nodes, and with no secondary thickening. The stem typically terminates in an inflorescence on which are formed sexual flowers, apomictic flowers, or vegetative proliferations. There are stems that do not terminate such as blind shoots or possibly the rhizomes of some bamboos. With the exception of these types of stems, a shoot or stem has a determinate life span; and perennialness is not imparted by maintenance of the primary shoot as in a tree but by virtue of continued production of new shoots. Thus when reproduction is defined as below, the basic unit of reproduction in grasses is a stem (Langer, 1963).

In this chapter reproduction is defined as any mechanism by which a species perpetuates itself and by which it is enabled to colonize new areas. This definition includes not only the obvious sexual systems of reproduction, but also various forms of asexual reproduction. For convenience reproduction shall be divided into vegetative reproduction and floral reproduction.

334

Under vegetative reproduction is included the formation of such structures as rhizomes, stolons, tillers, bulbs, and corms that impart perenniality to grass. Under floral reproduction are included all structures that develop on the inflorescence. This category includes cleistogamous and chasmogamous sexual flowers, various kinds of apomictic flowers, and proliferations.

Vegetative Reproduction

All that is needed to propagate most grasses is a piece of stem. The stem piece will form roots at the nodes and the axillary buds will grow out and form new shoots. Indeed this is the only way to propagate some sterile hybrids such as Coastal bermudagrass (Beaty, 1966). Although propagation of grasses by means of "sprigs" or pieces of stem with at least one node and a bud is common practice, one might question whether such mechanisms are true reproduction in the sense that they have evolved as a means by which grasses are able to both maintain themselves over many years and invade new areas. In this regard earlier writers have made a distinction between the major individual and the minor individual (Pallis, 1916; Arber, 1934). The major individual is a vegetative clone, that is, "the total vegetative output which one egg cell is capable of initiating" (Arber, 1934, p. 217), and the "'minor individuals' are those into which the major unit dissociates." Hitchcock and Chase (1931) consider that most of the buffalograss (*Buchlöe dactyloides*) of the Great Plains of North America were derived from plants started after the last ice age. In a more recent study Harberd carefully analyzed a field of *Festuca rubra* in Scotland. On the basis of morphologic and genetic analysis he found several natural clones. One clone was detected over a radius of 240 yd. On the basis of estimated spreading rate he concluded that this clone (major individual) must be over 1000 years old (Harberd, 1961). In a similar study of *Festuca ovina* he concluded that one clone of this species was also over 1000 years old (Harberd, 1962).

An indefinite life span for the major individual does not exist in all perennial grasses, however. For instance, Pallis (1916) indicated that in the common reed *Phragmites communis*, the rhizomes get progressively thinner each vegetative generation until senscence and death occurred.

Colonization of new areas would be rather slow by growth of rhizomes or stolons. The ability of clones to colonize wider areas through dissemination of pieces of plant would necessitate transport by wind, water, animals, or through the intervention of man. There do not seem to be any records of obvious dispersal mechanisms for pieces of vegetative material. Arber does, however, tell of cases in which whole plants were torn out of the ground and carried by windstorms for miles and of clumps of grasses that were growing along waterways and were broken off and carried down stream to become re-established on the shore or even transported on ocean currents (Arber, 1934, pp. 349–350).

Kikuyugrass (*Pennisetum clandestinum*) has been dispersed over several continents by deliberate action of man because it is a good forage grass in certain areas (Arber, 1934) and has been useful for erosion control. It seems able to spread over wider areas than desired, and has become a pest in southern California due to the spread of stolon pieces as well as of seed (Youngner, 1961).

Some of the morphological units involved in vegetative reproduction follow.

TILLERS

If axillary shoots grow upward within the sheath of their subtending leaf, they are called "tillers," "suckers," or "stools." In many grasses the internodes of such a shoot typically do not elongate unless that tiller is developing an inflorescence. If on the other hand the developing shoot breaks through the enclosing leaf sheath and begins to grow horizontally, it is no longer a tiller but becomes a stolon if it is growing above the ground surface and a rhizome if below (Arber, 1934, p. 254). Such horizontal stems characteristically have more elongated internodes than tillers.

In his review of tillering in herbage grasses, Langer (1963) distinguishes three types of tillers on the basis of longevity and life history. More than one of these types may be present on a given plant at one time: (1) tillers that develop, flower, and die in the year of their appearance are annual; (2) those that flower and die in the year after they begin to develop are considered biennial; and (3) there are tillers that fail to flower and may live from a few weeks to a year or more. In annual grasses, shoots that are present when conditions are favorable for flowering die after flowering, and little or no further tillering occurs to prolong the life of the major individual. In perennial grasses, tillers flower and die each year and maintenance of the major individual depends on the balance between development of new tillers and death of old ones. This is illustrated by the study of Branson (1953). He showed that the relative sensitivity of several range species to grazing pressure was dependent on the fraction of tillers that flowered and on the fraction of vegetative meristems that were elevated above the minimum grazing height. *Panicum virgatum* and *Andropogon scoparius* are likely to decrease under heavy grazing because of elongated vegetative tillers and because a high proportion of the tillers flower each year. On the other hand

Poa pratensis and *Buchlöe dactyloides* are very insensitive to grazing pressure because the vegetative tiller meristems are maintained below the minimum grazing height and because a small fraction of the tillers flower in one season.

Spreading of a grass by tillers appears to be a slow process, but it does seem to occur. Harberd (1962) found ramets of a natural clone of *Festuca ovina* spread over a radius of 10 yd. He estimated that this clone must be 1000 years or more old because of his observation that a clump of grass spreads about $\frac{1}{8}$ in. each time a tiller is found on the outside of the clump.

STOLONS AND RHIZOMES

Stolons and rhizomes are horizontal stems with elongated internodes. Rhizomes of some species such as *Poa pratensis* will become negatively geotropic any time the tip is exposed to light (Etter, 1951). In other species, such as *Agropyron repens*, the rhizomes remain diageotropic (growing horizontally) although they do turn green (Palmer, 1954). They turn up at the end and a new plant is formed at certain seasons, usually in the spring (M. W. Evans and Ely, 1935).

Oakley and Evans (1921) suggested a fourfold classification of rhizomes and stolons:

Determinate Rhizome. An underground stem, thickened or unthickened, that tends to root at the nodes, and from which a single shoot or tuft of shoots is produced.

Indeterminate Rhizome. An underground stem that roots at the nodes and produces aerial shoots progressively.

Determinate Stolon. An aboveground stem that roots at the nodes but does not produce shoots progressively. Under this heading are included lax culms that have come in contact with the soil and rooted.

Indeterminate Stolons. An aboveground stem that roots at the nodes and from which aerial shoots are produced progressively.

It appears that a better definition of determinate and indeterminate would be whether or not the stem *ends* in an aerial shoot. With the possible exception of some bamboos, all the grass rhizomes that have been studied become negatively geotropic and terminate in an aerial shoot even in those rhizomes which Oakley and Evans consider indeterminate (Palmer, 1954; M. W. Evans and Ely, 1935). Since rhizomes commonly terminate, Oakley and Evans (1921) were really using the degree of apical dominance in the rhizome to distinguish between determinate and indeterminate. Later work has shown that apical dominance in rhizomes can be modified by cultural practices such as nitrogen fertilization (McIntyre, 1967, 1969). Also the pattern of branching and aerial shoot formation is different when the plant is spreading into unoccupied soil than when it is in a solid stand (Etter, 1951). Although most rhizomes terminate eventually, kikuyugrass rhizomes have been observed to grow 2 to 3 m through heavy clay soil before emerging (Stapf, 1921).

Determinate stolons are described as aboveground horizontal stems, rooting at the nodes and terminating in a shoot or tuft of shoots. Lax culms that have come in contact with the soil or have been buried and that root are included in this category by Oakley and Evans (1921). It is not clear from the literature how determinate stolons terminate. Presumably they do so by a change in geotropic response as in rhizomes (Arber, 1934, p. 213).

Conversely, indeterminate stolons are considered to be aboveground stems that root at the nodes and from which shoots are produced successively. *Cynodon dactylon* has been given as an example of a species with indeterminate stolons (Oakley and Evans, 1921). The stolons of bermudagrass have been shown to terminate in an orthotropic shoot by Montaldi (1967, 1969) under certain conditions. Here again the distinction between determinate and indeterminate seems to be based on the pattern of branching rather than on whether or not the shoot continues to grow horizontally for an indefinite period.

There have been very few studies on the stolons of grasses. One reason may be as Bogdan (1952) suggested that stoloniferous species are quite rare among temperate grasses. He studied the stolon-producing grasses of Kenya and found that they were of two types: the *Digitaria* type which has one bud and leaf at a node, and the *Cynodon* type which has groups of 2–6 nodes separated by an internode. The associated buds and leaves appear to arise from a single node, but the "node" can be regarded as compound without development of the internodes. Species bearing the two types of stolons are taxonomically separated, with the *Digitaria* type appearing primarily in the *Paniceae* tribe and the *Cynodon* type in the *Chlorideae* and closely akin tribes. Bogdan does not consider creeping stems, which root at the nodes but terminate in an inflorescence, as true stolons (Bogdan, 1952, p. 75). These were included, however, in the category of determinate stolons of Oakley and Evans (1921).

BULBS AND CORMS

Botanically, bulbs are defined as fleshy leaf bases enclosing a shortened stem such as in an onion or tulip; corms are defined as shortened, thickened, upright, underground stems such as in *Gladiolus*. The structures found in grasses do not exactly fit the classic definitions, but they fit sufficiently well to stretch the definitions a little rather than create new terms (Arber, 1934). M. W. Evans (1927), for instance, coins the term "haplocorm" to describe the enlarged basal 1–2 nodes of the Timothy culm. His justification is that a corm is defined as a "multinode," thickened short stem while the Timothy haplocorm consists of only one (occasionally two) thickened internode(s) with associated dormant buds.

There is not too much information about bulb-forming grasses although, according to Burns (1946) and Arber (1934, p. 267), species like *Poa bulbosa* L. do form true bulbs. Many of the *bulbosum* species names, however, refer to plants that form corms rather than bulbs—for example, *Hordeum bulbosum* (Ofir, *et al.*, 1967).

After a survey of corm- and bulb-forming grasses from the literature and herbarium specimens, Burns (1946) concluded that most bulb- or corm-forming grasses are found in an area with a Mediterranean climate or in areas that show a seasonal physical or physiological drought. The function seems to be to help carry the plant over the stress condition even though many grass species are able to survive the same conditions without having such organs.

Earlier writers speculated that corms and bulbs must serve to store water as in succulents (Hackel, 1890; Nishimura, 1922), but several studies have shown that the corms depend on deep, relatively unbranched roots to maintain their hydration and will in fact stand very little desiccation before dying (Laude, 1953; Ofir *et al.*, 1967; McWilliam and Kramer, 1968).

In a classic study of two Mediterranean species of *Phalaris*, McWilliam compared *Phalaris minor*, an annual, with *P. tuberosa*, a corm-forming perennial (McWilliam and Kramer, 1968; McWilliam, 1968). Uptake of tritiated water and ^{32}P by the deep roots of *P. tuberosa* but not by deep roots of *P. minor* indicates a functional difference between the species. This was confirmed by anatomical studies of roots. Those of *P. tuberosa* have large metaxylem cavities and extensively suberized vascular bundles whereas the roots of *P. minor* appear partially collapsed and the vascular bundles are not as heavily suberized.

Whereas species having stolons seem to be found in the *Panicoid* and in the *Chloridoid* grasses, those species with bulbs or corms are found only in the Festucoid group of tribes with the exception of *Panicum bulbosum* from the highlands of Mexico. At least this was true of those species reviewed by Burns (1946). The genus *Beckmannia* which he classified in the *Zoysieae* has since been moved from the *Festucoideae* subfamily as an unclassified genus to the *Phragmitoformes* subfamily (Prat, 1960), but still most examples of species with bulbs or corms are in the *Festucoideae* subfamily.

Rhizomes, Bulbs, and Corms as Storage Organs

Although the point has been made that rhizomes, stolons, tillers, bulbs, and corms are reproductive units of a grass as much as fruits or proliferated spikelets, it should be emphasized that these structures must serve as carbohydrate storage organs in order to carry the dormant meristematic reservoir over some stress period such as winter cold or summer drought.

Seasonal changes in carbohydrate levels in grass plants suggest that regrowth following winter or drought is dependent on carbohydrates stored in rhizomes (Weinmann and Reinhold, 1946; Brown, 1943), crowns and roots (McCarty and Price, 1942), corms (Jefferies, 1916), or bulbs (Arber, 1934, p. 272). In a study of seasonal growth of range grasses, McCarty and Price (1942) found storage of carbohydrates in roots and stem bases to be inversely related to herbage growth. Growth of leaves and roots prior to disappearance of snow used up 70% to 75% of the carbohydrates stored the previous fall.

In the corm-forming grasses the studies on *Molina caerulea* (Jefferies, 1916), *Phleum pratense* (Trowbridge *et al.*, 1915; Nishimura, 1922), *Hordeum bulbosum* (Ofir *et al.*, 1967), and *Phalaris tuberosa* (McWilliam, 1968) show that the new tillers grow out from buds either just above or just below the enlarged internodes and that the corm withers and dies as the new tillers become sulf-sufficient. That carbohydrate is translocated from the corm to the developing bud has been shown by the redistribution of ^{14}C labeled photosynthate in *Phalaris tuberosa* (McWilliam, 1968).

In general it seems that a grass plant stores carbohydrates during periods of slow herbage growth. These reserves are then used during periods of rapid herbage growth. If a plant is defoliated at any time, however, reserves are utilized for production of new leaves or new shoots (May, 1960; Sullivan and Sprague, 1953).

Floral Reproduction

After the plant is induced to flower by conditions that are rigorously defined for a species or ecotype, (Sachs, this volume) the vegetative meristem of a tiller becomes a floral meristem by a series of morphogenetic events that have been described but are poorly understood (L. T. Evans, 1969). The floral meristem then develops into an inflorescence that may vary in morphology from a panicle with several orders of branching to a spike with only short primary branches. These branches are terminated by a highly specialized shoot system, the spikelet, which consists of one to several florets. The spikelet is replaced in certain species partially or completely by a vegetative shoot system called a "vegetative proliferation," or bulbil (Youngner, 1960). The subject of inflorescence and floral development in grasses has been studied by several workers (Sharman, 1947; Nishimura, 1922; M. W. Evans and Grover, 1940; and others) and is reviewed in this volume by Latting.

SEXUAL REPRODUCTION

In grasses several types of sexual reproduction occur which impart varying degrees of genetic variability or stability to a species or species complex. These include monoeciousness and dioeciousness, cleistogamy and chasmogamy, and self-fertilization and cross-fertilization.

Self-Fertilization and Cross-Fertilization

Self-fertilization occurs in most cereals and in many wild annual grasses (L. T. Evans, 1964). Self-fertilization occurs primarily because masses of pollen are shed very close to the stigmatic surface. There is of course always the possibility that pollen from another plant will fertilize a floret and introduce new gene combinations.

On the other hand many perennial grasses are normally cross-fertilized. The most common mechanism is self-incompatability in which pollen tube growth is inhibited by stigmatic tissue. Other mechanisms include protogyny in which the stigma is exerted before the anthers as in *Pennisetum clandestinum* (Youngner, 1961).

Self-fertilizing populations and cross-fertilizing populations behave differently in the way genetic variability is preserved and exploited. In cross-fertilizing species variant genes can be preserved in the heterozygous state and be exploited when the proper gene combination takes place if the new combination offers some competitive advantage to the plant. On the other hand, normally self-fertilizing populations, purge gene variants quickly unless they offer immediate advantage in the homozygous state. If the new character offers some advantage, self-fertilization provides the possibility of stabilizing and perpetuating the new genetic combination. Stebbins (1957) considers self-fertilization and the annual growth habit as being more evolutionarily advanced than cross-fertilization and the perennial habit.

Monoecious and Dioecious

Other sexual breeding systems in grasses include moneocious flowering in which the male and female flowers are on different parts of the same plant.

Zea mays is the classic example. In contrast to the monoecious condition some species have the male and female flowers on different plants such as buffalograss (*Buchlöe dactyloides*). Dioecious species are obligately cross-fertilized. Monoecious species are at least partly cross-fertilized because of the physical separation of the male and female flowers.

Cleistogamy and Chasmogamy

In cleistogamous flowers fertilization takes place before the floret opens. The "normal" condition in which the floret opens and the anthers and stigma are exerted is called "chasmogamy." Cleistogamy is rarely obligate and usually occurs on the terminal spikelet under conditions less favorable for flowering (Harlan, 1945). In some species cleistogamous flowers or cleistogenes occur as solitary florets in axillary positions (Dobrenz and Beetle, 1966) or even on underground stems (Weatherwax, 1934).

ASEXUAL REPRODUCTION

Reproduction that substitutes for sexual reproduction in higher plants is called "apomixis" if it partially involves the sexual mechanism. According to the definition of Winkler (1934), "apomixis is the substitution for sexual reproduction of another asexual reproductive process that does not involve nuclear or cellular fusion (that is, fertilization)." This definition includes vegetative proliferation and various types of agamospermy. The subject of apomixis has been reviewed by Stebbins (1941), Nygren (1954), and Gustafsson (1946, 1947).

Apomixis, like self-fertilization, is an evolutionary dead end if it is completely obligate. Many species that had been considered to be obligately apomictic were, however, found to have some mechanism for producing variability (Clausen, 1954). Clausen considers that truly obligate apomixis probably never occurs.

Facultative apomixis enables plants to store genetic variability for later release and through asexual reproduction to produce copies without losing the potential variability. Whereas self-fertilization appears to act as an evolutionary mechanism at the subspecies to species level, apomixis appears to operate at the species to species-complex level (Clausen, 1954).

Vegetative Proliferation

Apomixis as defined by Winkler (1934) includes both vegetative proliferation (vivipary) and agamospermy (apomixis through seed production). The development of vegetative proliferations is covered by Latting in this volume.

Agamospermy

In "normal" sexual reproduction in flowering plants, a distinctive mega-sporocyte or embryo-sac mother cell (EMC) appears in the developing ovule. The nucleus undergoes meiotic or reductive division which results in a tetrad of nuclei each of which has one half the chromosome number of the sporophytic tissue. By one of several possible developmental sequences, a mature embryo sac (gametophyte) arises that contains a distinct egg cell, two adjacent synergid cells, two or more free polar nuclei, and three anti-podal cells (Maheshwari, 1950). In grasses, at least in *Zea mays*, the mature embryo sac has two polar nuclei (Randolph, 1936).

At fertilization two haploid nuclei from the pollen grain, or male gameto-phyte, enter the embryo sac. One nucleus fuses with the egg cell to form the diploid zygote, and the other nucleus fuses with the polar nuclei to form a triploid (or polyploid) endosperm mother cell. The zygote then develops into the diploid embryo and the endosperm mother cell into the nutritive tissue, the endosperm (Wardlaw, 1955).

Two fundamental steps are thus involved in sexual reproduction. In the first step the sporophytic or diploid complement of chromosomes is reduced by one half. In the second step the haploid egg is fused with a haploid pollen nucleus. The resulting diploid cell, the zygote, has a set of chromosomes which is similar to but not exactly like that of either of its parents.

In agamospermous reproduction substitutions occur for one or both steps, which if embryogenesis is completed, result in a haploid or diploid embryo with the same genetic constitution as the parent plant. There are several known substitutes for each step and the substitutions for one step are independent of those for the other step.

Substitutions for Meiosis. Two broad categories are used to describe these phenomena by Gustafsson (1946). They are diplospory and apospory. In diplospory, the gametophyte (embryo sac) arises directly or indirectly from the megaspore mother cell. The mechanism varies from one group of di-plosporous plants to another or even between flowers on the same plant, but it always involves a failure in meiotic division. The forms that meiotic failure may take vary from those that resemble meiosis to those which appear mitotic. The result is the same however, the nuclei of the developed embryo sac having the same chromosome number as the somatic tissue (Gustafsson, 1946).

Stebbins (1941) has divided diplospory into three categories: diplospory, semiapospory, and generative apospory on the behavior of the first nuclear division. Care must be taken though in rigidly categorizing the behavior of early nuclear divisions because low temperature may change a meiotic-type division to a mitotic type (Gustafsson 1946, p. 19).

In apospory (Gustafsson, 1946) or somatic apospory (Stebbins, 1941), one or more cells other than the embryo-sac mother cell enlarge and develop into a functional embryo sac. Being able to identify the agamospermic process as diplospory (generative apospory) or as apospory (somatic apospory) presupposes identification of the megaspore mother cell. In those species with a single progenitor cell (archeospore) the sequence is reasonably clear. In aposporous species of *Heracium* a cell from the surrounding ovular tissue develops simultaneous with or following embryo-sac mother cell meiosis. The aposporous embryo sac may crush the meiotic embryo sac or they may both develop (Gustafsson, 1946). Distinguishing the true archeospore from potential archeospores or from somatic cells is more difficult in such plants as species of the Rosaceae (Gustafsson, 1946, p. 21). Somatic apospory has been found in the grasses in *Poa arctica* (Nygren, 1954) and *Poa pratensis* (Nielsen, 1946).

Substitutions for Fertilization. Substitutes for fertilization include parthenogenesis, in which the embryo develops from the egg cell and endosperm from the endosperm mother cell without fertilization, pseudogamy, in which endosperm development requires partial fertilization while the egg cell develops without fertilization, and apogamety, in which the embryo develops from some other cell in the embryo sac (Stebbins, 1941). Apogamety is rare and it has not been reported in grasses (Gustafsson, 1946).

If the egg cell of a haploid gametophyte develops pathenogenetically or by pseudogamous stimulation, a haploid plant results. Stebbins (1941) calls this "nonrecurrent apomixis." Gustafsson (1946) on the other hand refers to these events as "haploparthenogenesis" and "haplopseudogamy." The result is a sterile plant, hence the name "nonrecurrent."

In the grass family apomictic species of *Calamogrostis* are diplosporous (generative apospory) and develop embryos parthenogenetically; apospory followed by parthenogenesis is found in *Paspalum dilatatum*; haploparthenogenesis has been shown in some *Zea mays* crosses; and apospory is suspected in *Saccharum*, *Panicum*, and *Sorghum* (Nygren, 1954).

In the genus *Poa*, which has been studied extensively in Europe and America, apospory, diplospory, and vivipary have been described (Nygren, 1954; Gustafsson, 1946; Clausen, 1954; Nielsen, 1946; Youngner, 1960; Stebbins, 1941; and others). Diplospory occurs in *Poa alpina*, *P. glauca*, *P. nemoralis*, *P. palustris*, and *P. nervosa*. Apospory occurs in *P. ampla*, *P. arctica*, *P. arida*, *P. compressa*, and *P. pratensis*. In addition some subspecies of *P. alpina*, *P. arctica*, and *P. pratensis* produce viviparous propagules (Nygren, 1954).

Adventitious Embryony. Adventitious embryony, which is the development of an embryo from nucellar tissue or integumental tissue, is another important method of apomictic reproduction. It can be found in such plants as onion, cactus (Stebbins, 1941), and citrus (Swingle, 1932). Adventitious embryony has not, however, been recorded in the grass family.

Bibliography

Arber, A. (1934). "The Gramineae." Cambridge Univ. Press, London and New York.

Beaty, E. R. (1966). Sprouting of coastal Bermudagrass stolons. *Agron. J.* **58**, 555–556.

Bogdan, A. V. (1952). Observations on stoloniferous grasses in Kenya. *J. E. Afr. (Uganda) Natur. Hist. Soc.* **20**, 71–76.

Branson, F. A. (1953). Two new factors affecting resistance of grasses to grazing. *J. Range Manage.* **6**, 165–171.

Brown, E. M. (1943). Seasonal variations in the growth and chemical composition of Kentucky bluegrass. *Mo., Agri. Exp. Sta., Res. Bull.* **360**, 1–56.

Burns, W. (1946). Corm and bulb formation in plants, with special reference to the Gramineae. *Trans. Proc. Bot. Soc. Edinburgh* **34**, 316–347.

Clausen, J. (1954). Partial apomixis as an equilibrium system in evolution. *Proc. 9th Inter. Genet. Cong. Carylogia* 6(suppl.). 469–479.

Dobrenz, A. K., and Beetle, A. A. (1966). Cleistogenes in *Danthonia. J. Range Manage.* **19**, 292–296.

Etter, A. G. (1951). How Kentucky bluegrass grows. *Ann. Mo. Bot. Gard.* **38**, 293–375.

Evans, L. T. (1964). Reproduction. *In* "Grasses and Grasslands" (C. Barnard, ed.), pp. 126–153. Macmillan, New York.

Evans, L. T. ed. (1969). "The Induction of Flowering. Some Case Histories". Cornell Univ. Press, Ithaca, New York.

Evans, M. W. (1927). The life history of Timothy. *U.S., Dep. Agr., Bull.* **1450**, 1–55.

Evans, M. W., and Ely, J. E. (1935). The rhizomes of certain species of grasses. *J. Amer. Soc. Agron.* **27**, 791–797.

Evans, M. W., and Grover, F. O. (1940). Developmental morphology of the growing point of the shoot and the inflorescence in grasses. *J. Agr. Res.* **61**, 481–520.

Gustafsson, A. (1946, 1947). Apomixis in higher plants. Parts I, II, and III. *Lunds Univ. Arsskr., Afd.* Z [N. S.] **42**, No. 3, **43**, Nos. 2, and 12.

Hackel, E. (1890). Ueber einige Eigenthümlichkeiten der Gräser trockener Klimate. *Verh. Zool. Bot. Ges. Wien.* **40**, 125–138.

Harberd, D. J. (1961). Observations on population structure and longevity of *Festuca rubra. New Phytol.* **60**, 184–206.

Harberd, D. J. (1962). Some observations on natural clones in *Festuca ovina. New Phytol.* **61**, 85–100.

Harlan, J. R. (1945). Cleistogamy and chasmogamy in *Bromus carinatus* Hook and Arn. *Amer. J. Bot.* **32**, 66–72.

Hitchcock, A. S., and Chase, A. (1931). Grass. Old and new plant lore. *Smithson. Sci. Ser.* **11**, 201–250.

Jefferies, T. A. (1916). The vegetative anatomy of *Molinia caerulea*, the purple heath grass. *New Phytol.* **15**, 49–71.

Langer, R. H. M. (1963). Tillering in herbage grasses. *Herb. Abstr.* **33**, 141–148.

Laude, H. M. (1953). The nature of summer dormancy in perennial grasses. *Bot. Gaz.* **114**, 284–292.

McCarty, E. C. (1938). The relation of growth to the varying carbohydrate content of mountain brome. *U.S., Dep. Agr., Tech. Bull.* **598**, 1–24.

McCarty, E. C., and Price, R.(1942). Growth and carbohydrate content of important mountain forage plants in Central Utah as affected by clipping and grazing. *U.S., Dep. Agr., Tech. Bull.* **818**, 1–51.

McIntyre, G. I. (1967). Environmental control of bud and rhizome development in the seedling of *Agropyron repens* L. Beauv. *Can. J. Bot.* **45**, 1315–1326.

McIntyre, G. I. (1969). Apical dominance in the rhizome of *Agropyron repens*. Evidence of competition for carbohydrate as a factor in the mechanism of inhibition. *Can. J. Bot.* **47**, 1189–1197.

McWilliam, J. R. (1968). The nature of the perennial response in Mediterranean grasses. 2. Senescence, summer dormancy and survival in *Phalaris. Aust. J. Agr. Res.* **19**, 397–409.

McWilliam, J. R., and Kramer, P. J. (1968). The nature of the perennial response in Mediterranean grasses. I. Water relations and summer survival in *Phalaris. Aust. J. Agr. Res.* **19**, 381–395.

Maheshwari, P. (1950). "An Introduction to the Embryology of angiosperms." McGraw-Hill, New York.

May, L. H. (1960). The utilization of carbohydrate reserves in pasture plants after defoliation. *Herb. Abstr.* **30**, 239–245.

Montaldi, E. R. (1967). Modification del crecimiento diageotropico de los estolones de *Cynodon dactylon* (L.) Pers. par medio del ácido giberelico. *Rev. Invest. Agropecuar., Ser. 2* **4**, 55–68.

Montaldi, E. R. (1969). Gibberellin-sugar interaction regulating the growth habit of Bermudagrass (*Cynodon dactylon* (L.) Pers.). *Experientia* **25**, 91–92.

Nielsen, E. L. (1946). The origin of multiple macrogametophytes in *Poa pratensis. Bot. Gaz.* **108**, 41–50.

Nishimura, M. (1922). Comparative morphology and development of *Poa pratensis, Phleum pratense,* and *Setaria italica. Jap. J. Bot.* **1**, 55–85.

Nygren, A. (1954). Apomixis in the angiosperms. II. *Bot. Rev.* **20**, 577–649.

Oakley, R. A., and Evans, M. W.(1921). Rooting stems in Timothy. *J. Agr. Res.* **21**, 173–178.

Ofir, M., Koller, D., and Negbi, M. (1967). Studies on the physiology of regeneration buds of *Hordeum bulbosum. Bot. Gaz.* **128**, 25–34.

Pallis, M. (1916). The structure and history of Plav: The floating fen of the delta of the Danube. *J. Linn. Soc. (London). Bot.* **43**, 233–290.

Palmer, J. H. (1954). Effect of shoot orientation on leaf and shoot development. *Nature (London)* **174**, 85.

Prat, H. (1960). Vers une classification naturelle des Graminées. *Bull. Soc. Bot. Fr.* **107**, 32–79.

Randolph, L. F. (1936). Developmental morphology of the caryopsis in maize. *J. Agr. Res.* **53**, 881–916.

Sharman, B. C. (1947). The biology and developmental morphology of the shoot apex in the gramineae. *New Phytol.* **46**, 20–34.

Stapf, O. (1921). Kikuyugrass (*Pennisetum clandestinum* Chiov.). *Kew Bull.* 85–93.

Stebbins, G. L. (1941). Apomixis in the angiosperms. *Bot. Rev.* **7**, 507–542.

Stebbins, G. L. (1957). Self-fertilization and population variability in the higher plants. *Amer. Natur.* **91**, 337–354.

Sullivan, J. T., and Sprague, V. G. (1953). Reserve carbohydrates in orchardgrass cut for hay. *Plant Physiol.* **28**, 304–313.

Swingle, W. T. (1932). Recapitulation of seedling characters by nucellar buds developing in the embryo-sac of *Citrus. Proc. 6th. Int. Congr. Genet., 1932* Vol. **2**, pp. 196–197.

Trowbridge, P. F., Haigh, L. D., and Moulton, C. R. (1915). Studies of the Timothy plant. Part II. *Mo., Agr. Exp. Sta., Res. Bull.* **20**, 1–67.

Wardlaw, C. W. (1955). "Embryogenesis in Plants." Wiley, New York.

Weatherwax, P. (1934). Flowering and seed production in *Amphicarpon floridanum. Bull. Torrey Bot. Club* **61**, 211–215.

Weinmann, H., and Reinhold, L. (1946). Reserve carbohydrates in South African grasses. *J. S. Afr. Bot.* **12**, 57–73.

Winkler, H. (1934). Fortpflanzung der Gewächse. 7. Apomixis. *Handwörterb Naturwiss.* **4**, 451–461.

Youngner, V. B. (1960). Environmental control of initiation of the inflorescence, reproductive structures, and proliferations in *Poa bulbosa. Amer. J. Bot.* **47**, 753–757.

Youngner, V. B. (1961). Observations on the ecology and morphology of *Pennisetum clandestinum. Phyton (Buenos Aires)* **16**, 77–84.

Chapter 25

Inflorescence Induction and Initiation

ROY M. SACHS

There are several excellent reviews on reproductive development in higher plants (Hillman, 1963; Lang, 1965; Salisbury, 1961; Schwabe, 1968; Searle, 1965; Zeevaart, 1963) and two dealing specifically with the problem in grasses and cereals (Calder, 1966; Evans, 1964b). Emphasis in this chapter is placed on certain aspects of inflorescence initiation and induction that may be useful for breeders and ecologists seeking new varieties or by agronomists working to improve cultural practices.*

Four stages of development, or processes, are commonly recognized to precede the appearance of functional reproductive structures in higher plants. These processes are (1) maturation, (2) induction, (3) initiation, and (4) development.

Maturation is most commonly discussed in terms of juvenility. Regardless of the conditions in which they are grown most plants grow vegetatively for some time, producing only leaf, stem, and axillary bud tissue. So long as a plant is in the juvenile phase vegetative growth proceeds and the plant is insensitive to conditions that later promote flowering. In grasses the mini-

---

*The following abbreviations are used in the text: GA, gibberellic acid, gibberellin A_3; Alar, succinic acid 1,1-dimethyl hydrazide; CCC, 2-chloroethyltrimethylammonium chloride.

348

mum leaf number to spike formation is commonly used as a measure of the length of the juvenile phase although this is not an entirely accurate measure of the period (Lang, 1965). In annual grasses inflorescence primordia have been found in the embryo, or at the third or fourth node shortly after germination, or in perennial grasses requiring vernalization the obligate vegetative phase may be of several weeks duration.

A mature plant is one that can be "induced" to flower; that is, it becomes sensitive to conditions that eventually cause inflorescence initiation. Since the conditions required for initiation need not be continued up to the time of chemical or morphological transformation of the shoot apical meristem, these conditions are termed "inductive," and the process is called "induction." There are two kinds of induction. Most studies suggest that induction by low temperatures, "vernalization," occurs in the shoot apex whereas day-length induction occurs in the leaves. The product(s) of vernalization are probably not transmissible. Thus perennial grasses need to be vernalized each year, and even late-forming (summer) apices on a vernalized plant do not initiate inflorescences until the plant has been revernalized. On the other hand the product(s) of day-length induction must be translocated from the leaves to the shoot apical meristem.

"Initiation" is the transformation of the shoot apical meristem from a vegetative axis to a potentially reproductive axis. Although initiation requires gross chemical modifications of the apical meristematic cells prior to morphological change (Evans, 1969b), one usually waits for expansion of the inflorescence axis and floret formation to proclaim that initiation has occurred.

Table 1 (adapted from Calder, 1966) lists six classifications of require-

TABLE 1.

REQUIREMENTS FOR INFLORESCENCE INDUCTION AND INITIATION[a]

A.	Maturation (juvenile stage) + vernalization, day length (*Festuca pratensis*, *Lolium perenne*, *Dactylis glomerata*)
B.	Vernalization + daylength (*Agrostis* sp, *Bromus* sp, *Festuca* sp, *Poa pratensis*)
C.	Daylength (may not be easy to distinguish from F) *Lolium* sp, *Phalaris* sp, *Phleum* sp, spring cereals
D.	Maturation (juvenile stage) only; no environmental requirement
E.	No environmental requirement; no juvenile stage *Bouteloua curtipendula*, *Poa annua*, *Trisetum spicatum*
F.	Maturation, no vernalization, + daylength (*Oryza sativa*, *Saccharum officinarum*)

TABLE 2.

DAYLENGTH AND VERNALIZATION REQUIREMENTS ACCORDING TO TRIBES AND FAMILIES[a]

Tribes and Families Festucoideae	Vernalization	Daylength
Festuceae	±	All LD[b] or indifferent
Hordeae	±	All LD[b] or indifferent
Agrostideae	±	All LD[b] or indifferent
Aveneae	±	All LD[b] or indifferent
Phalarideae	±	All LD[b] or indifferent
Stipeae	−	All LD[b] or indifferent
Panicoideae		
Paniceae	−	LD, SD,[c] and intermediate
Andropogoneae	−	Mostly SD, some LD, and Intermediate day
Maydeae	−	SD or indifferent
Chloridoideae		
Chlorideae	−	Mostly SD, some LD, some Intermediate day
Zoysieae	−	All SD
Eragrosteae	−	All SD or indifferent

[a]Adapted from Evans, 1964b.
[b]LD—long day
[c]SD—short day

ments for inflorescence induction and initiation in grasses, with examples of each type cited. These six classes represent the total possible combinations (not permutations) of three processes: maturation, vernalization, and day-length induction. Table 2 (adapted from Evans, 1964b) summarizes published data concerning vernalization and day-length induction requirements according to tribes and families. There is a remarkable segregation of low temperature or day-length responses according to family. For example, almost every member of the *Festucoideae* is a long-day plant or indifferent to day length. None of the *Panicoideae* or *Chloridoideae* have low temperature requirements and most are short-day plants.

Inflorescence initiation is the first of many steps that must occur before gametogenesis and anthesis. The steps following initiation are commonly grouped under the term "inflorescence development" which is the subject of Dr. Latting's chapter in this book and is fully reviewed in her thesis (Latting, 1966).

Control of Reproductive Development

MATURATION

There is considerable literature on the general subject of juvenility, not only as it pertains to reproductive development but other age-related morphogenetic phenomena (Allsopp, 1965a; Lang, 1965; Leopold, 1964).

Although the juvenile phase has been well-investigated, the processes necessary for response to inductive conditions remain unknown.

Low light intensities tend to lengthen the obligate vegetative phase in some plants and mineral starvation reduces the minimal leaf number in others. There is some evidence that high carbohydrate nutrition shortens the juvenile period (Allsopp, 1965a). In *Hedera* gibberellic acid (GA) prolongs it (Robbins, 1957; Goodin and Stoutemeyer, 1961). Also, GA delays the node to flower initiation in peas (Barber *et al.*, 1958). Thus there are environmental and chemical influences on the juvenile stage, but it is not always clear whether the effects are on the capacity of the leaves to synthesize substances required for flower initiation, or the ability of the apical meristems to respond to chemical stimuli formed in the plant, or both. Reciprocal grafts between early and late varieties of peas show that the root systems of late varieties synthesize a substance (probably gibberellinlike) that is transported to the shoot system and prevents the response of the apical meristematic tissues to flower-forming stimuli (Paton and Barker, 1955; Barker *et al.*, 1958). There is strong evidence that GA-induced delay in flower initiation, where maturation is not a factor, is due to an effect on the receptor buds (Sachs *et al.*, 1967). Evans (1969b) has shown that in the long-day grass, *Lolium temulentum*, sensitivity to long days increases with plant age. The age effect is not related to increased leaf area or to the sensitivity of the shoot apex in the older plants, but to greater effectiveness of the older leaves per unit area. Thus, depending on the species, either the bud or leaf may be the site of maturation processes.

Whatever the operative factors regulating the length of the juvenile phase, the practical significance for the breeder and agronomist is that juvenility is a heritable factor that affects earliness to inflorescence initiation. It is of some importance in selection programs in which modification of earliness is the goal to be able to distinguish between factors affecting the length of the juvenile phase from those affecting response to low temperature or day length. Also, in species that have no vernalization requirement and are insensitive to day length, variation in the dates of inflorescence initiation, heading, and harvest can be the result only of changes in the juvenile period.

INDUCTION

The two kinds of induction, vernalization and day length, are different altogether and hence they are discussed separately.

Vernalization

In most cases the vernalization requirement is satisfied by exposure of imbibed seed or established plants to 0°C to 10°C for two to eight weeks. There is considerable ecotypic variation in the length of the requirement; usually the colder the place of origin, the longer the low temperature requirement. Cooper concluded that in *Lolium perenne* the vernalization factor was under polygenic control. Thus it should be possible to breed selectively grass varieties that will produce seed under mild winter conditions and still be adapted to cold climates. What is more likely in turfgrasses, however, is to select for varieties with a long low temperature requirement that will not be satisfied in mild climates. Such varieties would probably remain vegetative for long periods and be excellent for turf production.

In many grass species, however, the low temperature requirement can be met by prolonged exposure to short day lengths at temperatures well outside the vernalizing range; this is often called "short-day vernalization." Thus the short days of winter in mild climates can greatly hasten inflorescence initiation. In *Poa pratensis* however, short days are effective only at vernalizing temperatures. All evidence to date shows that the low temperature effect is perceived and localized in the shoot apical meristem. Short days are perceived by the leaves and the effect is either translocated to the shoot apex, preparing it for other floral stimuli coming from the leaves, or remains in the leaves preparing them for subsequent inductive treatment which cause the production of transmissible floral stimuli.

In some plants one or more of the gibberellins may replace the vernalization requirement (whether low temperature or short day) for inflorescence initiation suggesting that one of the effects of low temperatures is to increase endogenous gibberellin levels. Since all species that require vernalization for inflorescence initiation do not so respond to applications of the known gibberellins (usually GA), there is good reason to believe that special, but as yet unknown, gibberellins are involved, or that low temperatures may be activating other systems—for example, those reducing abscisin levels—necessary for the onset of reproduction. Also, since the low temperature effect is not transmissible and the known gibberellins are, some explanation must be found to account for this discrepancy.

Day length

Perhaps the most complex adaptation that plants have made to their environment is that to the day-length factor. There are at least five kinds of timing mechanisms by which inflorescence induction can be attuned to a particular day length. Three of these will be described here. The more complex short- long-day response, found in many grasses with a vernalization requirement, and long- short-day type are well covered by Best (1960). One mechanism exists in short-day plants in which inflorescence initiation is promoted as the day length is decreased (Fig. 1A); another is found in long-day plants in which initiation is promoted as the day length is increased (Fig. 1B); and still another is found in intermediate day plants in which initiation occurs when the day length is between certain critical limits (Fig. 1C). The critical day length, between 13 and 15 hours, for 19459 strain of *Phleum pratense* (Fig. 1A), *Trioda flava* (Fig. 1B), and *Sorghastrum mutans* (Fig. 1C), for all three response types may overlap, such that plants belonging to different groups may flower at the same time of year depending on the time of planting, the length of the juvenile phase, and the temperatures prevailing between sowing date and the completion of the juvenile phase.

There is strong evidence from spectral dependency studies that the prime light-sensing pigment system is phytochrome, a phycocyaninlike pigment bound to a relatively small protein of molecular weight 60,000. Phytochrome can exist in two intraconvertible forms, one absorbing light maximally at 730 mμ (P_{FR}) and the other at 660 mμ (P_R). Radiation at 660 mμ drives P_R to P_{FR}; and light at 730 mμ drives P_{FR} to P_R. At the end of irradiation with sunlight most of the phytochrome exists as P_{FR}, but in darkness there is a slow, spontaneous conversion of P_{FR} to P_R as well as considerable destruction of P_{FR} (Hillman, 1967). In *Xanthium*, a short-day plant requiring one short day for induction, the dark conversion of P_{FR} to P_R or its destruction requires about three hours. Since the critical dark period in *Xanthium* is 8.5 to 9 hr (critical day length is 15.5 to 15 hr), phytochrome conversion accounts for only a fraction of the dark requirement. Nevertheless brief interruptions of the dark period up to the 8.5- to 9-hr mark with light at 660 mμ prevent induction. Thus for some reason P_R is required or, what seems more likely, P_{FR} must be suppressed, for at least 8.5 to 9 hr in a *Xanthium* leaf before induction can occur. Induction means the capacity to synthesize transmissible flower-inducing stimuli; hence P_{FR} must control reactions that regulate the synthesis of a flower hormone. In applying this argument to long-day plants it must be assumed that P_{FR} promotes the synthesis of floral stimuli. For intermediate-day plants or dual-day-length requiring plants the arguments concerning phytochrome are even more complex.

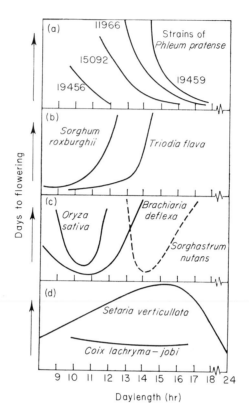

FIG. 1. Control of flowering by day-length. [Adapted from Evans (1964b); original references in his review.] (a) Long-day response type in four strains of *Phleum pratense* with markedly different critical day lengths. Strains 19459 and 11966 appear to be obligate long-day plants, whereas 15092 and 19456 are probably facultative long-day plants. (b) Short-day response type in *Sorghum roxburghii* and *Triodia flava*. Note the difference in critical day length. Both species are obligate short day plants. (c) Intermediate-day response type in *Oryza sativa* (a species in which many short-day varieties are known), *Brachiaria deflexa*, and *Sorghastrum nutans*. Again note the differences in critical day length or in the shape of the response curves. *Oryza* and *Sorghastrum* appear to have an obligate requirement for intermediate day lengths, whereas *Brachiaris* is a facultative type. (d) Day-length-indifferent response type in *Coix lachryma-jobi* and an ambiphotoperiodic type in *Setaria verticullata*. In the latter case flowering is promoted as the day length is increased above or decreased below 15 hr but will occur at all day lengths.

Moreover since temperature plays an important role in determining the response of a plant to day length, phytochrome-associated reactions are undoubtedly strongly temperature dependent. For example, at low temperatures *Xanthium* (J. P. Nitsch and Went, 1957) will flower in long days. Searle (1965) and Evans (1964b) cite many more cases in which day-length-controlled induction disappears or is modified in certain temperature regimes. In many long-day grasses temperatures above 12°C to 18°C inhibit long-day induction, whereas short-day grasses may not be induced if the temperatures during darkness are below 12°C to 16°C.

From this brief summary of day-length induction one must surely conclude that a great deal remains to be learned about (1) the level of phytochrome in closely related strains of certain species (for example, in *Phleum pratense*) (Fig. 1A) that may account for different critical daylengths, (2) how the level of phytochrome is controlled and, (3) the reactions dependent on P_{FR}, which may account for the different response types. Such information should provide more exact practical controls of induction and thus inflorescence initiation.

Induction and Hormonal Synthesis

It is well-established for many, though not all, cold-requiring and long-day plants that GA promotes inflorescence initiation under noninductive conditions (Lang, 1965; Evans, 1964a). Moreover endogenous gibberellin-like substances have been shown to increase in response to inductive conditions. Thus it is reasonable to conclude that gibberellin metabolism in some plants is under the control of reactions activated by low temperatures and/or long day lengths. Stoddart (1966) and Stoddart and Lang (1968) have shown that the proportional concentrations of three active gibberellins changed during long days. The GA-like component was present in highest amount in short days and decreased relative to the other two under long-day inductive conditions. Among several gibberellins tested on the forget-me-not, Michniewicz and Lang (1962) found specific effects on floral initiation different from those on shoot growth. Thus, a major weakness of many investigations on floral induction and initiation is that only GA is applied or in evaluating plant extracts, an assay is used that measures only vegetative growth.

Abscisic acid and related compounds that promote flowering in some short-day plants also seem to be under day-length control, increasing in short-day conditions (El-Antably and Wareing, 1966; Wareing and El-Antably, 1967).

Instances of day-length controlled formation or removal of inhibitors of initiation are well known. In some long-day plants, such as *Hyoscyamus niger* and *Lolium temulentum*, leaves in short-day conditions inhibit long-day induction, and in the latter case the evidence is good that a transmissible inhibitor is formed that interferes at the shoot apex with floral stimuli coming from long-day-induced leaves (Evans, 1960). Similar observations have been made in short-day plants, too (Bhargava, 1963, 1965); Guttridge, 1959; Harder and Bunsow, 1958; Schwabe, 1956). Evans (1968, 1969b) suggests that in *Lolium* the short-day inhibitor may be an abscisinlike compound. In some short-day plants the inhibitor may be a gibberellinlike compound (Harder and Bunsow, 1958; Thompson and Guttridge, 1959), the level of which is increased in long-day conditions.

Studies by Zeevaart and Lang (1962) and Zeevaart (1969a) suggest that in *Bryophyllum daigremontianum*, a long-short-day plant, gibberellin is required in the *leaves* not the shoot apical meristem for the synthesis of a flower-inducing hormone. Their results show that GA can replace the long-day requirement and cause plants to flower in short-day conditions and that a GA-treated plant can act as a donor (via a graft union) of flower-forming stimuli to a receptor kept in long- or short-day conditions. Thus they concluded that a certain level of a gibberellinlike substance was reached during long-day induction and permitted the subsequent synthesis of flower-forming stimuli in the leaves in short-day conditions; in fact the level of gibberellinlike materials increases twentyfold in long-day conditions (Zeevaart, 1969b). In view of Stoddart and Lang's findings for *Trifolium*, it is possible that applied GA in *Bryophyllum* is converted to another type of gibberellin which is a flower promoter and acts at the apical meristem. But recently Zeevaart has shown that GA is very stable in *Bryophyllum* and does not appear in the naturally occurring gibberellin fractions isolated from *Bryophyllum* leaves (Zeevaart, 1969b).

INITIATION AND THE ROLE OF HORMONES

Evans (1969b) has cited two events in the shoot apex of *Lolium temulentum* which together constitute inflorescence initiation. One is the general elongation of the apex (spike initiation) and the other is the activation of "target cells" in the axillary bud region leading to double-ridge formation (spikelet initiation). Elongation of the shoot apex is part of the general long-day-induced activation of the apical meristematic region, including increased permeability and RNA and protein synthesis. Even when flower induction does not occur, as in young plants, long days cause an increased apical meristematic activity expressed as increased leaf initiation. And long day continues to cause increased activity after inflorescence development has begun. The long-day promoter appears to be a compound whose level is affected by gibberellins but cannot be GA, since the latter causes a different pattern of activation from that observed following long-day induction.

The second, more specific, activation of the "target cells" appears to be the result of derepression in the axillary bud region of the leaf primordia. Evans believes that here derepression is the result of a relative decrease in an abscisinlike inhibitor formed in short-day conditions and translocated to the apex. More recently, however, Evans (1969a) has provided strong evidence for an increase in a floral stimulus that acts in concert with gibberellins to cause floral induction (see below). Youngner (1960) provided strong evidence for two floral stimuli in *Poa bulbosa*, each controlling steps equivalent to those cited by Evans. The first stimulus, controlling inflorescence initiation, is produced by a vernalization long-day sequence, and the second, controlling floret differentiation, is produced in long day at high temperatures (21–27°C). If the temperature during long-day induction is 20°C or below, bulbils develop in place of normal florets. Clearly information on the effects of gibberellins or abscisic acid on inflorescence initiation in *Poa* would be valuable for comparison with results for *Lolium*.

The role of gibberellins in regulating differentiation at the apical meristem is of great importance to an understanding of inflorescence initiation. There is little doubt that gibberellins promote initiation, but there are many instances in which GA inhibits flower initiation or development (Sachs and Hackett, 1969; Fig. 2), most likely by preventing critical reactions from

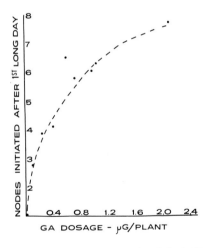

FIG. 2. GA-induced delay in flower initiation in *Fuchsia hybrida* "Lord Byron" (Sachs *et al.*, 1967; Sachs and Hackett, 1969). The dashed curve shows GA-induced inhibition of flower initiation in the receptor axillary buds as a delay in node to first flower. The ordinate represents the number of vegetative nodes initiated after the beginning of long-day induction. In control plants the first pair of axillary buds and each subsequent pair initiated below the apical meristem initiate flowers; whereas with increasing amounts of GA an increasing number of axillary buds initiated by the apical meristem remain vegetative. The GA is applied in a 10-μ l drop to the apical leaf cluster.

occurring at the shoot apical meristem. Growth retardants, such as Alar and CCC, often promote flower initiation and development, perhaps by lowering endogenous levels of certain inhibitory gibberellins or by increasing the level of floral-inducing substances. Evans (1969a) has shown CCC-induced promotion of floral initiation in *Lolium* when the plants are treated with gibberellic acid, too. Used alone, CCC is without effect; thus the interaction between CCC and GA is synergistic. Evans' explanation, which is subject to experimental testing, is that (1) gibberellins and floral stimuli share common precursors in *Lolium*, and (2) CCC blocks a late step leading to gibberellin synthesis, thereby causing an increase in precursors for synthesis of floral stimuli. The resulting increase in floral stimuli causes increased rate of floral initiation only if an exogenous gibberellin source is supplied since the latter is required for general activation of the apical meristematic tissues. In wheat and barley substantial increases in yield have been obtained by application of CCC; in those instances in which the prevention of lodging has been eliminated as a factor contributing to yield, it is clear that CCC-induced increases in yield are the result of more seed per spike or of more spikes per plant (Pinthus and Halevy, 1965; Primost, 1967).

Evans' hypothesis does not account for gibberellin-induced inhibition; at some stage of inflorescence initiation and development some gibberellins inhibit essential processes in the meristematic regions, perhaps at Evans' "target" areas. What are the essential processes affected by GA? Some clues may be found in the following section.

Light Intensity, Moisture Stress, and Carbohydrate Levels in Meristematic Tissues

In many species low-intensity light delays or inhibits floral initiation without inhibiting the differentiation of vegetative structures (Table 3). The most obvious explanation for the low light intensity effect is that products of photosynthesis are reduced below that required for inflorescence initiation and development. Allsopp (1965b) suggests, in fact, that inflorescence initiation has higher nutritional requirements, particularly for carbohydrates such as sucrose, than does differention of vegetative organs. A more general statement by Allsopp (1965b) is that " . . . sugar concentration appears to play a major role in morphogenesis . . . and . . . some of the effects of sugar concentration are probably relatively direct, whereas others represent a genetically determined response of the plant to a particular level of sugar concentration."

At sufficiently high light intensities bougainvillea, a short-day plant,

TABLE 3

A. *Bougainvillea "San Diego Red"* (Hackett and Sachs, 1966)

Light intensity (ft)	Node to first inflorescence
4000–4500	7.8
2000–2500	21.6
1500–2000	28.5

B. Marigold (*Tagetes patula*) (Harris, 1962)

Light intensity (ft)	Number of flowers initiated in 4 months
10,000	915
3,800	114
1,300	54

behaves like a day neutral plant, flowering as rapidly and profusely in 16-hr as in 8 hr day lengths. Short day lengths may in effect be conserving photosynthetic materials necessary for differentiation at meristematic sites (Hackett and Sachs, 1966). Since GA inhibits and growth retardants promote flowering in bougainvillea (Hackett and Sachs, 1967) and many other species, it is reasonable to suggest that these substances have major effects on the nutritional status of apical meristematic tissues.

Moisture stress occurs frequently under field conditions and at times in greenhouses, too. It is a factor that can have great effects on initiation and development of reproductive structures. The effect depends on the time when stress occurs as well as on the kind of crop. In corn, oats, and other plants with determinate inflorescences stress at the time of spike initiation may inhibit floret initiation (Shaw and Laing, 1966). Indeterminate crops, such as soybean, that initiate inflorescences for long periods are not as severely affected by stress.

There are reports, some from farmers and nurserymen, that moisture stress hastens the onset of flowering in many species; in these cases stress occurs before initiation. Allsopp (1965b) suggests that water stress may have this effect as a result of increased carbohydrate levels. In vitro studies (C. Nitsch and Nitsch, 1967; Kimura, 1963) reveal that the level of sucrose in the medium is of great importance in regulating reproductive development: Cumming (1967) has shown that glucose and sucrose can enhance and sustain an endogenous rhythm affecting inflorescence initiation in *Chenopodium rubrum*. In addition glucose can inhibit or promote flowering depending on the time of application during a long dark period, suggesting that there may be *optimal* levels of carbohydrates for reproductive development.

Conclusion

It is noteworthy that the only substances that have been found to affect inflorescence initiation also have more or less great effects on vegetative growth. Although there is circumstantial evidence that specific flower-inducing gibberellins may be found, no such hints of flower-inducing specificity exists for other families of growth substances. Abscisic acid inhibits flower initiation in some plants and promotes it in others; in all cases it strongly inhibits vegetative activity. Auxin-induced promotion of flowering in pineapple is duplicated by β-hydroxyethyl hydrazine and by an ethylene generating compound 2-chloroethane phosphonic acid (*ethephon*). Recently C. Nitsch and Nitsch (1969) have shown that *ethephon* induces flowering in *Plumbago indica*, a short-day plant. These substances inhibit vegetative development as well. Triiodobenzoic acid, a strong inhibitor of vegetative growth, increases the numbers of flowers initiated in tomato, beans, and soybeans (Galston, 1947; Gorter, 1954)—the effect on the latter is sufficient to warrant commercial application. The cytokinins, too, affect both flower initiation and growth in some plants (Michniewicz and Kamienska, (1964, 1965).

Probably all substances affecting vegetative growth activities of the shoot apical meristematic tissues will also affect inflorescence initiation and development. If this is true, there will be many more "floral stimuli," many of which will be naturally occurring compounds.

The evidence in favor of a single, specific flower-inducing substance, a *florigen* or *anthesin*, common to all flowering plants is based solely on reciprocal grafts between species in many families (no grafts have been successful on the grasses) and of different response types. Out of hundreds of attempts to isolate the transmissible flower-inducing substance, three laboratories have met with some degree of success (Lincoln *et al.*, 1961; Carr, 1967; Hodson and Hamner, 1970). Hodson and Hamner (1970) have achieved the most dramatic success with crude acetone extracts from flowering *Xanthium* plants; they show, furthermore, that GA applications are necessary to achieve a substantial response if *Xanthium* is used as the assay plant. However, if Lemna is used as the assay plant, GA inhibits the response. Here the dual action of GA is revealed most clearly.

Sufficient quantities of active floral-inducing extracts have never been available for extensive physiological or chemical testing, but Evans' hypothesis (1969a) concerning the role of CCC in increasing the level of floral stimuli in *Lolium* suggests that growth retardants should be tested in future attempts to extract floral-inducing substances.

Yet the major physiological problems will remain of how the level of such substances is controlled by inductive processes in the leaves and apical meristematic tissues and how they activate differentiation processes. But from the applied scientists point of view giant strides in control, whether towards promotion or inhibition, of inflorescence initiation and development will have been made. The papers by Aitken (1966) and Elliott (1967) reveal the great extent to which grasses are restricted to specific environments by virtue of temperature and day-length requirements for inflorescence initiation. Chemical control of initiation may well eliminate some problems resulting from year-to-year climatic variation and could extend the range of grasses to areas otherwise desirable for growth where proper inductive conditions do not exist.

References

Aitken, Y. (1966). The flowering responses of crop and pasture species in Australia. I. Factors affecting development in the field of *Lolium* species (*L. rigidum* Gand., *L. perenne* L., *L. multiflorum* Lam.). *Aust. J. Agr. Res.* **17**, 821–839.

Allsopp, A. (1965a). Shoot morphogenesis. *Annu. Rev. Plant Physiol.* **15**, 225–254.

Allsopp, A. (1965b). The significance for development of water supply, osmotic relations and nutrition. *In* "Handbuch der Pflanzen physiol" (W. Ruhland, ed.), vol. 15, Part 2, pp. 504–552. Springer-Verlag, Berlin and New York.

Barber, H. N., Jackson, W. O., Murfet, I. C., and Spent, J. L. (1958). Gibberellic acid and the physiological genetics of flowering in peas. *Nature (London)* **182**, 1321–1322.

Best, R. (1960). Photoperiodism in plants as studied by means of response curves. *Proc., Kon. Ned. Akad. Wetensch., Ser. C* **63**, 676–691.

Bhargava, S. C. (1963). A transmissible flower bud inhibitor in the short day plant *Salvia occidentalis*. *Proc., Kon. Ned. Akad. Wetensch.* **66**, 371–376.

Bhargava, S. C. (1965). A transmissible flower bud inhibitor in *Perilla crispa*. *Proc., Kon. Ned. Akad. Wetansch.* **68**, 63–68.

Calder, D. M. (1966). Inflorescence induction and initiation in the *Gramineae*. *In* "The Growth of Cereals and Grasses" (F. L. Milthorpe and J. D. Ivins, eds.), pp. 59–73. Butterworth, London.

Carr, D. J. (1967). The relationship between florigen and the flower hormones. *Ann. N.Y. Acad. Sci.* **144**, 305–312.

Cumming, B. G. (1967). Circadian rhythmic flowering responses in *Chenopodium rubrum*: Effects of glucose and sucrose. *Can. J. Bot.* **45**, 2173–2193.

El-Antably, H. M. M., and Wareing, P. F. (1966). Stimulation of flowering in certain short day plants by abscisin. *Nature (London)* **210**, 328–329.

Elliott, C. R. (1967). Factors affecting grass seed yields. *Can. Agr.* summer issue.

Evans, L. T. (1960). Inflorescence initiation in *Lolium temulentum* L. II. Evidence for inhibitory and promotive photoperiodic processes involving transmissible products. *Aust. J. Biol. Sci.* **13**, 429–440.

Evans, L. T. (1964a). Inflorescence initiation in *Lolium temulentum* L. V. The role of auxins and gibberellins. *Aust. J. Biol. Sci.* **17**, 10–23.

Evans, L. T. (1964b). Reproduction. *In* "Grasses and Grasslands" (C. Barnard, ed.), pp. 126–153. Macmillan, New York.

Evans, L. T. (1968). Abscisin II. Inhibitory effect on flower induction in a long day plant. *Science* **15**, 107–108.

Evans, L. T. (1969a). Inflorescence initiation in *Lolium temulentum* L. XIII. The role of gibberellins. *Aust. J. Biol. Sci.* **22**, 773–786.

Evans, L. T. (1969b). *Lolium temulentum* L. *In* "Induction of Flowering—Some Case Histories" (L. T. Evans, ed.). Macmillan, New York.

Galston, A. W. (1947). The influence of 2, 3, 5-triiodobenzoic acid on the growth and flowering of soy beans. *Amer. J. Bot.* **34**, 350–360.

Goodin, J. R., and Stoutemeyer, V. T. (1961). Effects of temperature and potassium gibberellate on phases of growth of Algerian ivy. *Nature (London)* **192**, 677–678.

Gorter, C. J. (1954). The flowering response of *Phaseolus vulgaris* to 2, 3, 5-triiodobenzoic acid and its Cl- and Br-analogues. *Proc., Kon. Ned. Akad. Wetensch., Ser. C* **57**, 606–616.

Guttridge, C. G. (1959). Evidence for a flower inhibitor and vegetative growth promoter in the strawberry. *Ann. Bot. (London)* [N. S.] **23**, 351–360.

Hackett, W. P., and Sachs, R. M. (1966). Flowering in *Bougainvillea* "San Diego Red." *Proc. Amer. Soc. Hort. Sci.* **88**, 606–612.

Hackett, W. P., and Sachs, R. M. (1967). Chemical control of flowering in *Bougainvillea* "San Diego Red." *Proc. Amer. Sci. Hort. Sci.* **90**, 363–364.

Harder, R., and Bunsow, R. (1958). Uber die Wirkung von Gibberellin auf Entwicklung und Blutenbildung der Kurztagpflanze *Kalanchoe blossfeldiana. Planta* **51**, 201–222.

Harris, R. W. (1962). Unpublished data on flowering in garden plants in relation to shading. University of California, Davis.

Hillman, W. S. (1963). "The Physiology of Flowering." Holt, New York.

Hillman, W. S. (1967). The physiology of phytochrome. *Annu. Rev. Plant Physiol.* **18**, 301–324.

Hodson, H. K., and Hamner, K. C. (1970). Floral inducing extract from *Xanthium. Science* **167**, 384–385.

Kimura, K. (1963). Floral initiation in *Pharbitis nil* subjected to continuous illumination at relatively low temperatures. II. Effect of some factors in culture medium on floral initiation. *Bot. Mag.* **76**, 351–358.

Lang, A. (1965). Physiology of flower initiation. *In* "Handbuch der Pflanzenphysiologic" (W. Ruhland, ed.), Vol. 15, Part 1, pp. 1380–1536. Springer-Verlag, Berlin and New York.

Latting, M. J. (1966). Floral morphogenesis and proliferation in several viviparous grasses. Ph.D. Thesis, University of California, Los Angeles.

Leopold, A. C. (1964). Juvenility. *In* "Plant Growth and Development," pp. 185–193. McGraw-Hill, New York.

Lincoln, R. G., Mayfield, D. L., and Cunningham, A. (1961). Preparation of a floral initiating extract from *Xanthium. Science* **133**, 756.

Michniewicz, M., and Kaminkska, A. (1964). Flower formation induced by kinetin and Vitamin E treatment in a cold-requiring plant (*Achorium intybus* L.) grown under non-inductive conditions. *Naturwissenschaften* **51**, 295–296.

Michniewicz, M., and Kamienska, A. (1965). Flower formation induced by kinetin and Vitamin E treatment in a long day plant (*Arabidopsis thaliana*) grown in short day. *Naturwissenschaften* **52**, 623.

Michniewicz, M., and Lang, A. (1962). Effect of nine different gibberellins on stem elongation and flower formation in cold-requiring and photoperiodic plants grown under non-inductive conditions. *Planta* **58**, 549–563.

Nitsch, C. and Nitsch, J. P. (1967). The induction of flowering *in vitro* in stem segments of *Plumbago indica* L. II. The production of reproductive buds. *Planta* **72**, 371–384.

Nitsch, C. and Nitsch, J. P. (1969). Floral induction in a short-day plant, *Plumbago indica* L. by 2-choroethane phosphonic acid. *Pland Physiol.* **44**, 1747–1748.

Nitsch, J. P., and Went, F. W. (1957). The induction of flowering in *Xanthium pennsylvanicum* under long days. *In* "Photoperiodism and Related Phenomena in Plants and Animals," Publ. No. 55, pp. 311–314. *Amer. Assoc. Advan. Sci.*, Washington, D. C.

Paton, D., and Barber, H. N. (1955). Physiological genetics of *Pisum*. I. Grafting experiments between early and late varieties. *Aust. J. Biol. Sci.* **8**, 230–240.

Pinthus, M. J., and Halevy, A. H. (1965). Prevention of lodging and increase in yield of wheat treated with CCC (2-chloroethyl trimethyl ammonium chloride). *Isr. J. Agr. Res.* **15**, 159–161.

Primost, E. (1967). Der Einfluss von Chloro Cholin Chlorid (CCC) auf den Ertragsaufbau von Winter—und Sommerwiesen. *Z. Acker-Pflanzenbau* **126**, 164–178.

Robbins, W. J. (1957). Gibberellic acid and the reversal of adult *Hedera* to a juvenile state. *Amer. J. Bot.* **44**, 743–746.

Sachs, R. M., and Hackett, W. P. (1969). Control of vegetative and reproduction development, *Hort. Sci.* **4**, 103–107.

Sachs, R. M., Kofranek, A. M., and Shyr, S. Y. (1967). Gibberellin-induced inhibition of floral initiation in *Fuchsia hybrida. Amer. J. Bot.* **54**, 921–929.

Salisbury, F. B. (1961). Photoperiodism and the flowering process. *Annu. Rev. Plant Physiol.* **12**, 293–326.

Schwabe, W. W. (1956). Evidence for a flowering inhibitor produced in long day in *Kalanchoe blossfeldiana. Ann. Bot. (London)* [N. S.] **20**, 1–14.

Schwabe, W. W. (1968). The initiation of flowering. *Sci. Progr. (London)* **56**, 325–336.

Searle, N. E. (1965). Pysiology of flowering *Annu. Rev. Plant Physiol.* **16**, 97–118.

Shaw, R., and Laing, D. R. (1966). Moisture stress and plant response. Chap. 5 pp 73–94. *In* "Plant Environment and Efficient Water Use," (W. H. Pierre *et al.*, eds.), Amer. Soc. Agron. and Soil Sci. Soc. Amer., Madison, Wisconsin.

Stoddart, J. L. (1966). Studies on the relationship between gibberellin metabolism and day-length in normal and nonflowering red clover (*Trifolium pratense* L.). *J. Exp. Bot.* **17**, 96–107.

Stoddart, J. L., and Lang, A. (1968). The effect of day length on gibberellin synthesis in leaves of red clover (*Trifolium pratense* L.) pp. 1371–1383. *In*: "Biochemistry and Physiology of Plant Growth Substances." F. Wightman and G. Setterfield, eds.) Runge Press Ltd., Ottawa, Canada.

Thompson, P. A., and Guttridge, G. C. (1959). Effect of gibberellic acid on the initiation of flowers and runners in the strawberry. *Nature (London)* **184**, 72–73.

Wareing, P. F., and El-Antably, H. M. M. (1967). The possible role of endogenous inhibitors in the control of flowering. *Int. Symp. Cell. Mol. Aspects Floral Induction*, Abstracts, 12.

Youngner, V. B. (1960). Environmental control of initiation of the inflorescence, reproductive structures, and proliferations in *Poa bulbosa. Amer. J. Bot.* **47**, 753–757.

Zeevaart, J. A. D. (1963). Climatic control or reproductive development. *In* "Environmental Control of Plant Growth" (L. T. Evans, ed.), Chapter 16, pp. 289–310. Academic Press, New York.

Zeevaart, J. A. D. (1969a). The leaf as the site of gibberellin action in flower formation in Bryophyllum daigremontianum. Planta **84**, 339–347.

Zeevaart, J. A. D. (1969b). Gibberellin-like substances in *Bryophyllum daigremontianum* and the distribution and persistence of applied gibberellin A_3. *Planta* **86**, 124–133.

Zeevaart, J. A. D., and Lang, A. (1962). The relationship between gibberellin and floral stimulus in Bryophyllum daigremontianum. Planta **58**, 531–542.

Chapter 26

Differentiation in the Grass Inflorescence

JUNE LATTING

Other authors of this volume have emphasized the tremendous complexity of environmental and genetic factors and their interactions which profoundly affect both vegetative growth and development in grasses and the flowering process of induction, initiation, and subsequent reproduction. Differentiation in the grass inflorescence encompasses the whole of morphological and physiological development from the first initiation of "double ridges" to the final phase of reproduction in which fruit set occurs. During this period the floral primordium, from the earliest morphological transition of vegetative to floral apex, is continuously under the influence of interacting environmental and genetic factors. Adverse environmental conditions may reduce or nullify the biochemical processes promoting floral differentiation so that the floral apex undergoes a dedifferentiation or reversal toward the vegetative condition, or under optimal environmental conditions the apex continues its progress toward completion of its function as a fully reproductive organ.

The literature concerned with the physiology of flowering is quite extensive and exhaustive. The most comprehensive treatises on this aspect of plant physiology spanning the whole of the plant kingdom are contained in the Handbuch der Pflanzenphysiologie (Ruhland, 1961a,b, 1965, 1967). These are fascinating and absorbing compilations of all available information at the time, old as well as new, intended to provide a broad and solid foundation for future literature and experimental studies. Other recent pertinent works are *The Induction of Flowering—Some Case Histories* (L.T. Evans, 1969) and *Cellular and Molecular Aspects of Induction* (Bernier, 1971). For the grasses, specifically, recent comprehensive reviews of growth and development are found in *Grasses and Grasslands* (Barnard, 1964), *The Growth of Cereals and Grasses* (Milthorpe and Ivins, 1966), and *Turfgrass Science* (Hanson and Ruska, 1969).

It has become clearly established that vegetative and floral meristems are fundamentally alike and that leaves and floral organs are therefore homologous. As discussed by Lang (1965) the transition to flowering occurs through the transformation of an existing, highly organized system producing vegetative primordia into one that reorganizes the histological and morphological pattern to produce floral primordia. He states that this is a unique mode of morphogenesis that poses distinct challenges to the developmental biologist.

This chapter is concerned primarily with the general pattern of differentiation in the floral apex of Festucoid grasses and the changes wrought on this general pattern by environmental factors. It also concerns vivipary in the Festucoid grasses, a phenomenon that occurs with considerable frequency and which, although usually referred to only in passing observations, is an expression of the shifting balance of factors controlling vegetative or floral development; as such, it deserves more attention as an important field of research in elucidating the mysteries of the flowering process.

Systematics

The grass family has traditionally been divided into two major subfamilies, the Festucoideae and the Panicoideae (Hitchcock, 1951). In recent years, however, there have been numerous revisions of subfamilies, tribes, and genera, with continual reassessment of findings. The need for a new and comprehensive treatment, to the generic level, of the family on a world-wide scale has been pointed out by Burbidge (1964) in a review of the history of grass systematics and discussion of the recent works and syntheses of efforts to bring together knowledge accumulating in the various fields of anatomy, biochemistry, cytogenetics, ecology, morphology, physiology, and taxonomy. These works reflect the necessity of intercommunication among the various specialists to bring about further clarification and identification of the natural relationships of the grasses and still retain adequately defined, documented, and useful categories.

Under the new systems of classification, divisions at the tribal and generic level are based on characters that show better correlation with each other and with the ecological and physiological characteristics of the genera than did inflorescence characters that were emphasized under the older system. The most significant of these are structure of spikelet and lodicule, size and structure of embryo, caryopsis and seedling, leaf anatomy, and chromosome size and number (Stebbins, 1956; Stebbins and Crampton, 1959; Reeder, 1957, 1962; Gould, 1968).

It appears that future classification of the Gramineae will be based on division into at least three major groups, the Panicoideae and the Chloridoideae, which developed primarily in the tropics, and the Festucoideae, which are the principal grasses of temperate zones; and into a number of minor groups, which may or may not have affinities with one or another of the major groups.

We may say then, in general, that the Festucoid grasses occur mostly in the temperate zones and are long day plants in which floral initiation must usually be accompanied by cool nights and preceded by vernalization (Arber, 1934). The inflorescences are usually many flowered and indeterminate, with spikelets dehiscing above the glumes. The apices usually have a two-layered tunica (Brown *et al.*, 1957), and the apical meristems of the mature sexual spikelets are usually only aborted rudiments that terminate further development of the florets on the spikelet. Festucoid grasses are specialized largely by reduction in the leaf epidermis, caryopsis, embryo, and seedling. They usually have large chromosomes with a basic number of seven (Avdulov, 1931).

Additional characters that distinguish the Festucoideae are the possession of compound starch grains; epidermal cells in the root hair zone which are of two types, long and short—only the latter of which give rise to root hairs—which emerge from the apical end of the cells and project forward at an angle of about 45 degrees with the axis of the root (Row and Reeder, 1957); flowering culms in which the 3-4 nodes below the inflorescence never bear branches; leaves in which the cells surrounding the vascular bundles are relatively little developed (Stebbins, 1956). Finally, the Festucoid grasses are easily killed as germinating seedlings by weak doses of the weed-killing chemical, isopropyl-*N*-phenyl carbamate (IPC) (Al-Aish, 1956).

In contrast the Panicoid–Chloridoid grasses occur mostly in the tropics, are short- or intermediate-day plants requiring warm nights at the time of initiation, and apparently have no need for preliminary vernalization. The inflorescences are usually one-flowered and dehisc below the glumes. Histologically, the apex usually has a one-layered tunica. Chromosomes are smaller than in the Festucoid grasses and have a basic number of 9, 10, or 12. There is also in this group a retention of primitive features in the leaf epidermis, caryopsis, embryo, and seedling, but with specializations in the leaf anatomy, inflorescence, and spikelet.

Other characteristics of the Panicoid group are simple starch grains; epidermal cells in the root hair zone all of one type, any one of which can give rise to a root hair which emerges from the middle of the cell and at a right angle to the axis of the root; flowering culms in which all nodes but the uppermost one immediately below the inflorescence bear either branches or axillary buds; leaves in which the cells surrounding the vascular bundles, and the chloroplasts contained in those cells, are highly specialized. Finally, the Panicoid grasses are strongly resistant to IPC.

Inflorescence Development

The earliest comprehensive studies on anatomical and morphological development of the inflorescence were those of Arber (1926, 1929, 1934) who worked with the bamboos and over 70 other species of grasses. She discussed ecological and morphological relationships and illustrated them with numerous drawings of serial sections of inflorescences and florets.

Morphological development of the grass apex and its transition from vegetative to reproductive state have been painstakingly and beautifully documented by Bonnett (1935, 1937, 1938, 1940, 1953, 1961, 1966) in barley, wheat, oats, sweet corn, maize, and rye; by Sharman in *Anthoxanthum odoratum* (1960a) and in *Agropyron repens* (1947), which he used as a representative of numerous other species he examined; and by M. W. Evans and Grover (1940) who described morphological development of the inflorescence in eight species of important grasses: *Phleum pratense, Agropyron repens, Euchlaena mexicana, Lolium perenne, Phalaris canariensis, Arrhenatherum elatius, Setaria italica,* and *Dactylis glomerata.* Cooper (1951) described the development of *Lolium italicum, L. perenne,* and *L. multiflorum.*

Anatomical development was included in Bonnett's studies of maize (1953) and oats (1961) and in Sharman's studies of *Anthoxanthum odoratum* (1960b) and *Agropyron* repens. Histology of the female gametophyte and caryopsis of *Poa pratensis* and *P. compressa* was well described and pictured in a detailed study by Andersen (1927) who traced the development of these structures from the time of anthesis to seed maturity. Vascular development in the spikelets of Pooideae and Paniceae has been studied by Chandra (1962a,b, 1963). Apart from the works just listed, the near dearth of histological studies was well overcome by Barnard (1955, 1957) in studies on the histogenesis of the inflorescence and flower of *Triticum aestivum, Bambusa arundinacea, Lolium multiflorum, Bromus unioloides, Danthonia setacea, Erharta erecta,* and *Stipa hyalina.*

Barnard compared the histogenesis of glume, lemma, palea, lodicules, and carpel with that of the vegetative bud as described by other workers, particularly Sharman (1945). He concluded that the stamen, lateral spikelet, and flower primordia are homologous with axillary vegetative shoots (cauline structures). The glume, lemma, palea, lodicules, and carpel are homologous to foliar structures. Barnard stated, however, that the carpel is not comparable to a leaf folded along its midrib and bearing ovules along its margin as the classical theory postulates. His interpretation of carpel development was that the gynaeceum may be composed of three and possibly four foliar structures which fuse to form the gynaeceum. Additional evidence for this interpretation was given by Williams (1966) in his study of the physiology of growth of the wheat plant in which interpretation of growth curves suggested that the gynaeceum is composed of several foliar structures fused together. Sharman, however, stated (1960b) that in *Anthoxanthum odoratum* the mode of initiation and early anatomical development of the carpel clearly resembles a single leaf primordium. Further clarification of the number of foliarlike initials involved in the grass flower is therefore dependent on study of other species, and indeed this characteristic may be variable among species. The significant feature is that the carpel is foliar in origin.

Barnard (1957) determined from his studies that there was very little difference in the histology of floral organogenesis in the seven species examined, which represented a reasonable cross section of gramineous types. He therefore concluded that the pattern of floral histogenesis, as found in these seven species, occurs generally throughout the Gramineae, and may be summarized as follows: "The flower in the Gramineae may be regarded as a branch system. The lemma is a bract which subtends the branch system; the palea and lodicules are foliar structures upon its main axis; the stamens represent reduced lateral branches bearing microsporangia; the gynaeceum is composed of fused foliar structures upon the distal portion of the main axis and the ovule is the ultimate reduction of a lateral branch bearing a megasporangium."

The only objection one might make to this interpretation would be to question why the lemma should be referred to as a "bract" rather than a "foliar" structure when it was clearly shown that the lemma is foliar in origin. The lemma also serves a very significant function as a foliar organ when proliferation of the spikelet occurs, as discussed below in the section on vivipary.

Measurement of Flowering

Many workers have recognized the necessity in experimental work concerning the flowering response of having a grading system for measurement of flowering from the earliest through the most advanced stages. Various developmental stage systems have been proposed for the dicotyledons by Lincoln *et al*. (1956), Salisbury (1955a, b, 1969), Takimoto (1955), Borthwick and Cathey (1962), Cathey (1969), Cumming (1969), and Wellensiek (1969). Other systems may be required for particular groups due to the immense variation in flowering habit through the dicotyledonous plants.

In the grasses the general uniform pattern of early inflorescence development allows the use of a stage system based on changes that are readily distinguishable in the transition from vegetative to floral apex and subsequent development. Although Cooper (1956) utilized a system of measurement based on leaf number on the main shoot before the time of floral initiation to determine the changeover from vegetative to reproductive state, this does not give positive evidence of floral development. In evaluation of the degree of flowering response it is usually preferable to note more precisely the stage of floral differentiation, even though more plants may be needed for sampling. Stage systems somewhat similar to those for the dicotyledons have been developed for the grasses by Purvis and Gregory (1937), Rice (1950), Anderson (1952, 1954a), Jeater (1956), Koller *et al*. (1960), and Latting (1966). Stages of differentiation are given numbers, either 0 or 1 denoting the vegetative stage, which progress through a series usually to 10 or 11, the

TABLE 1.

Stage of development	Stage index
Vegetative	0
Elongation: predouble ridge	1
Double ridge: first morphological change	2
Branch or spikelet primordia	3
Differentiation (budding) of spikelet primordia as shown by appearance of glume primordia and budding of spikelet apex	4
Differentiation of florets, indicated by appearance of lemma primordia and floret apices	5
Differentiation of stamens, from first budding to lobed anthers; palea and lodicule primordia appear at this stage	6
Glumes not enclosing, or half enclosing, spikelet, anthers fully lobed, ovaries infolding; preboot stage, just before elongation of the inflorescence	7
Glumes enclosing spikelet; early boot stage, when elongation of the panicle rachis has begun	8
Spikelets expanding above glumes; late boot stage, panicle and sheathing boot leaf elongating above vegetative leaves	9
Open panicle, preanthesis	10
Mature panicle, at anthesis; fertilization, if any	11

final number denoting the stage of the fully emerged inflorescence. The stage system given in Table 1 (adapted from Latting, 1966) may be readily expanded or condensed to fit the needs of the investigator.

Types of Apices

Sharman (1947) has pointed out that the length of the vegetative apex of grasses is fairly constant for species but variable between species, and can best be considered in three groups—short, intermediate, and long—although of course there is actually a complete gradation of types. These groups are separated on the basis of the number of leaf primordia making up the vegetative apex. The short type of apex, as in *Deschampsia caespitosa* (Fig. 1A), consists of two to three leaf primordia and seems to be common in the cereal grasses such as *Avena, Oryza, Saccharum, Secale, Sorghum, Triticum,* and *Zea.* This type remains short throughout the vegetative phase, elongating rapidly at the time of inflorescence initiation. The intermediate apex, as in *Agropyron cristatum* (Fig. 1B) and *Poa alpina* (Fig. 1C), is the most common and consists of five to ten leaf ridges. This type is found in the herbage grasses such as *Agrostis, Festuca, Glyceria, Holcus, Phleum, Phalaris, Poa,* and *Lolium.* Elongation seems to occur just prior to inflorescence initiation. The long type, as in *Cynosurus cristatus* (Fig. 1D,E,F), is found in those species having apices that bear over ten leaf primordia, or ridges, and which may bear up to 30 apparently vegetative ridges with no suggestion of spikelet buds, as in *Lolium multiflorum, Anthoxanthum odoratum,* and *Melica altissima.* There appears to be a continuous elongation and increase in number of ridges up to the time of inflorescence initiation with no very marked elongation just prior to changeover.

Sharman states that both the rate and site of initiation of provascular strands in the apex differ with species and suggests that the length of the apex may be in part dependent on how quickly such strands are initiated and link up with older strands. If vascular development is slow, leaf primordia would tend to stack up at the apex for lack of sufficient substances needed for growth; conversely, if vascular tissue differentiated rapidly, leaf development would in turn proceed at a more rapid rate.

Although apex types are more or less consistent with species, several reports indicate that the length of the apex may be considerably influenced by environmental factors. In *Lolium temulentum,* apex size was smaller and growth rates were lower during winter months than during the long days and higher temperatures of summer months (Rijven and Evans, 1967). In winter rye, short day length and low temperature caused faster growth of the apex,

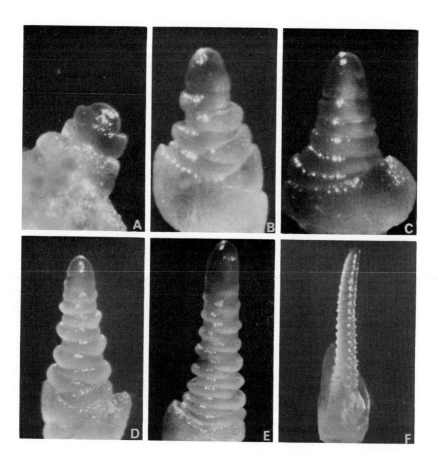

Fɪɢ. 1. A-F. The three types of vegetative apices common in the grasses according to Sharman's classification (Stage 0).

A. Short type, *Deschampsia caespitosa*, Two leaf primordia, or ridges, below the rounded apex (0.15 mm). Tissue below the second leaf primordium consists of basal tissue of leaves which have been removed.

B. Intermediate type, *Agropyron cristatum*. Seven-ridged apex subtended by a basal leaf primordium which partially encloses the two lower ridges (0.45 mm).

C. Intermediate type, *Poa alpina*. Seven-ridged apex (0.45 mm).

D, E, F. Long type, *Cynosurus cristatus*.

D. Twelve leaf primordia, or ridges (0.75 mm).

E. Seventeen leaf primordia (0.97 mm).

F. At least 30 ridges are present, but very faint apically (2.0 mm). Variations in apex length and ridge number commonly occur in the long apex type.

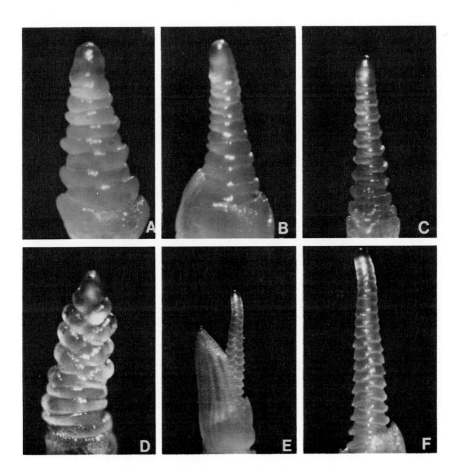

Fig. 2. A-F. Double-ridge and primary branch or spikelet primordia stages, intermediate- and long-type apices. Rounded protuberances in the axils of the ridges are incipient primary branch or spikelet primordia, depending on whether the inflorescence is a panicle or a spike (Stages 2, 3).
A, B. *Trisetum spicatum*, intermediate-type apex, early double-ridge stage.
A. Ten-ridged apex (0.68 mm).
B. Sixteen-ridged apex (1.13 mm).
C. *Cynosurus cristatus*, long-type apex, early double-ridge stage, 24 ridges (1.25 mm).
D, E, F. Spikelet primordia stage. D *Trisetum spicatum*, 12 nodes with spikelet primordia (0.71 mm).
E. *Cynosurus cristatus*. Apex with 38 to 39 ridges with axillary spikelet primordia (2.0 mm). The condition as shown in E, in which the youngest elongating leaf half encloses the floral apex, is usual for this stage of development.
F. *C. cristatus*, apex in E with partially enclosing leaf removed.

Fig. 3. A-D. Differentiation of apical spikelet, glumes, and lemmas. Glume development well advanced on apical spikelets, less so on lower spikelets (glume primordia are saucershaped structures below the apex) (Stages 4, 5).

A. *Deschampsia caespitosa.* The short, thick apex has six nodes (0.60 mm), short-apex type.

B. *Trisetum spicatum.* Apex with 12 nodes (0.82 mm), intermediate-apex type.

C. *Poa arctica.* Apex with 12 nodes (1.02 mm), intermediate type. Glumes of apical spikelet and lemma of its first floret are well differentiated.

D. *Agropyron cristatum.* Apex with 20 nodes (1.25 mm), intermediate type.

also elongation of the apex, and short day length favored leaf development (Purvis, 1934). Cooper (1956) found that after induction of strains of *Lolium perenne* and *L. temulentum* elongation of the apex was limited mainly by temperature. Although length of apex would appear to have no phylogenetic significance and is variable depending on environmental conditions, there is still ample evidence to assume that there is a general average number of leaf primordia for each species.

Morphology

The earliest morphological change in the grass apex indicating transition from vegetative to flowering state is elongation of the apex and the appearance of swelling protuberances in the axils of the leaf primordia (Fig. 2A,B, C). During their early development these protuberances, or floral primordia, plus their subtending leaf primordia give the general appearance of a double ridge at each incipient node, hence the common term "double ridge" for this stage of differentiation. The first double ridges appear in the midregion of the apex, with later protuberances appearing both distally and proximally. As M. W. Evans and Grover (1940) noted, "The nascent inflorescence presents the anomaly of having protuberances originating in acropetal succession in the distal region of the meristematic cylinder and at the same time in basipetal succession in the proximal region." The axillary protuberances of the double-ridge stage become further differentiated into branch or spikelet primordia depending on whether the inflorescence is a panicle or a spike (Fig. 2D,E,F).

Double-ridge increment continues apically until the apical meristem differentiates glume primordia and forms a spikelet (Fig. 3). With the differentiation of the apical spikelet the number of nodes of the inflorescence is determined. In the later primary branch stage, secondary lateral branch primordia arise on each side of the primary branches. Spikelet differentiation continues from the branch primordia, still advancing distally and proximally from the upper midregion of the inflorescence.

Within the spikelet, however, floret differentiation occurs acropetally (Fig. 4). The flat ridges of the lemmas appear, each subtending its floret bud. The palea is next initiated on the inner side of the floret apex and stamen initials arise as rounded buds on the surface of the floret apex, entirely different in appearance from the leaf-ridge, or foliar, aspect of the glumes, lemma, and palea. As the anthers become bilobed and the lobes bilocular, the floret apex develops differentially into an infolding ovary surrounding the differentiating ovule (Fig. 5). The ovary appears dimpled at this stage,

FIG. 4. A-H. Apical spikelet differentiation, anther budding and floret development (Stages 5, 6).

then two conical protuberances appear on the upper surface and later develop into the stigmas. Lodicules develop at the base of the ovary at the same time stamens are initiated.

At the preboot stage, elongation of the axis has begun (Fig. 5). Development of apical and midlevel spikelets and primary branch spikelets is advanced over that of lower and basal spikelets and secondary branch spikelets. All stages of floret differentiation may be found on the inflorescence. Anthers of upper florets are lobed, those of lower florets budding around the floral apex. Ovaries are infolding or tipped with stigma primordia. The glumes expand upward around the lower portion of the spikelets.

During boot stage, further elongation of the panicle axis takes place concurrently with rapid expansion of the glumes over the spikelet (Fig. 6). In those species that have awned lemmas, the awns, which are greatly advanced over the lemmas, continue their elongation followed by that of the lemmas. Stigmas elongate and become feathery in appearance. Anthers, green at this stage, become yellow as pollen ripens. Filaments of the stamens do not elongate until a very late stage, just before anthesis. During late boot stage and panicle emergence from the boot leaf, glume expansion ceases, florets expand above them and, at anthesis, lodicules swell, forcing apart the lemma and palea, and the stamen filaments elongate. Anthers become exserted and stigmas spread apart. Florets may or may not become fertilized at this time.

In the Festucoid grasses one or more apical florets in each spikelet become

FIG. 4
A-D. *Poa arctica*. A. Lemmas and floret buds of apical spikelet and glumes are becoming well differentiated; those of lower spikelets are less advanced (0.75 mm panicle).
B. Apical spikelet and next two lateral spikelets from A. Saucershaped glumes are below flat lemma ridges of the apical spikelet.
C. Apical spikelet with lateral spikelets from a 0.95 mm panicle. Three floret buds of the apical spikelet appear as rounded protuberances in the axils of the lemmas above the saucershaped glumes.
D. Panicle (1.70 mm) with small, rounded anthers budding on the florets of the apical spikelet.
E, F. *Trisetum spicatum* inflorescences with prominent anther buds on distal florets (E, 1.75 mm panicle; F, 1.55 mm panicle).
G. *Poa arctica*. Panicle with nine ridges, anther buds on distal florets (2.0 mm). As floral development proceeds, the ridges form the nodal regions of the inflorescence.
H. Primary (left) and secondary (right) spikelets from midlevel of panicle in G. Primary spikelet has elongating glumes. Its basal floret has prominent anther buds, but anther buds have not yet arisen on the next distal floret which appears as a rounded protuberance in the axil of the flat lemma. On the spikelet at right, basal glumes and two lemmas with axillary floret buds are obvious. Lemma and floret bud of the next distal floret appear as slight bulges on upper left of apical dome.

FIG. 5. A-H. Preboot stage. Anthers bilobed to bilocular, spikelets and rachillae beginning elongation. All are *Poa arctica* (Stages 6, 7).

aborted and remain as apical rudiments (Fig. 8A). During early differentiation and development, however, the most distal florets have the complete complement of floral parts, all normal in every respect, except that
there is a gradual decrease in overall floret size from the most proximal floret
in the spikelet to the most distal. Apparently the genetic response to the
flowering stimulus which permits the differentiation of a larger number of
florets than the number that actually matures is still further evidence of the
trend toward floral reduction in the grass family.

Overwintering of Initiated Inflorescences

Although flowering in most grasses is seasonal, there is a growing number
of reports of grasses that have evidently adapted to the shorter season of

---

FIG. 5

A. Panicle with 10 nodes, or ridges (1.87 mm). Upper spikelets with anthers budding around
floret apex, lower spikelets less advanced.
B. Panicle with 11–12 nodes (2.31 mm). Anthers becoming bilobed in distal spikelets, budding
in proximal spikelets. Secondary branch, or rachilla, primordia show spikelet development
to glume and floret stage.
C. Panicle (2.30 mm) with well-differentiated anthers distally, anthers budding on proximal
spikelets. Elongation of internodes and panicle rachillae is just beginning.
D. Panicle with at least eight nodes (3.45 mm) at slightly more advanced stage of differentia-
tion than in B and C. All spikelets have sexual florets, many with bilobed anthers and infolding
ovaries. Glumes are expanding around the florets. Panicle and branch axes have begun
elongating toward boot stage.
E. Basal spikelets from panicle in D. Anther lobing in basal florets, budding in second florets.
Primordia of third and fourth florets are visible below the spikelet apices.
F. Apical spikelet from panicle in D. Anthers lobed in lower three florets, budding on fourth.
Ovary infolded, or dimpled, on basal floret at left. Stigmas later arise from the distal initials
on either side of the infolding ovary. Lemmas of basal, second, and third florets appear as
flat ridges below the anthers. The two glumes appear tightly appressed against the basal
portion of the spikelet. Apical and other distal spikelets are always more advanced than basal
spikelets, as in E.
G. Panicle with at least nine nodes (4.50 mm). Preboot stage, just prior to elongation and
emergence from boot leaf. All spikelets are sexual, that is, with florets at least at the anther
bud stage.
H. Basal spikelet (0.67 mm) from panicle in G. Other spikelets are in left and right background.
Glumes and branch axes are elongating; anthers are deeply bilobed on basal and second
florets, and ovaries are deeply infolded. Lemma of second floret appears as flat ridge below the
anthers. Lobed anthers of third floret are prominent at upper left of the spikelet, and the fourth
floret appears as a small protuberance on the right and just below the apex.

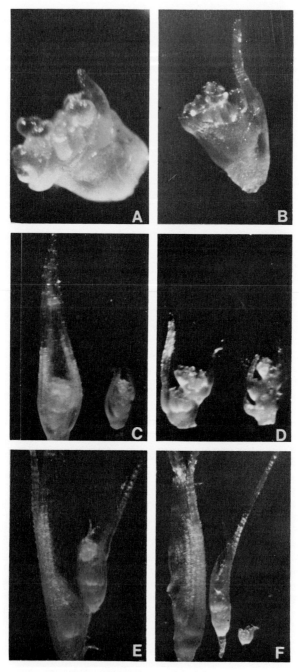

FIG. 6

growth in high altitudes or latitudes by initiating inflorescences in autumn which then overwinter without apparent reversion and complete their floral development the following spring.

In New Zealand snow tussock species of *Chionochloa* flowering occurs at irregular intervals of up to five years (Mark, 1965a,b,d, 1969). Mark found that in experiments conducted with *Chionochloa rigida* flowering is controlled by the combined effects of temperature and day length exceeding 14 hours, plus the reserves of the plant. At the experimental sites, subfreezing temperatures occur throughout the year. The high-temperature effect is cumulative during the 3-month inductive period and results in increased intensity of flowering with increased duration of high temperatures. Floral induction occurs only during warm summers and long days; inflorescences are initiated during autumn but do not actually emerge until the following summer. Thus there is a delay of 12 months between induction and anthesis. Inflorescence development appears to be temperature dependent but insensitive to day length, unlike that in many other long-day grasses, although inflorescence height is significantly increased with long days. Mark also demonstrated (1968) that autumn initiation and overwintering of the partially developed inflorescence occurs in *Chionochloa crassiussula, C.*

FIG. 6. A-F. Examples of spikelet development at preboot and boot stage in *Trisetum spicatum*, a species with awned lemmas (Stages 7, 8).

A. Spikelet from 3.5-mm preboot stage panicle. Awned lemma of basal floret, which has bilobed, bilocular anthers, extends above the two subtending glumes. Second floret at upper left has budding anthers above saucershaped lemma with its awn tip just appearing. Third floret, at right just below spikelet apex, has differentiating lemma (spikelet apex is the elongate dome seen at top left center of spikelet).

B. Spikelet from 9.28-mm early boot-stage panicle. The concave, U-shaped structure just above the large bilobed, bilocular anthers of the basal floret is the pistil with developing stigmas. Awn development of basal floret greatly exceeds that of the lemma.

C. Two spikelets from 24-mm boot-stage emerging panicle illustrating rapid glume and awn elongation at this stage and advanced development of apical over basal spikelet. Apical spikelet (3.0 mm) glumes (left) extending far beyond florets. Basal spikelet (1.0 mm) glumes (right) just enclosing florets. Glumes of both are almost transparent.

D. Same two spikelets as in C, with glumes removed. Both have florets with lobed anthers. Awn development is greatly advanced over that of lemmas. Apical spikelet on left (0.45 mm), basal spikelet on right (0.40 mm).

E. Apical spikelet (6.0 mm) from boot-stage emergent panicle. Glumes have been removed. Rate of lemma elongation in relation to that of glume elongation is greatly increased at this stage.

F. Basal, second, and third (from left to right) florets from spikelet in E. Only the base of the awn of the basal floret is shown; awn of second floret is shown almost entirely. Note that floret development within the spikelet proceeds from basal to apical whereas in the panicle as a whole, floral development proceeds from the more distal portion toward the base.

flavescens and *C. oreophila*. In a study of ecotypes (1965c) he found that differential flowering followed reciprocal transplanting of *C. crassiussula, C. flavescens*, and *C. rigida*, indicating ecotypic differentiation in the temperature control.

A utumn initiation is also common in Alaskan grasses as reported by Hodgson (1966). Thirteen species of Alaskan grasses collected from various parts of the state and grown in nurseries at Palmer, Alaska, initiated inflorescences in autumn; the partially developed inflorescences overwintered with little injury and completed development in the spring. The thirteen species were *Bromus pumpellianus, Poa alpigena, P. pratensis, P. arctica, Festuca rubra, Agropyron sericeum, Elymus mollis, E. innovatus, E. sibiricus, Hordeum jubatum, Deschampsia caespitosa, Hierochloe odoratum*, and *H. alpina*. As Hodgson pointed out, very high levels of cold resistance must accompany autumn initiation in these northern grasses because the developing floral structures are exposed to very severe temperatures. He suggested that induction, initiation, and partial floral development in autumn appear to be normal behavior for the majority of Alaskan grasses.

In addition to the above cool-season grasses Elliott (1967a) in a study made in the Peace River region of Alberta, Canada, found that in tillers of Russian wildrye that had previously overwintered in the vegetative stage floral initiation occurred in early autumn with overwintering of floral primordia and subsequent development the following spring, thus differing from most other cultivated species.

Autumn initiation also has been noted in two warm-season grasses. Youngner (1961a) reported that *Digitaria sanguinalis*, normally an annual, survives through the winter in southern California by means of new shoots arising from the rooted nodes of old plants. In such overwintering plants, flowers and seed were produced in early spring, indicating that many of the inflorescences had been initiated and partially developed the previous season. Further development, prevented by the cool winter weather, was resumed as temperatures increased in the spring. The other warm-season grass, *Bouteloua gracilis*, was found to have initiated inflorescences in autumn in Kansas that successfully overwintered in an immature stage and completed development the following spring (Launchbaugh and Hackerott, 1969).

Floral Inhibition

The normal developmental sequence of flowering as described previously occurs under optimal environmental conditions for floral differentiation. The prime environmental factors involved are temperature and photoperiod, acting either independently or in unison on the differentiating apex. As discussed in the chapter on floral induction by Dr. Sachs, the temperature and/or day-length requirements for floral differentiation may be the same as for induction or may be entirely different.

The persistence of induction, either by photoperiod or vernalization, is quite variable among species. If the inductive stimulus is slight, reversal or lowered flowering may result. It is therefore apparent that less than optimal environmental conditions may cause a shift in quantitative balance from the floral-promoting substance/s toward the vegetative-promoting, or floral-inhibiting, substance/s which results in decrease in the flowering response or reversion to the vegetative condition. These are expressed throughout the flowering period by many irregularities of development.

Some examples ot temperature and/or day-length inhibition on early floral differentiation and development in several species of Festucoid Arctic–Alpine grasses are shown in Fig. 7. These grasses are normally sexually reproductive; but under environmental conditions that are marginal for full sexual reproduction, they become viviparous, producing vegetative proliferations or propagules in place of sexual spikelets.

In the early stages of the double-ridge and primary branch differentiation, the floral apices may be distorted and depressed (Fig. 7A); the spikelet or branch primordia in the axils of the leaf ridges may be transformed into structures that are typically vegetative, appearing as a lateral vegetative apical meristem with leaf primordia (Fig. 7B,C); or the leaf ridges may develop into leafy structures at the expense of floral primordia development (Fig. 7D,E,F). Upper portions of the apex may continue floral differentiation, even with the development of stamen buds, while at the lower nodes floral primordia revert to a vegetative nature (Fig, 7G,H,I).

Other forms of floral inhibition in the grasses may be expressed by abortion of the whole inflorescence during elongation, throughout the boot stage, and even after emergence of the panicle or spike; by fusion of floral parts; by sterility of sexual florets; and by proliferation of spikelets, in which vegetative propagules are formed in place of spikelets, as discussed below under "Vivipary."

In normal floral development the proximal spikelets of the inflorescence are always less advanced than the distal, and in many species floral primordia never appear in the axils of the most proximal leaf primordia or ridges. When reversion occurs, the floral primordia or leaf ridges in the lower portion of the floral apex are always those that are influenced by the shift toward the vegetative condition. It would therefore appear that the floral stimulus is most active apically.

It has been reported by a number of workers that gibberellins play some as yet unknown role in reversions to the vegetative state at very early stages

FIG. 7

of floral differentiation. Koller *et al.* (1960) found that gibberellic acid had distinct morphogenic effects on the stem apices of three nonvernalized grasses, *Hordeum vulgare* var. "Kentucky," *Hordeum bulbosum*, and *Secale cereale* var. "Winter Petkus." Gibberellic acid caused the initiation of double ridges under both short- and long-day conditions, but these axillary protuberances differentiated into vegetative apices in lateral positions on the floral apex. In the *Hordeum* species distinct spikelet primordia were developed distally, while proximal lateral primordia developed into vegetative apices on the basal portion of the apex. In *Secale* no further development from the double ridge stage occurred distally, but vegetative lateral apices developed basally. In both *Hordeum* and *Secale* normal floral apices occurred, although more advanced, well-developed inflorescences were found more frequently in *Hordeum* than in *Secale*.

Caso *et al.* (1960) reported that in *Secale* the effect of gibberellic acid when applied at the third- to fifth-leaf stage was quite different than when it was applied at the ninth- to tenth-leaf stage. In the former many abnormalities were found such as formation of subsidiary "ears" from basal primordia and leafy outgrowths below the spikelets. However, when the plants were treated

---

FIG. 7. A-I. Inhibition of early floral differentiation by adverse environmental conditions. A. *Cynosurus cristatus*. 28-ridged apex (1.45 mm), early double-ridge stage, apical distortion. 50°SD.

B. *Poa alpina*. Eleven-ridged apex (0.75 mm). Double ridges above, lateral branch primordia below transformed into vegetative apices having two to five ridges. 50°SD, C-I *Trisetum-spicatum*.

C. Twelve-ridged apex (0.60 mm), double-ridge stage. Ridges are wide, leaflike. Branch primordium at lower left has become transformed into a typically vegetative apex. 50°SD.

D. Thirteen-ridged apex (0.85 mm), branch primordia stage. Branch primordia are well developed distally, but have widened into leafy appendages proximally. 50°SD.

E. Eight-ridged panicle (0.68 mm). All lateral branch primordia and the apical spikelet have become definitely vegetative, each with several ridges as in a typical vegetative apex. Lower two panicle ridges have expanded, partially enclosing the panicle and becoming leaflike. 50°SD.

F. Thirteen-ridged apex with lateral branch primordia and early spikelet differentiation (1.50 mm). Ridges are becoming leafy in appearance. 60°LD.

G. Nine-ridged panicle (1.0 mm). Apical spikelet has differentiated anthers, but lateral spikelets exhibit widening ridgelike primordia. Lower ridges are leafy and expanding above the lateral branches. 50°SD.

H. Nine-ridged panicle (0.90 mm). Apical spikelet with large glumes, two florets, and apex. Spikelet at lower left of apical spikelet has floret with lobed anthers. Remaining lateral spikelets have differentiated glumes, but floret differentiation is weak. Basal branch primordia resemble ridged vegetative apices. 50°SD.

I. Panicle with at least 15 nodes (1.30 mm), spikelet differentiation stage. Apical spikelet has well-developed glumes, lemma and floret buds of basal floret at upper right; second floret budding on left flank of apex. Lateral spikelets and branch primordia lag in floral differentiation, exhibit a vegetative aspect. Panicle is centrally compressed. 50° LD.

at the ninth- to tenth-leaf stage, ears appeared free of morphological abnormalities. Purvis (1960) reported quite similar results in treatment of unvernalized Petkus winter rye with gibberellic acid. He also found that in plants treated at the fifth-leaf stage, abnormalities occurred such as floral apices with lateral subsidiary ears, leafy outgrowths below the spikelets, and shortening or distortion of the peduncle, but at the ninth-leaf stage, floral apices were free from morphological abnormalities.

James and Lund (1965) found that when unvernalized Wong winter barley was treated at early stages of growth with gibberellin, floral primordia were initiated 3–4 weeks earlier than in control plants, but developed into either precocious anthers or supernumerary spikes. Allen *et al.* (1959) reported spike emergence up to 10 days earlier in three of six winter wheat varieties (*Triticum aestivum*) treated with gibberellic acid. In a quantitative study of endogenous substances Nicholls and May (1964) found that for barley plants (*Hordeum distichon*) grown under continuous illumination, from the time double ridges first appeared until shortly before ear emergence, the highest concentration of gibberellinlike substances coincided with the initiation of cell division in the pith region, while at the same time stamen initials first appeared and internode elongation of the inflorescence began. Both Purvis and Caso *et al.* concluded from their findings that gibberellic acid apparently is not directly involved in the induction of flowering in unvernalized Petkus winter rye but does have an accelerating effect on stem extension during floral initiation.

It would therefore appear that gibberellins activate axillary meristem activity and increase the tendency toward staminate development but are not directly involved in floral differentiation. However, even though the action of gibberellins stimulates development of leaf ridges and lateral vegetative apices on the floral apex, their action in stimulating activity at the axillary site from which the floral primordium is initiated and in the promotion of anther differentiation suggests that their role is not simply confined to cell elongation and vegetative development.

Effects of 2, 4-D on floral development have been reported by Anderson (1954b) among others. When barley plants were sprayed with 2,4-D during the early stages of floral differentiation, floral primordia were inhibited. Some leaf ridges apparently developed into nodal rings, from which spikelets developed irregularly about 3 weeks after spraying was discontinued, but in time the spikelets achieved flowering and fertilization as in uninjured tissue. The effect of 2,4-D therefore seems to be temporary repression of the flowering capacity and enlargement of the leaf primordia on the floral apex.

An interesting pathological aspect has been reported by Casady (1969). In sorghum, panicle proliferation is caused by head smut, *Sphacelotheca reilana*, and by loose kernel smut, *Sphacelotheca cruenta*. Casady found that when plants of *Sorghum bicolor* were inoculated with the head smut organism, proliferated spikelets were produced and could be grown to normal mature plants in the field except that all had symptoms of head smut infection. This leads one to suspect that the smut organism produces, or causes to be produced, some substance that inhibits the flowering stimulus or promotes the vegetative stimulus and results in proliferation.

Even though full floret development occurs in which stamens and pistil are fully differentiated, floral inhibition may be manifested by many flowering irregularities. Sharman (1944, 1947, 1967) found many naturally occurring "abnormalities" in the inflorescence of *Triticum aestivum* which he attributed to genetic factors operating under the influence of photoperiod and perhaps temperature. These "abnormalities" consisted of the development of the following structures: (1) leaf primordia subtending lower spikelets; (2) growth of a lateral bud into a miniature side head; (3) "miracle" heads, in which many of the lowest floral primordia grow out into miniature side heads —this type of development seems to arise only in tetraploid wheats or material derived from crosses of tetraploids and hexaploids, but the greatest development of the side heads occurs under short day lengths; (4) twin lateral spikelets in place of the usual single one, a condition that appears more frequently in certain lines or cultivars, which may be aneuploids. Other features were spikelets with unusually long rachillas, and forked, or Y-shaped heads, caused by a true bifurcation of the axis. Sharman also noted the occurrence of forked inflorescences in *Agropyron, Lolium, Phleum,* and *Triticum*. Bonnett (1966) reported the occurrence of supernumerary spike development in wheat which was thought to be the result of short day length and low temperature.

Other evidence for floral inhibition has been reported by Clements and Awada (1960). In field studies of sugarcane in Hawaii 70% of the canes in the field initiated inflorescences in the September–October period, but in November–December only 20% produced tassels. In January, however, different "monstrosities" began to appear in the field, consisting primarily of "multiple top," a condition in which numerous vegetative shoots develop from the initiated inflorescence. One or more of these shoots later reestablish normal cane growth, or, in many cases, the shoot buds remain dormant, but if they are planted they develop into normal vegetative shoots.

In support of the findings of Clements and Awada, Moore (1969) found that in controlled environmental experiments with sugarcane, after inflorescence development has begun, the application of noninductive photoperiods to plants at various stages of development leads to several types of altered vegetative structures. These include (1) apparently normal vegetative plants except for the persistence of malformed internodes; (2) multiple-leafed plants; and (3) multiple-topped plants. Tanimoto (1968) reported that in sugarcane the rate of development of the flower buds, which are initiated within a 10-day period from about September 7, and the final emergence of the tassels are dependent on the strength of the flowering stimulus; clusters of shoots instead of stalks were produced when the flowering stimulus was weak.

Temperature appears to be the most influential factor involved in sterility of sexual florets, as shown by Leighty and Sando (1924), Stephens and Quinby (1933), Pope (1943), Hovin (1957), Youngner (1961b), L. T. Evans (1964), and Maun *et al.* (1969).

Rate of Inflorescence Development

The rate of inflorescence development is particularly subject to the effects of day length and temperature, but in most grasses the time from inflorescence initiation to earing in the field falls in the range of 25 to 70 days (L. T. Evans, 1964). Continued favorable photoinduction and optimal temperature –day-length conditions result in acceleration of the rate of development toward mature reproductive structures and in initiation of a larger number of flowers and inflorescences, as reported by many workers, and may differ considerably with species (Lang, 1965). The vernalization effect, however, may be reversible by higher temperatures, as in Petkus winter rye and other winter cereals, and results in decreased flowering response.

The application of knowledge of environmental cycles has resulted in significantly greater production of forage and seed crops. Elliott (1967b), by determining the light and temperature requirements for each stage of development in creeping red fescue, bromegrass, and intermediate wheatgrass, found that these grasses could be grown through one complete life cycle in eight months as compared to 24 months for field-grown plants. In the Peace River region of Alberta, Canada, where his studies were conducted, the creeping red fescue annual seed production is 20 million pounds, so that acceleration of the life cycle is therefore very significant in this crop. In addition Elliott found that time and rate of nitrogen application significantly affected production because of the "very specific requirements for nitrogen" during the period of floral initiation and he recommended that seed growers apply supplemental nitrogen just prior to this stage. The application of nitrogen is a common practice for grass seed production and its effect on yield has been demonstrated for many species; as noted by Wilson (1959) and L. T. Evans (1964) the time of application influences earlier floral initiation and ear emergence and increases the number of inflorescences.

Cooper (1960) also reported that acceleration of flowering can be attained by the use of controlled environmental conditions in *Lolium multiflorum* and *Bromus inermis*, which can be made to give two generations per year, and in oats, which can be made to produce four generations per year. Cooper stated that after the photoperiodic threshold is reached, rate of inflorescence development is limited mainly by temperature.

Vivipary

Viviparous grasses undergo the same sequence of floral induction, initiation, and development as other grasses, but at some time during the developmental phase the factors initiating the flowering response may be nullified or inhibited, resulting in the proliferation of vegetative bulbils or propagules within the grass spikelet.

Terminology concerning "vivipary" and "proliferate" is confused and ambiguous. Linnaeus (1737, 1759) first gave the name of "vivipary" to the phenomenon in which bulbils are formed in the floral region of plants, particularly those belonging to the grass and lily families. Webster (1967) gives several definitions for both terms and their derivatives, in which "vivipary" may refer to either (1) the development of vegetative shoots among the reproductive organs of a plant, or (2) the germination of a seed while still attached to the mother plant, as in the mangrove; "proliferate" may refer to reproduction either (1) from some part of the inflorescence, or (2) from a vegetative organ. Interpretation of the terminology, primarily for the grasses, has been discussed at length (Mattfeld, 1920; Sernander, 1927; Arber, 1934; Gustafsson, 1946; Wycherley, 1953; Youngner, 1960; Barnard, 1964; Latting, 1966; Nygren, 1967). It would appear that the preponderance of evidence as to the meaning of the terms from these discussions and from actual usage in the literature indicates that the definitions as set forth under (1) of both terms are applicable to the grasses and are in common use.

"Vivipary" and its derivatives are used in the ecological sense and describe an apomictic form of reproduction. "Proliferate" and its derivatives are used in a morphological and physiological sense and describe the manifestations of vivipary. These interpretations are followed herein.

In normal sexual inflorescences of Festucoid grasses the apical meristems of spikelets cease development and one to several of the distal florets of the spikelet become dry rudiments while the proximal florets are fully reproductive (Fig. 8A). When proliferation occurs, floret development is arrested, usually during or after emergence of the inflorescence and anthesis. When partial proliferation occurs, the lower florets within a spikelet may be fully sexual and fertilization may take place while the lemmas of the distal florets become elongate (Fig. 8B). In a fully proliferated spikelet the lemmas of all the florets elongate to become miniature leaves, each consisting of sheath, ligule, and blade, and the apical meristem continues its growth, producing leaflike lemmas in place of the uppermost florets (Fig. 8C). No sexual parts are present, having become completely aborted (Latting, 1966). The proliferated spikelets form propagules which, if the inflorescence droops so that they come in contact with the soil, will initiate roots and under favorable conditions develop into normal plants. If they do not make contact with the soil, they dry on the plant and may become dormant for a short period; but they can later be planted and grown to maturity.

Vivipary is common in the Festucoid grasses (Gustafsson, 1946; Hitchcock, 1951; Wycherley, 1953). It has been particularly well studied in *Deschampsia, Festuca*, and *Poa*, and in all three genera the tendency of vivipary increases with the chromosome number (Nygren 1949, 1967; Flovik,

Fɪɢ. 8. A-C. Comparison of sexual, partially proliferated, and completely proliferated spikelets of *Poa bulbosa.*

A. Fully sexual spikelet with seven florets above the glumes. Anthers have dehisced and fertilization taken place. Apical floret is rudimentary (7 mm).

B. Partially proliferated spikelet from which the glumes have been removed. Lower florets are sexual, anthers exserted, dehisced and drying. Upper florets are proliferated; lemma of apical floret is leaflike (12 mm).

C. Fully proliferated spikelet in which lower lemmas are elongate and thickened basally. Upper lemmas have differentiated into typical leaf characteristics of sheath, ligule, and blade. The apical leaflike lemma encloses a typical vegetative primordium (20 mm).

1938; Heyn, 1962; Turesson, 1926). A diploid viviparous grass was reported, however, in 1952, by Skalinska who described a viviparous *Poa alpina* ($2n = 14$) which was restricted to the Tatra district of Poland.

In certain Arctic-Alpine grasses, such as *Festuca prolifera, F. vivipara, Poa alpina* var. *vivipara, P. bulbosa*, and *Deschampsia alpina*, proliferation is constant in occurrence (Gustafsson, 1946). However, the shift to vivipary as a usual method of reproduction is not irreversible. Schwarzenbach (1956, reported that normally viviparous biotypes of *Poa alpina* become non-viviparous when cultivated in Switzerland, and Turesson (1926) noted that some types of *Festuca ovina* classed as wholly viviparous would under certain conditions late in the season produce normal flowers and seed.

There are many accounts of normally sexually reproductive grasses of temperate zones that exhibit vivipary when flowering, particularly during the short days and cool temperatures of early autumn. However, Lawrence (1945) and Nygren (1949) were among the first to test experimentally the expression of vivipary by exposing several biotypes to different environments. Lawrence transplanted originally nonviviparous Swedish and Finnish biotypes of *Deschampsia caespitosa* to California where they became viviparous. Nygren subjected Norwegian and Swedish biotypes of *D. caespitosa* to artificial 8-hr day lengths and found that the northernmost biotype became viviparous. He concluded that, "Everything speaks in favor of different hormones and the moment of their action being genetically fixed and combined with a special life rhythm. Disturbances of this normal rhythm will, depending on their degree, cause irregular meiosis, diplospory, apospory, or vivipary."

Youngner (1960) was able to control the expression of vivipary in *Poa bulbosa* by varying the photoperiod and temperature conditions after vernalization. Although *P. bulbosa* has been introduced from the Middle East into North America where it reproduces primarily by propagules, in its native habitat reproduction is chiefly sexual. Youngner found that in several strains of *P. bulbosa* originating in the Middle East, full sexual reproduction could be promoted by long day length and high temperature, whereas full proliferation of spikelets was promoted by short day length and low temperature. Mixed vegetative and sexual spikelets in the panicles were produced when low temperatures were combined with long day lengths or high temperatures were combined with short day lengths (as in Fig. 8).

Nygren and Almgård (1962) verified Youngner's findings that the expression of vivipary is dependent on photoperiod and temperature. In *Poa bulbosa, P. alpina, P. Chaixii*, and in hybrids of *P. Chaixii* × *P. longifolia* and *P. longifolia* × *P. pratensis*, they determined that short day length and moderate temperature promoted proliferation of spikelets, whereas long day length and higher temperatures promoted sexual reproduction.

In controlled environmental studies of developmental morphology and the expression of vivipary in Arctic-Alpine grasses, Latting (1966) found that varying responses resulted among the several ecotypes and species used experimentally. Plants were subjected to 50° F, 60° F, and 50° F night to 70° F plus day temperatures in combination with either 8-hour or 16-hour photoperiods. Of two ecotypes of *Trisetum spicatum*, the Wyoming ecotype produced only sexual spikelets and flowered only at 50° F temperatures, but the Alaskan ecotype produced both sexual and proliferated panicles in all temperature-day-length combinations, and the intensity of proliferation was greatest under short day lengths and increased with temperature. This is more fully discussed below.

Poa arctica, an ecotype native to Canada, received vernalization but no long-day pretreatment and initiated floral primordia in all treatments. Under short day lengths, inflorescences attained the level of preboot stage differentiation with completely sexual florets; but there was no further elongation and flowering, indicating a requirement for long day lengths for full flowering, which did occur under the long day treatments. There was some proliferation in the high temperature long-day treatment.

Ecotypes of *Cynosurus cristatus*, obtained from England and Finland, produced sexual spikes under 50° F long-day length treatments and both proliferated and sexual spikelets under the high temperature long-day treatments. Proliferation in the plants under these treatments was attributed to the very high temperatures (over 90° F at times) that occurred during treatment. A greater degree of proliferation occurred in the ecotype from Finland than in the one from England. No flowering occurred in plants under short days. All ecotypes of *C. cristatus* received vernalization, but no long-day pretreatment, therefore long day-lengths are apparently required for full development and emergence of the inflorescence. These results are in agreement with Wycherley's findings (1952) that long days may be essential for inflorescence emergence. Wycherley also reported that *C. cristatus* produced proliferated spikelets under short day lengths. In his experiments when plants with proliferated spikelets still attached were placed in continuous light, the proliferated spikelets produced secondary inflorescences. However, propagules that had been removed from the mother plant, rooted, and placed in continuous light did not flower, although detached propagules that had first been exposed to cold temperatures for three months flowered after one month in continuous light. Wycherley concluded that the factor lacking in the detached proliferated plantlets but present in the parent plant was produced by vernalization. L. T. Evans (1960) also worked with *C. cristatus* and reported that the degree of proliferation was directly related to the number of long days under which the floral stimulus was induced.

These results indicate that in these Arctic-Alpine grasses sexual reproduction is favored by low temperatures and long day lengths, and proliferation is more intense under short day lengths but increases within either short days or long days under excessively high temperatures.

The varying morphological expressions of the intensities in which proliferation occurs were reported by many early workers as discussed by Philipson (1934). Their descriptions show a wide variation in the morphological expression of vivipary. Philipson's study was undertaken with the intent to establish the homology of the lemma, excluding awn, if present, to the sheath, ligule, and blade of the vegetative leaf. Because of the many variations in expression of vivipary generally, he chose proliferous material from *Deschampsia caespitosa* and *Dactylis glomerata* as a tool to trace the morphological transition from lemma to leaf. He showed that the lemma is a modified leaf, with the potential of developing into a typical leaf consisting of sheath, ligule, and blade; and he found that when the lemma elongated, growth was renewed in the central zone of the lemma, producing ligule and blade. Growth of the awn was greatly reduced or absent as the lemmas became more leaflike. Philipson thereby established the homology of the lemma to the leaf. He also reported that the lemmas are the only floral parts that develop into leaves; the other floral parts retain their characteristic morphological aspect.

One other anatomical study of change in the lemma at a late stage of differentiation has been reported by Yagil (1965) on Nepal, or hooded barley (*Hordeum vulgare*). In this variety the lemmas terminate in a trifurcated structure called a "hood." The center lobe is an accessory floret with stamens and pistil but usually infertile. Yagil reported that a single-gene effect was involved by which a meristematic region in the central portion of the lemma was activated at a late stage in floret development with the subsequent production of a supernumerary floret. If short day lengths or low temperatures were applied just prior to and during the initiation and formation of the supernumerary floret from the lemma meristem, the expression of the genetic factor was weakened or almost canceled and resulted in the hooded structure becoming elevated as an awn instead of a supernumerary floret. This is further evidence of the existence of the intercalary meristem in the lemma and the effect of environmental and genetic interaction.

Wycherley (1953) in a taxonomic study of viviparous races in British grasses, noted in comparing *Deschampsia caespitosa* var. *pseudoalpina* with *D. alpina* that the tendency of the awn to become longer, more clearly distinguished, and inserted at a lower level on the lemma increased directly as the flower-bearing tendency increased. He could not completely separate the two species morphologically, noting that transitional forms existed, characterized by differences in lemma and awn. Neither could he separate them cytologically. However, he maintained them as distinct taxa because of the differences in ecological range. Taxonomic classification of these species, as well as other species complexes in which proliferation occurs, is confused due to the varying intensity of proliferation reported at different times in the different forms.

Reduction and disappearance of the awn, concomitantly with elongation of the lemma, are distinctive features of proliferous development when awned lemmas are involved. In the controlled environment experiments with *Trisetum spicatum*, a day-neutral Alpine grass of North America, it was found (Latting, 1966) that plants which were exposed to an 8-hr photoperiod either at a constant temperature of 50°F or a diurnal temperature of 50°F night to 70°F plus day produced both sexual and proliferated spikelets, but the intensity and quantity of proliferation was much greater in those plants subject to the high-day-temperature treatment. As the lemma became more vegetative, or proliferous, awn development was reduced. When the lemma was completely leaflike, no awn development was morphologically apparent. In *T. spicatum* during early floret differentiation, awn development and elongation is greatly advanced over that of the lemma, as shown earlier in Fig. 6, although during the late boot stage and panicle emergence, its growth rate falls behind as the lemma elongates until both lemma and awn attain their normal mature size in the sexual spikelet. In the proliferated spikelet this early differentiation of awn and lemma proceeds in a similar manner, but in the later stages of development, with more rapid and greater elongation of the lemma, awn development may cease completely so that it appears as a rudiment, if at all, in the mature proliferated lemma.

It is apparent from findings as discussed above that there are two meristems in the grass spikelet which are involved in the shift toward the vegetative condition–the apical meristem of the spikelet and the intercalary meristem of the lemma. No other floral parts are morphologically involved in proliferation. These two meristems become reactivated by the controlling genetic system in response to certain environmental influences.

These instances provide evidence that the different intensities of proliferation are influenced by the intensity of the environmental effect, countered or enhanced by the strength of the inherent tendency toward sexuality or proliferation. The expression of vivipary may be attributed to the influence of photoperiod and/or temperature which may be decisive in controlling the production of inflorescences that are predominantly sexual or predominantly vegetative.

Vivipary therefore has a significant function in the Gramineae. In those environments adverse to sexual reproduction, vivipary allows the maintenance of the species and accelerates reproduction. In this manner such grasses are enabled to exist under extremes of environmental conditions which they possibly could not otherwise endure.

Conclusion

The flowering response in grasses as expressed by degree of differentiation of the inflorescence reflects the influence of both temperature and photoperiod on differentiation and development of the floral primordium, and indicates further that the floral expression is achieved through a biochemical system that may fluctuate in favor of either the flowering or the vegetative condition depending on the quantitative balance between the floral-promoting substance/s and the vegetative-promoting, or floral-inhibiting, substance/s. This system acts on the meristematic regions of the grass apex to shift from vegetative to floral and back to vegetative in response to external and endogenous stimuli.

References

Al-Aish, M. (1956). The effect of isopropyl-n-phenyl carbamate on the germination of grass seeds and the bearing upon systematics of the Gramineae. Ph.D. Thesis, University of Texas.

Allen. R. E., Vogel, D. A., and Craddock, J. C., Jr. (1959). Comparative response to gibberellic acid of dwarf, semidwarf and standard short and tall winter wheat varieties. *Agron. J.* **51**, 737–740.

Andersen, A. M. (1927). Development of the female gametophyte and caryopsis of *Poa pratensis* and *Poa compressa*. *J. Agr. Res.* **34**, 1001–1018.

Anderson, S. (1952). Methods for determining stages of development in barley and oats. *Physiol. Plant.* **5**, 199–210.

Anderson, S. (1954a). A method for determining stages of development in wheat. *Physiol. Plant.* **7**, 513–516.

Anderson, S. (1954b). Effects of 2, 4-D on ear development in barley. *Physiol. Plant.* **7**, 517–522.

Arber, A. (1926). Studies in the Gramineae. I. The flowers of certain Bambuseae. *Ann. Bot. (London)* **40**, 447–469.

Arber, A. (1929). Studies in the Gramineae. VIII. On the organization of the flower in the bamboo. *Ann. Bot. (London)* **43**, 765–781.

Arber, A. (1934). "The Gramineae: A Study of Cereal, Bamboo and Grass," Cambridge Univ. Press, London and New York (reprint, p. xi J. Cramer, Weinheim, Germany, 1965).

Avdulov. N. P. (1931). Karyo-systematische Untersuchungen der Familie Gramineen. *Bull. App. Bot.* **44**, *Suppl.*, 1–428.

Barnard, C. (1955). Histogenesis of the inflorescence and flower of *Triticum aestivum* L. *Aust. J. Bot.* **3**; 1–20.

Barnard, C. (1957). Floral histogenesis in the monocotyledons. I. The Gramineae. *Aust. J. Bot.* **5**, 1–20.

Barnard, C., ed. (1964). "Grasses and Grasslands." Macmillan, New York.

Bernier, G., ed. (1971). "Cellular and Molecular Aspects of Induction." Longmans, Green, New York.

Bonnett, O. T. (1935). The development of the barley spike. *J. Agr. Res.* **51**, 451–457.

Bonnett, O. T. (1937). The development of the oat panicle. *J. Agr. Res.* **54**, 127–131.

Bonnett, O. T. (1938). Hood and supernumerary spike development in barley. *J. Agr. Res.* **57**, 371–78.

Bonnett, O. T. (1940). Development of the staminate and pistillate inflorescence of sweet corn. *J. Agr. Res.* **60**, 25–38.

Bonnett, O. T. (1953). Developmental morphology of the vegetative and floral shoots of maize. *Ill., Agr. Exp. Sta., Bull.* **568**, 1–47.

Bonnett, O. T. (1961). The oat plant: Its histology and development. *Ill, Agr. Exp. Sta., Bull.* **672**, 1–112.

Bonnett, O. T. (1966). Inflorescences of maize, wheat, rye, barley and oats: their initiation and development. *Ill., Agr. Exp. Sta., Bull.* **721**, 1–105.

Borthwick, H. A., and Cathey, H. M. (1962). Role of phytochrome in control of flowering in chrysanthemum. *Bot. Gaz.* **123**, 155.

Brown, W. V., Heimsch, C., and Emery, W. H. P. (1957). The organization of the grass shoot apex and systematics. *Amer. J. Bot.* **44**, 590–595.

Burbidge, N. T. (1964). Grass systematics. *In* "Grasses and Grasslands", (C. Barnard, ed.), pp. 13–28. Macmillan, New York.

Casady, A. J. (1969). Propagation from proliferated sorghum spikelets caused by head smut infection. *Crop Sci.* **9**, 381–382.

Caso, O. H., Highkin, H. R., and Koller, D. (1960). Effect of gibberellic acid on flower differentiation in Petkus winter rye. *Nature (London)* **185**, 477–479.

Cathey, H. M. (1969). *Chrysanthemum morifolium* (Ramat.) Hemsl. *In* "The Induction of Flowering—Some Case Histories" (L. T. Evans, ed.), pp. 268–290. Cornell Univ. Press. Ithaca, New York.

Chandra, N. (1962a). Morphological studies in the Gramineae. I. Vascular anatomy of the spikelet in Pooideae. *Proc. Nat. Inst. Sci. India* **28**, 545–562.

Chandra, N. (1962b). Morphological studies in the Gramineae. II. Vascular anatomy of the spikelet in Paniceae. *Proc. Indian Acad. Sci., Sect. B* **56**; 219–231.

Chandra, N. (1963). Morphological studies in the Gramineae. III. On the nature of the gynaecium. *J. Indian Bot. Soc.* **42**, 252–259.

Clements, H. F., and Awada, M. (1960). Multiple top in sugar cane. *Hawaii Farm Sci.* **9**, 1–3.

Cooper, J. P. (1951). Studies on growth and development in *Lolium*. II. Pattern of bud development of the shoot apex and its ecological significance. *J. Ecol.* **39**, 228–270.

Cooper, J. P. (1956). Developmental analyses of populations in the cereals and herbage grasses. I. Methods and techniques. *J. Agr. Sci.* **47**, 262–279.

Cooper, J. P. (1960). The use of controlled life-cycles in the forage grasses and legumes. *Herb. Abstr.* **30**, 71–79.

Cumming, B. G. (1969). *Chenopodium rubrum* L. and related species. *In* "The Induction of Flowering—Some Case Histories" (L. T. Evans, ed.), pp. 156–185. Cornell Univ. Press, Ithaca, New York.

Elliott, C. R. (1967a). Factors affecting grass seed yields. *Can. Agr., Publ.,* Summer.

Elliott, C. R. (1967b). Creeping red fescue. *Can. Dept. Agr., Publ.* **1122**, 1–15.

Evans, L. T. (1960). The influence of environmental conditions on inflorescence development in some long-day grasses. *New Phytol.* **59**; 163–174.

Evans, L. T. (1964) Reproduction. *In* "Grasses and Grasslands" (L. T. Evans, ed.), pp. 126–153. Macmillan, New York.

Evans, L. T., ed. (1969). "The Induction of Flowering—Some Case Histories." Cornell Univ. Press, Ithaca, New York.

Evans, M. W., and Grover, F. O. (1940) Developmental morphology of the growing point of the shoot and the inflorescence in grasses. *J. Agr. Res.* **61**, 481–520.

Flovik, K. (1938). Cytological studies of Arctic grasses. *Hereditas* **24**, 265–376.

Gould, F. W. (1968). "Grass Systematics." McGraw-Hill, New York.

Gustafsson, A. (1946). Apomixis in higher plants. I. The mechanism of apomixis. *Lunds Univ. Arrsska, Afd. Z.* [N.S.] **42** No. 3.

Hanson, A. A., and Ruska, F. V. eds. (1969). "Turfgrass Science." Amer. Soc. Agron., Madison, Wisconsin.

Heyn, C. C. (1962). Studies of bulbous *Poa* in Palestine. I. The agamic complex of *Poa bulbosa. Bull. Res. Counc. Isr., Sect. D* **11**, 117–126.

Hitchcock, A. S. (1951). Manual of the grasses of the United States. U.S., *Dep. Agr., Misc. Publ.* **200**.

Hodgson, H. J. (1966). Floral initiation in Alaskan Gramineae. *Bot. Gaz.* **127**, 64–70.

Hovin, A. W. (1957). Bulk emasculation by high temperatures in annual bluegrass, *Poa annua* L. *Agron. J.* **49**, 463.

James, N. I., and Lund, S. (1965). Shoot apex development of winter barley as influenced by potassium gibberellate. *Amer. J. Bot.* **52**, 877–882.

Jeater, R. S. L. (1956). A method for determining developmental stages in grasses. *J. Brit. Grassland Soc.* **11**, 139–146.

Koller, D., Highkin, H. R., and Caso, O. H. (1960). Effects of gibberellic acid on stem spices of vernalizable grasses. *Amer. J. Bot.* **47**, 518–524.

Lang. A. (1965). Physiology of flower initiation. *In* "Handbuch der Pflanzenphysiologie" (W. Ruhland, ed.), Part 1, Vol. 15, pp. 1380–1536. Springer-Verlag, Berlin and New York.

Latting, J. (1966). Floral morphogenesis and proliferation in several viviparous grasses. Ph. D. Dissertation, University of California, Los Angeles, Publ. no. 67–7374 University Microfilms, Ann Arbor, Michigan.

Launchbaugh, J. L., and Hackerott, H. L. (1969). Early-spring blue grama inflorescences from fall-initiated spikes. *Crop Sci.* **9**, 631–633.

Lawrence, W. E. (1945). Some ecotypic relations of *Deschampsia caespitosa. Amer. J. Bot.* **32**, 298–314.

Leighty, C. E., and Sando, W. J. (1924). The blooming of wheat flowers. *J. Agr. Res.* **27**, 231–244.

Lincoln, R. G., Raven, K. A., and Hamner, K. C. (1956). Certain factors influencing expression of the flowering stimulus in *Xanthium*. I. Translocation and inhibition of the flowering stimulus. *Bot. Gaz.* **117**, 193–206.

Linnaeus, C. (1737). "Flora Lapponica". Amsterdam.

Linnaeus, C. (1759). "Flora Alpina," Vol. 4: Holmiae. Amoenitates Academicae.

Mark, A. F. (1965a). Flowering behavior of a New Zealand mountain grass. *Naturwissenschaften* **167**, No. 7, 52.

Mark, A. F. (1965b). Flowering, seeding and seedling establishment of narrow-leaved snow tussock, *Chionochloa rigida. N.Z. J. Bot.* **3**, 180–193.

Mark, A. F. (1965c). Ecotypic differentiation in Otago populations of narrow-leaved snow tussock, *Chionochloa rigida. N.Z. J. Bot.* **3**, 277–299.

Mark, A. F. (1965d). Effects of management practices on narrow-leaved snow tussock, *Chionochloa rigida. N.Z. J. Bot.* **3**, 300–319.

Mark, A. F. (1968). Factors controlling irregular flowering in four alpine species of *Chionochloa. J. N. Z. Ecol. Soc.* **15**, 55–60.

Mark, A. F. (1969). Ecology of snow tussocks in the mountain grasslands of New Zealand. *Vegetatio, Acta Geobot.* **18**, 1–6.

Mattfeld, J. (1920). Über einen Fall endocarper Keimung bei *Papaver somniferum* L. *Verh. Bot. Ver. Brandenburg* **62**, 1–8.

Maun, M. A., Canode, C. L., and Teare, I. D. (1969). Influence of temperature during anthesis on seed set in *Poa pratensis* L. *Crop Sci.* **19**, 210–212.

Milthorpe, F. L., and Ivins, J. D., eds. (1966). "The Growth of Cereals and Grasses." Butterworths, London.

Moore, P. H. (1969). Personal communication (reported at the 12th International Botanical Congress).

Nicholls, P. B., and May, L. H. (1964). Studies on the growth of the barley apex. II. On the initiation of internode elongation in the inflorescence. *Aust. J. Biol. Sci.* **17**, 619–630.

Nygren, A. (1949). Studies on vivipary in the genus *Deschampsia*. *Hereditas* **35**, 27–32.

Nygren, A. (1967). Apomixis in the Angiosperms. *In* "Handbuch der Pflanzenphysiologie" (W. Ruhland, ed.), Vol. 18, pp. 551–596. Springer-Verlag, Berlin and New York.

Nygren, A., and Almgard, G. (1962). On the experimental control of vivipary in *Poa*. *Kgl. Lantbrukshögsk. Ann.* **28**, 27–36.

Philipson, W. R. (1934). The morphology of the lemma in grasses. *New Phytol.* **33**, 359–371.

Pope, M. N. (1943). The temperature factor in the fertilization and growth of the barley ovule. *J. Agr. Res.* **66**, 389–402.

Purvis, O. N. (1934). An analysis of the influence of temperature during germination on the subsequent development of certain winter cereals and its relation to the effect of length of day. *Ann. Bot.* (*London*) **48**, 919–955.

Purvis, O. N. (1960). Effect of gibberellin on the flower initiation and stem extension in Petkus winter rye. *Nature* (*London*) **185**, 479.

Purvis, O. N., and Gregory, F. G. (1937). Studies in vernalization of cereals. I. A comparative study of vernalization of winter rye by low temperature and by short days. *Ann. Bot.* (*London*) [N. S.] **1**, 569–592.

Reeder, J. R. (1957). The embryo in grass systematics. *Amer. J. Bot.* **44**, 756–768.

Reeder, J. R. (1962). The bambusoid embryo: A reappraisal. *Amer. J. Bot.* **49**, 639–641.

Rice, E. L. (1950). Growth and floral development of five species of range grasses in central Oklahoma. *Bot. Gaz.* **111**, 361–377.

Rijven, A. H. G. C., and Evans, L. T. (1967). Inflorescence initiation in *Lolium temulentum* L. IX. Some chemical changes in the shoot apex at induction. *Aust. J. Biol. Sci.* **20**, 1–12.

Row, H. C., and Reeder, J. R. (1957). Root hair development as evidence of relationships among genera of Gramineae. *Amer. J. Bot.* **44**, 596–601.

Ruhland W., ed. (1961a). "Handbuch der Pflanzenphysiologie," Vol. 14, Springer-Verlag, Berlin and New York.

Ruhland W., ed. (1961b). "Handbuch der Pflanzenphysiologie," Vol. 16, Springer-Verlag, Berlin and New York.

Ruhland, W., ed. (1965). "Handbuch der Pflanzenphysiologie," Vol. 15, Part 1. Springer-Verlag, Berlin and New York.

Ruhland, W. ed. (1967). "Handbuch der Pflanzenphysiologie," Vol. 18. Springer-Verlag, Berlin and New York.

Salisbury, F. B. (1955a). Kinetic studies on the physiology of flowering. Ph.D. Dissertation, California Institute of Technology, Pasadena.

Salisbury, F. B. (1955b). The dual role of auxin in flowering. *Plant Physiol.* **30**, 327–334.

Salisbury, F. B. (1969). *Xanthium strumarium* L. *In* "The Induction of Flowering—Some Case Histories" (L. T. Evans, ed.), pp. 14–61. Cornell Univ. Press, Ithaca, New York.

Schwarzenbach, F. H. (1956). Die Beeinflussung der viviparie bei einer gronlandischen rasse von *Poa alpina* L. durch den jahreszeitlichen licht- und temperaturewechsel. *Ber. Schweiz. Bot. Ges.* **66**, 204.

Sernander, R. (1927). Zur Morphologie und Biologie der Diasporen. *Nova Acta. Regiae Soc. Sci. Upsal.* Vol. extra ordin. ed.

Sharman, B. C. (1944). Branched heads in wheat and wheat hybrids. *Nature* (*London*) **153**, 497.

Sharman, B. C. (1945). Construction of the shoot apex in cereals and other grasses. *Nature* (*London*) **158**, 291–296.

Sharman. B. C. (1947). The biology and developmental morphology of the shoot apex in the Gramineae. *New Phytol.* **46**, 20–34.

Sharman, B. C. (1960a). Development of the inflorescence and spikelets of *Anthoxanthum odoratum* L. *New Phytol.* **59**, 60–64.

Sharman, B. C. (1960b). Developmental anatomy of the stamen and carpel primordia in *Anthoxanthum odoratum*. *Bot. Gaz.* **121**, 192–198.

Sharman, B. C. (1967). Interpretation of the morphology of various naturally occurring abnormalities of the inflorescence of wheat (*Triticum*). *Can. J. Bot.* **45**, 2073–2080.

Skalinska, M. (1952) Cyto-ecological studies in *Poa alpina* L. var. *vivipara* L. *Bull. Acad. Pol. Sci. Lett., Cl. Sci. Math. Natur., Ser. B.* No. 1, pp. 253–283.

Stebbins, G. L. (1956). Cytogenetics and evolution of the grass family. *Amer. J. Bot.* **43**, 890–905.

Stebbins, G. L., and Crampton, B. (1959). A suggested revision of the grass genera of temperate North America. *Recent Advan. Bot.* **1**, 133–145.

Stephens, J. C., and Quinby, J. R. (1933). Bulk emasculation of sorghum flowers *J. Amer. Soc. Agron.* **25**, 233–234.

Takimoto, A. (1955). Flowering response to various combinations of light and dark periods in *Silene armeria*. *Bot. Mag.* **68**, 308–314.

Tanimoto, T. T. (1968). Floral differentiation in sugarcane and the subsequent rate of development, *Hawaii Plant Rec.* **60**, 275–278.

Turesson, G. (1926). Studin über *Festuca ovina* L. I. Normalgeschlechtlihe halb- und ganzvivipare Typen nordischer Herkunft, *Hereditas* **8**, 161–206.

Webster. (1967). "Webster's Third New International Dictionary, Unabridged." G. & C. Merriam Co., Springfield, Massachusetts.

Wellensiek, S. J. (1969). *Silene armeria* L. *In* "The Induction of Flowering–Some Case Histories" (L. T. Evans, ed.), pp. 350–363. Cornell Univ. Press, Ithaca, New York.

Williams, R. F. (1966). The physiology of growth in the wheat plant. III. Growth of the primary shoot and its inflorescence. *Aust. J. Biol. Sci.* **19**, 949–966.

Wilson, J. R. (1959). The influence of time of tiller origin and nitrogen level on the floral initiation and ear emergence of four pasture grasses. *N. Z. J. Agr. Res.* **2**, 915–932.

Wycherley, P. R. (1952). Temperature and photoperiod in relation to flowering in three perennial grass species. *Mededel, Landbouwhogesch. Opzoekingssta, Staat Gent* **52**, 75–92.

Wycherley, P. R. (1953). Proliferation of spikelets in British grasses. I. The taxonomy of the viviparous races. *Watsonia* **3**, 41–56.

Yagil, E. A. (1965). A morphogenetic comparison between awned and hooded genotypes of barley. Ph.D. Dissertation, University of California, Davis.

Youngner, V. B. (1960). Environmental control of initiation of the inflorescence, reproductive structures and proliferations in *Poa bulbosa*. *Amer. J. Bot.* **47**, 753–757.

Youngner, V. B. (1961a). Winter survival of *Digitaria sanguinalis* in subtropical climates. *Weeds* **9**, 654–655.

Youngner, V. B. (1961b). Low temperature induced male sterility in male-fertile *Pennisetum clandestinum*. *Science* **133**, 577–578.

Chapter 27

Seed Production and Cultural Treatments

I. J. JOHNSON

Certainly an important aspect of grass breeding must include as one objective the development of varieties having good seed yields since the success of any variety is closely related to the economics of seed production. One of the most clear-cut means of improving seed yields of grasses has been through the proper application of fertilizers, especially nitrogen, in relation to tiller formation and the transition from vegetative to reproductive growth. Inflorescence induction and development are primary requisites for seed formation. One might almost conclude that a considerable portion of the biology of grasses is related to its reproductive stages of growth and ultimately to seed production.

The question of seed production may be examined in several ways. The most important phase of any seed production (and ultimately seed marketing) program is an analysis of current trends in seed usage as reflected by the complex changes occurring today in American agriculture. There can be no question, as so well-stated by Louis Wise, Vice President for Agriculture and Forestry, Mississippi State University (1968), that the United States will continue to be a meat eating and dairy products consuming nation. To meet the needs of a growing population it will be necessary to have more acres of forage crops than are grown today. The estimated demand for beef will increase 45% by 1975 and by year 2000 the demand for beef will double. By 1975 it will be necessary to increase beef cattle numbers by 7 million in feed lots and by 21 million on pastures. If these estimates prove to be correct there will be a greater demand for grass seed than exists today and good sense in land use will dictate that seed yields either will need to be increased or a disproportionate part of our existing (and shrinking) crop land acreage will need to be used for seed production.

One of the most striking features of today's livestock industry has been the mechanization of feed production and processing to reduce labor imputs. Today it is possible by converting herbage to haylage for a single operator to deliver an appropriately balanced ration for 1000 or more dairy or beef cattle from storage to feed bunks in 1 hr per feeding—and to do this without a great deal of expenditure of physical labor.

The pressures for mechanization of livestock feeding have had a major effect on the kinds of forage crops and the acreage needed to each. The recent trend is strongly away from perennial grasses and legumes and toward annual grasses that have higher yield potentials. This is not equally true in all regions in the United States because of the differences that exist in land use and cropping potentials. For example, in the Southern states, the almost revolutionary expansion in livestock numbers has resulted in a six-fold increase of sorghum-sudan and sudangrass hybrids. New legumes for pasture seedings and new grass and legume crops for hay production are needed to match feed supplies for this expanding livestock industry.

In the Northeastern states, where dairy cattle have been of greatest importance because of the need for milk, the pattern of seed usage for the past 10 years in part dramatically reflects changes in livestock feeding practices.

During this 10-year period, the usage of legume seeds has decreased by about 40% and of perennial grasses by 50%, but forage sorghums, including sorghum-sudans, have decreased only slightly. Although data on use of corn for silage were not included, if the practices in the Northeast are comparable to those in the Midwest, the use of corn silage has steadily increased.

In the Southwestern states numerous new grasses for rangelands have been developed in recent years. These range grasses become important in supplying feed for future expansion of livestock numbers on land that normally was too dry for more intensive feed crop production.

In the Midwest where the farm economy and machinery are closely related to corn and soybean production, livestock feeders have been decreasing their use of grasses and legumes in rotations and stepping up acreage of corn for silage. This appears to be particularly true in the feeding of beef cattle where protein requirements can be supplemented with soybean meal and urea. Dairy farmers may not be in accord with the practice of buying feed from off the farm.

The total acreage of land used for seed production in the United States is surprisingly large. Data from the USDA Crop Reporting Board, Annual

Summary for 1967 shows that over 2-million acres of land were used for this purpose. This acreage includes only ten of the major grass and legume species. The total value of seed produced was over 81-million dollars in 1967. The value of legume seeds greatly exceeded that of the grasses. Seed production is extremely variable, especially in those areas in which seed crops do not compete favorably with income from other crops. In the highly specialized seed-growing areas under irrigation in the Western states the variations in seed yields are considerably less than in the marginal areas.

Changes in livestock feeding practices obviously have a direct relationship to the kinds and quantities of grass seed needed in our economy and also provide important guidelines for crops on which greatest research emphasis is needed. With the present-day need to use effectively available funds for the greatest benefit in research it would seem inappropriate to place emphasis on those crops in which the results obtained might have limited value.

If the current crop trends really are indicators of future practices in seed needs, pertinent questions may well be asked about research and development with forage grass and grass seed production and needs. There can be little doubt that the seed industry itself will play an increasingly important role in variety developments and that variety development by industry also is closely allied to seed production and marketing of its own products. A prime example is the large investment in funds on development of sorghum-sudan hybrids, on sudangrass hybrids, and on forage-type sorghums. From a status virtually unknown a decade ago, the total usage and seed production of proprietary hybrids have now become a dominant feature in the total livestock feed programs. One of the unique features of private research is the controlled seed production of an item so as to match essentially its sales opportunity. A second feature is that the extent of private research funding of development programs must by necessity be related to the future potentials for recovery of its investment. Both of these qualifications are closely related to the variety protection that is needed to insure maintenance of exclusive merchandising rights for the products developed with its own capital investment.

In the current decade a great deal of effort has been made by the seed industry itself and in cooperation with experiment stations and the USDA to clarify viewpoints on the need and the form of plant variety protection that would give greater incentive to private industry to establish new and expanded programs on variety (and hybrid) development.

The role industry can play in changing existing patterns of agriculture is well documented through such actions as given by the hybrid corn industry to the Market Development Committee of the Feed Grains Council and the actions of the American Soybean Association to expand its foreign markets.

The total research on seed production in grasses for the United States is extremely limited and has been primarily restricted to studies on time and rate of nitrogen application, row spacing, and so on. In recognition of this limitation a special task force was established to explore the types of studies needed to assure a more effective seed production program. The study committee recommended that expanded research be initiated on the following specific fields in seed production:

1. Pollination control, including development of superior pollinators.
2. Improved techniques for measuring seed yields in experimental plot trials.
3. Pest control in seed fields, including both insects, weeds, and diseases.
4. Post harvest management of seed fields, including stubble burning.
5. Stand establishment and management.
6. Seed shattering.
7. Isolation requirements for maintaining genetic control.
8. Genetic shifts in generations of multiplication.
9. Hard seed and seed dormancy.
10. Varietal identification.
11. Drying and processing seed.

The committee also recommended that new basic research be initiated to obtain a better understanding of the biochemical and biophysical changes that occur in seed formation and development as related to germination and longevity.

Reference

Wise, L. (1968). *Proc. 14th Annu. Farm Seed Conf., 1968.*

Chapter 28

Future Needs in Grass Research

FUTURE NEEDS IN RANGE RESEARCH

WESLEY KELLER

All research on arid lands should be geared to explain why any given result is obtained, not merely to report what happened. This will require much better instrumentation, and close attention to one or a very few sites, in contrast to general observation of many sites. Only when we know why can we hope to project our findings from areas experimented upon to those not experimented upon. The Western range is so heterogeneous that only a few of the many conditions can be studied.

Management practices must be developed that maximize the value of the range resource when fully integrated with all other available feed resources and when the range has been freed of all unwanted vegetation. Loss of water by runoff must be reduced to a minimum. Thorough economic analyses will be acquired.

Basic physiological, genetic, and pathological research must be accelerated to determine the basis for adaptation to heat, cold, drought, longevity, productivity, nutritive value, water use efficiency, disease resistance, and other desirable characteristics, such as response to an associated legume.

Legumes must be developed and introduced into the range that are capable of contributing nitrogen to grass and that are compatible with feasible management practices.

For the more arid rangelands, and possibly for all Western ranges, grazing management systems must be developed that are based on the physiology of the plant in response to its environment rather than from conventional grazing trials.

A comprehensive census of grazing lands is necessary. It is no more possible to conduct a highly efficient range improvement program without an adequate range census than it is to breed for resistance to a disease whose cause is not known.

A much greater awareness of the specific conditions essential to success in range seeding is needed, and the development of economical procedures for insuring their contribution to the success of the range seeding operation. These include moisture, temperature, seeding, and seed-bed requirements in advance of seeding, to insure success on any given soil with any given species at any season of the year, and with various probabilities of future precipitation, wind and temperature relationships.

RESEARCH NEEDS IN THE FORAGE GRASSES

A. A. HANSON

A very substantial amount of the 700-million acres of forage-producing land on farms in the United States is occupied by perennial forage grasses and grass-legume mixtures. Research needs must be defined in terms of use, which, as noted, may combine both livestock feed and improved soil management. Forage-grass research should also be considered within the framework of changes that are taking place in agriculture and especially in livestock production. Some of the variables that could influence trends in future research include the availability and cost of feed grains; problems in managing large dairy herds on pasture; the relative cost of handling many forages; the use of nonprotein nitrogen in supplying ruminants with a substantial fraction of their nitrogen requirements; and the possible development of low-cost chemical treatments to improve the digestibility of low quality, high-lignin roughage. There is every reason to expect that perennial grasses will remain important in cow-calf operations and in the production of replacement dairy heifers. The very obvious role that they can assume in reducing feed costs and in improving the efficiency of animal production will require intensive research and technological progress.

There is an urgent need for major improvements in the conservation of forages for use in the confined feeding of dairy and beef animals. Better methods must be developed to reduce harvesting and storage losses, to reduce handling costs, and to facilitate mechanical feeding. The success of engineering and nutritional research involved in these projects will be enhanced by concomitant progress in grass production.

In production research greater emphasis and effort must be given to the improvement of yield potential, dry-matter digestibility, persistence, and retention of quality in accumulated pasture herbage and field stored hay. Particular attention should be devoted to the development of grasses that will produce optimum yields over a relatively wide range in management inputs, soil fertility, and soil water. The complexity of forage improvement and utilization research demands the organization of well integrated multidiscipline research programs that can draw on the talents of geneticists, physiologists, agronomists, plant breeders, pathologists, entomologists, animal and soil scientists, biochemists, and engineers.

FUTURE NEEDS IN TURFGRASS RESEARCH

J. R. WATSON

In the past few decades landscaping has taken on a new and significant emphasis in our cities, towns, villages, and communities. Beautification projects have gained national fame and many changes have occurred in outdoor recreation. Large segments of all ages of the population have become involved as participants or spectators in all kinds of outdoor activity. The National Golf Foundation estimates there are some 9600 golf courses in the United States today—up some 4000 in the past decade—and that the number is increasing at a net rate of about 400 annually. And who would care to estimate the number of Little League teams, organized and unorganized, that will play baseball this summer? Concurrent with the increase in numbers of people using turfgrass facilities has been an ever-increasing and very vocal demand for continuing improvement in turf quality.

The basic need for turfgrass areas as places to relax, to play, and to filter the atmosphere of our urban, suburban, and perhaps even some rural areas will become increasingly important. Projections for population increases and availability of leisure time with a concomitant increase in disposable income practically assure a continuing need for such facilities. Turfgrass surveys at state and national levels clearly indicate the magnitude and the importance of the turfgrass industry.

Breeding and selection of turfgrasses to meet the esthetic needs and the use demands must clearly move forward at a more rapid rate. It seems necessary that plant breeders will direct their efforts in two directions: (1) grasses for landscape and esthetic purposes and (2) grasses for heavy, intensive use.

In many countries today lawns are grown and maintained solely for their esthetic value. They receive very little traffic and are never played upon. On the other hand sports fields and golf courses are heavily used. The two types of areas clearly have different functions and maintenance requirements.

Turfgrasses for the future should be developed along the two lines proposed and possess the following characteristics: available color choices, response to grooming, resistance to pests and diseases, tolerance to environmental stresses, and desirability in general appearance or wearability.

Author Index

Numbers in italics refer to the pages on which the complete references are listed.

Subject Index